Union in Truth

An Interpretive History of the Restoration Movement

James B. North

UNION IN TRUTH

An Interpretive History of the Restoration Movement

Standard PUBLISHING
Bringing The Word to Life

Cincinnati, Ohio

Published by Standard Publishing, Cincinnati, Ohio
www.standardpub.com

13 12 11 10 09 08   9 10 11   .

Library of Congress Cataloging-in-Publication Data

North, James B.
     Union in truth : an interpretive history of the Restoration
movement / James B. North.
          p.   cm.
     Includes bibliographical references and index.
     ISBN 0-978-7847-0197-0
     1. Restoration movement (Christianity)--United States--History.
2. United States--Church history.   I. Title.
BX7316.N67   1994
286.6'09--dc20   94-16583
                                                         CIP

to Don Hargrave,
who first stimulated my interest
in the Restoration Movement

to Enos Dowling,
my mentor in the study
of Restoration History

to Hugh and Rebecca Brownlee,
my great-great-grandparents,
who were married at Cane Ridge in 1802,
probably by B.W. Stone

Contents

Preface

THE TIME OF THIS WRITING is exactly two hundred years after James O'Kelly and his followers left the Methodist Episcopal Church and began the first of several movements in America that coalesced into what later came to be called "The Restoration Movement." Over the next couple of decades, numerous other individuals also left their denominational moorings and sailed toward a new identity as "Christians only."

Over the last century, numerous histories have been written about these groups, particularly around the turn of the century as the Disciples were preparing to celebrate their Centennial Convention in Pittsburgh in 1909—one hundred years after Thomas Campbell first penned the *Declaration and Address*. Many of these published histories reflected a particular perspective. Apparently the first history was written by B. B. Tyler in 1894, *A History of the Disciples of Christ* in the "American Church History" series, which proudly presented the Disciples of Christ as one of the significant denominations in the country.[1] James Harvey Garrison edited a series of contributions to present another treatment, *The Reformation of the Nineteenth Century*, in 1901.[2] Errett Gates wrote *The Disciples of Christ* in 1905 to reflect his liberal perspective and argue for Christian union and against the pattern of apostolic Christianity upon which Alexander Campbell had focused.[3] In 1909 J. H. Garrison wrote

---

[1]Benjamin B. Tyler, *A History of the Disciples of Christ,* American Church History Series (New York: The Christian Literature Co., 1894).

[2]James Harvey Garrison (ed.), *The Reformation of the Nineteenth Century* (St. Louis: Christian Publishing Company, 1901).

[3]Errett Gates, *The Disciples of Christ* (New York: The Baker & Taylor Co., 1905).

a popular history, *The Story of a Century*, in honor of the centennial.[4] The same year William Thomas Moore put out an even larger volume, appropriately entitled *A Comprehensive History of the Disciples of Christ*, running to 800 pages.[5] M. M. Davis put out *The Restoration Movement of the Nineteenth Century* in 1913,[6] and then two years later produced a condensation (almost as many pages, but with larger print), *How the Disciples Began and Grew*.[7] In 1919 W. W. Jennings published his Ph.D. dissertation from the University of Illinois, *The Origin and Early History of the Disciples of Christ*,[8] wanting "to show the origin and early history" of the movement; he stops his coverage in 1866. P. H. Welshimer put out a small book in 1935, *Concerning the Disciples: A Brief Resume of the Movement to Restore the New Testament Church*, but this popular treatment only goes up to the Campbell-Purcell Debate, and then he covers doctrinal issues to present current beliefs. Other than this latter item, all the previous books were written prior to the explosive tensions that hit the Disciples in the 1920s, so none of these books treat this decade. Welshimer's book comes after the 1920s, but by the nature of his purpose, he does not deal with it either.

W. E. Garrison entered new scholarly territory in 1931, however, when he published *Religion Follows the Frontier*.[9] This work analyzed the growth of the Restoration Movement from the perspective of the Turner Frontier Thesis.[10] Garrison also provided a new popular history in 1945, *An American Religious Movement*,[11] but because of its popular nature, it does not deal with the divisions of the 1920s either. Garrison and

---

[4]J. H. Garrison, *The Story of a Century* (St. Louis: Christian Publishing Company, 1909).

[5]William Thomas Moore, *A Comprehensive History of the Disciples of Christ* (New York: Fleming H. Revell Company, 1909).

[6]M. M. Davis, *The Restoration Movement of the Nineteenth Century* (Cincinnati: The Standard Publishing Company, 1913).

[7]M. M. Davis, *How the Disciples Began and Grew: A Short History of the Christian Church* (Cincinnati: The Standard Publishing Company, 1915).

[8]Walter Wilson Jennings, *The Origin and Early History of the Disciples of Christ* (Cincinnati: The Standard Publishing Company, 1919).

[9]Winfred Ernest Garrison, *Religion Follows the Frontier: A History of the Disciples of Christ* (New York: Harper and Brothers, 1931).

[10]For a study of this in context, see W. Clark Gilpin, "Faith on the Frontier: Historical Interpretations of the Disciples of Christ," in *A Case Study of Mainstream Protestantism: The Disciples' Relation to American Culture, 1880-1989*, edited by D. Newell Williams (Grand Rapids: William B. Eerdmans Publishing Company, 1991), pp. 260-275, particularly pp. 267-272.

[11]Winfred Ernest Garrison, *An American Religious Movement: A Brief History of the Disciples of Christ* (St. Louis: Christian Board of Publication, 1945).

DeGroot wrote their *Disciples of Christ: A History* in 1948; they do cover the issues, but they defend the liberal drift of the Disciples, castigating the narrow-minded fundamentalists who had resisted liberal efforts over the past couple of decades. Oliver Read Whitly wrote *Trumpet Call of Reformation* in 1959, but his purpose was to use a socio-cultural framework for understanding the movement, applying the concepts and insights of sociology.[12] James DeForest Murch in 1962 wrote *Christians Only* to present a conservative interpretation of the history and to counter much of the presentation of Garrison-DeGroot.[13] Enos Dowling's brief *The Restoration Movement: Study Course for Youth and Adults* published in 1964, while valuable as a study course, is not oriented toward a thorough or scholarly discussion of the issues.[14] Earl I. West's four-volume *The Search for the Ancient Order* (1950-1987) is a presentation of the detail from the Noninstrumentalist perspective.[15] He does in greater length what Homer Hailey had attempted earlier in his 1945 *Attitudes and Consequences in the Restoration Movement.*[16] In 1975 McAllister and Tucker wrote an officially recognized history of the Disciples, again endorsing the liberal Disciples drift and perspective.[17] Leroy Garrett's 1981 *Stone-Campbell Movement* was an attempt to talk about the movement's three branches in an objective, accurate manner; but he was also pushing his interpretation that restorationism is impossible, even intentionally abandoning the label "Restoration Movement" in his title.[18] More recently (1990), Henry Webb has written *In Search of Christian Unity* as a thorough middle-of-the-road treatment from the Christian Church/Church of Christ perspective.[19]

With all these histories having been written—many in the last couple of decades—why does this author presume to present yet another volume

---

[12]Oliver Read Whitly, *Trumpet Call of Reformation* (St. Louis: The Bethany Press, 1959).

[13]James DeForest Murch, *Christians Only* (Cincinnati: The Standard Publishing Company, 1962).

[14]Enos E. Dowling, *The Restoration Movement: Study Course for Youth and Adults* (Cincinnati: Standard Publishing, 1964).

[15]Earl Irvin West, *The Search for the Ancient Order: A History of the Restoration Movement,* 4 vols. (Nashville: Gospel Advocate Company, 1974-1987).

[16]Homer Hailey, *Attitudes and Consequences in the Restoration Movement,* Second Edition (Rosemead, California: The Old Paths Book Club, 1952).

[17]Lester G. McAllister and William E. Tucker, Journey in Faith: *A History of the Christian Church* (Disciples of Christ) (St. Louis: The Bethany Press, 1975).

[18]Leroy Garrett, *The Stone-Campbell Movement: An Anecdotal History of the Three Churches* (Joplin, Missouri: College Press Publishing Company, 1981).

[19]Henry E. Webb, *In Search of Christian Unity: A History of the Restoration Movement* (Cincinnati: The Standard Publishing Company, 1990).

to the reading public? Mostly because he believes that his approach is sufficiently different from all the rest as to warrant its publication. He is calling this volume "an interpretive history." When he mentioned this to his colleague, Henry Webb, that scholar commented, "Now, Jim, all history is interpretive!" Webb's observation is surely true. All history is written from a certain perspective and presents the author's interpretation—some books more candidly than others. But this is intended to be an openly candid presentation.

It is the perspective of this author that the Restoration Movement has two central foci—the concern for Christian union and the concern for biblical authority. Everything that happens in the history of the Restoration Movement is the direct result of one or the other or both of these concerns. Sometimes these concerns work in tandem; sometimes they are polarized. But it is the ebb and flow of these twin concerns that has created the Restoration Movement. Hopefully the reader will see these twin concerns as the skeleton of development within the Movement; the flesh is simply developed around these skeletal ideas.

The author has tried to use a title for this work that will adequately reflect both the Movement and the interpretation presented here. The phrase "Union in Truth" was used by Thomas Campbell in his key writing *Declaration and Address*.[20] The phrase reflects both the commitment to Christian unity as well as the commitment to base that union on biblical authority (truth).

One result of this interpretive history approach is that the author does not feel compelled to cover *everything* in the history of the Movement. There are numerous things he has bypassed—many of them interesting, rewarding, and informative. But they were not central to his main task, which is to interpret the history of the Restoration Movement in the light of the twin concerns. Therefore, there is a good deal about missionary outreach, educational development, international contacts, and some fascinating personalities that are omitted in this treatment. This is not to say such items are unimportant; it is only to say they have not been crucial for the development of the thesis of this volume. The author acknowledges that his presentation is not a comprehensive history. For some topics, the reader will have to go elsewhere. But the author does hope that what he is presenting is a viable and valuable understanding of what the history of the Restoration Movement is all about.

---

[20]"Union in truth has been, and ever must be, the desire and prayer of all such [Christians]; 'Union in Truth' is our motto." Thomas Campbell, *Declaration and Address* (Lincoln, Illinois: College & Seminary Press, n.d.), p. 28.

One additional word about terminology. The author has usually talked about the Restoration Movement in capitals. This is not always standard usage, but it appears to him that this development really is a proper noun. To talk about *the* restoration movement and then use lower case seems a contradiction. There are restoration movements in art, architecture, music, politics, and probably any other discipline. But to talk about the Restoration Movement is to talk about a particular topic that members of Restoration Movement churches will immediately identify.

Unfortunately, there is always confusion with terminology in discussing some of the details and labels in this Movement. For the majority of this treatment, the author will use the terms "Christian Church," "Church of Christ," and "Disciples of Christ" as basically interchangeable. Not until the twentieth century do these terms begin to take on nuances of specificity. One exception is the Christian Churches of the Christian Connection, or the Smith-Jones Movement, later officially called the Christian Denomination in America. Thus the term "Christian Church" does carry a bit more complicated freight than the other terms. Today, of course, the Noninstrumentalists virtually exclusively use the term "Church of Christ," although not all congregations called Churches of Christ are noninstrumental. The term "Disciples of Christ" has a specific application today that it did not have in the previous century when it was a generic for the entire Movement. "The Christian Churches/ Churches of Christ" is an awkward label referring to those churches that are neither Disciple nor Noninstrumentalist. Yet these twentieth century nuances should not cloud the fact that in the nineteenth century such nuances did not exist. We should never use modern labels with retroactive application.

The mere fact of the explanations of this last paragraph is a comment on the tragedy that a movement that began to create a renewed sense of unity within the body of Christ on earth now exists in several identifiable parts. How great it would be if we could all just be Christians working for the advancement of the kingdom of Jesus Christ. That was the goal of the original founders of this Restoration Movement. What went wrong along the way is the story of the following pages.

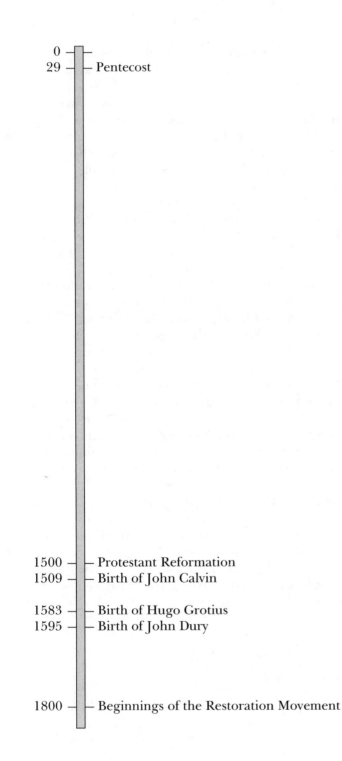

0	
29	Pentecost
1500	Protestant Reformation
1509	Birth of John Calvin
1583	Birth of Hugo Grotius
1595	Birth of John Dury
1800	Beginnings of the Restoration Movement

Chapter 1

Background

C HRISTIANS HAVE ALWAYS seen Pentecost, as recorded in Acts 2, as the birthday of the Church. Here was the occasion of the first known preaching of Jesus as the Christ after His resurrection, and the prospect of salvation offered in His name. Under this apostolic preaching, several thousand responded and "the church" became an identifiable group of people in first-century society. The church continued to grow as we see the record unfold in the book of Acts, with followers appearing in Judea, Samaria, Cyprus, and Antioch. Under the missionary travels of Paul, churches were also established in Asia Minor and Greece, and a church was in Rome by the time Paul got there under imprisonment. We need not trace out the details here, only to remark that the Christian Church soon spread throughout the entire Roman Empire and beyond.

Periods of Reform

That early church and its congregation, under the leadership of the apostles, has remained primary in the history of the church ever since. Later generations of Christians have always looked back to it as the model for Christian understanding, theology, and practice. To state this truism, however, is also to admit that later developments within the Church often deviated significantly from the early Christian churches. Questions of imperial persecution and later imperial favor caused the church to evolve structures of clerical hierarchy that were not represented in the earliest churches. Accommodating the Christian message to the world views and thought forms of the Greek and Latin worlds caused theological abstractions. While most of these remained true to original

1

Christian teaching as recorded in the New Testament, they still added theological nuances and concepts that were not in the original apostolic preaching. The mere fact of survival in the ancient world meant that the Church adapted itself to its environment. Later generations of Christians often identified with the adaptations rather than with the original model of the apostolic churches.

As a result, the church has constantly gone through cycles of revival in order to cast off some of the accretions that have built up around the structure of the church. Some of these revivals were significant cleansings, while others only added a new ecclesiastical form to the corpus of Christian activity. In time many of the institutions that began as revivals had to be either revived or abandoned.

Probably the most significant of the reviving and cleansing movements was the Protestant Reformation. By the latter Middle Ages, the Church had developed theological forms and church structures that departed radically from the original New Testament teachings regarding the function of the church, the process of salvation, and the basic activities of the Christian life. Major reformers like Martin Luther, Ulrich Zwingli, and John Calvin challenged much of the status quo of Catholicism and formulated changes to cleanse the Church from papal despotism and theological error. In many ways these men were successful in their endeavors. They eliminated many of the mechanical forms of religion, they renewed a proper sense of God's grace and a trust in Christ for salvation, and they pointed people back to the Bible and the early church as the source for true Christian teaching and practice.

Unfortunately, the Protestant Reformation also bequeathed some major liabilities to the corporate church. Luther's break from Catholicism was only the first of many that occurred in that century. Once he started the trend there were further divisions: the Reformed churches, first under Zwingli, then later under Calvin. The Anglican Church in England separated from Roman Catholicism and added to the divisions. The Anabaptists produced numerous small bodies of believers, many of which grew to respectable-sized denominations: the Mennonites, the Swiss Brethren, and others. The continuing existence of some pre-Reformation bodies added to the number of new groups: the Hussite Moravians, and the Waldensians who became Italian Presbyterians. The English Reformation produced its own dissenters in the form of Puritan Congregationalists, Presbyterians, and later, Quakers. Within a century after Luther, Protestantism had spawned a number of denominational churches.

These individual churches considered themselves true to the form of Christian teaching and there was great rivalry between them. Some were more intolerant of rivals than others, but most of them bitterly denounced their competitors; many of the larger groups severely persecuted the smaller groups in various national territories. These theological divisions became a major scandal to the church of the Protestant era and beyond. Most of these divisions formed their own theological statements to which the adherents were often fanatically loyal. Lutherans had their Augsburg Confession (1530); Presbyterians had their Westminster Confession (1648); Reformed bodies had their Heidelberg Catechism (1562). These statements of faith were each seen as equivalent to biblical teaching and became standards of orthodoxy for each group. These creeds did their part in perpetuating denominational divisions.

A second liability bequeathed from the Protestant Reformation was the fact that many of the major reformers carried over some of the presuppositions and concepts of Roman Catholic theology and practice. In many details the reformers abandoned Catholic concepts to recapture biblical teaching, but in some measure they saw scriptural teaching through eyes that had been accustomed to seeing Catholic doctrine. As a result, they often continued practices that came from Catholicism rather than from Scripture. On occasion they sincerely thought these practices were endorsed in Scripture (a clergy system, sacramentalism in the Lord's Supper); at other times they saw the positions as matters of indifference that could be continued without any difficulty (infant baptism, infrequent communion). Either way, such practices usually discouraged uniformity among the different Protestant churches and paved the way for denominational isolationism.

The American Context

When the American continent was being colonized, these same problems appeared in America. Most colonists were from Europe, and they brought their religious attitudes and practices with them to the New World. All the various denominational churches that were established in the area that came to be called the United States of America were imported. At the time of American independence, there were about a dozen major religious groups in America—all of them European transplants. All of this had several direct influences on religious life in America in general and the fortunes of the Restoration Movement in particular.

For one thing, the denominations continued in their divided state, often with great rivalry between them. One of the greatest sports engaged in by frontier clergy in America was "sheep stealing"—that is, converting members out of opposing denominational churches. At a time when 90 percent of the American population was unchurched, preachers often spent more time on trying to convert members of somebody else's flock than converting the unconverted. Part of this was also reflected in the continuing passionate loyalty people had to their denominational creeds. It was often merely the identification with a particular theological standard that kept people members of a particular denomination. Thus the Presbyterians strongly adhered to the Westminster Confession and the Lutherans to the Augsburg Confession, while Baptists firmly upheld their more recent Philadelphia Confession of Faith (1742). These creeds were held to be identical with true New Testament teaching. Any question about them within a denomination was cause for serious concern and often dismissal.

A second influence on the development of American religious life was the mere fact of multiple Protestant groups. We have already seen some of the problems this caused. It also occasioned some blessings and opportunities. This was a situation that took some time for recent European immigrants to get used to. In their homeland, normally there was only one dominant church—Lutheranism in much of Germany; the Anglicans in England; the Reformed in Switzerland, the Netherlands, and the Rhineland; and Catholicism in France, Spain, and elsewhere. Coming to a land where there was no dominant church called for an adjustment.

In the American colonial period, most colonies had state churches that were supported by public tax money in the colony. The Congregational Church enjoyed this privilege in three of the New England colonies (New Hampshire, Massachusetts, and Connecticut; Rhode Island, with its strong tradition of separatism under Roger Williams, was the only exception). The Anglican Church was the official church in the south: Georgia, both Carolinas, Virginia, and Maryland. Yet neither of these churches was dominant enough to become the state church for the new country. If anything, they cancelled each other out, and no other denomination had the influence to fill the gap. Consequently, there was no national church establishment, and the First Amendment to the Constitution guaranteed that Congress would make no established religion. This did not interfere, however, with the states that continued to maintain their state churches—as did the Congregationalists in New England for another several decades.

Because America had a number of viable denominations, none of them dominant over all the others, religious pluralism became a fact of American religious life and has remained so ever since. Consequently, each denomination had as much legal protection and freedom as did its rivals. If the churches were to survive, the people of the churches would have to take the initiative. This created a very activist laity that has also remained one of the dominant features of American religious life— much more so here than in Europe where religious pluralism was a late arrival in most countries. This lay activism became an extremely important factor in explaining the early growth and spread of the Restoration Movement across the middle of the country.

A further result of the fractured religious situation in America was that many people were unhappy with the current situation. Many people lost concern with religion because the denominations could not get their act together or even agree on the basic doctrines of the faith. When the Restoration Movement came along with its appeal to Christian unity and the basic common denominator of Christianity, many of these people heard a message they had awaited for a long time. They were not opposed to religion as much as they were opposed to the petty squabbles among the myriad religious groups. They readily identified with the positive and unitive message of the Movement.

Additionally, much of the frontier was permeated with a trait that historians have called "primitivism." People on the frontier were rugged individualists who were dependent upon their own resources. They expected very little from their central government, and they wanted it that way. Across the entire country there was the deep-seated feeling that the governments of Europe had become too corrupt, too top-heavy, too interfering in the lives of the people. The people who moved to the American frontier wanted to escape the degradation and decadence of European court life and urban prisons. They saw the raw frontier as an opportunity to build a new life—a life of simplicity, living close to the soil.

Although these people wanted to escape from the degenerating civilization of Europe, that does not mean they were anti-cultural or anti-intellectual. They wanted schools, churches, and stable institutions. But they saw themselves as desiring to recapture a simpler lifestyle. Their models were not the contemporary ones of Europe; their vision was more directed at the ancient cultures of Greece and Rome. There breathed a true democracy in the Greek city states and in the Roman republic before it fell to the Caesars. This primitivism was a major factor in the world view of the frontier. Notice how many towns on the frontier were given classic names: Rome, Utica, Athens, Sparta, Corinth, Argos, Syracuse, Memphis, and others. These people were also wide open to the basics of the Restoration Movement as it harked back to the simple gospel message and church structure of the New Testament. Ideologically, the frontier had already opted for that kind of viewpoint in society, politics, and culture. Since the Restoration Movement presented the same idea as a religious option, many people accepted it wholeheartedly. Thus the American frontier was a ready-made field for the message of this Restoration Movement. The preachers got nods of agreement when they pointed negatively to the hierarchical structures of numerous denominations—they were the religious counterparts of the elite societies of Europe that the frontiersmen despised. The preachers got the same agreement when they called for an elimination of the legalism and restrictions that marked denominational control over the lives of church members. The frontiersmen felt the same way about social regulations in general, and the words of these preachers perfectly matched their sociology. For these reasons, the Restoration Movement was able to get a running start on evangelizing the frontier.

Ideology of the Restoration Movement

So far we have been saying quite a bit about the Restoration Movement without defining the term. Since this entire book is about that, we don't need to say everything at this point. Suffice it to say that the Restoration Movement is a movement that began in America about the year 1800, in order to restore the church to the ideals that are pictured in the New Testament. This movement becomes the history of the Christian Churches and Churches of Christ. It will be the thesis of this book that the Restoration Movement is built upon two key concerns: the concern for the unity of all Christians in the one body of Christ, and the concern for the Bible as the only authority for the faith and practice of Christians. Everything that happens within the Restoration Movement is the direct result of one or both of these twin concerns. This book will be a history of this Movement as interpreted in light of these two concerns.

Before we get into the history of the Movement proper, it will be helpful to look at both of these concerns, particularly to note that neither of them is unique to the Restoration Movement. Christians earlier than 1800 were sensitive to the need for Christian unity, just as many were convinced that the Bible alone was authoritative for Christian faith and practice. Perhaps it will be useful to look at some earlier expressions of these concerns.

As soon as there was division within the Church, there was concern about unity. This is even a mark of the apostolic church, as seen in the Jerusalem conference of Acts 15 and Paul's writings to the Corinthians.

In later years unity concerns surfaced in the wake of the cyclical divisions between eastern and western halves of Christendom—in the sixth century, the ninth century, and the thirteenth century, to name only a few. After the Protestant Reformation got under way, the Marburg Colloquy (1529) attempted union between the Lutherans and the Zwinglians. When the Lutherans split over theological minutiae, the Formula of Concord (1580) was designed to draw them back together. Hugo Grotius (1583-1645) spent much of his life trying to draw various Protestant groups together. John Dury (1595-1680) did much the same thing, trying to work out a theological statement that all major denominations could agree with. All these efforts, however, are only the highlights of a much longer story: the efforts to unite Christians of different sorts into a unity on earth.[1]

The unity that was to take place within the Restoration Movement was more of a preparation for service. The design was to eliminate sectarian divisions not just to ease a conscience pricked by scandal, but to pave the way for the evangelization of the world according to the prayer of Jesus. The night before His crucifixion, Jesus prayed for the unity of His followers: "That they all may be one; as thou, Father, art in me, and I in thee, that they also may be one in us: that the world may believe that thou hast sent me" (John 17:21, KJV). In Jesus' prayer, the purpose of unity was for the conversion of the world. The existence and competition of the rival denominations was a stumbling block to the smooth progress of the gospel. Removing the stumbling block was to be the goal of the Movement.

If the Christian Churches were not the first to talk about unity, neither were they the first to be sensitive that the Bible only was to be the standard for the church. The teachings of the apostles had a major place in the doctrinal formulations of the early church, and virtually every generation thereafter looked to original apostolic teaching as the standard to follow. Not every generation was accurate in its perception of apostolic teaching, and some generations paid only lip service to the standard; but for most generations there was a genuine intent to walk in the pathway of primitive Christianity.

By the time of the Protestant Reformation, this was an overt principle. The Renaissance scholars made famous their slogan *ad fontes* ("to the

---

[1]For a fuller treatment, see Ruth Rouse and Stephen Charles Neill (eds.), *A History of the Ecumenical Movement, 1517-1948* (Philadelphia: Westminster Press, 1954). None of them were significantly successful, partially because most of them had unity as the goal for self-serving purposes.

sources!"), and this influenced the Christian humanists to examine the source documents of Christianity (the New Testament and early patristic writings) and compare them to the teachings of contemporary Christianity. When Luther was challenged by the Catholic Church during the Diet of Worms (1521), he declared he would not recant unless he could be proven wrong by reason or Scripture. When John Calvin dedicated the first edition of his *Institutes of the Christian Religion* to King Francis I of France in 1536, he defended the Protestants against the charge of innovation by stating they based their teachings on the New Testament, while the Catholics traced their teachings back only to the late Latin fathers. Constantly throughout the Reformation era, the leaders looked to the New Testament as the basis for their teachings. We may argue about whether they properly interpreted or applied biblical teaching, but there is little reason to doubt they were sincere in trying to recapture the essence of original Christian teaching and practice. In the two centuries following the Reformation the various denominations continued the same claim and purpose. Throughout the writings of the Anabaptists, the Puritans, the Baptists, and others, there runs the same concern for using the New Testament as the standard of orthodoxy.

If, then, the Restoration Movement is based on the twin concerns of unity and biblical authority, and if these two concerns are not unique to the Restoration Movement, what is so significant about the Movement? It was the first time in the Movement that these two concerns were combined. Others previously concerned themselves with unity; still others with the restoration of biblical authority as the standard for the church. But not until the Restoration Movement got under way was anyone concerned about restoring the unity of the church by restoring the original standard of the church. Restoration of biblical authority, that the Church may be united, in order that the world might be won according to the prayer of Jesus—that is the pre-eminent purpose of the Restoration Movement. Nothing else has the importance as does this premier goal of evangelism. Unity and biblical authority are means to an end, not ends themselves.

Another factor that needs to be kept in mind, one that this book will focus on considerably, is that these twin concerns are designed to be compatible, but often appear to be antagonistic. That is, ideally, unity and biblical authority should work together in harmony and balance; in certain conditions, however, the two concerns can tend to go off in different directions, thus producing tremendous strain on one's understanding of the *raison d'etre* of the Movement and how the Movement is supposed to function. From time to time we will note the pressures that are brought to separate these two concerns, as well as the emphasis that was originally placed to coordinate the two in the early years.

Thus what is presented here is an interpretive history of the Restoration Movement. We will try to analyze what the Movement has stood for and what it has accomplished. In light of its intended purposes, how successful has it been? In light of its intended purposes, what is our task now? It is not enough that we simply perpetuate a Movement if we have no perception of the real purpose of that Movement. It is hoped that this book will both enlighten and challenge: enlighten as to the detail and meaning of the events of Restoration history, but also challenge us to greater effort to bring about a greater measure of restoration, unity, and evangelism. We can be inspired by the examples of previous trailblazers and servants as well as challenged to intelligent productivity as we see the tasks and issues that await the Church today. For this purpose this book is written.

Before we go on to the detail of the Movement, however, one more item ought to be mentioned. The Restoration Movement has put such emphasis on the restoration of the apostolic church and the idealization of early Christianity, that we often forget that there were seventeen centuries of church history separating the apostles from the Restoration Pioneers around the year 1800. It is too easy, though appallingly attractive, to just skip from the apostolic period to the Restoration Movement. We are not alone in this, by the way. When this author was in seminary, several Lutheran colleagues told him of the folk-myth that after the Apostle John died, Martin Luther was born—conveniently overlooking fourteen centuries of church history. Yet Luther was born into a certain context, and it is impossible to fully understand Luther and the Reformation he inaugurated without understanding that context. One cannot divorce Luther from history and his precedents.

The same needs to be understood about Restoration history. Some of us joke, "The Apostle John died, and Alexander Campbell was born." Yet Alexander Campbell came out of a context that helped to fashion him, just as much as Luther's context fashioned him. The same can be said of Thomas Campbell, B. W. Stone, Walter Scott, and other Restoration leaders. There are seventeen centuries of church history that cannot be overlooked. Thus the story of Restoration origins calls for a serious study and acquaintance with the historical context in which the Movement developed. While most of this has to do strictly with historical awareness, some of it also has to do with the thin balance line that separates historicity and theological presuppositions.

For instance, there is the oft-repeated idea in much of modern

Restoration thinking that the pure apostolic church has had a continued institutional embodiment down through the ages. This theory has been variously called "the church of the remnant," "the underground church," or as E. H. Broadbent entitled it in his full-length book treatment, "the pilgrim church." This theory holds that ever since the death of the apostles there has been a continuing, connected string of pure Christians who have kept the faith. James DeForest Murch, in his work *Christians Only,* defended this position: "In spite of severe limitations, a large body of trustworthy evidence enables us to trace through history the fact that the true church, often a remnant flock, has existed continuously since Pentecost."[2]

He then illustrated the theory by reference to such groups as the Priscillians, Paulicians, Bogomils, and Albigensians. He criticized the Roman Catholic Church for calling these people heretics and working for their extermination. However, all of these groups were teaching false doctrine and were thus heretics. Historically speaking, there is no "trustworthy evidence" that Murch refers to. The evidence that is available points to the fact that all of these groups were heretical.

The "pilgrim" church concept has always been a popular one, for it mingles pride with historical romance, nostalgia, and one-upmanship against the Catholics. There is something inherently attractive in being able to say that "the true church (of which I am a part)" has existed continuously since Pentecost apart from any corruptions inherited from the Catholics or Eastern Orthodox. The only difficulty, of course, is that it isn't true. Murch claims, "Churches that never departed from the faith and were not influenced by the evils prevailing in the Catholic system existed in the Alpine valleys of the Piedmont from the earliest days of the Christian era."[3]

But he gives no documentation to prove this. The pilgrim church idea is an attractive concept, but it is void of historical substance.

Thus we cannot say that John died and Alexander Campbell was born, nor can we say that the Campbells were the nineteenth century embodiment of a pilgrim church that has a clear, connected history through the ages. When various individuals began the Restoration Movement, they were coming out of their own individual context. They did not inherit a pure church that they kept alive and increased. Instead, each had to fight his own way through an inherited body of Protestant tradition in order to come to a clearer understanding of the significance of the

---

[2]Murch, *Christians Only*, p. 11.
[3]*Ibid.*, p. 12.

Scriptures and the function of the church in his generation. This is not to diminish their accomplishment; it is to heighten it. For these men did not descend through a perpetuated pure church. Each man had his own struggle to find the impact of the Word on his situation. Together these men established a Movement dedicated to a pure church in faith and practice. This, then, is their story.

1735	James O'Kelly born
1745	Francis Asbury born
1760	O'Kelly arrives in America
1769	Elias Smith born
1772	Abner Jones born
1773	William Guirey born
1784	Methodist Episcopal Church organized
1787	Elias Smith converted
1792	Right of Appeal raised
	Jones converted
1793	Republican Methodists loosely formed
1794	Southern Christians organized
	Guirey in Jamaica
1797	Guirey leaves Methodists
1801	Smith leaves Baptists
	Jones begins a Christian Church in Vermont
1808	Smith begins *Herald of Gospel Liberty*
	contact between Smith-Jones and O'Kelly Movements
1810	O'Kelly movement divides over baptism
1811	Guirey joins with Smith-Jones Movement
1815	Virginia delegates attend U.S. General Convention

Chapter 2

Beginnings

CHRONOLOGICALLY, THE FIRST INDIVIDUAL of prominence in the Restoration Movement was James O'Kelly (1735-1826).[1] Much of the information on his early life is scanty and questionable, but the basic outline seems to begin from his birth in Ireland in 1735. Even this is uncertain. Some evidence suggests that he may have been born in Virginia or North Carolina. But the better evidence places it in Ireland and his immigration to Virginia about 1760.

James O'Kelly

O'Kelly's wife apparently converted to Methodism early in the 1770s and O'Kelly himself was only a year or two behind. He began preaching as a lay exhorter for the Methodists about 1775, although his name is not listed in Methodist documents as a lay preacher until 1778.[2] Because O'Kelly came out of the Methodists, and because so much of what he experienced was directly influenced by Methodist concepts, it may be helpful to review Methodist beginnings in America.

Under John Wesley's (1703-1791) leadership, the Methodists increased their number not only in England, but throughout the English-speaking world. But although the Methodists in England had their own structure and clergy, they were not a separate denomination until after Wesley's death. Wesley himself was a priest in the Anglican Church.

---

[1] The best source for the life of O'Kelly is W. E. MacClenny, *The Life of Rev. James O'Kelly and the Early History of the Christian Church in the South* (Indianapolis: Religious Book Service, 1950). MacClenny is somewhat prejudiced toward his subject, but the information is still invaluable and the viewpoint often helpful.

[2] MacClenny, pp. 13–22.

Officially Methodists were Anglicans, commonly seen as a pietistic movement within Anglicanism. Methodist preachers were just that—preachers. They were not ordained and thus could not perform baptisms, weddings, or provide communion.

Early Methodist preaching in America was in the same situation.
Methodist preachers preached, but they were not ordained. They established societies, not churches; for that reason their places of worship
were called chapels. For the sacraments Methodist laymen were dependent upon the local Anglican clergy. Relations between Anglicans and
Methodists were not always cordial, however, particularly during the
American Revolution. Most Anglican clergymen were loyal to the British
crown, and most of the southern clergymen left the rebellious colonies
and returned to England. This left the Methodists—most of whom were
loyal to the patriotic cause—without the sacraments that even their own
preachers could not perform.

So it was that after the Revolution the Methodist leaders gathered in
Baltimore, Maryland, on December 24, 1784, to organize a new denomination. About sixty Methodist preachers assembled, including three men
who had recently arrived directly from John Wesley to help give guidance
to the Americans. At this conference a number of the American preachers
were ordained as ministers, including James O'Kelly. He was soon
appointed as presiding elder of southern Virginia, where he served for
eight years. Also at the conference Francis Asbury (1745-1816), who had
arrived in America in 1771, was made superintendent (a title that was
soon changed to "bishop"); he was the dominant influence in American
Methodism for the next third of a century.[3] The title chosen for the new
denomination was the Methodist Episcopal Church. The word *Episcopal*
simply meant they were governed by a bishop, which was Asbury.

He soon exercised full control over the fledgling denomination, since
he was its only bishop. At that time, virtually all Methodist preachers
were traveling circuit riders, moving from church to church rather than
being resident ministers with a particular congregation. As bishop,
Asbury assigned all the men to their circuits. Thus all the ministers were
under Asbury's authority, and his influence was dominant at the meetings. It was this that began to irritate a number of men in the denomination, particularly O'Kelly.

O'Kelly had served in the North Carolina militia during the
Revolution, and he feared that American Methodists were replacing their

---

[3]One of the best treatments of Asbury is L. C. Rudolph, *Francis Asbury*
(Nashville: Abingdon Press, 1966).

recently won political liberty with ecclesiastical tyranny and despotism. From 1787 on, O'Kelly had discussions and arguments with Asbury about such things, but he could win no relief on these points. Things came to a head in 1792.

The Methodists gathered for another General Conference in Baltimore on November 1. The next day O'Kelly presented what has come to be called the "Right of Appeal." If a preacher were assigned to a circuit by the bishop, but he did not like that assignment, what could he do? Up to this point, he could do nothing. O'Kelly and a number of others felt there ought to be some sort of appeal process, so the disgruntled preacher could get a hearing and perhaps a new assignment. Asbury, however, was opposed to this, feeling that if an appeal were allowed, everybody would soon be appealing for the better circuits and the poorer circuits would have no preaching whatsoever.[4]

The petition for appeal took up three days at the conference, not counting recess over Sunday. For better handling, it was soon broken down into two parts: (1) shall the bishop be the one to make the appointments? and (2) shall there be a right of appeal? The first part of the proposal was accepted without any difficulty—the bishop would continue to assign the circuits. But the real issue was in the second portion. Asbury argued for the negative. O'Kelly and others argued for the positive. At one point in the debate, O'Kelly stood up with a New Testament in his hand and stated, "Brethren hearken unto me, put away all other books, and forms and let this be the only *criterion* and that will satisfy me." O'Kelly thought that Christian ministers would surely agree to such a proposal. But one replied, "The Scripture is by no means a sufficient form of government. The Lord has left that business for his ministers to do suitable to times and places."[5] Apparently a large number of the preachers agreed in essence with O'Kelly, but in the process of the discussions those for the appeal began to liken Asbury to a venomous tyrant and slave owner. Some who originally supported the motion finally voted against it, and it was soundly defeated.

But O'Kelly was not willing to yield the point. The next day he and his followers sent a letter to the conference announcing they would withdraw from the conference and the circuit ministry.[6] Early in 1793

---

[4]MacClenny, pp. 87–97.

[5]*Ibid.*, p. 91.

[6]*Ibid.*, p. 98; for a careful treatment of this whole issue, see Charles Franklin Kilgore, *The James O'Kelly Schism in the Methodist Episcopal Church* (Mexico City: Casa Unida De Publications, 1963).

O'Kelly and his followers drew up a petition proposing some changes in church government and submitted it to Asbury. Asbury would not honor their request.[7] They met again on August 2, 1793, at Piney Grove, Virginia, to send a second petition to Bishop Asbury. In this they specifically requested a meeting with him and others to discuss their proposed changes and bring about peace and union. They were concerned that the present Methodist form of government was despotic and unscriptural, and they desired to follow the Holy Scriptures as their guide. Asbury refused to call such a meeting, saying he had no authority to do so. Thus, O'Kelly and his followers met by appointment at Manakin Town, Virginia, on December 25, 1793, and formed themselves into a new religious identity. They called themselves Republican Methodists and within a few days reported one thousand members of their new church. They stipulated that their ministers would all be equal—no bishops or presiding elders. The laity would also have a balance of power in their decisions.[8] The name of this group is significant. They still considered themselves Methodist, but they were *Republican* Methodist rather than Methodist *Episcopal:* Their framework of government was congregational rather than episcopal. Episcopalism they felt was unscriptural; their congregational government reflected that of their new country, a republic.

This is the first instance we have had to note the insistence on working within scriptural guidelines from a person to be associated with the rising Restoration Movement. In the petition O'Kelly and others sent to Asbury on August 2, there is concern that the episcopal power over the Methodists was both despotic and unscriptural. They wanted the New Testament to be the criterion of their government.[9] Their hope was to work something out with Asbury in order to reunite with the Methodist organization; they were also concerned about union. But when it became obvious that Asbury would entertain no intention to amend episcopal government, the reformers felt they had no choice but to leave the Methodist Episcopal Church. Unity and the concern for biblical authority both emerge in this incident, but not unity at the *expense* of biblical guidelines.

The next summer the Republican Methodists felt the necessity of meeting in order to work out a more permanent organization. This meeting took place at the Lebanon church in Surry County, Virginia,

---

[7]Kilgore, p. 28.

[8]*Ibid.*, pp. 30–31.

[9]A copy of their proposals can be found in Kilgore, p. 30, quoting from William Guirey's *History of Episcopacy*, pp. 379–380.

August 4, 1794.[10] After several resolutions on government were passed, it was obvious that a minority of men were extremely dissatisfied with the developments. O'Kelly himself recommended the whole situation should be reconsidered, and a committee of seven men was appointed to draw up a plan of government and lay it before the complete conference the next day. These seven men met, but they could accomplish nothing. Finally they decided they would lay aside every manuscript except the Scriptures, and take the Word of God alone as their guide. They then gave attention to their corporate name, the Republican Methodist Church. After some discussion, Rice Haggard, with a New Testament in his hand, stood up and stated: "Brethren, this is a sufficient rule of faith and practice, and by it we are told that the disciples were called *Christians,* and I move that henceforth and forever the followers of Christ be known as Christians simply."[11] The motion was adopted unanimously. Mr. Hafferty of North Carolina then moved that the Bible was to be their only creed, which was also accepted by the group.

The next day the committee reported to the remainder of the conference. Their decisions pleased the assembly. From this beginning, the assembly went on to decree equality among the preachers. There would be no gradations, no superiority or subordination among them. All preachers were to be allowed the liberty of private judgment, so far as it did not conflict with the teachings of the New Testament. The laity were also to be granted more liberty than they had under the Methodist episcopal system. Furthermore, they agreed that all plans and regulations made at the conferences would be only advisory. The annual conference would have no authority over the churches, each of which was free to call its own preacher and enjoy the greatest possible freedom.[12]

In referring to this gathering, O'Kelly commented that they still felt the pain of division from "our Episcopal brethren."[13] But since the Methodists would not reform their government along scriptural lines, the Christians felt they had no alternative but to depart and establish their own organization. Notice again how in this 1794 meeting, it is the centrality of scriptural authority that was the impetus for their decisions, from the name they were to wear, to the liberty of each man's judgment. This earliest Christian Church movement was motivated by the twin concerns of biblical authority and Christian union.

---

[10]MacClenny, pp. 114ff.
[11]*Ibid.,* p. 116.
[12]*Ibid.,* pp. 117–118.
[13]*Ibid.,* p. 118.

"CARDINAL PRINCIPLES OF THE CHRISTIAN CHURCH" (O'KELLY MOVEMENT)

1. The Lord Jesus is the only Head of the Church.
2. The name Christian to the exclusion of all party and sectarian names.
3. The Holy Bible, or the Scriptures of the Old and New Testament, our only creed, and a sufficient rule of faith and practice.
4. Christian character, or vital piety, the only test of church fellowship and membership.
5. The right of private judgment, and the liberty of conscience, the privilege and duty of all.[14]

This O'Kelly Movement seemed to grow significantly in the next few years. There were thirty preachers in the group at its beginning,[15] and then several additional preachers came out of the Methodists to join them. Because of O'Kelly's eight years as presiding elder in southern Virginia, he had been popular with many of the younger Methodist preachers. Many of the Methodist ministers who now joined the Christian Church brought their chapels and members with them. According to statistics provided by a Methodist historian,[16] the Methodists in these years suffered a decline in membership of about 6,000, actually a time of great and successful evangelism for them. It is likely that most of these defections went to the O'Kelly Movement. Asbury's biographer states that by 1793, O'Kelly had pulled ten thousand Methodists into his group.[17]

The principles of the O'Kelly Movement were stated much later in the document called "Cardinal Principles of the Christian Church," but O'Kelly's biographer, MacClenny, insists that they were already embodied in 1794. These principles are stated under the heading above.

To anyone acquainted with the later leadership of Stone and Campbell in the Restoration Movement, these principles will seem very familiar, with the exception of #4. Followers of Campbell would more than likely say something about baptism in any test of church membership, or at least some such phrase as "obedience to the gospel." Herein is already an indication of some of the differences that will plague the O'Kelly and Campbell Movements.

---

[14]MacClenny, pp. 121–122.

[15]*Ibid.*, p. 126.

[16]James M. Buckley, *A History of Methodism in the United States* (New York: Harper & Brothers, Publishers, 1898), vol. 1, p. 346.

[17]Rudolph, p. 65.

In spite of the positive accomplishments of the 1794 conference, there was still discontent within the O'Kelly Movement. Shortly after that meeting, some of the preachers became dissatisfied with the name "Christian Church" for fear it would appear exclusivist. They reasoned, "If we are the Christian Church, it will imply that there are no Christians but our party." Four of the preachers broke away from O'Kelly's leadership and resumed the name "Republican Methodists."[18]

William Guirey

Another individual very important to the story of the O'Kelly Movement was William Guirey (1773-1840), born probably around Philadelphia because it was here that he was converted and became a Methodist in 1788. In 1792 or 1793 he began preaching, although the sources are not clear whether he was more than a lay exhorter. Probably he was not at the 1792 General Conference because he became aware of O'Kelly only later. If he had attended the 1792 Conference, he certainly would have known of O'Kelly at that time. In 1794 he went to Jamaica. He found it destitute of religion, feeling that the formalities of Anglicanism, performed by a dissolute parson, did not count. He began to preach and had about sixty converts in a few weeks. But the Anglican authorities resented his activities. They had him arrested, imprisoned, and finally expelled back to the United States.

In America, he became a trial member of the Methodist Conference in 1795 and traveled in Virginia. In 1797 his name disappeared from all Methodist records, and it must be about this time that he left that church. For some time, beginning with his difficulties in Jamaica, he had been concerned about pure doctrine and church polity. He became convinced the Methodists were in error, so he left them. Episcopalism prevented him from uniting with Catholics, Episcopalians, and Methodists, and Calvinism prevented him from uniting with Baptists or Presbyterians, and there were no other churches in his area. He described his dilemma in these words:

> What was to be done? to stand alone was disagreeable—to unite on bad conditions was worse. Thus circumstanced, I perused the scriptures, and from them gathered a system, which I conceived to be correct; after my mind was perfectly satisfied on the subject.[19]

---

[18]*Ibid.*, pp. 155–156.
[19]*Herald of Gospel Liberty*, April 14, 1809, p. 65.

Here again we see a man driven by two concerns: concern for scriptural teaching and concern for Christian union. He did not want to stand alone as a Christian, yet he could not compromise his conviction that the existing churches he knew were all in error on one subject or more. He wanted to unite with other Christians, but he could not compromise biblical teaching.

Guirey does not provide any exact chronology, but it was apparently some years later that he was in Georgia and heard of a group that called themselves "Christians." He had never heard of such a group, and he wanted to meet them. They were, of course, a congregation of the O'Kelly Movement. In his interview with them, he was delighted because he discovered that the only principle difference between them and him was on the subject of baptism. The O'Kelly Movement was practicing infant sprinkling and adult pouring (affusion); Guirey, through his independent study of the Scriptures, had come to believe in immersion—although he himself had not yet been immersed. But Guirey was as concerned about Christian unity as about scriptural purity. He wanted to unite with someone in Christian fellowship, and this group was closer to his beliefs than any other he had met. So Guirey united with their fellowship on the condition that they would allow him to have his opinion on baptism and to act as he thought proper on the subject.

It was not long, however, before someone began to ask about baptism. Guirey encouraged the discussion and explained his understanding of Scripture. As a result, four of the group, including Guirey, determined to be immersed. They sent for a minister who had been immersed on a profession of faith in Christ. The man came and baptized the quartet. Soon every Lord's day Guirey was baptizing a handful of people until more than a hundred immersed believers were a part of the congregation.[20]

There may be something very significant in this episode in Guirey's life. He had come to this group in Georgia in Christian union, realizing that there was disagreement between them on the subject of baptism. But his tolerant acceptance and his patient teaching soon created a congregation with over a hundred immersed believers. What would have happened to Guirey's potential for witnessing and teaching if he had approached these people with a belligerent attitude of spiritual superiority? He could have said, "You people are wrong on baptism, and if you don't straighten up I can have nothing to do with you." He could have said that and his influence on them would have been zero. He was concerned about biblical purity, but he was also concerned about Christian

---

[20]*Ibid.*

unity. He did not compromise his beliefs, but he was open in his acceptance of others and his desire to be able to teach the Word of the Lord
more perfectly. He did not argue; he did not condemn. He maintained
his integrity to the Bible, but he also maintained a sensitivity about the
implications of Christian union. He did not allow his biblical commitment to become exclusivist to the point of washing out his desire for
unity, nor did he allow his commitment to unity to become so inclusivist
as to nullify his desire to be true to biblical teaching. Between the two
poles there was a thin line of sensitive appraisal. In Guirey's case, this situation turned out quite well. The combination of unity and biblical
authority created a healthy church fellowship that grew in understanding
of biblical practice.

The lesson here that later generations need to learn, including our
own, is that all too often we have staked out the limits of our inclusivism
and demanded that others yield to it or else. Particularly in the area of
baptism, we have typically been unwilling to make any gesture of unity
lest our biblical integrity be compromised. This is not to ask for a surrendering of the biblical teaching on baptism, but it is asking for a sensitive
consideration of the healthy tension between the twin concerns of
Christian unity and biblical authority. Guirey's patience and willingness
were amply rewarded.

O'Kelly-Guirey Conflict

Unfortunately, but all too typically, the harmony and openness of this
congregation in Georgia was not to be widely repeated a little further
north. In 1806 Guirey moved into North Carolina, and in 1808 he located in Virginia. He came into contact with James O'Kelly for the first time
and was soon recognized as one of the leading ministers of the Christian
Churches. However, O'Kelly, as much as he talked about following the
Scriptures, was not in favor of immersion. Friction soon developed
between himself and Guirey on this very issue.

Guirey had led three or four other ministers to be immersed and he
continued to practice immersion.[21] But he did not want it to become a
test of fellowship. In a letter of 1809, he reflected on this sensitive issue.

> Notwithstanding the union that existed between me and my brethren, yet I
> frequently mourned in secret, that infant baptism was practiced. All my
> brethren knew my sentiments, but through fear of disturbing the peace of the

---

[21]*Herald of Gospel Liberty,* January 19, 1809, p. 43.

church, I have said as little on the subject as possible; the many good things I find among them endear them to me; and I never expected during my life to find a church more conformable to the Apostolic order in every particular. As to infant baptism, I had long reconciled it to myself, to bear with my brethren, knowing that imperfection is the portion of mortals.[22]

Obviously Guirey was still wrestling with the tension between unity and biblical authority. He did not have to wrestle much longer.

In 1810 the annual conference of the Christians took place at Pine Stake, Orange County, Virginia. The practice of baptism by immersion came into serious discussion at this meeting. As MacClenny records it, "Guirey and his fellow immersionists were not willing to give over their position in regard to the ordinance, and Mr. O'Kelly and his fellow affusionists [sic] were not willing to give up their position, and so a debate was begun to try to settle the matter."[23] Joshua Livesay, an eyewitness immersionist, recorded that at the meeting, the O'Kelly people presented three resolutions whose "tendency was to proscribe baptism," and the presentation indicated that this was the only way union of the churches could be preserved. Of the fourteen preachers present, nine of them were for "liberty of conscience": that is, that baptism not be made a test of fellowship. Three ministers were opposed to this position, wanting a repudiation of immersion; two ministers remained neutral. The "liberty of conscience" ministers held up the Bible in opposition to the man-made articles, but O'Kelly and his men would not yield.[24] In the heat of the discussion, O'Kelly demanded of Guirey, "Who rules this body, you or I?" Guirey simply replied, "Neither of us brother; Christ rules here."[25]

Resolution of the conflict appearing impossible, the two leaders decided to dissociate their forces. Most of Guirey's followers were in Virginia, and they soon organized the Virginia Conference. O'Kelly and his followers were mostly located in North Carolina and they returned to their state; before the year was out, they organized the "Old North Carolina Conference." Guirey and his group were soon being called the "Independent Christian Baptist Church." However, even in North Carolina there was a group of immersionist churches that refused any meeting with groups unless they were immersionist. Some Baptists who left that

---

[22]*Ibid.*, April 14, 1809, p. 65.
[23]MacClenny, p. 158.
[24]*Christian Palladium*, August 2, 1841, p. 104.
[25]MacClenny, p. 158.

denomination because of closed communion merged with these North
Carolina Christians, and some of their churches were still known as
Christian Baptists as late as 1854.[26]

The actions of the 1810 conference are significant for several reasons.
First of all, they show that Guirey and his followers wanted to practice
"liberty of conscience," but they would not accept dictation. They were
willing to tolerate unscriptural practices on baptism without making
them a test of fellowship. But when the affusionists demanded that they
yield on immersion, they refused. There may be a thin line between tolerating error and rejecting truth, but Guirey and his followers felt they
were justified in their position.

Secondly, this conference is significant in that it demonstrates a deviation from the original position of 1794. At that time, the conference
agreed that all plans and regulations made at the conferences would be
advisory only. Now O'Kelly himself was willing to use the conference to
push through some articles demanding uniformity on the churches and
preachers. How far he had come in sixteen years! This is only another
indication of how far a man may be willing to go in order to "bend the
rules" to defend his own position.

A third observation that comes out of this conference has to do with
the selective desires of O'Kelly about following the Scriptures only. In his
struggles against episcopacy, he constantly called for defense from the
Scriptures. In his struggle against immersion, he was deaf to the same
plea now being advanced by the other side. This raises the question as to
how sincere O'Kelly was in his desire to follow the New Testament alone.
From the standpoint of the mainstream of the Restoration Movement,
O'Kelly appears quite inconsistent.

This may be unfair, of course. It may not be a matter of sincerity as
much as a matter of understanding and perspective. O'Kelly may have
sincerely believed that affusion was proper biblical baptism. But one
would at least think he would be willing to tolerate immersion even if he
felt it was unnecessary. At the very least, the three articles presented in
1810 were intolerant, whether or not he was sincere in his understanding.

It is interesting that early in 1809, O'Kelly wrote to the *Herald of Gospel
Liberty* and included "A Plan of Union Proposed." In his discussions he
pointed out he could not unite with the Baptists because "the door into
that church is *water*—and I can not enter because of unbelief."[27] He went

---

[26]*Ibid.*, pp. 158–159.
[27]This document is reprinted in MacClenny, p. 248, quoting from *Herald of
Gospel Liberty,* pp. 39 and 44.

on to remark, "Let the *Baptists* open a more charitable door, and receive to their communion those of a Christian life and experience; and they themselves eat bread with their Father's children."[28] At least he is consistent here in asserting the only test of church fellowship or membership is that of Christian character or piety, the same position that had marked the Christian Church of the O'Kelly Movement all through its years. They never accepted the limitation of Christian immersion.

Smith and Jones

At this point it is necessary to leave the O'Kelly Movement temporarily and look at a movement that was occurring at almost exactly the same time in another part of the country. This movement was coming to almost identical positions even though there was no contact between the two in these early years. Guirey and O'Kelly had come out of a Methodist background in Virginia and North Carolina. Elias Smith (1769-1846) and Abner Jones (1742-1841) came out of a Baptist background in New England.

Elias Smith[29] was born in Connecticut but grew up in the backwoods of Vermont. His father was a Baptist, but his mother was a Congregationalist. When Elias was about eight, at a time when his father was out of town, his mother made the arrangements to have him sprinkled in the local Congregationalist church. When young Elias got the idea of what was about to happen, he bolted out the church door. His uncle was alerted to this, however, and ran him down, bringing him back to church where he was baptized rather against his will. It did not endear the Congregationalist Church to him.

When he was sixteen, he began to experience religious concern and wondered about his own salvation. One day he was out in the woods when a heavy log fell on him, pinning him down in the snow and frightening him considerably. He was able to get out from under the log without significant injury, but the experience provided him with the typical saving conversion experience that Calvinism expected at that time. Smith professed both physical and spiritual regeneration. He began to search the Scriptures and found no basis there for infant baptism. He was already inclined against the church of his mother, and the issue of baptism led him to the church of his father, the Baptists. Apparently,

---

[28]MacClenny, p. 249.

[29]The best source for the life of Smith is his autobiography, Elias Smith, *The Life, Conversion, Preaching, Travels, and Suffering of Elias Smith* (Portsmouth, New Hampshire: Beck & Foster, 1816), vol. 1 [there was never a vol. 2].

about the age of twenty, he became a member of the Baptist Church and was immersed.

By the next year he was reading sermons from the pulpit and was soon actively preaching. In 1792 he was ordained by the Baptist ministers of Boston. For the next ten years or so he continued as a Baptist minister, seriously studying the Bible, while he was making his living as a school teacher and by practicing medicine. As he continued to study the Scriptures, he became convinced that orthodox Calvinism was in error and that all standardized bodies of doctrine and creeds were wrong. He wanted to abandon all theological systems as tests of fellowship, abandon ecclesiastical forms as bonds of unity, and instead restore the simple faith and practice of the New Testament church. It is useful to note that Smith came to these positions pretty much on his own. He had never heard of James O'Kelly or William Guirey or the Christian Churches in the South.

Unfortunately, however, Smith had a major tinge of instability in him. In 1801 he abandoned the Baptists under the influence of his brother and became a Universalist. This was but the first of several times he joined the Universalists and then later left them. On this occasion he was a Universalist for fifteen days. He continued his searching and in the next year he discovered Abner Jones who stabilized him temporarily and brought him into the Christian Church Movement of New England.

Abner Jones[30] was born in Massachusetts, but he also grew up in Vermont. His rural upbringing was very similar to that of Smith and at about age twenty, he had a religious conversion and joined the Baptists. He soon felt he would like to preach, so he began to study the Bible. He felt it was necessary to study the Scriptures directly rather than what people said about the Scriptures. As did Smith, he made his basic livelihood by teaching school and practicing medicine in addition to preaching.

Through the 1790s, Jones began to have increasing doubts about his identity as a Baptist. Three things bothered him: (1) He could find no scriptural warrant for the name "Baptist Church." (2) He was bothered about portions of Calvinism that he could not find sanctioned in Scripture, particularly predestination. (3) He developed doubts about typical Baptist church polity, the organization of Baptist churches in local associations. Technically, the Baptists claimed congregational independence, but Jones could see that the associations could exert influence and control over the local churches. He was convinced this practice had

---

[30]The best source for the life of Jones is his autobiography, Abner Jones, *Memoirs of the Life and Experiences, Travels and Preaching of Abner Jones* (Exeter, New Hampshire: Norris & Sawyer, 1807).

no New Testament foundation and was even dangerous for the churches. Even with these doubts, however, he continued as a Baptist preacher.

Then sometime in the late 1790s he heard Elias Smith preach and realized he was not alone in some of his doubts and misgivings about Baptist identity. So he broke from the Baptists, although Smith continued as one. Smith's influence on Jones at this point is significant, even though that influence led Jones into a position that was in advance of where Smith was at the time.

Having broken with the Baptists, Jones continued to preach as occasion offered. In September of 1801, he began a new church in Lyndon, Vermont, and called it simply a "Christian church." He had become convinced that was the only name in Scripture that the followers of Christ should be called. There were soon other churches, and in either 1802 or 1803 Jones received the cooperation of Smith to begin a church in Portsmouth, New Hampshire. Smith remained here for several years, while Jones went on to start a church in Boston in 1804, and even others. Smith recorded that in 1807 there were fourteen churches and twelve ministers in the movement.[31] From meager beginnings in 1801, the Christian Church in New England was well under way.

Smith's Leadership

At this point in the story, Abner Jones fades somewhat into the background. He had begun the first Christian Church in the area and began numerous others. But he was a quiet worker. Once Smith came into the movement he soon began to exercise more visible leadership. This is not to say that he elbowed Jones out of the way and took things over. It simply recognizes that Smith was a more dynamic and aggressive leader. He became the most visible leader for the next couple of decades. Part of this was personality; part of it was also innovation, creativity, and journalism. Both of these men were important to the establishment of the northern Christian Churches. Smith initially influenced Jones; Jones began the first Christian Church; Smith joined him in the movement and ascended to greater leadership. This is why this movement is generally called the Smith-Jones Movement.

In 1805 Smith began a quarterly with the impressive title, *The Christian's Magazine, Reviewer, and Religious Intelligencer.* This advent into religious publishing magnified Smith's leadership role and placed him in

---

[31]*The Morning Star and City Watchman,* ed. by Elias Smith, vol. 1 (January, 1828), p. 173.

a position of great influence. Religious journalism developed into one of the major tools of the Restoration Movement. The significance of religious journalism in the Movement dare not be minimized. We will have numerous occasions to see this throughout the remainder of this book, but the whole thing began with Elias Smith. Smith's quarterly magazine soon developed into something bigger and more frequent. On September 1, 1808, he published the first issue of *The Herald of Gospel Liberty*, a biweekly publication that has been called the first religious newspaper in the world. That claim has been questioned, but there is no question that this was a most important move.

The significance of Smith's journalistic ventures became evident within two months as he received a letter from Robert Punshon in Philadelphia. Punshon had gotten hold of a book written by Smith, *The Age of Inquiry*, and he found in it a religious position exactly like his own. Punshon then described the origin of the Christian Church in Virginia and how the Virginia Christians started the congregation in Philadelphia.[32] In the next couple of weeks, several additional letters came to Smith from individuals in the southern Christian Churches. They asked for information on the background of the northern Christians and for details on doctrine and practices. William Lanphier wrote from Alexandria, Virginia, on November 9, 1808, and said, "If I have not mistaken as to your order, I think the Christian Church in this part of the U.S. would rejoice to give you the right hand of fellowship."[33]

Two things stand out in these early letters. The writers from the South were awed at the realization that there were others in the country who apparently had the same beliefs as they did. They had labored under misrepresentation and attack from Methodists and others so long that they were gratified to discover they were not alone. They had renewed confidence in their position and a longing to see these other people who shared their precious faith. Secondly, we note again that one of their initial concerns was for Christian union. It is not surprising that as soon as these groups began to discover each other, their thoughts turned to unity. They wanted to be simply Christians on the basis of the Bible, and their hearts and hands went out to others who shared the same convictions.

The next significant letter received in the north was from William Guirey, dated Caroline County, Virginia, December 18, 1808. He stated his anxious desire to know more about the northern Christians, and he

---

[32]*Herald of Gospel Liberty,* November 10, 1808, p. 23.
[33]*Ibid.,* December 8, 1808, p. 3.

also pointed out the variance that existed in the south over the form of baptism. (Recall that this is 1808, before the 1810 division over baptism.) He concluded his letter with this telling paragraph:

> I should be exceedingly glad to receive a letter from you stating the doctrines and government of the church to which you are united, and if there should not be any thing like Episcopacy or Calvinism in the way, my soul would exult if a union between us could be effected, should only a prospect of this kind present itself gladly would I pay you a visit the ensuing spring.[34]

Two things stand out in Guirey's letter: concern for proper scriptural teaching and concern for Christian union.

Smith's response to Guirey partook of the same spirit. He stated his wish that the southern brethren had a better understanding of baptism, but he affirmed they would learn more as time went on. Smith finished his letter to Guirey in these words:

> There is nothing to hinder a general union among the brethren from north to south, that I can see: but there is something to be done; that is, to let all our brethren through the whole know that we are striving for the same thing.
>
> It is wonderful to me, that while I was laboring to convince men that Christ is all; not knowing there was another person on earth striving for the same thing, that others in the South should be doing the same. Had I known it before now, I might have leaned on them; but we have done like those in the days of Nehemiah; each built the wall over against his own house till they joined all in one, and set up the gates. . . .
>
> My. Br. have we not built long enongh [sic] to join the wall? I think we have. With pleasure I look forward to a day, I hope, not far off; which I shall meet some of my brethren in the south, to join in *Christian Union*, endeavoring to promote harmony and love among thousands of our brethren widely spread throughout the United States of America.[35]

Guirey was delighted to receive this letter because it indicated that in the three crucial areas of baptism, episcopacy, and Calvinism, he and Smith stood in the same position. In addition, the general goals of Christian union and adherence to the Bible alone were also duplicated.[36] On May 27, 1809, a general meeting of elders and brethren of the Christian Church in the south met at Pittsylvania, Virginia. The seventeen ministers assembled (including Guirey, but not O'Kelly) wrote a letter to the northern brethren explaining their doctrinal position in

---

[34]*Ibid.*, January 19, 1809, p. 43.
[35]*Ibid.*, February 2, 1809, p. 47.
[36]*Ibid.*, April 14, 1809, pp. 65–66.

three basic points: (1) Christ the only head of the church; (2) the New Testament the only law for the church; and (3) the name "Christian" the only name for Christ's followers.[37] On June 23, twelve ministers from the north gathered at Portsmouth, New Hampshire, and sent a similar letter in reply, using almost identical terminology in the doctrinal points.[38]

Things had reached this point in 1809. The next year was the divisive meeting at Piney Stake, Virginia, where Guirey and O'Kelly separated their followers. For years Guirey had "mourned in secret" about their differences on baptism, but no separation occurred until *after* the contact between the Virginia immersionists and the New England Christians, who were also immersionists. Is there any connection between these two events? Was Guirey emboldened by the awareness of immersionist brethren in the North to take a firm stand against O'Kelly, a firmer stand than he might have taken if he had not been aware of his colleagues in the North? Until now, he had stated he did not expect to find "a church more conformable to the Apostolic order" than the O'Kelly people, and he was willing to tolerate their weakness on baptism. Had his acquaintance with the Smith-Jones Movement increased his "lowest common denominator" on which he would practice Christian union? These questions have no answer, but they may suggest a change in the tension exerted by the twin poles of unity and biblical authority.

Regardless of this speculation, what is certain is that correspondence between North and South flourished in 1809 and that the O'Kelly Movement divided in 1810. It may also be significant that it was the immersionist brethren that continued the correspondence with the North. In August of 1810 editor Elias Smith announced his intention of encouraging elders from both North and South to meet in Philadelphia. By the summer of 1811 Smith even moved to Philadelphia and edited the *Herald* from there. Thus when the Virginia Christians held their annual meeting on October 4, 1811, in Caroline County (home of Guirey), Smith himself was present. From Friday afternoon until Monday, Smith preached seven sermons and other ministers preached eight more. There were a total of about fourteen preachers present. On the last morning of the meeting an historic event took place.

Monday morning, the preachers met together in an upper Chamber in order to attend to the important question so often asked—*"Can the Christian Brethren in the South, unite with the Christian Brethren in the North?"* This question had frequently been asked in the South, and by many answered in the negative.

---

[37]*Ibid.*, June 23, 1809, p. 87.
[38]*Ibid.*, July 21, 1809, pp. 95–96.

Some at the beginning of this meeting concluded that on account of Baptism, a union could not take place, though they wished it might. After some conversation upon the subject, one of the Elders observed, that an Elder from the North was present (E. Smith), that he was in fellowship with the other Elders and Brethren in New England; that it was the desire of the Brethren in Philadelphia, and many in New England, that he should meet with the Brethren here—and that it was his and their desire, that a general union should take place through the whole; that the walls should be joined. He observed that all who felt free to receive him as a brother, a member with them, and a fellow laborer, would manifest it by giving him the right hand of fellowship. He began, and each one did the same without hesitation; all agreeing to exalt Christ, to preach him as the only way, to obey his commands as far as understood, and teach others also. This meeting was truly solemn, joyful, and glorious; God was among us of a truth.[39]

Thus union occurred between the Guirey portion of the O'Kelly Movement and the Smith-Jones Movement. One wonders if Smith himself was the elder who made the "observation" that led to the handshaking consummation. Two movements that started out of entirely different backgrounds, from different parts of the country, but came to the same ideology and concerns, now united their forces in the common cause of being simply Christians on the basis of the New Testament alone. But O'Kelly was not pleased. He worked both to prevent and break up this union between North and South. O'Kelly wrote to some of the churches that had gone into the union, but apparently they ignored him.[40] This again casts doubt upon O'Kelly's consistency as a "restorationist." He resisted biblical purposes and even endeavored to break up Christian union because of his pettiness.

The union between the Virginia Christians and the Smith-Jones Movement was a solid one. By 1815 the Virginia Conference was sending a representative to the United States General Convention that met that year in Windham, Connecticut.[41] This points out the fact that not only had the Smith-Jones Movement developed local conferences, but they had assembled a national conference as well. As innocent as this may appear, one wonders what Jones would have thought about it, because the Baptist regional associations were one reason why Jones became restive with Baptist identity in the 1790s. Furthermore, when contact developed between the Stone Movement and the Smith-Jones Movement, this national conference may have been a cause for concern.

---

[39]*Ibid.*, October 25, 1811, p. 331.
[40]*Ibid.*, January 17, 1812, p. 355.
[41]MacClenny, p. 165.

But Virginia representatives appeared at the national conference in 1815 as well as in later years. The union between the North and South was also typified in the fact that occasional northern preachers went on preaching tours in the South where they were well received. These itinerant preachers became another link in the connection between the two parts of the country and the two initially different movements.

1772	B.W. Stone born
1779	Stone family moves to southern Virginia
1790	Stone attends Caldwell Academy
1792	Stone "convicted" by McGready's preaching
1793	Stone "converted" by Hodge's preaching
1796	Stone licensed to preach; goes to Kentucky
1798	Stone ordained to Presbyterian ministry
1800	Revivalism spreads out from Logan County, Kentucky
1801	Stone marries Eliza Campbell
	Cane Ridge revival
	Heresy charges against Richard McNemar
1803	McNemar convicted of heresy by Synod of Kentucky
	Stone and others leave Presbyterian organization; form Springfield Presbytery
1804	Springfield Presbytery publishes *Apology*
	Springfield Presbytery dissolves; adopts *Last Will and Testament*
1805	Shakers arrive in the West; McNemar and Dunlavy join them
1810	Stone immersed
1811	Marshall and Thompson rejoin Presbyterians
1825	Joseph Badger comes west; Stone and Smith-Jones "unite"
1826	Badger's second visit causes controversy
	Stone begins *Christian Messenger*

Chapter 3

The Stone Movement

AS SIGNIFICANT as the movements under O'Kelly and Smith-Jones were, however, they never came into the mainstream of the Restoration Movement, for reasons which will be discussed later and in Chapter Seven.[1] They represent the initial desire of implementing Christian union upon the basis of the Christian Scriptures, but they failed to follow through in an ultimate commitment to that goal. A fuller realization of the Restoration Plea had to come in the movements led by Barton W. Stone (1772-1844) and the father-son team of Thomas (1763-1851) and Alexander Campbell (1788-1866).

Barton Warren Stone

Stone was born near Port Tobacco, Maryland, on December 24, 1772.[2] Port Tobacco was a small town on the Potomac River about thirty miles south of modern Washington D.C. Of course, at the time of his

---

[1]See pp. 62-69 of this chapter as well as Chapter Seven, pp. 179-185.

[2]The best source for the life of Stone is still his autobiography: John Rogers (ed.), *The Biography of Eld. Barton Warren Stone, Written by Himself: With Additions and Reflections,* (Cincinnati: J. A. & U. P. James, 1847). It has appeared in numerous editions since its first appearance. The edition and pagination used here are from Hoke S. Dickinson, *The Cane Ridge Reader* (no place, no publisher, 1972), although Dickinson's pagination is exactly that of the original and several of the other editions. Other helpful treatments of Stone include Charles C. Ware, *Barton Warren Stone, Pathfinder of Christian Union: A Story of His Life and Times* (St. Louis: The Bethany Press, 1932); William Garrett West, *Barton Warren Stone: Early American Advocate of Christian Unity* (Nashville: The Disciples of Christ Historical Society, 1954) Cane Ridge in Context: Perspectives on Barton W. Stone and the Revival (Nashville: Disciples of Christ Historical Society, 1992)."

birth the city of Washington did not exist; the American colonies were still part of the British Empire, although that was about to change in just a few years. Stone was born into a family with a rich history in the colony of Maryland. His great-great-great grandfather, William Stone, was the first Protestant governor of Maryland (1648-1653) when it was still a Catholic colony under the Calverts.[3] It was under this governor that Maryland adopted a Religious Toleration Act in 1649, heavily influenced by the Puritan Civil War in England at the time.[4]

In spite of Maryland's Roman Catholic beginnings, the Church of England was actively becoming the dominant religion in the colony by the end of the seventeenth century. King William III took over the colony as a royal one in 1692 and made the Church of England the official religion, although the law approving such was not officially adopted until 1702. By 1750 the Anglican Church was the largest church in the colony. It was into this church that infant Barton was baptized shortly after his birth.

Young Barton was born into a large family—he had six brothers and one sister. In 1775 his father, John, died. But the family was still comfortably well off, living on a plantation with fifteen slaves. In 1779, however, the widow Mrs. Stone decided to leave Tidewater Maryland for the hills of south central Virginia. The exact reasons are not clear, but the British invasion up the Chesapeake Bay in 1777 might have had something to do with her plans. She settled the family in Pittsylvania County, near Danville.[5] Thus before his seventh birthday Stone had moved to the frontier. All his life he bore the marks of his frontier upbringing. This does not mean he was crude; it only means he was more comfortable with frontier settlers than with developed society on the eastern coast.

Even in southern Virginia, however, the Stone family could not escape the war. Two of Stone's elder brothers served in the militia. To save some of their valuable horses from being confiscated by military scouting parties, Barton and two brothers once hid them in a thicket of brushwood not far from their home. When Generals Greene and Cornwallis fought the Battle of Guilford Court House (March 15, 1781) about thirty miles away, Stone and his family could hear the roar of the

[3]McAlister and Tucker, pp. 62-63.

[4]For this Act of Toleration and a discussion of William Stone, see William Warren Sweet, *Religion in Colonial America* (New York: Cooper Square Publishers, Inc., 1965), pp. 177-178.

[5]Rogers, p. 1.

artillery and fearfully awaited the result.[6] The Americans lost the battle, but the British could not keep up the fight. Cornwallis moved up to Virginia, where he surrendered at Yorktown in October.

Early in Stone's youth, he was sent to a schoolmaster who was rather a tyrant, one who took pleasure in whipping and abusing his pupils on the slightest pretext. Stone was so intimidated through his fear of the teacher that he could learn nothing. Called on to recite, young Barton was so afraid of a whipping and confused in mind that he could not recite at all. After a few days, his mother noticed that the process was making no progress, so she sent Barton to a different teacher. This one had a different temperament and Stone easily learned the essentials of reading, writing, and arithmetic. Ever afterward Stone praised this teacher, Robert W. Somerhays, for his kindness, patience, and encouragement. In four or five years Stone learned all that Somerhays could teach him and was pronounced a finished scholar.[7]

It is always risky and perhaps even ill-advised to attempt to psychoanalyze a person long after his death, but Stone's experience with his first two teachers seems to establish a pattern that will appear later in his life as well. Faced with an intimidating authority, Stone could not respond properly; when that authority was replaced with one of gentle understanding, Stone blossomed. As we will soon see, Stone's conversion experience had some interesting parallels to this, as will his experience with the religious authorities in Kentucky.

The lack of Christian unity between the various American denominations had an influence on Stone while he was still a youth. He remembered the Baptist preachers who came through his part of Virginia converting multitudes of the settlers. Stone himself was a constant attendant upon their services, interested in hearing the converts relate their conversion experiences. Then the Methodist preachers began to arrive and were greeted with a great deal of abuse. The Baptists attacked them as denying the doctrines of grace and teaching salvation by works. Baptists warned the people that these Methodists were the locusts of the Apocalypse and urged the people not to receive them. Stone was much concerned, and he vacillated between the two groups. He retired both morning and evening for private prayer, trying to decide what to do. But he became discouraged over the conflict, quit praying, and decided to enjoy the youthful sports of the day instead.[8] Already it is evident that

---

[6]*Ibid.*, p. 2.

[7]*Ibid.*, pp. 3-4.

[8]*Ibid.*, pp. 5-6.

Stone was concerned about Christian unity. At the time he could only confess confusion over the differences, but later he committed himself to trying to resolve some disputes.

When the family split up their inheritance from their father, Barton decided to take his share and go to college with the intention of becoming a lawyer. His family encouraged him in this, so in February of 1790 he enrolled in the David Caldwell (1725-1824) Academy in Guilford, North Carolina. He devoted himself seriously to his studies, limiting himself to only six to seven hours of sleep a day, and to a diet of milk and vegetables. He was so intent upon his academic progress that he felt religion would impede him. He joined that part of the student body that made light of religious things, even though he was forced to admit that many of the students recently converted displayed overt signs of sincere piety and happiness.[9]

But Stone could not escape religion at the Caldwell Academy. At one point he resolved to transfer to Hampden-Sidney College in Virginia, but a stormy day prevented his departure. Upon reflection he decided to stay at Guilford, stick to his own affairs, and maintain his resolution to ignore religion. But one night his roommate invited him to a revival service where James McGready (1760-1817) was preaching. McGready was a revivalist preacher of the hellfire-and-damnation style. He normally depicted the horrors of hell so vividly that a person could almost smell the sulphur. McGready concluded by urging the sinners to forsake the wrath to come. Under the impact of that influence Stone decided to "seek religion." Thinking these things through, he walked into a nearby field and prayed to God for mercy.[10]

But the technicalities of Calvinism caught him short. He waited to "get religion" but he spent a year in torment. He wanted to be saved, but no one could tell him how. According to Calvinism, he must wait upon the moving of the Holy Spirit to cleanse his unregenerate heart and work faith and repentance in him. In the meantime he was despondent, almost despairing of ever getting religion. Hearing a sermon on Daniel 5:27 ("Thou art weighed in the balance and found wanting"), he lost all hope and fell into an indescribable apathy. A visit home with his relatives brought no help, although his mother was so shocked by his appearance that she immediately joined the Methodists.[11]

Soon after, however, Stone attended another preaching service near

---

[9]*Ibid.*, pp. 6-7.
[10]*Ibid.*, pp. 7-9.
[11]*Ibid.*, pp. 9-10.

Guilford and heard William Hodge, a young Presbyterian minister. His text was 1 John 4:8, "God is love." Hodge described what God's love had done for sinners. Stone was elated and hopeful, but he still wondered how this message correlated with the expectation of a mighty conversion wrought by the Holy Spirit. After the sermon, he retired to the nearby woods with his Bible. Through prayer and searching Scripture, Stone grew convinced that God was love, that Jesus came to seek and save the lost, and that He would not cast out those who came to Him.

> I yielded and sunk at his feet a willing subject. I loved him—I adored him—I praised him aloud in the silent night—in the echoing grove around. I confessed to the Lord my sin and folly in disbelieving his word so long—and in following so long the devices of men. I now saw that a poor sinner was as much authorized to believe in Jesus at first, as at last—that *now* was the accepted time, and day of salvation.[12]

The parallels between this experience and Stone's earlier experience with his first teacher are intriguing. Stone could not respond positively to his first teacher because of fear and intimidation through punishment. Yet when he met a teacher who was gentle and understanding, Stone performed readily. McGready's picture of God as a wrathful deity sending sinners to the torments of hell froze Stone into religious despair and hopelessness. Yet Hodge's presentation of a loving God melted Stone's heart and brought him to conversion. The similarities seem more than superficial. We will see the pattern again in Stone's relationship with the Synod of Kentucky.

Now converted and a Presbyterian, Stone finished out his school days at Caldwell's Academy as a Christian, living his life devoted to God. Studying "dead languages" and even the sciences were pleasant tasks as he realized he was doing it for the glory of God. But Stone's life had changed sufficiently for him to abandon any plans to become a lawyer. Now he wanted to become a minister of the gospel. Right there another problem loomed. His Presbyterian Calvinism expected that a preacher would receive a special call from God to enter the ministry. Stone felt no such call. In discussing this with Caldwell, however, the latter advised Stone that a strong desire to preach was a call from God. Thus emboldened, Stone prepared for the ministry.[13]

His first step was to be licensed by the local presbytery of the Presbyterian Church. He would need to study theology as well as prepare

---

[12]*Ibid.*, p. 11.
[13]*Ibid.*, pp. 11-12.

a trial sermon on an assigned doctrinal text. Stone was assigned the topic of the Trinity for his trial sermon. Previously he had never read any book on theology except the Bible, and, except for passing reference by preachers, he had never heard a sermon on the Trinity in his life.

The presbytery gave him a copy of *The Divine Economy* by Herman Witsius (1636-1708), a Dutch theologian, who explained that there was one God, but three persons in Him. It was idolatry to worship more than one God, yet equal worship must be given to all three persons—Father, Son, and Holy Spirit. Stone became so confused that he did not even know how to pray any more, afraid that he would approach God improperly. Previously Stone had enjoyed prayer because he had been in ignorance of such theological abstractions as he now read in Witsius. He even considered giving up the study of theology and following some other line of business. But he finally laid down Witsius as unprofitable and unintelligible and instead found Isaac Watts' (1674-1748) little book on the Trinity. This he read with pleasure and understanding,[14] not fully realizing that Watts' views tended toward subordinationism; toward the end of his life, Watts leaned toward Unitarianism.

Note that Stone had no problem with studying the Bible; it was only the study of men's theologies that gave him difficulty. By his own words, he had never read a book of theology previously except the Bible, and he had not even felt the lack. It was such experiences that later helped Stone come to the commitment to the Bible alone. As long as he had followed the Scriptures exclusively, his mind had been unbothered by theological speculation and abstraction. Later in his life Stone wished to return to such simplicity.

Having studied Watts, Stone prepared his sermon. Technically the views he enunciated in his sermon were contrary to the Presbyterian standard of faith, the Westminster Confession. But the man in charge of examination of the candidates on theology was Henry Patillo (1726-1801), who himself held Watts' views on the Trinity. Consequently, his questions in this area were brief, touching none of the irregularities of Watts' system. Stone's answers were honest and satisfactory to the examining committee, and he was approved for his preaching license.[15]

This preaching license is not to be confused with ordination. The Presbyterians did not allow just anyone to preach. They had to be approved by the local presbytery. Receiving the preaching license was the first step. This gave permission for the candidate to practice preach-

---

[14]*Ibid.*, pp. 12-13.
[15]*Ibid.*, pp. 13-14.

ing. He still was not allowed to baptize or preside at the Lord's Supper, but licensing did allow him to develop his preaching skills. Later such a licentiate could come back to the presbytery and request ordination, which included another test over theology.

Stone was now approved to be licensed, but it would be several months before the full presbytery met in North Carolina to grant the license. In the meantime, Stone became emotionally and psychologically depressed. Study of abstract theology and Calvinistic systematics left him with a deflated, comfortless spiritual life. He had accepted some abstruse doctrines as true even while he could not reconcile them with others that were plainly taught in the Bible. Again, he decided to give up the idea of preaching and pursue some other vocation. In addition, he was also financially destitute. He scraped up all his available resources (fifteen dollars) and headed to Georgia to visit his brother. He became ill along the way and had to spend several months recovering once he got to Georgia.[16]

While there, however, he received an offer to teach languages at Succoth Academy, a Methodist school near the town of Washington. He started about the beginning of 1795 and greatly pleased the administration and trustees of the academy, but the most important thing about his stay in Georgia was his contact with two men there.

Mr. Hope Hull (1763-1818) was the principal of the academy as well as a Methodist preacher. In fact, in 1792 he had been present with James O'Kelly at the Methodist Conference where the Right of Appeal was brought up. Hull sided with O'Kelly at the beginning of the discussion, but switched to Asbury's side as the debate got vociferous. However, it may be significant that Stone spent some considerable time with Hull, who had indicated his desire for liberty in the Methodist church. It is difficult to determine how much Hull might have influenced Stone along these lines, but it is reasonable to assume there was at least some influence exerted here.

In addition, Stone often attended the preaching of John Springer (1744-1798), a Presbyterian minister in the area of Washington. Springer was a tolerant evangelical, not interested in conducting his parish along sectarian lines. He had warm contacts with the neighboring Baptists and Methodists. Again, it is not easy to assess how much influence Springer might have had on Stone, but in light of Stone's later activities and inclinations, it is easy to think that Springer became somewhat of a model and pattern for the younger man. Stone's later ministry had

---

[16]*Ibid.*, p. 14.

many similarities to that of Springer. Furthermore, it was under Springer's preaching that Stone felt the desire to preach the gospel again. Such feelings grew until the spring of 1796 when he resigned his position with the Succoth Academy and returned to North Carolina to receive his license from the Orange Presbytery.[17]

At the formal meeting of the presbytery, Stone and several other candidates received their formal license to preach. The charge to the candidates was given by Henry Patillo. At its conclusion, he gave each one a Bible, but not the Westminster Confession. Stone called particular attention to this in his autobiography, suggesting again the distinction between his love for the Scriptures and his confusion with the Confession.

Arrangements were soon made for Stone and another candidate, Robert Foster, to conduct a preaching tour through the "lower parts" of North Carolina, probably the southeastern portion. They arrived there, made the arrangements for Sunday preaching, but then both lost their resolve. Foster stated he did not feel qualified for such a solemn work. Stone had felt the same way but thought Foster was superior to him in spirituality; if Foster felt he was unworthy, how could Stone carry on? Stone slipped away on Saturday night, intending to go to Florida where no one would know him. This was early May, 1796.[18]

He attended worship services the next day and was recognized by an elderly woman, who guessed his intentions. She accused him of being a Jonah, running out on God. Under her chastisement, Stone decided to follow her advice and go west to preach. Along the way, he was again recognized in southern Virginia by a pious friend from North Carolina. This friend prevailed upon Stone to tarry until Sunday and preach. Stone begged off, but finally consented. While he was singing and praying in the early part of the service, his anxieties left him, and he preached with boldness, to the delight of the congregation. This led to other invitations, and he spent the next two months preaching in Wythe and Montgomery Counties, Virginia.[19]

In July, Stone headed further west, left Knoxville on August 14 and travelled on to Nashville, which at the time was only a small town of a couple hundred inhabitants. He preached in this area for a while and made the acquaintance of Thomas Craighead, minister of the Presbyterian church in Nashville.[20] Years later, when Stone had gotten into difficulty

---

[17]*Ibid.*, pp. 15-16.
[18]*Ibid.*, pp. 16-17.
[19]*Ibid.*, pp. 17-18.
[20]*Ibid.*, pp. 20, 24.

with the Presbyterian authorities, several of his opponents said it was Craighead that had corrupted him.[21] Again, it is impossible to say how much Craighead influenced Stone in the weeks they were in and around Nashville together, but apparently it was enough for at least some to make the connection.

Craighead (1753-1825) was a Presbyterian minister from North Carolina trained at Princeton.[22] Ordained by the Orange Presbytery (the same one that had just licensed Stone), he arrived in Nashville in 1785 and preached for what is today the downtown, First Presbyterian Church. In 1805 Craighead was suspected of holding Pelagian tenets. In 1806 he preached a sermon rejecting the special work of the Holy Spirit upon the mind of the unbeliever. In 1809 he gave an address that not only insulted the Synod, but attacked every distinctive tenet of Calvinism. Finally, in 1811, Craighead was permanently suspended from the ministry.[23] Apparently Craighead got his rebelliousness legitimately. His father was also a Presbyterian minister and had been suspended by his presbytery in 1741 "for contumaciously declining their jurisdiction." The dates of Thomas Craighead's difficulties in Nashville are considerably after his encounter with Stone, but it is possible that some of these ideas were already in his head and even in his preaching in 1796 when Stone was present. Certainly Craighead's final positions are very similar to those of Stone at the very same period. Perhaps Stone was led to some of his position by his elder colleague.

From Nashville, Stone and a friend moved north into Kentucky, preaching as they went. On January 4, 1797, they were officially acknowledged by the Transylvania Presbytery, allowed to preach in the territory, and recommended to the churches.[24] Stone's friend soon settled near Lexington, while Stone went on to Bourbon County where he took two churches, a country church called Cane Ridge, and a church in the small town of Concord (now in Nicholas County). Here he learned the value of study and located ministry. Itinerant preaching lent itself to superficiality—a few sermons, repeated often, sufficed. But being

---

[21]W. E. Garrison and Alfred T. DeGroot, *The Disciples of Christ: A History*, Revised Edition (St. Louis: The Bethany Press, 1958), p. 97.

[22]Much of this information is derived from Hugh Walker, "The Apostasy of Craighead," *The Tennessean* (Nashville, February 27, 1977), pp. 6-8.

[23]William Warren Sweet (ed.), *Religion on the American Frontier, 1783-1840: A Collection of Source Materials*, vol. 2, *The Presbyterians* (New York: Cooper Square Publishers, Inc., 1964 [originally published by Harper & Bros. in 1936]), pp. 228, 343-347, 384-387.

[24]*Ibid.*, p. 167.

stationary meant reading and study, discipline and improvement. The result was an addition of about fifty members to the church in Concord, about thirty to the church at Cane Ridge.[25]

Stone began his settled ministry with the two congregations in the winter. In the fall of 1797, he returned to Georgia on some unsettled business, and went to Charleston, South Carolina, officially for the Transylvania Presbytery to solicit some funds for a college in Kentucky. These travels took him most of a year. When he returned to Kentucky in 1798, he officially applied to the Transylvania Presbytery to be received under their care, transferring his credentials and recommendation from the Orange Presbytery of North Carolina. The Transylvania Presbytery accepted him on April 10, and at the same time presented him with the official calls from the congregations of Cane Ridge and Concord, which he accepted, becoming their permanent settled minister.[26] Up to this time he had only been their regular supply minister. He was still preaching only with a license and was not able to perform baptisms, weddings, or other clerical duties. There was nothing Stone wanted more than to be a fully ordained Presbyterian minister, but the prospect also filled him with foreboding.

At each ordination service, the candidate was always asked to state his acceptance of the Westminster Confession as the system of biblical doctrine. Previously Stone had stumbled over its teachings on the Trinity, but he now resolved to give the Confession a thorough examination again. In doing so, he not only had renewed difficulty with its doctrine of the Trinity, he also developed doubts about its position on election, reprobation, and predestination. From older ministers he had learned the habit of modifying these doctrines, removing some of their harsh edges and accepting them as true but incomprehensible. Thus he never preached on these topics, but instead restricted himself to practical religion and subjects within his understanding. But his renewed study of these doctrines now led him to conclude that they were necessary to the whole system of Calvinism—a system he could no longer honestly accept.[27]

On the day of his ordination he decided to tell the presbytery his dilemma and ask them to defer his ordination until he could become better informed and mentally settled. Stone was sorrowful at the realization that this would mean the end of his ministry among the

---

[25]Rogers, p. 25.
[26]Rogers, pp. 25-26, 29; Sweet, *Religion on the Frontier*, vol. 2, p. 172.
[27]Rogers, p. 29.

Presbyterians but still committed to follow the lead of his conscience and integrity. Before the meeting got under way, he took two of its leading members aside, James Blythe and Robert Marshall, both of whom he had known as preachers in North Carolina in 1791. They tried to satisfy his objections, but in vain.[28]

Finally they asked him how far he was willing to receive the confession; he said, as far as he saw it consistent with the Word of God. They said that was sufficient. Thus he went into the presbytery meeting, held at the Cane Ridge building. At the appropriate moment he was asked, "Do you receive and adopt the Confession of Faith as containing the system of doctrine taught in the Bible?" He answered, in a loud voice that could be heard by the entire assembly, "I do, as far as I see it consistent with the word of God." The minutes of the presbytery do not record Stone's qualified answer, just that he answered "in the affirmative." He was duly ordained, October 4, 1798.[29]

It is interesting that no one caught Stone's reservation or made anything out of it. Later there was some controversy over whether in fact Stone had made these reservations. Some accused him of going back on his statement at his ordination that he accepted the Westminster Confession. He insisted that he had voiced his reservations and that is also the reason why he stipulated in his autobiography that he said it in a loud enough voice to be heard by all in the room. To further support his defense, in a booklet *An Address to the Christian Churches of Kentucky, Tennessee and Ohio,* he quoted affidavits from six men who were present at his ordination and swore that he had made the qualification.[30]

Actually this whole affair of an expressed qualification with regard to the Westminster Confession was not a rare situation. Back in the 1720s, the same kind of question had come up within the colonial Presbyterians. In 1722 Jonathan Dickinson preached a sermon before the new synod affirming that the Scriptures alone were the only sufficient rule of faith and practice and that the human interpretations of the Bible were too fallible to be made into official doctrinal definitions of Scriptural truth. In 1727 John Thompson introduced a resolution to the synod that all

---

[28]*Ibid.*

[29]Rogers, pp. 29-30; Sweet, *Religion on the Frontier,* Vol. 2, pp. 177-178, 180-181. In a footnote on p. 181, Sweet calls attention to the discrepancy between the official minutes and Stone's answer as recorded in his autobiography.

[30]This document can be found in James M. Mathes (ed.), *Works of Elder B. W. Stone, to which is added a few Discourses and Sermons (original and Selected),* Second Edition (Cincinnati: Moore, Wilstach, Keys & Co., 1859), pp. 83-84. This volume was reprinted by The Old Paths Book Club in 1953.

ministers and licentiates must subscribe to the Westminster Confession. Dickinson led the opposition, and peace was restored in 1729 by the Adopting Act, which allowed any ministerial candidate who had scruples about the Confession to declare his sentiments to the presbytery or synod. If the synod or presbytery determined his scruples were about articles not essential or necessary, the candidate could be admitted in spite of his reservation.[31] In such an instance, however, the candidate would be expected to clarify exactly what his reservations were, and the presbytery or synod would make an informed decision as to whether these were sufficient problems to bar ordination or licensing. In Stone's case, there was no explicit reference to the grounds of his reservation. Whatever the rationale, the Presbytery did approve and ordain him. It is also important to note that Stone had gone on record as indicating that if there is ever any conflict between the Scriptures and the Confession, his loyalty was to the Scriptures rather than to the official doctrinal statement of the Presbyterians. His commitment was to biblical authority.

Even after his ordination, Stone continued to struggle with the doctrines of Calvinism. Often he would preach the doctrine of total depravity, and then urge people to repent and believe the gospel. He realized the contradiction and saw the preachers' intellectual theorizing and hairsplitting as weak attempts to resolve the dilemma. Increasingly he turned away from the works and doctrines of men and looked to the Bible for truth.[32]

One night he was engaged in deep devotion and prayer and was filled with comfort and peace. He felt an ardent love and tenderness for all mankind, longing for the salvation of them all. Overwhelmed by such feelings, he expressed the desire to a pious friend that had he the power, he would save the entire world. The friend, horror-stricken, asked if Stone loved the world more than God did, and why then did God not save the entire world? Stone studied the Bible more thoroughly and was convinced that not all people were saved. Did this mean that God did not

---

[31]A discussion of the conflict and the Adopting Act can be found in Clifton E. Olmstead, *History of Religion in the United States* (Englewood Cliffs, New Jersey: Prentice-Hall, Inc., 1960), pp. 152-154; in Sydney E. Ahlstrom, *A Religious History of the American People* (New Haven: Yale University Press, 1972), pp. 268-269; and in Lefferts A. Loetscher, *A Brief History of the Presbyterians*, Fourth Edition (Philadelphia: The Westminster Press, 1978), pp. 64-65. For further discussion, as well as lengthy quotations from Dickinson's reply to Thompson in 1728, see H. Shelton Smith, Robert T. Handy, and Lefferts A. Loetscher (eds.), *American Christianity: An Historical Interpretation with Representative Documents, Vol I, 1607-1820* (New York: Charles Scribner's Sons, 1960), pp. 262-268.

[32]Rogers, pp. 30-31.

love all the world, and that the spirit within Stone that did love all the world was thus not of God? Further reading and meditating brought Stone to the conclusions that God did indeed love the entire world, and that the reason the world was not saved was because of men's unbelief. Their unbelief was not because of any lack on God's part, but because people neglected and refused to receive the testimony concerning His Son.[33] Thus Stone shrugged off his Calvinism as an unbiblical doctrine, resting on an unbiblical view of God. Through all this, Stone remained true to his commitment that the Bible alone would be his authority, his sourcebook for faith and doctrine.

The Western Revival

The year 1801 was an eventful one for B. W. Stone. He got married in July, but on both sides of that date he became involved in revivalism that would change his life. Revivals were not new to American religious history. The Great Awakening occurred in 1740-1745 in the middle and New England colonies and had a major influence on the churches. The southern colonies did not begin to experience the Great Awakening until 1750. It began in Virginia and then went through the remainder of the southern colonies/states until 1790. One of the last great preachers in the southern Great Awakening was James McGready, the one who had such an influence on Stone in 1792. In 1796 McGready left his pastorate in North Carolina and settled in Logan County, Kentucky. (Ironically, this was the very same year that B. W. Stone also left North Carolina and settled in Kentucky.) McGready took over three small frontier churches: Muddy River, Red River, and Gaspar River. He also had the members of these churches sign a covenant—that they would pray for revival every Saturday night, every Sunday morning, and one entire Sunday a month.

It took a while, but within two years McGready got a revival going in Logan County. Soon unusual things were taking place under his preaching. The activities drew even larger crowds, and the revival began to take on increasing power. By 1799 other ministers became involved, and either late in the year or early in 1800, the first "camp meeting" took place. People came from miles around in their wagons, brought provisions for the weekend, camped out on the church grounds, had an outdoor revival, and started the trend toward camp meetings. At first just Presbyterian ministers were involved, then Baptists and Methodists also joined in. The crowds were much larger than could be accommodated

---

[33]*Ibid.*, pp. 31-33.

inside the small log church buildings, thus the need for outdoor meetings. Soon thousands were involved.

Word of these large gatherings began to spread throughout Kentucky, as well as the report of the unusual "religious exercises." Stone heard these reports while up in the bluegrass area of north central Kentucky, and in the spring of 1801 he traveled to Logan County to see it for himself. He was baffled by the people being "struck down," unconscious sometimes for hours, and then coming to and delivering a powerful testimony to their deliverance and an encouragement to others to repent and come to Jesus. Stone believed that there was much fanaticism involved, but he also concluded that this was a genuine work of God.

Stone hurried back to Bourbon County, arriving at Cane Ridge on a Sunday morning. A large crowd had already gathered to hear his report from Logan County. He related what he had seen and heard and emphasized the Great Commission. He urged that all could be saved if they desired, that faith was the condition of salvation, and he urged sinners to believe and be saved. He answered numerous objections to this very un-Calvinistic doctrine, and many were moved to tears by his remarks.[34]

He then hurried over to Concord and preached at night to the congregation there. Under his preaching two little girls were struck down, just as so many had been down in Logan County. Their entreaties for others to accept Christ made a deep impression upon the congregation. The next day he returned to Cane Ridge where he had made an appointment to preach at a neighbor's house. Stone arrived there at the same time as another man, who then began shouting praises to the Lord. Hearing the commotion, the crowd left the house, hurried to the scene, and in less than twenty minutes scores of them had fallen to the ground. A deist in the area was present and reproached Stone for this activity. Stone took pity on him, addressed a few mild words to him, and this man also fell. When he got up, he claimed Christ as Savior.[35]

Soon thereafter Stone held a protracted meeting at Concord. Multitudes from the countryside came, from various denominations. All groups seemed to unite in the work, in Christian love. Partisanship disappeared. The meeting lasted five days and nights without stopping.[36]

Perhaps it was on his trip to Logan County in the spring that Stone met Elizabeth Campbell at Greenville in neighboring Muhlenberg

---

[34]*Ibid.*, p. 36.
[35]*Ibid.*, pp. 36-37.
[36]*Ibid.*, p. 37.

County. He made a return trip to southwest Kentucky in June and married Eliza on July 2, 1801. Shortly after the wedding, they hurried back to Cane Ridge. About two years previously, Stone had purchased a hundred acres of land about five miles east of Cane Ridge and built a log cabin. It was to this home that Stone brought his bride.[37]

The reason for their haste in returning to Bourbon County was that a meeting had been advertised to be held at Cane Ridge beginning Thursday or Friday, that is, about August 13 or 14, 1801. This has been judged to be the largest camp meeting of all frontier history and the typical example of what frontier revivalism was all about. Estimates of attendance ranged from ten thousand to thirty thousand. Obviously this number could not crowd into the Cane Ridge meeting house. In fact, none of the services were held inside. The building was used only for preacher meetings for prayer and strategy. There were often five or six preachers speaking at once on the church grounds, each with a group of people gathered around, out of earshot of other preachers. Some spoke from a tree stump, others from the back of a wagon. Preaching went on day and night without interruption for six or seven days and nights. The revival would have continued even longer, but the food supplies in the neighborhood simply ran out. Again, there was interdenominational harmony in the work. Baptist and Methodist preachers worked along with Presbyterians for the salvation of sinners. As Stone reported, "We all engaged in singing the same songs of praise—all united in prayer—all preached the same things—free salvation urged upon all by faith and repentance."[38] The application of Christian unity was one of the fruits of the revival preaching as was also the concern for souls' salvation, regardless of denominational identity.

Probably the most controversial aspect of the frontier meetings was the "religious exercises." Stone devotes an entire chapter to these in his autobiography.[39] The most common exercise was probably the "falling exercise," which we have already described. A person fell, often with a piercing scream, lay unconscious for some time, and then came to, relating his love for Jesus and urging the hearers to repentance. The "jerking exercise" was more complicated. People were seized by a series of "jerks," violent muscular convulsions. Documented stories attest of people standing flat-footed on the ground with their whole body jerking back and forth so violently that at one end of the jerk, the forehead

---

[37]*Ibid.*

[38]*Ibid.*, p. 38.

[39]Chapter Six, from which the following information is derived; Rogers, pp. 39-42.

almost touched the ground in front, and at the other end of the jerk, the
back of their head almost touched the ground behind. Women who came
to the revival meetings in all their finery were often taken with the jerks.
In their jerking, their hat ribbons came undone, and bonnets, ribbons,
and hats began flying all over. Their hair came undone (women wore
long hair in those days, either braided and wrapped around their heads,
or piled up on top and fastened with pins and bonnets). Documented
stories exist of women with long hair jerking so violently that at each end
of their jerk their hair made exactly the sound of a bull whip being
snapped.[40]

The "barking exercise" was often in conjunction with the jerks. A person jerking back and forth made a grunting or barking noise from the
suddenness of the jerk. The "dancing exercise" usually began with jerking and then slowed down into a dance, either fast or slow. It did not
cause others to be amused but appeared as a heavenly motion to those
who saw it. Similarly, the "laughing exercise" did not cause others to
laugh. Stone called it loud and hearty, but rapturously solemn at the
same time. It is difficult to imagine a "solemn" laugh, and one under-
stands his problem when he called it "truly indescribable."[41] The "running exercise" consisted of people apparently trying to run away from
such feelings, but instead, falling down or becoming so physically agitat-
ed that they could run no further. The "singing exercise" was a melodi-
ous song, uttered not from the mouth nor nose but from the chest.
Those who heard it concluded it was most unusual and unnatural. Stone
said it was "more unaccountable than any thing else I ever saw."[42] Stone
also points out that the dancing and laughing exercises were confined
only to believers. The other exercises were likely to affect either believers
or unbelievers, including the falling exercise. Some believers were so
concerned about their relatives, friends, and neighbors that they fainted
and later related their vision of heaven.[43]

There is no doubt that Stone took a sympathetic view toward these
religious exercises. He acknowledges that there were eccentricities and
fanaticism, yet he also insists that much good was done and the exercises
silenced sectarian contention by promoting unity. "The blessed effects
would have continued, had not men put forth their unhallowed hands to

---

[40]Peter Cartwright, *Autobiography of Peter Cartwright* (New York: Abingdon
Press, 1956), p. 45.

[41]Rogers, p. 41.

[42]*Ibid.*

[43]*Ibid.*, p. 39.

hold up their tottering ark, mistaking it for the ark of God."[44] In another place he states:

> My conviction was complete that it was a good work—the work of God; nor has my mind wavered since on the subject. Much did I then see, and much have I since seen, that I considered to be fanaticism; but this should not condemn the work. The Devil has always tried to ape the works of God, to bring them into disrepute. But that cannot be a Satanic work, which brings men to humble confession and forsaking of sin—to solemn prayer—fervent praise and thanksgiving, and to sincere and affectionate exhortations to sinners to repent and go to Jesus the Savior.[45]

He estimated the number of conversions at Cane Ridge between 500 and 1,000.[46]

But not every one had the same sanguine view of the revivalistic exercises. Even John Rogers, who edited Stone's autobiography, had deep reservations. He went so far as to say:

> To regard them as tokens of the divine favor, is of the essence of fanaticism—that to suppose they are divine attestations of the truth of any dogma, is the most consummate nonsense, not to say presumption.[47]

Rogers explains that such exercises came from an improper preaching of the gospel, one that did not provide a correct understanding of the *assurance* of salvation. Calvinistic and Arminian orthodoxy alike found that assurance of pardon in a feeling—and thus these exercises were used to create such a feeling. But Rogers found that pardon in the divine promise of baptism for the remission of sins.[48]

Moreover, Rogers was not the only one who was disinclined to accept the religious exercises as a genuine work of the Lord. Many individuals, particularly the leadership of the Presbyterian Church in Kentucky, saw not the conversions and lives changed, but the fanaticism, the eccentricities, and the disorder. During the emotional excesses of the revivals, some girls got pregnant.[49] Although this was a rarity rather than a commonplace, it was enough of a scandal to embarrass the entire cause of revivalism. A further factor that led to tension was that in order to provide enough revivalistic ministers, some presbyteries began to

---

[44]*Ibid.*, p. 42.
[45]*Ibid.*, p. 35.
[46]*Christian Messenger*, vol. 1, no. 4 (February, 1827), p. 76.
[47]Rogers, p. 384.
[48]*Ibid.*, pp. 396-397.
[49]Sweet, *Religion on the Frontier*, vol. 2, p. 87.

approve men for preaching who were not sufficiently educated. This not only violated the strict rules of the church, it also seemed to approve of the excesses that a maturer education would resist. Thus the controversy over ministerial educational standards became more a symbol of where one stood with regard to the revival than to educational attainment in its own right. This was the most important single factor in the schism of the Cumberland Presbyterians, which occurred in 1810.

Another factor of conflict between the revivalists and the anti-revivalists was the strict observance of Calvinism. As a rule, the Presbyterians were close observers of the traditional teachings of Calvinistic predestination and limited atonement. Stone and others used the revivals to urge people to believe *now*. Rather than remaining in unbelief until the Spirit was given to them, people could believe before the Spirit or salvation came. Jesus died for all, and no previous qualification was required than simply to believe in Jesus. Under such preaching, people began to see that they were responsible for their own situation and a refusal to believe was in itself a damning sin.[50]

At first the more orthodox writhed silently under these doctrines. They saw that both Baptists and Methodists were united with the revivalistic preachers, and they believed that all would become good Presbyterians. So they winked at the doctrinal aberrations for a while. But as soon as they saw that the Methodists and Baptists were not going to become Presbyterians, they returned to a strict preaching of Calvinism and the Westminster Confession. In turn, the Methodists and Baptists, who had lived in peace with the Presbyterians and with each other, also responded with sectarian belligerence and defensiveness.[51]

In this situation, the friends of the Confession were indignant at the revivalist preachers. The Washington Presbytery focused the brunt of its attack upon Richard McNemar (1770-1839), making an example of him and the revivalistic preaching. McNemar was preaching for a congregation at Cabin Creek, near Maysville, Kentucky. On November 3, 1801, three elders from the church sent a letter to the Washington Presbytery that included accusations that McNemar denied a limited atonement and that he stated a sinner has power to believe at any time. Included in their letter was also the statement that McNemar "would be bound by no system but the Bible."[52] The Presbytery, however, meeting in Springfield,

---

[50]Rogers, p. 45.

[51]*Ibid.*, p. 46.

[52]*Ibid.*, p. 150."This information comes from the document, "An Apology for Renouncing the Jurisdiction of the Synod of Kentucky."

Ohio, on November 11, refused to consider the case against McNemar because no one came forward to personally substantiate the charges offered against him.[53] Afterwards, however, McNemar asked liberty to explain his ideas. In his explanations he clearly stated his Arminian views, but nothing was done against him. In fact, by March 20, 1802, he and the three elders from the Cabin Creek church signed a statement of reconciliation, agreeing to forget "past altercations, and cordially unite in communion for the future."[54]

Soon thereafter, McNemar was called to the church at Turtle Creek, just outside Lebanon, Ohio, still within the jurisdiction of the Washington Presbytery. But by that fall, complaints were again being raised against McNemar concerning his views about free will salvation rather than strict Calvinism. When the presbytery met in Cincinnati on October 6, 1802, formal verbal complaint was lodged against McNemar as a propagator of false doctrine. The Presbytery's examination of McNemar led them to conclude that he was indeed Arminian. McNemar had been dismissed from the meeting as they discussed his situation, and when he returned and was informed of their decision, he protested. According to proper procedure, no charge should be entertained unless in written form; and these charges against McNemar were not. Furthermore, there were no witnesses cited or called for testimony.[55] McNemar's complaint was one mostly of procedure, rather than of substance.

In April of 1803, the Presbytery met again in Springfield and heard an additional petition to reexamine McNemar, this time to include John Thompson in the examination, minister of the Presbyterian church in Springfield. But revivalistic men were in the majority at this meeting, and the petition was rejected as being out of order. If the Presbytery had fully entertained the petition, the expectation was that it would have been overruled, and even the decision against McNemar at Cincinnati the previous October overturned. In fact, there were two presbyteries working at this time. Whenever the Presbytery met at Springfield, it was favorable to McNemar; whenever it met at Cincinnati, the stricter Calvinists succeeded in having the Presbytery take action against McNemar. From a later standpoint, this provided grounds for the question of asking which "presbytery" was the more proper in its actions. McNemar, Stone, and others contended that the Cincinnati actions were illegal even by Presbyterian standards.[56]

---

[53]*Ibid.*, p. 153.
[54]*Ibid.*, p. 154.
[55]*Ibid.*, pp. 154-158.
[56]*Ibid.*, pp. 159-162.

Then in the fall of 1803, the Synod of Kentucky exercised its normal function of looking over the records of its member presbyteries. What it discovered in the Washington Presbytery seemed inconsistent. The committee appointed to examine the Washington Presbytery's minutes concluded that the Presbytery acted wrongly in rejecting the petition on April 6, 1803, at Springfield. When it came to a vote on upholding the examination of McNemar at the October 1802 meeting in Cincinnati, the result was 17 in favor, six opposed. This took place on Thursday, September 8, 1803. On Friday, there was more discussion on the implications of McNemar's case, all to the point of McNemar's theological heresy and the inappropriateness of the Presbytery's allowing him to remain in his pulpit.[57]

On Saturday, September 10, five of the ministers present took advantage of one of the recesses to meet privately. They realized the actions taken against McNemar were an indictment of their common revivalism, and that if they did not hang together now, they would all hang separately later on. Thus they wrote out a protest against the actions of the Synod and took it back into the meeting. Ironically, at that very time the Synod was discussing whether to proceed with the proposed examination of McNemar and Thompson requested in the April petition. Interrupting the discussion, Robert Marshall presented the protest on behalf of himself and the other four—B. W. Stone, Richard McNemar, John Thompson, and John Dunlavy (McNemar's brother-in-law).

In their protest the men declared they were no longer members of the Synod and rejected the jurisdiction of the Synod and its member presbyteries. They gave three reasons for this: (1) the original minutes against McNemar in October of 1802 were not a true representation of McNemar's beliefs; (2) they claimed the privilege of interpreting the Scriptures by itself, as the Westminster Confession itself stated in its first chapter; (3) they stated their continued adherence to the doctrines of grace according to the Protestant Reformation, but they felt some phrases in the Westminster Confession were used to strengthen sinners and enslave the pious. They concluded by stating they did not wish to break communion with the members of the Synod, but they must depart until the Synod adopted "a more liberal plan respecting human Creeds & Confessions."[58]

---

[57]Sweet, *Religion on the Frontier*, vol. 2, pp. 315-317.
[58]*Ibid.*, pp. 318-319.

The Springfield Presbytery

The Synod was rather surprised by this proceeding, but it soon appointed a committee to deal with the dissidents and bring them back into the fold; the committee's work was not successful. (However, one of its members, Matthew Houston, became so interested in the position of the small group that he soon left the Presbyterians and joined them.) In the discussions between the dissident preachers and the Synod, the preachers stated they were willing to return to the Synod if the Synod would agree to recognize them as a separate presbytery and then judge their teachings according to the Word of God. When the Synod did not respond to this, the disaffected preachers organized their own presbytery naming it the Presbytery of Springfield. They selected a moderator and clerk and wrote a circular letter to the churches explaining their actions. They stated they still desired to be known as Presbyterians and remain in Presbyterian communion. They did not intend to create a new party or sect. But they felt as long as they remained under the Synod, they could not enjoy the liberty of reading, studying, or explaining the Word of God for themselves.[59] As a consequence of such actions, the Synod suspended these five men from the ministry on September 13, 1803, and then permanently deposed them from the ministry on October 15, 1803.[60]

In January of 1804, the group published their famous *Apology for Renouncing the Jurisdiction of the Synod of Kentucky*, which consisted of three parts. Part I was written by Robert Marshall and contained their explanation of what had happened. Much of the material in this section has been referred to here in the previous few pages. Section II of the Apology was "A Compendious View of the Gospel," written by B. W. Stone. This is an overview of doctrine, particularly attacking the Westminster Confession on election and limited atonement. Section III was written by John Thompson, "Remarks on the Confession of Faith," which pointed out that all creeds and standards of faith were harmful and useless when used as a test of faith.[61]

The Springfield Presbytery, now organized, consisted of fifteen churches—seven in Ohio and eight in Kentucky—but apparently never more than the original five ministers. Some of these churches were those who had followed their ministers into the new Presbytery; others were

---

[59]*Ibid.*, pp. 320-323; Rogers, pp. 173-175.
[60]Sweet, *Religion on the Frontier*, vol. 2, pp. 322-323, 371-372.
[61]This entire document was appended by John Rogers to Stone's autobiography; see Rogers, pp. 147-247.

new ones constituted after the Presbytery was organized. Publication of
the *Apology* plus other items defending the new movement brought about
a response from the Presbyterians, who now published items attacking
the new group. This pamphlet warfare probably did little good to either
side, except that it brought the new group to the attention of some who
probably would never have heard of it otherwise.

Soon after the events of September, 1803, Stone called a meeting in
the two churches where he was preaching and explained the events to
them. In addition, he stated he could no longer preach the normal
Presbyterian doctrines but would preach only to support the Redeemer's
Kingdom, regardless of party. He tore up the salary obligation they had
with him, but he continued to preach, though without obligation on their
part. He released his slaves and sought to support himself by his own
labors on his farm. He still preached, almost every night, and often during the day. He sometimes had to weed his corn at night while others
were asleep. But he was happy in his ministry. Fatigued in body, his
mind was happy.[62]

But the Presbytery of Springfield did not last long. By the next summer its founders decided it reflected a partisan spirit. Rice Haggard had
moved to Cumberland County, Kentucky, in either 1802 or 1803,[63] and
he soon became acquainted with the Springfield Presbytery. He had also
written a little pamphlet entitled *The Sacred Import of the Christian Name*.
The Presbytery had this document printed, and herein Haggard argued
that the only appropriate name for the followers of Christ was the term
Christian. Thus, when the leaders of the Springfield Presbytery soon dissolved their organization and their Presbyterian label, they took instead
only the name "Christian."

The Sacred Import, however, was not the only document the Springfield
Presbytery published that summer of 1804. For when they met at Cane
Ridge on June 28, they adopted a unique document entitled *The Last
Will and Testament of the Springfield Presbytery*. In this brief, humorous, and
even sarcastic statement they announced the dissolution of their organi-
zation, stated why, and reflected on the principles that led them to do so.

The authorship of the document has been the matter of some conjec-
ture. It is signed by all the leaders of the group, but not in such a way as
to indicate which was the author. In his autobiography, Stone gives no
indication as to authorship. In his textbook treatment, James DeForest

---

[62]*Ibid.*, pp. 49-55.
[63]Colby D. Hall, *Rice Haggard: The American Evangelist Who Revived the Name
Christian* (Fort Worth: University Christian Church, 1957), p. 34.

Murch suggests it was done either by McNemar or Stone, with the weight of probability favoring Stone.[64] In this he may be following C. C. Ware who credits Stone with the idea.[65] Yet William Garrett West points conclusively to McNemar. He quotes from a pamphlet written by Robert Marshall and John Thompson in 1811 that definitively credits McNemar with the authorship.[66] Stone only states in his series of articles, "History of the Christian Church in the West," that he was in favor of the matter of the document, but not the manner.[67] Regardless of the question of authorship, however, whether or not Stone wrote it, he certainly remained as the most steadfast spokesman for it and never in the remainder of his life willfully abandoned its principles.

This brief document (it runs less than five pages) encapsulates the ideas of these preachers at the time, and set the course for much of their future. Three basic ideas stand out: (1) Christian unity; (2) exclusive biblical authority; and (3) local congregational autonomy.

After some preliminary paragraphs, the document includes a list of items, much like bequests in a will. But these are headed with an *Imprimis* (Latin, "in the first place"), which states: "We *will,* that this body die, be dissolved, and sink into union with the Body of Christ at large; for there is but one Body."[68] In the "Witnesses' Address," a two-page explanation added to the list of items, the six writers noted that they were concerned with division and a party spirit among Christians. While they tried to cultivate a spirit of love and unity among themselves, they discovered it was difficult to escape the realization that they were a party just as separate as the others. Hence they stated "in the first place" their desire to die as a presbytery and be simply Christians, in union with the body of Christ at large, having no other identification than this. They took the name of "Christian" as urged by Rice Haggard, which the O'Kelly Movement had taken a decade earlier. Apparently, the major goal of this group of ministers was to unite with other Christians.

---

[64]Murch, p. 88.

[65]Ware, p. 141, as cited by West, p. 76.

[66]Robert Marshall and John Thompson. *A Brief Historical Account of Sundry Things in the Doctrines and State of the Christian, or as it is Commonly Called, the Newlight Church* (Cincinnati: J. Carpenter and Company, 1811); cited by West, p. 77; contained also in Levi Purviance (ed.), *The Biography of Elder David Purviance* (Dayton, Ohio: B. F. and G. W. Ells, 1848; [reprinted by Alva Ross Brown, 1940]), pp. 253-274; see particularly p. 256.

[67]B. W. Stone, "History of the Christian Church in the West, No. VIII," *Christian Messenger,* vol. 1, no. 11 (September 25, 1827), p. 241.

[68]This document can be located in a number of places. For convenience purposes, we are quoting from Rogers, p. 51.

In order to accomplish this, they determined they must use the Bible
and the Bible alone as their basis. They noted the divisions and party spirit among Christians "principally owing to the adoption of human creeds
and forms of government."[69] It was these human creeds and forms that
precluded unity in Christ. While they tried to establish "the beautiful simplicity of Christian church government, stript of human inventions and
lordly traditions," they discovered "there was neither precept nor example in the New Testament for such confederacies as modern Church
Sessions [the Presbyterian equivalent of a church board], Presbyteries,
Synods, General Assemblies, etc."[70] Thus they concluded that as long as
they remained organized as a presbytery, they were off the foundation of
the New Testament Church. This was the reason they dissolved their own
Presbytery. To be a scriptural body, they must abandon such an organization. One of the items in the Will itself emphasized "the Bible as the only
sure guide to heaven."[71] Throughout all of this, they clearly enunciated
their concern that the Bible and the Bible alone was to be their guide and
resource. Things that were unscriptural they would abandon.

The third major theme that comes out of the Last Will and Testament
is the concern for local congregational autonomy. "The church of Christ,"
they stated, ought to "resume her native right of internal government."
Each particular church ought to "choose her own preacher," and "never
henceforth *delegate* her right of government to any man or set of men
whatever." Furthermore, the presbytery's "power of making laws for the
government of the church, and executing them by delegated authority"
would forever cease—that the people might have free course to the
Bible.[72] Thus this new movement was similar to the movements already
begun in Virginia and New England—independent churches under the
Bible alone, with no rules other than biblical teachings, and no denominational structure. The similarity between the three groups on these points
is remarkable, even down to the name they chose—"Christian."

The loss of their name and identity as Presbytery of Springfield did
not mean, however, the demise of the new group. They continued to
flourish and grow. Matthew Houston soon left the Presbyterians and
joined the new group of Christians.[73] Many other Presbyterians,
intrigued by the synod's orders to not associate with the Christians, came

---

[69]*Ibid.*, p. 54.
[70]*Ibid.*
[71]*Ibid.*, p. 52.
[72]*Ibid.*, pp. 51-52.
[73]*Ibid.*, p. 47.

to the new group to be informed and stayed as converts.[74] There was other growth as well. Members of the O'Kelly Movement from Virginia and North Carolina began to move into Kentucky, made contact with these kindred Christians, and allied with the movement. Some stayed, others moved on. One such was Clement Nance (1756-1828). He had been a member of the O'Kelly Movement, but had moved into Kentucky and identified with the Christians there. After an eighteen-month stay, he moved on to Indiana in 1805 and became the first preacher of the Christian movement in that state.[75]

The Western Christians

But not all was sweetness and light among the new Christians. Not only did harassment and turmoil come from the Presbyterians and others, but problems also came from the inside of the movement as new ideas came to bear. The Shakers were a group of people who left England in 1774 under the influence of Mother Ann Lee (Stanley). This remarkable woman developed the idea that Christ had come once to earth as a man, but had more recently come to earth as a woman—herself. The technical and full name of her group was The United Society of Believers in Christ's Second Appearing—and Christ's second appearing was in the form of Ann Lee. In addition, the group prohibited marriage and sexual relations; they also adopted pure communism. Further, the Shakers developed a number of religious dances as part of their worship, hence their common name "Shakers." Ann Lee led them to form a farm commune in 1775 in upstate New York. Even though she died in 1784, the Shakers continued. When they heard of the frontier camp meetings and the religious exercises (including the "dancing exercise"), they became interested and sent three missionaries out west in 1805 to investigate.[76]

These individuals came first to Kentucky and talked to Stone. At first he was impressed with their obvious piety and their initial emphasis on Scriptural teaching. But as they talked, he learned of their other ideas and sternly opposed them. The Shaker missionaries then moved north into southwestern Ohio, where they met Richard McNemar and soon

---

[74]*Ibid.*, p. 61.

[75]McAllister and Tucker, p. 81.

[76]The best source for the beginnings of the Shakers is Edward Deming Andrews, *The People Called Shakers* (New York: Dover Publications, Inc., 1963). For Stone's account of their involvement with the western Christians, see Rogers, pp. 61-64.

converted him, his wife, and most of the Turtle Creek church to their beliefs. McNemar's brother-in-law, John Dunlavy, also converted to their position. On the lands of one of the elders of the Turtle Creek church, Malcom Worley, the Shakers established their first commune in the West, Old Union, just outside Lebanon, Ohio. Later they established Shaker-town in central Kentucky, their largest commune and center in the West.

The conversion of McNemar and Dunlavy to the Shakers was quite an embarrassment and scandal to the new Christian Movement. These were two of the original leaders who left the Presbyterians in 1803, and two who had signed the *Last Will and Testament* in June of 1804. Matthew Houston also joined them. The enemies of the Christians used this incident to point out what the movement would lead to—heresy and social revolution. Stone spent a good deal of his time fighting back against the Shakers directly and refurbishing the Christians' reputation in general. He could point out that Christians were not the only ones becoming Shakers; others had joined the celibate communitarian group straight out of the Presbyterians, Baptists, and Methodists. Even so, the loss of these two leaders was a serious loss for the Christians to sustain.

The next issue that came to the Christians was the topic of baptism. Regardless of their commitment to take the Bible only as their rule and guide, this group still followed several of their earlier practices as Presbyterians, including the practice of infant baptism. According to Stone, Robert Marshall had become convinced of the practice of believers' immersion even while he and Stone were yet Presbyterian preachers. Stone wrote him a lengthy letter trying to convince him of his error on the subject; Marshall wrote back a letter in which he so ably answered Stone's objections that Stone was convinced. He ceased to practice infant baptism. "About this time the great excitement commenced, and the subject of baptism was for a while, strangely, almost forgotten."[77] Apparently this refers to the Cane Ridge meeting and the revivals in general. Thus it was several years before baptism was again investigated.

By this time the western Christians had dissolved the Springfield Presbytery, but they had also determined that none of them would take up new practices without consultation with the others. So they held a meeting of elders and deacons to discuss their new thinking on baptism. David Purviance placed the event in 1807. Stone immersed a young woman that year at her request, and several others. Of the preachers who attended, David Purviance also requested immersion from Stone, and

---

[77]Rogers, p. 60.

then Purviance immersed Reuben Dooley.[78] It is ironic that Stone himself was not yet immersed. Yet Robert Marshall still had no faith in the ordinance,[79] and John Thompson remained a strenuous advocate for infant baptism.[80] At this meeting those present concluded that every brother and sister should make his/her own decision, and that each would forbear with the others. Those who wished to be immersed would not despise those who did not, and *vice versa*. They also discussed who would do the baptizing. Because they did not wish to join the Baptists, the Baptists would not immerse them. They decided, therefore, that if they were authorized to preach, they were also authorized to baptize. The preachers baptized each other and then in turn baptized the crowds who came.[81]

Concerning Stone's own baptism, the evidence is uncertain. He gives no details in his autobiography. W. E. Garrison states Stone was immersed "considerably later" than Purviance's baptism.[82] Garrett even raises the question whether Stone *was* in fact immersed at all, but he answers it by quoting Stone as saying:

> We were all pedobaptist when we determined to take the name and word of Jesus alone, as our name and our rule. Not long after, I with many others from reading the Scriptures, became convinced that baptism signified immersion; we submitted to be immersed.[83]

There is also a tradition that Stone was baptized in 1810 in Stoner Creek, just outside Paris, Kentucky. Regardless of Stone's own baptism, in the course of a few years the practice of immersion spread throughout the western Christians until by 1827 Stone remarked "The far greater part of the Churches submitted to be baptized by immersion, and now there is not one in 500 among us who has not been immersed."[84]

In the early years of the growth of the practice, however, there were some that resisted it. Although Robert Marshall introduced the subject to Stone in convincing terms, he never fully warmed up to it himself. John

---

[78]Purviance , pp. 179-180.

[79]Rogers, p. 61.

[80]Purviance, p. 179.

[81]Rogers, pp. 60-61.

[82]Garrison and DeGroot, p. 113.

[83]Unfortunately Garrett documents this statement by referring to p. 351 of the first volume. It had only 288 pages. Therefore this statement can not be referenced. See Garrett, pp. 117-118.

[84]B. W. Stone, "History of the Christian Churches in the West, no. VIII [should be no. IX]," *Christian Messenger*, vol, 1, no. 12 (October 1827), p. 267.

Thompson never accepted it. David Purviance stated that from the time that immersion began to grow in the movement, John Thompson and others began to look back to Presbyterianism.[85]

Because of the disturbance over baptism, some brethren even began to urge the necessity of making a stand on the truth they had already learned, but desisting from further search. Because of the growing lack of uniformity in belief and practice, some thought a bond other than the Bible and brotherly love was necessary to unite the growing churches and keep them pure. Differences existed on the doctrines of the trinity, the nature of Christ, the atonement, and now the practice of baptism. They called for a meeting to discuss these items and hopefully work out a solution and preserve uniformity. The meeting took place at the Christian Church in Bethel, about ten miles south of Lexington, August 8, 1810.[86] Marshall and Thompson were the leaders in this. They began to speak that the principle of following the Bible alone was too latitudinarian. One individual (perhaps Thompson?) even brought a doctrinal statement to read to the conference, but many thought it best to postpone it. The conference, did, however, appoint a committee to write a piece for publication containing the doctrinal topics that were under discussion: trinity, nature of Christ, and the atonement. The committee consisted of Robert Marshall, B. W. Stone, John Thompson, David Purviance, and Hugh Andrews. The committee was to report back to another general conference meeting at Mt. Tabor, east of Lexington, on March 11, 1811. The various members of the committee had prepared pieces for discussion, but at the meeting, the committee members discovered they could not resolve their differences. Marshall, Thompson, and Andrews advocated the views of the Westminster Confession with respect to the atonement and the trinity. Stone and Purviance were opposed to these views. When the committee reported to the entire group, the conference listened to the different papers presented by the two sides, but declined to entertain a debate of the issues, feeling the differences of opinion need not break fellowship.[87]

Marshall and Thompson, however, were not willing to accept this condition of affairs. They soon left the group, and that same year returned to the Presbyterian Synod of Kentucky. On October 12, they were interviewed by a committee of the Synod on their doctrinal beliefs, and pronounced orthodox. They gave their unhesitating assent to the

---

[85]Rogers, pp. 127-128.

[86]*Christian Messenger,* vol. 1., no. 12 (October, 1827), p. 267.

[87]*Ibid.,* p. 268; Rogers, pp. 65-66.

Westminster Confession. The Synod lifted the suspension against them and directed their local presbyteries to readmit and restore the two returning Presbyterian ministers.[88] (Hugh Andrews also left, but because he did not have proper education, he could not be received as a minister among the Presbyterians; he joined the Methodists instead.[89])

At that point, B. W. Stone was the only remaining minister of the original five that left the Presbyterians in the fall of 1803. McNemar and Dunlavy had gone to the Shakers, Marshall and Thompson had returned to the Presbyterians. For this reason, the movement has ever since been known as the Stone Movement—he was the only survivor of the original five. This, in spite of the fact that it was Marshall who was their first spokesman to the Synod and who also first introduced the topic of immersion, and it was McNemar who apparently wrote *The Last Will and Testament*.

Of the original six signers of that document, only Stone and Purviance were left. In 1807 Purviance moved to Ohio. He himself says this was a "happy circumstance" because after the departure of Marshall and Thompson, Stone was on the scene in Kentucky to counter Marshall's influence, and Purviance was on the scene in Ohio to counter that of Thompson.[90] Purviance also reported that Thompson told him that because of the differences, the little group of Christians would be better off to "dissolve and join the different sects." Purviance concluded that he had no doubt "that the aim of Marshall and Thompson was to abolish the Christian Church."[91]

In spite of such problems, however, the group of western Christians grew. They were basically committed to two ideas: the authority of the Bible and the Bible alone, and Christian unity. When the discussions over baptism emerged, Stone stated that it was "from reading the Bible" that these people became convinced that "immersion was the apostolic mode of baptism."[92] When the conference met at Bethel in 1810, they adopted a statement that they were "taking the word of God as their only rule and standard for doctrine."[93]

Their penchant for exercising Christian unity was also easily displayed. They adopted Rice Haggard's suggestion to be known as "Christians," partially because it was the most biblical appellation, but also because it

---

[88]Purviance, p. 278, quoting Robert Davidson, *History of the Presbyterian Church in the State of Kentucky* (New York: Robert Carter, 1847), pp. 207-212.

[89]*Christian Messenger,* vol. 1, no. 12, p. 269.

[90]Rogers, p. 129.

[91]*Ibid.*

[92]*Christian Messenger,* vol. 1, no. 12, p. 267.

[93]*Ibid.*, p. 268.

would serve as a common name uniting all those believers in Christ who accepted the authority of the Bible.

In the early correspondence that sprung up between the southern Christians and the New England movement under Smith and Jones, numerous references in the southern writing indicate that union had taken place between the O'Kelly and Stone Movements. Men like Rice Haggard and Clement Nance we have already noticed—men that went from the O'Kelly Movement to the west and met the Stone Movement. They represented the first early bridge between the two movements. But obviously there was more than this casual contact. Robert Punshon, in the first letter from the south to Elias Smith, editor of the *Herald of Gospel Liberty,* stated that "the Church" had spread through Virginia, the Carolinas, Tennessee, Kentucky, Ohio, and other parts of the west. He went on to say that "the Christian Church in the Western parts of this country" is "the sister Church of those in Virginia, and the Southern States."[94] Even Peter Cartwright, the famous Methodist circuit rider in Kentucky and later in Illinois, referred to a number of preachers from the O'Kelly Movement who "came out to Kentucky, and formed a union with these New Lights."[95] "New Lights" was another name for the Stone Movement, as was the term "Christian Connection" or even "Christian Connexion."

When William Guirey corresponded with Elias Smith, one of his early letters, dated December 18, 1808, contained this comment:

> Our sentiments on doctrinal points have been sufficiently explained in a pamphlet entitled *an apology for renouncing the jurisdiction of the Synod of Kentucky, to which is added a compendious view of the Gospel &tc*; those persons who are the authors of this pamphlet have since their separation from the Presbyterians united with us.[96]

It is tempting to read too much into this phrase, "united with us." By 1808, of course, we know of no formal union, no merging of organizations. For one thing, neither the Stone Movement nor the O'Kelly Movement had such organizations at the time. But through Haggard and Nance, the western Christians certainly knew of the O'Kelly Movement; and if William Guirey had a copy of the Springfield Presbytery's *Apology*

---

[94]*Herald of Gospel Liberty*, vol. 1 (November 10, 1808), p. 23. Further similar references can be found in the same periodical on p. 27 (November 24, 1808) and p. 32 (December 8, 1808).

[95]Cartwright, p. 35.

[96]*Herald of Gospel Liberty*, vol. 1 (January 19, 1809), p. 43.

and knew of their separation from the Presbyterians, then certainly the O'Kelly Movement had knowledge of the Stone Movement. The intriguing phrase "united with us" probably means little more than an acknowledgment that the two groups knew of each other and accepted each other as occupying the same positions and working for the same ends. Regardless of these uncertainties, it is instructive that these two groups, both committed to Christian union, acknowledged it when they both got under way and met each other. For them, this was the very essence of what their movement was all about.

Thus a union of some meaningful sort was achieved between the Stone and O'Kelly Movements. Soon, of course, the O'Kelly Movement, or at least the Virginia immersionists led by William Guirey, also achieved union with the Smith-Jones movement, symbolized by their action of accepting Elias Smith in 1811. Thus the southern Christians developed a union with both of the other groups; it only remained for the Stone and Smith-Jones Movements to discover each other and reach out in Christian union.

The first indication of any awareness on the part of the eastern Christians about their counterparts in the west occurred in the very first issue of the *Herald of Gospel Liberty*. On page two of the first issue, Elias Smith reprinted *The Last Will and Testament of the Springfield Presbytery*. In a couple of introductory paragraphs, Smith explained a little bit about the western revivals, the reforming views that came out of them, and the dissolution of the Springfield Presbytery.[97] How a copy of the *Will* got up to Smith in New Hampshire at the time is unknown, but it appears that Smith did not know much more about the Stone Movement at this time. In fact, in an 1835 address at a New England conference of Christians, the speaker, Ira Allen, mentioned that "it was not until twenty years after the first churches were formed in the east, that any specific information was received in relation to the progress of the same state of things beyond the Alleganies [sic] in the west. But by degrees information was received."[98]

It seems that as migration out of New England moved into northern and central Ohio, migration from Kentucky also moved into central Ohio. Here Christians from the Stone Movement and from the Smith-Jones Movement probably first met each other. Word of this began to filter back to the east, and this led to the decision to follow up on the contact. Joseph Badger, an elder of the Christian Churches in New York,

---

[97]*Herald of Gospel Liberty*, vol. 1 (September 1, 1808), p. 2.
[98]*Christian Palladium*, vol. 4 (August 15, 1835), p. 125.

was approved by the New York Western Conference to visit the west and "obtain a history of our brethren there, and to open a correspondence between them and the brethren of the northern and middle states."[99] This decision was also confirmed at the United States General Conference held on September 2, 1824. Badger did not start out on his trip until the fall of 1825, but it was a momentous journey indeed.

Throughout September and October, Badger travelled through New York and Ohio. In December, a conference of Christians in Kentucky was held, which officially welcomed Joseph Badger from New York and adopted a statement that included the following comments:

> We with gladness receive you and your communications, and cordially reciprocate the sentiment of your brethren in New-York, to correspond with each other, at least by letter.[100]

> Brother Badger, . . . we love you—we thank you for your labors of love—we feel the sweet spirit of union, a union which death cannot dissolve. . . . Salute your brethren and our brethren in the east for us; tell them we feel them as one family with us—governed by the same rule, directed by the same spirit, animated by the same hope, and engaged in the same cause.[101]

On January 9, 1826, a conference of elders and brethren was held in Ohio, which again hosted Badger. They reported on the status of churches in the west and recorded the following statement:

> Whereas this conference deems it highly necessary that a conference of the Christian Elders and brethren in the states of Ohio, Kentucky, Indiana, Illinois, Missouri, Alabama and Tennessee, or so many of the brethren in the aforementioned states as can be convened, the first Monday after the last Sabbath in October next. Meeting to commence Saturday previous. The object of this conference is to form a correspondence throughout the Churches, in the western States, and acquire a correct knowledge of the churches in general—and also to consult about establishing a *periodical work* to be edited in the western country. And Elders Barton W. Stone, Thomas Adams, and Matthew Gardner, are hereby appointed a committee, to consult the brethren where conference will be held, and to locate the meeting.[102]

Three things stand out in significance from this paragraph. First is the suggestion of having a general conference of individuals from the

---

[99]*Christian Herald*, vol. 7 (September, 1824), p. 105.
[100]*Gospel Luminary*, vol. 2 (April, 1826), p. 83.
[101]*Ibid.*, p. 87.
[102]*Ibid.*, p. 88.

Christian Churches of the various western states, to meet during the last week of October, at a place unspecified. Second, there is the suggestion of considering a periodical to be published in the west. Stone himself was on this committee. In fact, Stone began publishing the *Christian Messenger* the next November. This development is probably directly related to Badger's presence and suggestion; the eastern Christians already had several such magazines and knew their importance. Third is the suggestion of a continuing correspondence to be kept up between western and eastern Christians. In fact, this also was done. Numerous letters from western Christians, particularly from Ohio, appeared in the eastern journals over the next several years.

With all this accomplished, Badger headed home, delighted that he had been the instrument of such contact and goodwill between the two groups. So good did he feel about it, that he decided to return to the west the last week of October to participate in the planned western general conference. No place had been set, but Badger concluded that it would take place in Cincinnati.[103] So to Cincinnati he went in October of 1826. As we shall see later, however, there was no meeting in Cincinnati the last week of October. Regardless, Badger reported on this visit that he was "everywhere received with much friendship."[104] Continuing correspondence from Ohio and Kentucky followed his visit, and both sides talked of a "union" being achieved between the two groups. In an 1835 statement, one speaker in the east reported that in the 1820s, "union and co-operation" were established between east and west.[105] In an official statement written in 1827, a committee of eastern Christians referred to the separate Christian movements in New England, the south, and the west and stated, "These bodies, however, shortly became acquainted with each other, and have long since been considered as forming one extensive denomination of Christians, and have co-operated together in promoting the general cause of truth and piety."[106]

Another indicator of what happened as a result of this initial visit came from a letter of Simon Clough. It was about this time the Smith-Jones movement opened up a correspondence with the General Baptists in England. A correspondence committee was appointed by the U. S. General Conference, and Simon Clough was made Corresponding

---

[103]*Ibid.*, p. 87.
[104]*Christian Herald,* vol. 10 (March, 1827), p. 7.
[105]*Christian Palladium,* vol. 4 (August 15, 1835, p. 125.
[106]*Gospel Luminary,* vol. 3 (July, 1827), pp. 165-166.

Secretary. In a letter to the England Baptists, he explained some background of who these Christians were. In explaining their origins, he mentioned their own beginnings in New England, plus other beginnings in the south (the O'Kelly Movement) and the west (the Stone Movement). He then stated, "These bodies, however, shortly became acquainted with each other, and have long since been considered as forming one extensive denomination of Christians, and have co-operated together in promoting the general cause of truth and piety."

He mentioned the formation of conferences, each of which sends a delegate to the United States General Christian Conference. In listing their conferences, he listed the fourteen conferences of the western Christians, but also stated, "No delegate, however, as yet has met with us from the Western States. It is expected they will be represented at the sitting of the next Conference." He also mentioned that "we have now established among us three periodical works," specifically including the *Christian Messenger* edited by Stone in Georgetown, Kentucky.[107]

It seems obvious, thus, that a union was consummated between the Stone Movement and the New England movement in 1826. This does not mean that there was a tight organizational merger. It was probably union only in the sense of groups of people acknowledging each other as comrades in the same cause identified together. Considering their common background in commitment to Scripture and Christian union, their uniting does not seem unusual.

Unfortunately, however, the union of the groups under Stone and Smith-Jones also had some misunderstandings. These misunderstandings provided the foundation for some bitter controversy in the next two decades. One of the problems lies in the difficulty in determining what did and did not happen in 1826 with regard to the two visits of Joseph Badger.

One indication of a problem came in a letter from Thomas Adams, a Christian in Ohio from the Stone movement, to Joseph Badger after his first visit. Adams wrote,

> I do not think that you should give up the idea of visiting us again because your wish was not obtained the first time and not withstanding you feel disappointed and somewhat discouraged [,] your mission has been profitable in the west, and I am confident that there is not a society that you visited while here, but would unite in soliciting you to return.[108]

---

[107]*Ibid.*, pp. 165-167.
[108]*Gospel Luminary*, vol. 2 (October, 1826), p. 243.

What wish was not obtained? The tone of the letter indicates that it was something that would not necessarily be supplied by a second trip. Whatever the missing item was, it apparently hurt Badger's morale and confidence in the efficacy of his first visit. Regardless, Badger came west in October of 1826 and was even appointed by the U. S. General Conference in Connecticut to do so.[109] The General Conference even composed an official message to the Cincinnati Convention.[110]

In contrast, however, to the publicity and reports that accompanied Badger's first visit, this second one received little notice. The best account is a brief summary in the *Christian Herald* in which Badger mentioned that the western Christians looked forward to a correspondence with their brethren in the east and that he was personally "received with friendship."[111]

At the time, nothing more was recorded. The real detail of what happened with regard to this visit did not come out until years later—after the union between Stone and Alexander Campbell in 1832. These records are therefore strongly influenced by various value judgments from people who felt strongly either in support or opposition to this union. We will save the details of these feelings about the union until Chapter Seven. One indication of irritation, however, surfaced in 1833. The lead editorial for January in the *Christian Messenger* reported,

> A few years ago, our brethren in the east, forgetting that the churches were independent, and dazzled with the pomp of a general Conference, resolved among themselves to constitute one in the East—one in the South, and another in the West. We in the West were solicited to co-operate in this measure. We saw it unauthorized by the New Testament, and therefore refused our co-operation. The Eastern brethren soon discovered what we had plainly seen, and have lately dissolved the unscriptural thing among themselves.[112]

It seems obvious, therefore, that the erection of area conferences offended the western Christians. However, there is no indication that the eastern Christians ever noticed this observation in the 1833 *Messenger*. It was not until some editorial correspondence developed in 1841 that things were brought fully into the open.

In that year, Stone wrote to Joseph Marsh, editor of the *Christian Palladium,* noting the continual snipping going on against the western Christians and asking for "an explicit statement of the objections he and

---

[109]*Ibid.,* (October, 1826), p. 238.
[110]*Christian Herald,* vol. 9 (September, 1826), p. 110.
[111]*Ibid.,* vol. 10 (March, 1827), p. 7.
[112]*Christian Messenger,* vol. 7, no. 1 (January, 1833), p. 2.

the eastern brethren have against us as a people."[113] In reply Marsh pointed out that the eastern Christians have always been committed to unite with all Christians, and still are. In an insightful statement, he added,

> They, in former years labored to form a permanent union and co-operation with their brethren of the West. Messengers for this purpose were sent among them; but our friendly visits were not returned; our conferences were opposed, and finally our offers for union were rejected: this was virtually, if not officially, the case.[114]

Some months later Stone replied to this with some heat. Here finally, after a fifteen year lag—a period in which the situation changed dramatically because of Stone's union with Campbell—emerges the story of what happened with Badger's second visit in October of 1826.

> If I, as one, ever heard, that brothers Badger, Hathaway, Millard, and yourself were sent by the eastern Christians for these purposes, or that they were the messengers of the churches to us, the impression is entirely obliterated from my mind. But will any of you say, they were not received by us, and treated as brethren engaged in the same cause? You cannot. But in the second visit of one, we were not so well pleased; for he without any consultation with us, appointed a conference to be holden at Cincinnati some months ahead, at which the preachers in the West were all summoned to attend. He himself came; but none of us in the West attended the summons, because we did not acknowledge the authority. He was mortified, returned home and reported that we were opposed to conferences, &c. In truth we were opposed to them *then,* and equally so now, as they have been generally got up and managed. Such are the strong pillars of partyism. But, you say, "Our friendly visits were not returned." We were poor, and not able to bear the expense of so long a journey. Yet our brethren, Kinkade, Lane, and Thomas, and others did visit you and abode long time with you.
>
> You say, "finally our offers of union were rejected." Do, bro. Marsh, say, what union did we reject? Did we reject offers of Christian Union—the union of which the Bible speaks? No; never. Is it to reject Christian union, because we cannot unite in your district conferences—your central conferences—your general conferences, &c.—and aid in drawing up many *Resolves,* what the churches must do, and what the preachers must do, &c.
>
> My brother, and such as think with him, may act as they see proper; but do not reject us, because we cannot act in these things with you. Do you think that we, in acting thus, have refused Christian union? What saith the scripture? Do examine.
>
> Your old brother,
> B. W. Stone.[115]

---

[113]*Ibid.*, vol. 11, no. 7 (March, 1841), p. 243.

[114]*Christian Palladium,* vol. 10 (May 1, 1841), pp. 9-10.

[115]*Christian Messenger,* vol. 11, no. 12 (August, 1841), p. 420.

Here finally is an explanation of what happened fifteen years earlier. The western Christians had decided to have a meeting the last week of October, but they never specified the location. Badger assumed it would be in Cincinnati. He so announced it, but the western Christians seemed offended by his presumption. So they never came. In addition, when Badger did come, he reported that he was "received everywhere with friendship." This is hardly a candid account of what happened. Why did he gloss over the situation?

It is of further interest to note Stone's reaction to the eastern tendency toward conferences. The west had its conferences, but apparently they were not tightly organized. But when they learned that the east had local conferences with delegates to a national conference that passed resolutions—this probably appeared too similar to the Synod of Kentucky, and the western Christians (or at least Stone) wanted nothing to do with it. They received Badger as a friendly guest, but they wanted no organizational union with the eastern Christians, even though they continued to regard them as brethren. The discontent here became magnified in the 1830s.

1560 —├—Presbyterianism becomes Scotland's state church

1733 —├—"Lay patronage" leads to Seceder Presbyterian split

1747 —├—Burgher/Anti-Burgher split

1763 —├—Thomas Campbell born

1786 —├—Campbell begins studies for the ministry
1787 —├—Campbell marries Jane Corneigle

1795 —├—Old Light/New Light split

1805 —├—Synod of Ireland desires to unite with Burghers
1807 —├—Campbell leaves for America
       Heresy charges filed in Chartiers Presbytery
1808 —├—Campbell appeals to Synod in Philadelphia
       Campbell leaves Presbyterians
1809 —├—Christian Association of Washington formed
       Campbell writes *Declaration and Address*

Chapter 4

Thomas Campbell and the
Declaration and Address

O F EVEN MORE IMPORTANCE than the Stone Movement was the Campbell Movement. Two primary figures are involved here: Thomas and his son, Alexander. Although Alexander became the more famous of the two, the story rightly begins with his father.

Campbell's Early Life

Thomas Campbell was born February 1, 1763, in northern Ireland, the eldest of eight children.[1] The children were evenly divided between sons and daughters, but, sadly, all four of the daughters died in infancy. Thomas' father, Archibald, had been a soldier in the British Army and served under General James Wolfe at the victorious battle on the Plains of Abraham where the British captured Quebec in 1759. Archibald Campbell was also a Roman Catholic, but after his return from the wars, he changed to the Church of Ireland, which was part of the Anglican Church. He spent the rest of his life as a faithful member of the Anglicans.[2] One must be careful not to read too much into this shift of denominations, but it is interesting to note that Thomas was born to a man who was willing to transfer his religious loyalty. Thomas' later choice to join the Presbyterians rather than the Anglicans, as well as his even later decision to leave the Presbyterians, may have been somewhat influenced by the knowledge that his own father had not seen denominational loyalty as an irrevocable identity.

---

[1]The best biography of Thomas Campbell is Lester G. McAllister, *Thomas Campbell: Man of the Book* (St. Louis: The Bethany Press, 1954). Much of the material for this chapter reflects McAllister's work.

[2]*Ibid.*, pp. 21, 22.

Archibald provided a good education for his four sons, all of them enrolling in a military school not far from home. Since all four of the lads later served as school teachers, we can only assume that their early education was begun well. Each of them began teaching school at an early age, although exactly how early is not recorded.

Thomas grew up in his father's church, the Anglican. Even as a youth, he became earnest in his religious devotion and study of the Scriptures. Yet he felt the Anglicans were coldly formal, lacking both piety and warmth of religious expression. He began to attend the services of surrounding Presbyterian churches. Here he found what he felt was lacking. Soon he was seeking some sign of his election and assurance of salvation. While under these mental pressures, he was walking through the fields one day and had the following experience:

> In the midst of his prayerful anxieties and longings, he felt a divine peace suddenly diffuse itself throughout his soul, and the love of God seemed to be shed abroad in his heart as he had never before realized it. His doubts, anxieties and fears were at once dissipated, as if by enchantment. He was enabled to see and to trust in the merits of a crucified Christ, and to enjoy a divine sense of reconciliation, that filled him with rapture and seemed to determine his destiny forever.[3]

Following this conversion experience, Thomas Campbell became a Presbyterian. However, to understand the later course of Campbell's life and ministry, it is necessary to note that he was not just a Presbyterian, for the Presbyterians were divided into several factions. The Presbyterian Church was the state church of Scotland, dating from 1560 with the triumph of Protestantism in that country under John Knox. Catholicism remained a threat to the Scottish Presbyterians for a while, but by 1690, Presbyterianism was secure. By that time, however, new troubles arose in the form of lay patronage.

"Lay patronage" was the issue of whether the churches had the right to select their own preachers, or whether lay individuals, either landlords or the monarchy, could choose and assign ministers to the various congregations. An act of Parliament in 1712 reinforced the right of lay patronage, but a number of individuals in the church resisted this. They attempted to get the system reversed, but to no avail. Realizing defeat over this issue, Ebenezer Erskine in 1733 left the national church and

---

[3]Robert Richardson, *Memoirs of Alexander Campbell* (Cincinnati: The Standard Publishing Company, 1913), vol. 1, p. 23.

organized what was officially called the Associate Presbytery, but more commonly known as the Seceder Presbyterians.[4]

Because of the widespread dissatisfaction over this issue, the Seceders soon became a large group, only to be faced by another problem in 1747. One of the laws in Scotland was that all residents of towns (burghers) had to swear allegiance "to the religion presently professed in this realm." When the law was first adopted it meant only to keep Roman Catholics out of the towns and thus prevent their political comeback. But with the growth of the Seceder Presbyterians, the question now arose, did the "religion presently professed" mean Presbyterianism in general, or the National Church of Scotland in particular? If this latter interpretation were adopted, could Seceder Presbyterian residents of towns swear allegiance to a church of which they were not a member? The result of this dispute was another division. The Burgher Seceder Presbyterians felt the required oath referred only to Presbyterianism in general; the Anti-Burgher Seceder Presbyterians felt the oath required an allegiance to the National Church, which they could not profess.[5]

Both of these disputes were Scottish issues. Meanwhile, Scottish Presbyterians, under official encouragement from the monarchy, had been immigrating in large numbers into northern Ireland ever since the days of James I (1603-1625). They soon became the dominant force in that part of the island. Now the various groups in Scotland sent missionaries over to their fellow Presbyterians in Ireland informing them of the disputes back home and urging them to choose sides. Thus the Irish Presbyterians soon divided into National Church of Scotland Presbyterians and Seceder Presbyterians; these latter subdivided into Burgher Seceder Presbyterians and Anti-Burgher Seceder Presbyterians. The tragedy of this was that the issues themselves had nothing to do with the churches in northern Ireland. Fellow believers divided over theoretical questions of culture that meant nothing to how they functioned as Christians. The spiritual body of Christ divided over political and social issues—a development that many found very disturbing.[6]

Out of this situation, Thomas Campbell became a Presbyterian and

---

[4]Earle E. Cairns, *Christianity Through the Centuries: A History of the Christian Church*, Revised and Enlarged Edition (Grand Rapids: Zondervan Publishing House, 1981), p. 404.

[5]Garrison and DeGroot, p. 127. For a more contemporary account, see John Winebrenner (ed.), *History of All the Religious Denominations in the United States* (Harrisburg, Pennsylvania: n.p., 1849), p. 25.

[6]A treatment here is in David Stewart, *The Seceders in Ireland, With Annals of Their Congregations* (Belfast: Presbyterian Historical Society, 1950).

joined the Anti-Burgher Seceders, though he had no particular inclination on the disputes themselves. Thomas continued as a school teacher, although he now increasingly felt the desire to become a minister. His father would hear nothing of it. However, in his neighborhood was another Seceder, John Kinley, who urged Campbell to get enough education to qualify for ministerial studies. Kinley even provided the finances. After a prolonged period of urging, Archibald Campbell finally relented and allowed his son to prepare for the ministry.[7]

Campbell enrolled in the University of Glasgow in 1783 and finished his undergraduate course in 1786. At that time, he began specific studies for the ministry. He attended the theological seminary operated by the Anti-Burgher Seceders at Whitburn, Scotland. It was a small school, conducted by a single professor, Archibald Bruce, and it operated only during an eight-week summer session. It took five years to get through the normal program, so Campbell did not finish until 1791. Spending his summers in seminary studies, he spent the remainder of his time teaching school. In the meantime he met Jane Corneigle and married her in 1787. Their first child, Alexander, was born in September of 1788.[8]

Irish Ministry

Once Thomas finished his schooling, he returned to northern Ireland for his ministry. He first preached for several small congregations, then settled into a pastorate at Ahorey in 1798.[9] Here Campbell spent the next nine years of his life. Although his formal education had ended, his education in life and ministry had not. In fact, influences soon transformed him.

For one thing, it was in this period that the Presbyterian churches went through another division. The question arose in 1795 about the authority of governmental officials in religion. Whenever there is a state church, this dilemma exists. The Burgher Seceders first raised the question, but it soon spread to the Anti-Burghers as well. In 1806 Archibald Bruce, Campbell's seminary professor, led in the establishment of a presbytery along the new lines, and Campbell found himself affiliated with it. Those Presbyterians who were content with things the way they were were known as the "Old Lights." Those who wanted change professed to have new light on the subject, so were called "New

---

[7]McAllister, pp. 23-24.
[8]*Ibid.*, pp. 25-32.
[9]*Ibid.*, pp. 31-33.

Lights." Again, the tragedy was that this was a Scottish issue—in Ireland, the Anglican Church was the state church, and those officials had no authority in the Presbyterian churches anyway. But now both Burgher and Anti-Burgher Presbyterian Churches in Ireland divided over this Scottish political issue. This completed Thomas Campbell's religious identification. He was not just a Presbyterian; he was not just a Christian; he was an Old Light Anti-Burgher Seceder Presbyterian Protestant kind of a Christian. Worst of all, they officially believed they were the one true church, and all persons of any other denominational stripe ought to be disfellowshipped.

Thomas found it difficult to accept this narrow view of things. This was reinforced by recent experiences in his ministry in northern Ireland. While ministering to the church in Ahorey, Thomas lived near Rich Hill, a few miles distant. In Rich Hill was an independent church that generously made its meeting house available for use by a variety of religious speakers who came through the area. Thomas was often in the audience when these men spoke. He heard James A. Haldane, the famous evangelist Rowland Hill, and John Walker.[10]

John Walker (1768-1833) had been an Anglican priest, minister of Bethesda Chapel in Dublin, and a professor at Trinity College in the same city. But he left the Anglicans in 1804 because of their worldliness, even throwing aside their clerical vestments. His decision was based partly on his desire to follow precisely the precepts and precedents of Scripture. He was also somewhat of an eccentric. Not wanting to appear ostentatious, he sold his carriage and traveled on foot throughout Ireland to proclaim his message. He did not have much of a following, but Alexander Campbell later said his ideas were closer to those of John Walker than of any other man he knew.[11]

The Independents at Rich Hill were apparently also conversant with the ideas of John Glas and Robert Sandeman, although how much of an influence these were upon the congregation, and upon Thomas Campbell in particular, is difficult to say. John Glas (1695-1773) left the Church of Scotland in 1728 over the question of church-state relationships. He established a number of churches throughout Scotland, pointing out that each congregation should be autonomous, and that the precepts and examples of the New Testament church should be their major guide for church life. They followed Acts 2:42 as the divine order for worship.[12]

---

[10]*Ibid.*, pp. 46-49.

[11]For Walker, see Garrison and DeGroot, p. 128; also McAllister, pp. 48-49.

[12]McAllister, pp. 49-50; Garrison and DeGroot, pp. 46-47.

Glas' son-in-law, Robert Sandeman (1718-1771), became an active influence in this movement by 1755. He specifically developed the theological concept that the typical Calvinist view of "saving faith" was erroneous. Rather than seeing faith as a metaphysical substance granted as a special gift of God, Sandeman saw faith simply as "belief in testimony." People believe in Christ in much the same way they believe in any historical figure. This faith becomes "saving faith" because it leads them to obey Him. However, there is nothing miraculous in the act of faith itself—it is the simple act of a normal mind apprehending claims of truth.[13] As we will see later, this idea had significant impact upon the homiletical development of Walter Scott.

The views of Glas and Sandeman (their followers sometimes called Glassites, but more commonly Sandemanians) tended to be divisive, however. Some churches followed the "divine order of worship" so strictly that they declared nonfellowship with congregations that differed from them. Further divisions occurred over such things as whether the unordained may serve the Lord's Supper, the mode of baptism, plurality of elders versus one-man rule, and the erection of a church building. The Glas-Sandeman movement brought to light some important concepts of church life: weekly communion, mutual edification, the kiss of charity, weekly contributions for the poor, distinguishing the New Testament Lord's Day from the Old Testament Sabbath, and that the proper name for the church was "Church of Christ." But this emphasis on the restoration of New Testament teaching was not balanced with a concern for Christian unity, and the result was to see numerous divisions over various issues. The Restoration Movement in America inherited many of the concepts of Glas and Sandeman; unfortunately, some of the divisive tendencies were also passed along. We will return to these at a later point.[14]

The congregation at Rich Hill also exposed Campbell to the Haldane movement. Two Scot brothers, Robert (1764-1842), and James Alexander Haldane (1768-1851) were wealthy laymen in the Church of Scotland, both of whom had pursued careers in the navy.[15] But before the turn of the century, both had left the service and were converted to a more evangelical Christianity. Dissatisfied with the tepid services available through the National Church of Scotland, they had begun their own independent church by 1799 in Edinburgh, where James Alexander was

---

[13]McAllister, p. 50; Garrison and DeGroot, pp. 48-50.

[14]For Glas-Sandeman, see McAllister, pp. 49-50; also Garrett, pp. 48-57.

[15]The Haldanes are treated in Garrison and DeGroot, pp. 50-52; see also Randall, pp. 166-182.

the minister for almost fifty years. The brothers used their financial resources to establish theological institutes to train laymen for the work of the ministry. James Alexander preached the gospel in all parts of Scotland, and even traveled to Ireland, where Thomas Campbell heard him at Rich Hill. Robert was not a preacher as such, but from 1816-1819, he took an evangelistic tour through Switzerland and France and initiated a revival known as the *Reveil,* or "awakening."[16]

In 1797 the Haldane brothers established the "Society for the Propagation of the Gospel at Home," since the Church of Scotland was little interested in either home or foreign missions. Thomas Campbell later became a member of this group and supported their endeavors to preach the simple New Testament gospel throughout the land.[17] The Society also supported various evangelical preachers, including Rowland Hill (1744-1833). He was a well-known itinerant evangelist who remained in the Anglican Church in spite of its cool views toward his evangelistic efforts.

In 1805 J. A. Haldane published a book committed to the thesis that all church practices should be based on the precepts of the New Testament. Both the worship services and daily Christian conduct were to be gauged by conformity to the teaching and practices of the apostolic church. Two years later, the Haldane brothers become convinced that immersion was the apostolic practice. Not all Haldanean churches followed them in this practice, although many did and became known as Scotch Baptists. Scottish immigrants also planted many churches of the Haldanean movement in America. In addition, Robert Sandeman came to America in 1764, establishing several churches in New England. Sandeman was buried in Danbury, Connecticut. Through these various movements—Walker, Glas-Sandeman, Haldanes—concepts appeared that influenced numerous individuals who later played significant roles in the Restoration Movement.

In these formative years of his early ministry, Campbell was also influenced by the writings of John Locke (1632-1704). Locke was an English philosopher who was still being widely read in the eighteenth and nineteenth centuries. Locke's *Essay Concerning Human Understanding* (1690) influenced Campbell's concepts of man and man's ability to understand the Scriptures plainly. Even more significant was Locke's *A Letter Concerning Toleration* (1689). This significant work came out of the

---

[16]For a brief word on the place of this revival in the larger picture of European Christianity, see James Hastings Nichols, *History of Christianity, 1650-1950: Secularization of the West* (New York: The Ronald Press Company, 1956), pp. 139-141.

[17]McAllister, p. 51.

struggles in England between a Protestant Parliament and the Catholic King James II. The struggle resulted in James' forced departure from the country and his daughter Mary's arrival—along with her husband William—as the new monarch. They jointly occupied the English throne in 1689. In this context of religious strife, Locke appealed for religious toleration. In the process, he pleaded for the church to be guided solely on the basis of New Testament teaching. In arguing for the matter of biblical authority alone, Locke wrote:

> Some, perhaps, may object that no such society can be said to be a true church unless it have in it a bishop or presbyter, with ruling authority derived from the very apostles, continued down to the present time by an uninterrupted succession.
>
> To these I answer: In the first place, let them show me the edict by which Christ has imposed that law upon His church. And let not any man think me impertinent if in a thing of this consequence I require that the terms of that edict be very express and positive.[18]

Along the same line, emphasizing that any doctrine that is to be used as a test of fellowship must be very clear in Scripture, Locke added:

> Since such men are so solicitous about the true church, I would only ask them here, by the way, if it be not more agreeable to the church of Christ to make the conditions of her communion consist in such things, and such things only, as the Holy Spirit has in the Holy Scriptures declared, in express words, to be necessary to salvation; I ask, I say, whether this be not more agreeable to the church of Christ than for men to impose their own inventions and interpretations upon others as if they were of Divine authority, and to establish by ecclesiastical laws, as absolutely necessary to the profession of Christianity, such things as the Holy Scriptures do either not mention or at least expressly command? Whosoever requires those things in order to ecclesiastical communion, which Christ does not require in order to life eternal, he may, perhaps, indeed constitute a society accommodated to his own opinion and his own advantage; but how that can be called the church of Christ which is established upon laws that are not His, and which excludes such persons from its communion as He will one day receive into the Kingdom of heaven, I understand not.[19]

There is no doubt that these ideas became part of the fertile seed bed that Thomas Campbell developed into his later writing, *The Declaration and Address*.[20]

---

[18]John Locke, *A Letter Concerning Toleration;* Introduction by Patrick Romanell (Indianapolis: The Bobbs-Merrill Company, Inc., 1955), p. 21.

[19]*Ibid.*, p. 22.

[20]See below, p. 88ff.

In his immediate situation, exposure to the preaching of Hill and J. A. Haldane influenced Campbell toward a more evangelical view of the ministry. He was not happy with the spirit of bitter sectarian strife that characterized so much of the work of Protestant groups, both in Ireland and Scotland. Campbell saw not only the virtue of trying to recapture New Testament Christianity; he also became convinced that the partisan divisions were out of place. He decided to do something about the situation in northern Ireland.

Since the oath of allegiance "to the religion presently professed in this realm" was not required of citizens in the towns in Ireland, Campbell decided the division between the Burghers and Anti-Burghers ought to be removed, at least in Ireland. A "Committee on Consultation" met in Rich Hill on October 9, 1804, to discuss means of bringing the two branches of Seceder Presbyterians together.[21] Thomas drafted an address to the Synod of Ireland, which his *ad hoc* committee unanimously approved. In it he pointed out that the two branches of the Seceders were not divided over doctrine, worship, discipline, or government; the subject matter of their differences was found neither in the Old nor the New Testament. Since Christianity was intended for unity, and since the issue was a Scottish one and irrelevant to the Irish, the present division was an embarrassment to the work of both branches in Ireland. He concluded, "It appears that there is nothing to prevent the two bodies of Seceders in this land to unite in a bond of a common testimony adapted to their local situation."[22]

Apparently the Synod was in favor of the request, for in March of 1805, a meeting of Burgher and Anti-Burgher representatives announced a unanimous desire for union. The Synod then made formal application to the Scottish parent body for permission to carry on their own affairs without being in subordination to the General Synod. Thomas Campbell was elected to represent the ministers in Ireland, and he traveled to Glasgow to present their case. Unfortunately, the petition lost. In the words of one man, "While in my opinion he clearly outargued them, they outvoted him."[23] Campbell could not break down their partisan loyalties, but he did plant some seeds. After he left the country, the division between the Burghers and Anti-Burghers was dissolved in 1820 in the same Edinburgh church where the division had occurred seventy-three years previously.[24]

---

[21]McAllister, pp. 52-53.

[22]For the entire address, see Alexander Campbell, *Memoirs of Thomas Campbell* (Cincinnati: H. S. Bosworth, 1861), pp. 210-214.

[23]*Ibid.*, p. 9; also in Richardson, vol. 1, p. 58.

[24]Richardson, vol. 1, p. 58; Stewart, p. 383; McAllister, p. 55.

The 1805 refusal from the General Synod came as a severe disappointment to Campbell. He had put a great deal of energy into this unitive effort, and its death was a blow to his morale. In addition, he was suffering from overwork—he was preaching for two congregations and teaching school on the side to provide an income for his family, which now included seven children. On top of these concerns were other problems unique to northern Ireland. The Protestants and Catholics were already fighting each other, just as they continue to do in the present. Campbell was concerned for the safety of his family. He was also concerned about the economic future of his children. Northern Ireland could not be called a depressed economy, but neither could it boast of great economic opportunities; Campbell wanted something better for his family. Finally, this very period was in the midst of the great migration of Scotch-Irish to America. Numerous friends, neighbors, and members of his congregations had already moved to the United States, and several urged him to join them. To cure him of his nervous indigestion, Campbell's physician urged an ocean voyage, an enforced vacation from his overwork.[25]

He was still reluctant to go, but he was finally persuaded by an argument from his eldest son, Alexander that he himself determined to emigrate to the United States a little bit later. If Thomas were to go now, he could blaze the way for the rest of the family. Alexander agreed to continue teaching the school his father maintained; he had already been assisting him in that regard since the fall of 1805. It was now the spring of 1807; Thomas bid good-bye to his family and congregation and on April 1 went to Londonderry. There he boarded ship, sailed for America on April 8, and arrived in Philadelphia on May 13, after thirty-five days at sea.[26]

American Ministry

He had arrived in Philadelphia the week that the Anti-Burgher Seceder Presbyterians were having their annual meeting in that very city. In America there was no state church—therefore there was no problem with lay patronage. Neither proprietary landlords nor monarchy chose or assigned ministers to churches in America. The issue that brought on the Seceder division in Scotland in 1733 did not exist in America. But the division had been brought in with the immigrants when they arrived, and it continued nevertheless. Residents in towns in America did not

---

[25]McAllister, pp. 56-58.
[26]*Ibid.*, pp. 58-59, 68.

take any oath to support the "religion presently professed in this realm," yet the Anti-Burghers continued their existence as separate from the Burghers. There were not enough Burgher Seceders in America to have their separate organization, but the Anti-Burgher Seceders maintained their distinctiveness. At least the churches in America were not divided over the Old Light/New Light issue. But if it was tragic that churches in northern Ireland were divided over Scottish issues that meant nothing to them, it was even more tragic that the same issues divided Christians in America. They were three thousand miles from the source of the problems, but the lines laid down in Scotland continued in America. We have seen that Thomas could not tolerate these divisions in Ireland; even less could he accept them in America.

Campbell had with him letters of introduction from the presbytery in Ireland.[27] He presented these to the Synod meeting in Philadelphia, and they soon assigned him to the Chartiers Presbytery in western Pennsylvania. Actually, he requested assignment to this area since that was where many of his former neighbors and parishioners had located. Arriving in America on May 13, he presented his credentials to the Synod on May 16 and on May 18, he was appointed to his duties. The synod also advanced him fifty dollars for his travel expenses. His assignments within the Chartiers Presbytery were to begin July 1. Before he left Philadelphia, he sent his family a letter, dated May 27, in which he explained his cordial reception by the Synod, his plans to travel to the west, and also his prayers on their behalf.[28]

Campbell soon arrived in western Pennsylvania, and located in the town of Washington, about twenty-five miles southwest of Pittsburgh. Many of his friends from northern Ireland had already settled here and several additional families joined him shortly after his arrival.

Religious conditions on the western frontier were not at all similar to those of the Old Country, or even to the settled areas along the Atlantic seaboard of the United States. In many frontier communities, preachers were normally few and far between. Settlers had come from a variety of religious backgrounds; many had no religious affiliation whatsoever.

Ministers or preachers played a key role in frontier life. They fulfilled some functions in frontier society that no one else could. On the frontier there were no justices of the peace or any legal administrators that could perform weddings; only preachers married people. Yet many

---

[27]A letter of introduction from the Presbytery of Market Hill, County of Armaugh, Northern Ireland, is in A. Campbell, pp. 20-21.

[28]McAllister, pp. 68-69.

communities had no preacher, nor any access to one. The frontier records numerous instances of young men and women who wanted to get married but could find no preacher. As a result, they often made a public declaration of their intentions and began to live together as husband and wife. It was not considered immoral or scandalous; both sets of parents were completely aware of the situation. Whenever a preacher showed up, they went through the formal wedding ceremony, although sometimes the bride had one or two children in arms. Only preachers conducted funeral services; the dead were buried, but the official funeral service had to wait upon the arrival of a preacher. Thus when a preacher arrived, he caught up on all the marrying, baptizing, and conducting of any necessary funeral services.

This was further complicated by the common denominational practice of closed communion. That is, ministers could provide the Lord's Supper only for members of their particular denomination. Many people found it difficult enough to wait for *any* kind of preacher for weddings, funerals, and so on. But they also knew that a preacher from their particular denomination might *never* show up. Many were God-fearing and devout; they just had the misfortune to belong to a denomination that was only sparsely represented on the frontier.

The same applied to the various Presbyterian divisions in western Pennsylvania. Here were Church of Scotland Presbyterians as well as Seceder Presbyterians; Burgher Seceders as well as Anti-Burgher Seceder Presbyterians; there were even other groups represented by immigrants from Scotland. Each of these groups practiced closed communion. No preacher could allow people to partake of the Lord's Supper unless they were genuine members of the particular Presbyterian branch he represented. This is where Thomas Campbell got into trouble.

As we have already seen, the partisan divisions of Ireland did not set well with him. Those of western Pennsylvania were intolerable. Many of Campbell's former neighbors in Ireland were now his Pennsylvania neighbors, but they were outside the Anti-Burgher Seceder Presbyterian Church. Yet Thomas refused to treat them as enemies; he fellowshipped openly with them. One family in particular was that of James Foster, who had been a significant leader in the independent congregation at Rich Hill. Anti-Burgher Seceder Presbyterian ministers were disturbed at Campbell's open friendship with such people.[29]

More grist for their mill of denominational jealousy came in Campbell's visit to some scattered Anti-Burghers at the community of

---

[29]McAllister, pp. 71-73.

Cannamaugh, along the Allegheny river upstream from Pittsburgh. As Campbell prepared to celebrate a communion service here, he noticed that there were numerous individuals from other Presbyterian branches who had not been able to receive the Lord's Supper for a long time because no preacher from their branch had come to their community. In his sermon preceding the communion, Campbell lamented the divisions in the church and urged all those who felt disposed and prepared to join them in the Lord's Supper. The way Robert Richardson related this incident over half a century later, it is difficult to determine whether Campbell invited "all" to join them, or just "all Presbyterians."[30] Regardless, Campbell was authorized to provide the communion only to Anti-Burgher Seceder Presbyterians, and he had certainly done more than that. A younger minister, William Wilson, was travelling with him, and soon passed on word of Campbell's irregular action.

This began official action by the Chartiers Presbytery against Campbell. Official charges of irregularity and heresy came through the Chartiers Presbytery, and then went on to the Associate Synod in Philadelphia. All the details need not concern us here,[31] but enough needs to be told to explain what Campbell experienced and indicate the problems with denominational machinery.

The first charges against Campbell were filed in the Presbytery in October 1807. The accusations urged that Campbell did not believe in saving faith as Calvinists usually understood it, nor did he accept creeds and confessions as resting on anything other than human authority. We can see that Campbell is apparently already showing the influence of Sandeman's concept of faith ("belief in testimony") and his commitment to biblical authority as opposed to human, creedal authority.

A committee to investigate the charges came up with seven specifics: (1) Campbell challenged the normal understanding of "saving faith"; (2) he denied that there was a divine warrant for using creeds as terms of communion or fellowship; (3) he said it was all right for elders to preach and pray in the absence of ministers; (4) he said it was all right to visit other congregations to hear preaching when Anti-Burgher Seceder Presbyterian preaching was not available; (5) he questioned whether Christ was subject to the penalty of the law when he died on the cross;

---

[30]Richardson, vol. 1, p. 224; compare Garrison and DeGroot, p. 130; McAllister treats it as "all Presbyterians," p. 74.

[31]A full account of these, based upon detailed reporting from the minutes of both presbytery and synod, is in William Herbert Hanna, *Thomas Campbell: Seceder and Christian Union Advocate* (Cincinnati: The Standard Publishing Company, 1935).

(6) he said man could live without sin; and (7) he preached in another minister's territory without the latter's approval.

The first four charges probably fairly reflected Campbell's viewpoints, though the Seceders saw these as scandalous, whereas Campbell did not. Numbers (3) and (4) seem innocent enough to us, although they were violations of normal Presbyterian discipline. Number (5) was unclear and can be disregarded. Number (6) was flatly untrue. Campbell did not believe it, and no testimony was ever brought forward to prove that Campbell had said it. Number (7) was a simple matter of protecting the parish concept, which Campbell saw as inoperable on the frontier. In meetings in January and February of 1808, Campbell was finally given an opportunity to respond to the charges. He refuted some of them and protested the proceedings, but the presbytery voted to suspend his ministry among them. In March, 1808, three members met in a rump session after the normal adjournment of the meeting and voted his suspension to be permanent. Campbell appealed his case to the Associate Synod in Philadelphia.

On May 16, 1807, Campbell had appeared in the Synod as an immigrant minister from Ireland. On May 19, 1808, he appeared again, this time as a suspected heretic trying to clear his name. The Synod found some irregularities in the presbyterial proceedings against Campbell and decided to try their own case. The last three charges were dropped and, ultimately, the first three charges were resolved (somewhat curiously, for it is apparent that Campbell did believe what was charged against him). But the matter of encouraging what was called "occasional preaching," that on occasion it was all right to hear other preaching, could not be resolved. For this one issue, then, Campbell was voted guilty and sentenced to be rebuked and admonished by the moderator of the meeting. Campbell protested that he would submit to admonition on the grounds of imprudence and indiscretion, but he did not want to be censured. He asked for a reconsideration, which the Synod granted, but the decision stood. Thus on May 27, 1808, Campbell stood before the moderator. One man prayed, and the moderator appropriately "rebuked and admonished" Mr. Campbell.

Campbell was given preaching appointments in the Philadelphia area for June and July (perhaps as a cooling off period), but then sent back to the Chartiers Presbytery. When he arrived back in western Pennsylvania, the Presbytery refused to give him any preaching assignments or use him in any way. Clearly they did not want him. On September 13, Campbell declined the authority of the Presbytery and of the Synod and severed communion with the Anti-Burgher Seceder Presbyterians. He soon returned to the Synod the fifty dollars they had advanced him the previous year. For wanting to practice Christian unity under the authority of the Scriptures alone, he was not wanted. Still committed to those two principles, he left the Seceder Presbyterians to try his hand at Christian ministry in a different context.[32]

While he was still contending with the Chartiers Presbytery in the winter-spring of 1808, Campbell penned a "Protest and Appeal," which sheds light on where his thinking was proceeding. In the light of developments in the next two years, much of it is worth quoting:

> How great the injustice, how highly aggravated the injury will appear, to thrust out from communion a Christian brother, a fellow-minister, for saying and doing none other things than those which our Divine Lord and his holy apostles have taught and enjoined to be spoken and done by his ministering servants. . . . I dare not venture to trust my own understanding so far as to take upon me to teach anything as a matter of faith or duty but what is already expressly taught and enjoined by Divine authority. . . . I absolutely refuse, as inadmissible and schismatic, the introduction of human opinions and human inventions into the faith and worship of the church. Is it, therefore, because I plead the cause of the Scriptural and apostolic worship of the Church, in opposition to the various errors and schisms which have so awfully corrupted and divided it, that the brethren of the Union should feel it difficult to admit me as their fellow-laborer in that blessed work? . . .
>
> . . . For what error or immorality ought I to be rejected, except it be that I refuse to acknowledge as obligatory upon myself, or to impose upon others, anything as of Divine obligation, for which I can not produce a "Thus saith the Lord"? . . . Allegiance to Christ and fidelity to his cause and people constrain me to protest against making sins and duties which his word has nowhere pointed out.[33]

Departure from the Seceder Presbyterians in the fall of 1808 did not leave Campbell friendless. Many friends and neighbors appreciated the thrust of his ministerial concern. Even when the charges against him first came up at the meeting of the Synod in May, there also appeared five petitions from western Pennsylvania in support of him. Obviously Campbell had supporters.

Apparently Campbell regularly spent time during the next nine months or so speaking to assemblies of these friends, addressing them on the grand theme of unity on the basis of biblical authority. Sometimes these meetings were held out of doors, but more commonly held in the homes of his old Irish neighbors now living in Washington County.[34]

---

[32]McAllister, pp. 91-95.
[33]Campbell, pp. 12-14.
[34]Richardson, vol. 1, p. 231.

After a while, Campbell noticed that there was a common core of individuals who were regular in their attendance at these meetings. Many of them were Seceders or regular Presbyterians, still holding membership in these churches. Nonetheless, they were the core group of Campbell's support at this time. Up to this time the meetings had been for worship and preaching. But in the summer of 1809, Campbell proposed holding a meeting to formulate a statement of principles on which they were to proceed. The meeting took place at the home of Abraham Altars, a little distance north of Washington. Altars was not a member of any church, but he was friendly to the interests of this group.[35]

At this meeting Campbell rehearsed the course of recent events, mentioning specifically the problems that religious division created. Insisting that the divisions had come because men had gone outside the Bible for their religious teachings, he argued for a return to the Scriptures as the basis for religious instruction and discipline. He concluded by announcing a rule to guide them: "Where the Scriptures speak, we speak; where the Scriptures are silent, we are silent."[36]

There was quiet for some time after Campbell sat down. Finally, Andrew Munro, a Seceder bookseller and postmaster at nearby Cannonsburg, said, "Mr. Campbell, if we adopt *that* as a basis, then there is an end of infant baptism." Although Campbell did not see that conclusion as necessary, he simply replied, "If infant baptism be not found in Scripture, we can have nothing to do with it." Thomas Acheson, deeply moved, jumped up and said, "I hope I may never see the day when my heart will renounce that blessed saying of Scripture, 'Suffer the little children to come unto me, and forbid them not, for of such is the kingdom of heaven.'" Overcome with emotion, he broke into tears. But James Foster, an old friend of Campbell's from Ireland days, observed: "Mr. Acheson, I would remark that in the portion of Scripture you have quoted there is no reference, whatever, to infant baptism." Acheson, in tears, left the room, and everyone present realized they were dealing with issues that rested upon deep emotional attachments. Nonetheless, all concerned decided that Campbell's motto would be adopted.[37]

This moving dialogue is significant for two reasons. (1) It appears they were willing to adopt a principle without fully seeing where that principle would take them. It would be some time before Thomas Campbell gave up infant baptism, and some of them never did. Yet they saw the value of the rule, and expressed their adherence to it. (2) Furthermore, the deep

---

[35]McAllister, pp. 96-97.
[36]Richardson, vol. 1, 236.
[37]McAllister, pp. 98-99.

emotion showed by Acheson was symptomatic of the problems they soon encountered. It was one thing to discuss religion in the abstract; it was something else to make decisions that changed their lives and value structures. Most of those present had accepted infant baptism without question all their lives, as their ancestors had done for centuries before them. To call it into question required an objective detachment from feelings and identities that most, including Campbell, found very difficult. People are often able to make decisions with their heads that they are never able to implement with their hearts.

Yet this little group had now made a resolve to do something about restoring unity to the separated religious world. They planned to meet again on August 17, 1809. At this meeting, they decided to call themselves the Christian Association of Washington and formed a committee of twenty-one individuals to decide how they would carry out their determined purposes. There is no doubt that Campbell was the driving force behind this group. There is good reason to believe that the entire association did not number much more (if any) than twenty-one people. Campbell was empowered to write up a statement of their goals and the principles on which they would operate.

About this same time the group, deciding it was increasingly inconvenient to continue meeting in private dwellings, planned to erect their own meeting house. They built a log building on the Sinclair farm, about three miles south of Mount Pleasant and about seven miles north of Washington. The structure would also serve as a school building for the neighborhood. Near here lived a successful farmer named Welch, and Campbell moved into an upstairs bedroom in Welch's home. It was here that he labored the next few weeks over his famous work, the *Declaration and Address*.[38]

Campbell did not write this document off the cuff. It is obvious that these thoughts had been fermenting in his mind for some time. When the Christian Association of Washington met again on September 7, he read it to them. They unanimously agreed to it and ordered it to be printed. The galley proofs of the document were available about the second week of October, and the document was probably printed about the end of the year.[39]

---

[38]*Ibid.*, pp. 100-101.

[39]In the current "official" history of the Disciples of Christ, McAllister and Tucker state it was printed "sometime during the last two weeks of 1809," but they give no citation for this date; see their p. 111. Their conclusion is probably based on the fact that the original printing of the document included a Postscript that refers to a meeting on December 14.

The Declaration and Address

The *Declaration and Address* is probably the most significant document that the Restoration Movement has produced.[40] In it Thomas Campbell laid out the principles by which a reformation of the church according to the authority of the New Testament could be attained. Here is represented the distillation of a lifetime of thinking about the divisions that existed in the churches and what could be done about them. Campbell's ideas on unity and his observations on church history are brilliant insights into human nature and the applicability of the Word of God to the human situation. If more people followed Campbell's insights today, most troubles among churches would disappear.

The *Declaration and Address* is composed of four parts. First is the "Declaration," a brief statement of only a few pages explaining the origins of the Christian Association of Washington. Then follows the "Address," a further description of the divided state of Christendom, including thirteen propositions intended to discover the principles by which the church could again be united. The "Appendix" is lengthy (longer than all the rest of the document put together), but it is an attempt to answer objections to the proposals, as well as further clarify their methods and goals. Finally, there is the "Postscript," a brief statement written about three months later,[41] containing proposals for a catechism and a periodical publication.

The "Declaration" began by calling attention to the "bitter jarrings and janglings of a party spirit" that pervaded the churches of the time. Against this background, the Christian Association of Washington began. Nine resolutions provide information as to their intent.[42] They state the Association is formed "for the sole purpose of promoting simple evangelical Christianity, free from all mixture of human opinions and inventions of men." The Association did not consider itself a church (either a

---

[40]The *Declaration and Address* has appeared in numerous editions. The original was printed in Washington, Pennsylvania, in 1809. Other significant reprintings include: Alexander Campbell's *Memoirs* of his father, pp. 25-109; Charles A. Young (ed.), *Historical Documents Advocating Christian Union* (Chicago: The Christian Century Company, 1904), pp. 71-209; *Declaration and Address with The Last Will and Testament of the Springfield Presbytery* (St. Louis: The Bethany Press, 1955); and one of a series of documents edited by Enos Dowling of Lincoln Christian College and Seminary, *Declaration and Address* (Lincoln, Illinois: College and Seminary Press, n.d.). Because of the better availability of the edition published by Prof. Dowling, this is the source referred to here for pagination.

[41]Within the Postscript are references to meetings on November 2 and December 14.

[42]Campbell, pp. 2-3.

denomination or even a local congregation), but only "voluntary advocates for Church reformation." They also talked about forming similar associations and supporting ministers that would practice "that simple original form of Christianity, expressly exhibited upon the sacred page."

The "Address" contains what is probably the real meat of the document. Campbell spent several lengthy paragraphs describing the problems of a disunited Christendom, during which he observed, "Our differences, at most, are about the things in which the kingdom of God does not consist, that is, about matters of private opinion or human invention."[43] This idea he reinforced later. About midway through the "Address," Campbell presented his noteworthy propositions.[44] He introduced these by stating they are not intended as a creed, but only to open up the way for establishing clear and certain premises upon which to come to the original ground of New Testament Christianity.

Propositions I and II deal with the unity of the church, certainly one of Campbell's key concepts. Proposition I states: "The Church of Christ upon earth is essentially, intentionally, and constitutionally one." There are not many bodies of Christ, only one; not many churches, only one. Proposition II affirms that there will be many local congregations in that one church: "Although the Church of Christ upon earth must necessarily exist in particular and distinct societies, locally separate one from another, yet there ought to be no schisms, no uncharitable divisions among them." Obviously there will be different congregations in different geographical locations—but they are to acknowledge that they are one church, with no divisions or party spirit separating them.

Proposition III reflects Campbell's other major commitment—the authority of the Bible alone for the church. "Nothing ought to be inculcated upon Christians as articles of faith; nor required of them as terms of communion, but what is expressly taught and enjoined upon them in the word of God." Nothing is to be made essential to Christian identity or fellowship unless it is clearly stated as such in the New Testament, "either in express terms or by approved precedent." This would certainly eliminate all such divisions as the Seceders, the Burgher/Anti-Burghers, Old/New Lights, etc. Only what was *expressly* taught in the Bible was to be used as tests of faith and fellowship.

Proposition IV separated the authority of the two Testaments, stating that while the Old Testament was sufficient for the Old Testament people, it is the New Testament that is the unique authority for the New

---

[43]*Ibid.*, p. 13.
[44]*Ibid.*, pp. 22-26.

Testament church. The significance here is that the Old Testament by itself was not to be used as a proof text for New Testament doctrine or practices, such as Sabbath days, tithes, and a whole host of other Old Testament laws.

Proposition V deals with a sensitive issue:

> With respect to the commands and ordinances of our Lord Jesus Christ, where the Scriptures are silent as to the express time or manner of performance, if any such there be, no human authority has power to interfere, in order to supply the supposed deficiency by making laws for the Church.

It is relatively easy to follow the first half of Campbell's famous motto: "Where the Scriptures speak, we speak." It is much more difficult to apply the second half: "Where the Scriptures are silent, we are silent." Silence works both ways: Unless there is a clear New Testament teaching, we cannot insist that people do certain things; nor can we insist that they *not* do certain things. Either way is speaking where the Bible is silent. This will bring in certain problems that we will return to in Chapter Eight.

Proposition VI is a key observation:

> Although inferences and deductions from Scripture premises, when fairly inferred, may be truly called the doctrine of God's holy word, yet are they not formally binding upon the consciences of Christians farther than they perceive the connection. . . . No such deductions can be made terms of communion, but do properly belong to the after and progressive edification of the Church.

This idea is dynamite! Campbell is saying: Be sure to make a distinction between what Scripture says and what you think it means. Logical deductions are human conclusions, and they are not to be confused with the teaching of Scripture itself. When Jesus instituted the Lord's Supper, He picked up the bread and said, "This is my body"; He picked up the cup and said, "This is my blood." That's what He said. What does it mean? Catholics teach the Real Presence of Christ in transubstantiation, Lutherans in consubstantiation; John Calvin denied the physical presence of Christ in the elements, but affirmed His spiritual presence; Ulrich Zwingli denied all three of these and stated the communion is only a memorial service—Jesus said, "Do this in *memory* of me." But notice that all four of these interpretations are conclusions based on Scripture—none of them are the teaching of Scripture in express terms. Thomas Campbell would argue that such interpretations are never to be made tests of membership, faith, or fellowship. If Christians today could learn to separate their *conclusions* based on Scriptural statements from the actual teaching of Scripture itself and never make their own conclusions tests of fellowship, most doctrinal controversies would disappear.

Proposition VII picks up a thread from VI—Campbell states that although the creeds may be highly expedient for the work of the church, yet since they contain many inferred truths, they ought never to be used as tests of faith. Notice that Campbell is opposed to creeds only when they are used as a cause of division within the Church. If people feel comfortable with a creed, Campbell will grant its use as a personal statement of their faith. But he argues against forcing that statement upon others.

In Proposition VIII, Campbell states that the only things necessary for people to become members of the church are for them to: (1) know they are lost; (2) profess their faith in Christ; and (3) obey Him in all things according to His word. They need not become Bible scholars or memorize a profession of faith that goes far beyond their understanding at the time.

In Proposition IX, Campbell states simply that Christians should consider each other precious saints of God and act accordingly. Proposition X returns to the matter of divisions. Campbell affirms that division is "a horrid evil," being anti-Christian, anti-Scriptural, and anti-natural. "It is productive of confusion and of every evil work."

Yet if division is all that bad, then why are there so many denominations in the world? Campbell answers this in Proposition XI. He says that all corruptions and divisions that have ever taken place in the church are the result of two things: (1) a partial neglect of the revealed will of God; and/or (2) making human opinions a term of communion. A quick review of church history will indicate that Campbell is right. All divisions that have ever occurred come from one or both of these two problems. Some people neglect to observe the entire will of God. For instance, the Quakers refuse to practice any kind of water baptism at all. For people who want to follow Scripture, there will then be a division between them and the Quakers, because the Scriptures state quite plainly that baptism is expected of the Christian. If all professed Christians will observe all that the Scriptures plainly command, there will be unity on this score.

However, many people profess to accept the Scriptures but then add another layer of teaching on top of it—the Lutherans add the teachings of Luther, the Methodists add the teachings of John Wesley, the Presbyterians add the teachings of John Calvin, etc. Some people even add the teachings of Alexander Campbell! By doing so, and then by making these teachings required, they are in the same camp as the first three groups. Campbell's point is that the Scriptures are expected of all Christians, but nothing more is expected. If all people follow the Scriptures, and then do not make human opinions a test of communion, there will be unity of the church on the basis of the Scriptures. This is what the Restoration Movement is all about: unity and scriptural authority. Most divisions in the church today do not rest upon different interpretations of Scripture as much as they rest on the perpetuation of certain human teachings.

Proposition XII again has to do with the nature of the Church and her members. Campbell affirms that the only people who should become church members are those described in Proposition VIII. Their temper and conduct ought to reflect the reality of their profession, and if the church teaches nothing more than what the Scriptures enjoin, then the church will remain pure on earth—pure in membership as well as in doctrine.

Finally, in Proposition XIII, Campbell realizes that Scripture does not always cover every contingency for the Christian life. He says that if anything absolutely necessary to the work of the Church is not recorded in revelation, it can still be done, as long as it is understood that it is a human expedient. To an extent, this is a response to some of the problems that can come up with regard to areas of biblical silence. Where the Bible speaks, we speak; where the Bible is silent, we are silent. But there are times when we have to say something when the Bible is silent. The Bible clearly teaches that Christians are to assemble weekly for worship. But at what time? The Bible is silent here. The Bible clearly talks about elders having the oversight of the congregation and twice Paul gives the qualifications of the eldership. But how long is the elder's term of office? The Bible is silent here. In both of these instances, the church cannot simply refuse to act because of biblical silence. It must decide when it will gather for weekly worship, and it must decide how long elders will serve before reelection is necessary. But these decisions are human expedients and are not to be used as tests of fellowship.

Campbell's observation in this proposition gives the church room to act in these areas of silence. As long as the church realizes these matters are expedients, they will never become tests of fellowship. There can be room for disagreement. If people feel terribly strongly about whether elders are to have three-year terms or five-year terms, there may even be two congregations—but as Campbell warned in Proposition II, there is to be no schism or *uncharitable* division. Proposition XIII thus leaves room for the church to adapt to the needs of its society and culture. As long as people label these adjustments human expedients, and as long as these adjustments do not compromise any clear teaching of Scripture, there will be no problem. The total thrust of the *Declaration and Address*, and the thirteen propositions in particular, is to provide principles by which the church can restore the authority of the Scriptures. Unity on the basis of the Bible—that is the key concept of the entire Restoration Movement. This will require some liberty in the area of human opinions and the refusal to make such opinions tests of fellowship, but it still provides a workable scheme for restoring New Testament Christianity.

As mentioned earlier, Thomas Campbell did not write this document without deep reflection. Nor did he write it in a vacuum. It is easy to see how many of his experiences with the Old Light Anti-Burgher Seceders are reflected in its ideas, as well as his experiences with the Chartiers Presbytery. But even beyond this, Campbell was influenced by the writings of John Locke. Earlier, we quoted two passages from Locke's *A Letter Concerning Toleration* that carry the same ideas as Campbell's *Declaration and Address*. To show the parallel thinking of Campbell and Locke, notice these passages:

Declaration and Address
Nothing ought to be inculcated upon Christians as articles of faith; nor required of them as terms of communion, but what is expressly taught and enjoined upon them in the word of God. Nor ought anything to be admitted as of Divine obligation, in their Church constitution or managements, but what is expressly enjoined by the authority of our Lord Jesus Christ and His apostles upon the New Testament Church; either in express terms or by approved precedent.[45]

A Letter Concerning Toleration
Nothing in worship or discipline can be necessary to Christian communion but what Christ our legislator, or the apostles by inspiration of the Holy Spirit, have commanded in express words.[46]

Declaration and Address
Although inferences and deductions from Scripture premises, when fairly inferred, may be truly called the doctrine of God's holy word, yet are they not formally binding upon the consciences of Christians farther than they perceive the connection, and evidently see that they are so.[47]

A Letter Concerning Toleration
However clearly we may think this or the other doctrine to be deduced from Scripture, we ought not therefore to impose it upon others as a necessary article of faith because we believe it to be agreeable to the rule of faith.[48]

---

[45]T. Campbell, Proposition III, p. 23.
[46]Locke, p. 62.
[47]T. Campbell, Proposition VI, p. 24.
[48]Locke, p. 61.

Thomas Campbell began a movement in frontier America in 1809 to restore Christianity to its pattern in the New Testament. He was initially concerned with the divisions among Christian brethren, but he was convinced that only by following the precepts and examples of the New Testament could human teachings and human divisions be overcome. He saw no polarization between these two concerns—unity and biblical authority. The unquestioned authority of Scripture was the means to unity, and this in turn was the means to winning the world to the gospel of Jesus Christ.

One of the tragic misunderstandings of numerous writers is to fail to see that Thomas Campbell had both of these concerns in view. In 1905 Errett Gates wrote his scholarly history of the movement, *The Disciples of Christ,* and in it he argued that Thomas Campbell had focused his attention on the need for Christian union, but that it was Alexander Campbell who emphasized the need for the authoritative pattern of the New Testament church. Thus Gates contends that Alexander shifted the chief point of the movement away from union.[49] Gates was a liberal, educated at the University of Chicago Divinity School, so it is easy to see why he would want to downplay any concern for biblical authority on the part of the early leaders. However, it is even more disconcerting to see that the conservative Homer Hailey has picked up the same theme. Quoting Gates at this very point, Hailey contends that by 1813, the Campbells had "begun to shift the emphasis from the obligation of Christian union to the authority of primitive Christianity."[50] This seems to endorse the attitude of many conservatives that the main thrust of the Restoration Movement is to emphasize the pattern of New Testament Christianity. Many of these conservatives have no interest at all in unity.

Thus it is important to note what Thomas Campbell says in the propositions to the *Declaration and Address.* Propositions I, II, IX, and X deal with unity; but there is no doubt that Propositions III and XI deal with the necessity of basing all church teachings upon the New Testament alone. Campbell was concerned with New Testament authority just as much as he was with the need for Christian union. To picture him in any other posture is to misunderstand him.

---

[49]Errett Gates, *The Disciples of Christ* (New York: The Baker & Taylor Co., 1905), pp. 94-95, 112-113.

[50]Hailey, p. 67; the same thrust is carried through in the material on pp. 67-71.

1788 —	—Alexander Campbell born
1808 —	—Campbell family shipwrecked in Scotland
1809 —	—Campbell family arrives in America
1810 —	—Alexander preaches his first sermon
	Thomas applies for membership in the Synod of Pittsburgh
1811 —	—Alexander marries Margaret Brown
	Brush Run church organized
1812 —	—Thomas and Alexander accept immersion
1815 —	—Brush Run church joins Redstone Baptist Association
1816 —	—Alexander preaches the "Sermon on the Law"
1818 —	—Alexander begins Buffalo Seminary

Chapter 5

Alexander Campbell

W HEN THOMAS CAMPBELL LEFT Northern Ireland to sail for America, he left his family in the charge of his eldest son, Alexander (1788-1866). Alexander was eighteen years old at the time, but he was already showing signs of promise.[1]

Early Life

His father Thomas had taught school prior to entering the ministry, so Thomas was certainly capable of teaching his children at home. In this he was aided by his wife, Jane. Alexander also attended an elementary school in a nearby town, then for a couple of years was a student at an academy taught by two of his father's brothers. For several years of his

---

[1]The best biography of Alexander Campbell is the old standard written by his good friend and colleague, Robert Richardson, and officially sanctioned by the Campbell family, *The Memoirs of Alexander Campbell,* first published in two volumes in 1868 and 1870. It has been issued in various reprints, particularly by The Standard Publishing Company of Cincinnati, Ohio. Richardson had access to private files and notes from family sources that have not been available to later writers and historians. Therefore, much of what Richardson says cannot be verified by outside documentation, but it is assumed that he is correct because of the unparalleled sources that he had. A more recent study of Alexander Campbell is Louis Cochran, *The Fool of God: A Novel Based Upon the Life of Alexander Campbell* (New York: Duell, Sloan and Pearce, 1958). Since it is a historical novel, it has the great advantage of being easily readable, but it contains no documentation. Although told in novel form, the contents are very close to the known facts, except for such obvious things as the reconstitution of dialogue. There have been a variety of other studies of aspects of Campbell's life in monographs, but no significant biographies other than these two. The treatment presented here will closely follow that of Richardson.

youth, he also worked on the family farm with the day laborer, finding satisfaction in the field work and developing a healthy constitution that stood him well in future years.[2]

In the parsonage family there were also the daily rounds of Bible reading, Scripture memorization, and morning and evening prayers. Thus Alexander received instruction both in the ways of God and man, as well as the physical exercise to develop a sound body. As the result of his developing religious sensitivity, Alexander became

> fully persuaded that I was a sinner, and must obtain pardon through the merits of Christ or be lost for ever. This caused me great distress of soul, and I had much exercise of mind under the awakenings of a guilty conscience. Finally, after many strugglings, I was enabled to put my trust in the Saviour, and to *feel* my reliance on him as the only Saviour of sinners. From the moment I was able to feel this reliance on the Lord Jesus Christ, I obtained and enjoyed peace of mind.[3]

Soon thereafter he was received as a regular member of the church at Ahorey where his fathered ministered. His father's wish was that he should also devote himself to the ministry, and although he had not yet made this decision for himself, he acceded to his father's wishes at least to the extent of studying theology and church history. This study led him to a concern over the divisions in Christendom with which he now became acquainted, particularly Catholicism, Anglicanism, and Presbyterianism, including the various factions into which the Presbyterians were divided. Thus early on he became aware of the party spirit that he later resisted so much.[4]

It was Alexander's desire to go to the University of Glasgow as his father had done, but the family finances did not permit such an expense. Thomas had a family of seven children[5] and was again teaching a school in order to make a living for his family. In the fall of 1805, Alexander, now just turned seventeen, joined his father as an assistant in this endeavor. For a year and a half he so labored, in the process learning a good deal himself as he prepared to teach along with his father.[6]

Thus when his father became ill in the spring of 1807, it was Alexander who encouraged him to travel to the United States. When

---

[2]Richardson, vol. 1, pp. 31-32.
[3]*Ibid.*, p. 49; italics in original.
[4]*Ibid.*, pp. 49-50.
[5]*Ibid.*, p. 77.
[6]*Ibid.*, pp. 47-48.

Thomas was still reluctant, Alexander stated that he had decided to emigrate to that country himself when he became of age, and that perhaps Thomas could go there in advance and make suitable arrangements for the family, who could come later. Alexander would take over complete charge of the school, and thus provide an income for himself and the rest of the family. So encouraged, Thomas left in April of 1807, as we have already seen.[7]

On January 1, 1808, Thomas sent his family a letter from Washington, Pennsylvania, urging them to come to him as soon as possible. They made the necessary arrangements: before they could leave, however, their community at Rich Hill received a visit from small pox and some of the younger children caught the disease before they could be inoculated. As soon as all recovered, preparations were again made, but it was August before they were completed. The family left Rich Hill in late September 1808 to travel to Londonderry, but their ship did not leave harbor until October 1.[8]

The voyage did not proceed very swiftly. They ran into severe winds and had to take shelter in a bay on the coast of one of the islands of Scotland. Here the storm got even worse, and on the night of October 7, the winds increased to a gale, pushing the ship across the bay in spite of its dragging anchors, and into a submerged rock. The ship began to take on water and sink. The crew of the ship cut down the masts to lower the center of gravity and lessen wind resistance. This succeeded in righting the ship upon the rock where it remained through the rest of the uneasy night.[9]

In the midst of the storm, Alexander Campbell came to a significant decision. His father had always desired that Alexander enter the ministry of the Seceder Presbyterians. Alexander had begun studies toward this end but had not really decided upon this course as his own life's work. Now in the storm, however, after he had made all the preparations he could for himself and the family he sat down upon the stump of a mast and reflected upon life in general and his own life in particular. He concluded that the aims and ambitions of human life were all vanity and that human life had its highest excellence in a religious orientation. He thought of the godly life of his father, devoted to the gospel ministry, and he concluded that such a calling was the highest any man could aspire to. Thus he vowed that if the family were saved from its

---

[7]*Ibid.*, pp. 78-79. See Chapter Four, p. 80.
[8]*Ibid.*, pp. 88-95.
[9]*Ibid.*, pp. 98-101.

present peril, he would commit himself to the gospel ministry as his profession.[10]

With dawn came rescue from the surrounding shore. All the passengers were gotten off without loss of life, and later Alexander was able to return to the ship and rescue all the family's belongings. But they were now marooned on the island of Islay.[11]

Their chances of securing passage on another ship bound for America this late in the shipping season were unlikely, so Alexander and the family decided to take advantage of their location in Scotland and go to Glasgow where Alexander could enroll for classes through the winter. Earlier he had wanted to be a student at the University of Glasgow, but the family's finances did not allow it. Now, the family situation encouraged such a possibility. To help them when they arrived in the strange city, several of the leading families on Islay sent letters of introduction to ministers and merchants in Glasgow along with the Campbell family. One such letter was addressed to Rev. Greville Ewing, a former Church of Scotland minister who had previously led one of the Haldanean theological institutes in Glasgow, but was now ministering to a Haldanean congregation there.[12]

Armed with these credentials, the Campbell family traveled by water and land transport to reach Glasgow; Alexander arrived on November 3 to make arrangements for the family, who arrived on November 5. In this he was helped considerably by Greville Ewing, who not only helped them find lodgings initially, but by the end of the month decided their apartment was insufficient and helped them find an even better place. They also wrote to Thomas in America to let him know of their delay; he wrote back approving their interim arrangements.[13] Alexander enrolled at the University of Glasgow, where classes began on November 8, and he took classes in French, Greek, Latin, science, literature, and philosophy.[14]

But attending school was not all that Alexander Campbell did that winter. He of course attended church on Sundays, but he also took occasion to visit some other churches as well—other, that is, than the Old Light Anti-Burgher Seceder Presbyterian Church of which he was a

---

[10]*Ibid.*, pp. 101-102.

[11]*Ibid.*, pp. 103-106.

[12]*Ibid.*, pp. 114-128.

[13]*Ibid.*, p. 148.

[14]*Ibid.*, pp. 130-132. See also Lester G. McAllister, *Alexander Campbell at Glasgow University, 1808-1809* (Nashville: Disciples of Christ Historical Society, 1971).

member. Alexander had grown up in this denomination under his father's preaching, and accepted the idea that the Old Light Anti-Burgher Seceder Presbyterian Church was the one true church of God, and that all others were corrupt in one way or another. But exposure to the ideas of Greville Ewing softened Alexander's attitude.

Ewing was born in 1767 and was licensed to preach in the National Church in 1792. The next year he accepted a call to one of the churches in Edinburgh. In the course of the decade, he also came into contact with the Haldane brothers. In 1798 he resigned his pastorate as well as his relationship with the Church of Scotland and joined the Haldanes in forming a new congregational church movement. A church was erected in Edinburgh early in 1799 with over three hundred members, and large tabernacles were also erected in other major cities as well—particularly Glasgow and Stirling. Ewing was placed in charge of the tabernacle in Glasgow and the congregation that would meet there. The Haldanes also began a number of theological institutes to train young men for the ministry, and Ewing taught in these for a while—both in Edinburgh and later in Glasgow.[15]

But trouble developed even between these leaders committed to much the same cause. Robert Haldane purchased a large building in Glasgow to be turned into a tabernacle, which would cost about three thousand pounds. Ewing wanted Haldane to pay all of this; Haldane paid only one third. This itself led to some strain between the two leaders.[16] In 1808 James A. Haldane accepted the practice of immersion only as baptism, and the congregation in Edinburgh divided as a result. The division in the Haldane movement spread to Glasgow, and Ewing was vehemently opposed to immersion; he remained an earnest advocate of infant baptism. He and others even reached the point where they would have no visible communion with those who followed the new teaching of the Haldanes.[17]

In spite of this friction, however, Greville Ewing did have a significant impact on Alexander Campbell. Campbell was frequently a guest to Ewing's for dinner or tea. He often went to hear Ewing's preaching on Sunday evenings at the tabernacle, since the Seceder churches had day-time services only. Ewing's evening services generally drew a crowd of between one and two thousand people. Ewing frequently invited groups of students to his house, including Alexander. In the free discussions that

---

[15]Richardson, vol. 1, pp. 149, 166-167.
[16]*Ibid.*, pp. 165, 167, 174-175.
[17]*Ibid.*, pp. 181, 187.

developed, the topic was often of the general cause of church reform that the Haldanes had initiated, and the particular causes for which Ewing was most interested.[18] It was Ewing who was generally credited with the commitment of the movement to congregationalism. When the new churches were first formed, the leaders adopted the principle that church usages should be conformed to the practice of the apostolic churches. It was also Ewing's insights that led to celebrating the Lord's Supper every Sunday. This occurred first in the congregation at Glasgow, then it spread to Edinburgh and the other churches in the movement. But when Ewing followed too closely some of the ideas of the Glas-Sandemanians, the Haldanes removed the seminary under his direction back to Edinburgh.[19]

One concept that influenced Campbell, which came directly from James A. Haldane, was the practice of preaching without receiving remuneration. Haldane happened to be independently wealthy, but this ideal of preaching without charge held a fascination for Campbell. Thus he resolved that when he began his public ministry, he would preach the gospel "without fee or reward." He noted also that the clergy of Scotland had generally blocked the progress of the Haldane movement as much as possible. Campbell came to have fairly negative feelings against this class of men who were more characterized for their narrow sectarianism than the desire to reform the world according to the gospel. Although he had just vowed to pursue the vocation of a gospel minister, Campbell also vowed that he would never become like the professional clergy.[20]

Thus, through the course of that winter in Glasgow, Campbell had his mind stretched, his identity questioned, and his commitment to true biblical Christianity challenged. He wondered whether he could continue to be a part of a church that was sectarian and divisive. Yet he resisted leaving this denominational fold because of the tremendous respect he had for his father. All he and his family knew was that his father was still a faithful minister of the Old Light Anti-Burgher Seceder Presbyterian Church.

But he could not put off a decision for long. In the spring of 1809, the time came for the semi-annual communion service of the Seceders. Because he had brought no credentials with him from Ireland, Alexander had to take the pre-communion examination administered by the elders of the local congregation, but that presented no problems. He was

---

[18]*Ibid.*, pp. 149, 187-188.
[19]*Ibid.*, pp. 178-179.
[20]*Ibid.*, pp. 176-177.

handed a token that would admit him to the communion service. But then he wrestled with the question: Should he partake? It was not a question of whether he was worthy in the Lord's sight. It was a question of whether he ought to continue to identify with a sectarian group whose doctrine and viewpoint he no longer shared. Indeed, if the leaders of the congregation knew of his doubts concerning their status as *the* Church of Christ, he would not have been given the token. If he partook of *their* communion service, was he not giving tacit approval to their views? Was he not suggesting that he accepted them? Could he, ought he, to do so in all good conscience?

There were about eight hundred communicants, and about eight or nine tables to be served in succession. He waited at the last table, postponing as long as possible his decision. When the plate came around he dropped in his communion token, but he could not overcome his scruples when the elements of communion came past. He did not partake. In his own mind he dated his departure from the Presbyterians at this point. But he told no one. And when he left Scotland later that year, he took with him the usual certificate that indicated he was a member of the church in good standing.[21]

The university session concluded in May 1809. There was no immediate prospect of securing passage for the family on a ship bound for America, so Alexander took a tutoring job in a nearby community for about five weeks in June and July. He and his family were finally able to obtain passage on a ship, and they left Scotland August 4 for their voyage to America. It was quite a changed Alexander Campbell from the lad of twenty years who had been shipwrecked the previous fall.[22]

Preparation for Ministry

After a difficult crossing of the ocean, the ship finally reached New York on September 29. On October 5 the family started for Philadelphia, reaching it on the seventh. From there Alexander hired a wagon to transport the family to Washington, Pennsylvania, where Thomas was residing. It was a journey of about three hundred and fifty miles. They started off, following the major wagon road from Philadelphia to the west, and staying at various inns along the way.[23] About the eleventh day of their journey, they encountered Thomas Campbell who was riding east on the same

---

[21]*Ibid.*, pp. 189-190.
[22]*Ibid.*, pp. 190-195.
[23]*Ibid.*, pp. 204-205.

road to meet them. He had received their letter sent from New York
detailing their travel plans and had decided to travel east to meet them
rather than wait in Washington. Their meeting occurred about October
19. Thus the family was reunited, after two and a half years of separation.
It took three additional days to complete their journey to Washington and
during this time, Thomas and the various other members of his family got
caught up on what had happened in the interval.[24]

Alexander had been somewhat uncomfortable thinking of how he was
going to tell his father that he had left the church of which his father
was a minister. But to his surprise, his father told him how he had himself left the Seceder Presbyterians because of his experiences over the
past two years. Thus father and son, separated by a generation in age
and over three thousand miles of distance, had gone through different
experiences with sectarian bigotry but had come out at the same place—
desiring the union of all followers of Christ on the basis of the practices
and beliefs of the ancient church as indicated in the Scriptures. When
Thomas Campbell went on to explain the organization and plans of the
Christian Association of Washington, Alexander got even more excited.
He had committed himself to the Christian ministry, yet he was disgusted at the actions and demeanor of the clergy in Scotland. The
prospects of serving in an association such as the Christian Association of
Washington renewed his zeal.

There is an interesting legend that says Thomas Campbell had the
galley proofs of *The Declaration and Address* in his saddlebags as he rode
east to meet his family, and that father and son spent the first evening
gathered around a campfire discussing the principles behind the propositions of the *Address*. W. E. Garrison refers to this, but he provides no
documentation.[25] Leroy Garrett in his history discounts this anecdote,
citing a statement from Alexander in 1848 to the effect, "The first *proof
sheet* that I ever read was a form of *My Father's Declaration and Address,* in
press in Washington, Pennsylvania, on my arrival there in October,
1809."[26] But this seems a bit ambiguous. A further indication along the
same line, however, is his comment when he edited a volume of his
father's works in 1861. Here he refers to the *Declaration and Address* and
he stated, "It was first published A. D. 1809. It was being published when
I arrived in Washington, from Scotland, in the autumn of that year. I
read its proof sheets as it issued from the press, with special attention."[27]

---

[24]*Ibid.,* pp. 217-220.
[25]Garrison and DeGroot, p. 144.
[26]Garrett, pp. 174-175; *Millennial Harbinger,* 1848, p. 280.
[27]A. Campbell, *Memoirs of Thomas Campbell,* p. 23.

Although it is possible to interpret these two statements a bit figuratively to save the idea of the campfire legend, the simpler interpretation seems to indicate that Alexander did not see the pages of his father's writing until he got to Washington and saw them coming off the press.

Regardless of exactly where Alexander first saw the principles of the *Declaration and Address* in print, there is no doubt that he had decided to commit himself to the gospel ministry in its terms. Thomas was delighted and assisted his son in further studies for such a calling. James Foster and Abraham Altars were also at this time engaged in studies aimed at ministerial labors under the guidance of Thomas Campbell. But Thomas was gone from home so much in pastoring the families of the Christian Association of Washington that he only directed the general course of their studies, leaving Alexander to work out the details. In addition, Alexander was given responsibility for the education of his younger brothers and sisters, besides his own study for ministerial preparation. He spent four-and-a-half hours daily in studying Greek, Latin, Hebrew, and direct Bible study; an additional four-and-a-half hours daily were given directly to supervising the studies of Altars and the other Campbell children. Daily Bible study was the main ingredient in his preparations.[28]

In the spring of 1810, Thomas arranged to have Alexander speak to the assembled association after Thomas' sermon. This was more in the nature of a short exhortation than a full sermon for Alexander. Both he and his father were pleased with the result, however, so that Thomas soon urged him to prepare a full-length sermon, scheduled for Sunday, July 15. Alexander had written out his sermon in full and memorized it so that he would not be bothered by notes during the delivery. The result was a happy one for both speaker and audience, many of whom were thrilled to hear a message they considered even superior to Thomas'. Alexander was soon besieged with additional requests for preaching, and in his first year preached one hundred and six sermons, delivered at various points in western Pennsylvania and adjacent territories in western Virginia and southeastern Ohio. On July 22 he preached on Christian unity, sounding again an emphasis that remained with him throughout his life.[29] This sermon was not memorized but was preached from a few notes in outline, which was his general style for the future.[30] Both Thomas and Alexander were now receiving overtures from various

---

[28]Richardson, vol. 1, pp. 277-279.

[29]*Ibid.*, pp. 312-317.

[30]*Ibid.*, p. 321. A useful study of Campbell's preaching is Alger Morton Fitch, Jr., *Alexander Campbell: Preacher of Reform and Reformer of Preaching* (Joplin, Missouri: College Press Publishing Company, 1988).

denominations for them to enter the ministry among them. Some proposals also came asking them to establish schools and seminaries. But the
Campbells turned down such offers, desiring instead to continue to work
for the cause of restoring the Church to its original purity and unity and
breaking down the barriers of religious partyism.[31]

The members of the Christian Association of Washington continued to
meet regularly, including Sundays. To all intents and purposes, they
appeared to be a local congregation, in spite of the strong assertion of
the *Declaration* that they were not such. This grieved Thomas Campbell
particularly, for the one thing he did not want to do was to create one
more religious party in the world. He felt there were too many already;
he did not want to create another. But as long as the Christian Association
remained a religious group separate from others, its appearance belied
its intent.

For this reason, and also because some local Presbyterian members
and ministers approached him about it, Thomas decided to petition the
Synod of Pittsburgh for membership. This was a branch of the regular
Presbyterian Church, not the Seceders; at least Thomas need not worry
about the Chartiers Presbytery. There is a bit of confusion about exactly
what Thomas requested from them. The records of the Synod indicate
only that he desired "Christian and ministerial communion."[32] In their
response the Synod also talked about the Christian Association, and this
has led many historians to conclude that Thomas was speaking "as the
representative of the Christian Association."[33] One recent history goes to
the extent of stating that Thomas was applying to the Synod "for membership of the association in the regular Presbyterian church,"[34] but this
may be taking things a bit too far. Thomas' main motive was to prove
that he was not trying to start a new religious group. By having the
Presbyterians acknowledge him as a Presbyterian minister, Thomas could
deny the accusation that he was in fact initiating another religious group.
Alexander had predicted that the request was doomed to disappointment, and the Synod proved him correct.[35]

The Synod of Pittsburgh met in Washington, Pennsylvania, in early
October, and their minutes record Campbell's petition. On the afternoon of October 4, 1810, they entertained Campbell's request but turned

---

[31]*Ibid.*, pp. 309-310.
[32]*Ibid.*, p. 327; McAllister, p. 142, citing the *Records of the Synod of Pittsburgh,*
pp. 71f.
[33]Richardson, vol. 1, p. 329; McAllister, p. 143.
[34]McAllister and Tucker, p. 116.
[35]Richardson, vol. 1, p. 326.

it down out of hand, giving as their reasons that the Christian Association was destructive of religion by promoting division rather than union, by degrading ministerial character, and by allowing errors of doctrine and corruption of discipline.[36] The next morning, Campbell asked for a further explanation of these reasons. They listed: (1) Thomas' belief that some opinions taught in the Westminster Confession of Faith were not taught in the Bible, but he would not stipulate which ones; (2) stating infant baptism was unauthorized by Scripture and is a matter of indifference, but still practicing it; (3) encouraging his son to preach without regular authority; (4) opposing creeds and confessions as injurious to the interests of religion; (5) and finally that it was contrary to Presbyterian Church regulations for the Synod to have connections with any [independent] ministers, churches, or association.[37]

Certainly it was true that Thomas wanted to join the Presbyterians on *his* terms, not theirs. The reasons the Presbyterians gave for rejecting him were exactly the reasons the Campbells wished to maintain their independent status. They would not yield to Presbyterian regulations, nor limit preaching to the "regular authority" of ordination. They would insist that creeds and confessions were injurious to religion, and that unscriptural practices were matters indifferent to the church. Thomas pointed out to the Synod, however, that he did not believe baptism was a matter of "indifference," though he did treat the various practices of it with "forbearance."[38]

Thomas was disappointed by this rejection, but Alexander was infuriated by the things said against his father. The rejection took place on October 4, 1810. On November 1, 1810, the Christian Association of Washington held its regular semi-annual meeting and Alexander addressed the meeting, using as his text Isaiah 57:14 and 62:10— "Take up the stumbling block out of the way of my people," and "Go through the gates." He contended that anything was a stumbling block that caused people to stumble on their way to Zion; these hindrances were human opinions and inventions of men. Removing them was exactly what the Christian Association had been trying to do, as indicated in the principles of the *Declaration and Address.*

Alexander then replied particularly to seven objections that the Synod had levied against Thomas. (1) The Christian Association believed in the

---

[36]*Ibid.*, p. 327; McAllister, p. 142, citing the *Records of the Synod of Pittsburgh,* pp. 71f.

[37]Richardson, vol. 1, p. 328; McAllister, p. 142, citing the *Records of the Synod of Pittsburgh,* p. 75.

[38]McAllister, p. 143; Richardson, vol. 1, 348.

cause of Christian unity; if this caused them to be considered a party separate from others, it probably said more about the others than it did about them. (2) They did not intend to degrade ministerial character but wanted to support gospel ministers who were scripturally qualified. (3) They were not trying to corrupt discipline, but restrict discipline to those matters of the Christian faith expressly taught in the New Testament. They were unwilling to make matters of human opinion or even human inference from biblical texts the basis for disfellowshipping. (4) They did not want to make only a "nominal approbation of the Bible a satisfactory test of truth," as the Synod had charged. (5) With regard to infant baptism, Alexander admitted there was no Scriptural warrant for it, but he was desirous of seeing the issue as one of forbearance, as the early church did circumcision. Otherwise, Campbell observed, they must reject a number of God's children, which might violate one of God's commands, "Receive him that is weak in the faith." (6) He affirmed strongly a commitment to independent, congregational government. (7) Answering the charges of allowing "lay preaching," Alexander noted that the distinction between clergy and laity is unscriptural—for both terms are used in Scripture for God's people.[39]

Robert Richardson concludes that by this time, Thomas and Alexander regarded the denominations around them as possessing the substance of Christianity, but not the form of it; the object of the Christian Association was to have people adopt "the form of sound words" as the true basis of union. In addition, it appears the Campbells now expected that they would have to resolve the Christian Association into a church since the religious world would not accept them. Finally, the Campbells now realized that by insisting that no teaching or practice could be made essential unless it was expressly revealed, many things heretofore considered precious and important by the denominations must be excluded.[40] They also knew, of course, that doing so would antagonize those religious groups that wanted to hold on to such practices and ideas.

It was also obvious to many of the members of the Christian Association that in this address, Alexander took over a major share in the leadership of the organization. This is not to say that he was elbowing his father out of the way or aggressively "taking over." But it does indicate that Alexander is moving into premier leadership, soon to replace his father as the driving force and intellect behind the movement that his father had initiated. For the next several years, father and son worked in

---

[39]Richardson, vol. 1, pp. 341-346.
[40]*Ibid.*, pp. 348-349.

tandem, but Alexander's natural abilities now coming to the fore, and also the removal of his father to Ohio for a few years, placed Alexander in the unquestioned position of leader of the group that started out as the Christian Association of Washington.

Also in that same fall of 1810 Alexander Campbell became acquainted with the John Brown family of nearby Virginia, living on the shores of Buffalo Creek. Mr. Brown (1761-1835) had a daughter named Margaret (1791-1827) who soon caught Alexander's eye. Courtship developed through the winter, and the couple was married on March 12, 1811, by the minister of the Presbyterian church in West Liberty, Virginia, where the Browns were members. Mr. Brown and his wife (his second marriage; Margaret's mother had died previously) lived in a large two-story house, with plenty of room. For this reason, before the month of March was out, Alexander and his bride moved in with her parents.[41] Alexander lived in this house the rest of his life. He helped his father-in-law around the farm but still preached on numerous occasions in the area around.

It was the growing conviction of Thomas Campbell that it was becoming increasingly necessary for the Christian Association to formally organize itself into a local congregation—the very opposite of what they had determined for themselves initially. When the Christian Association met for its semi-annual meeting in May, Thomas mentioned that the obvious hostility of the Christian denominations around them made it necessary for them to constitute themselves into a church in order to provide Christian fellowship and relationships. Thomas would have preferred to be a parachurch organization influencing the churches, but it was obvious the churches were resistant to their influence.[42]

At this meeting, probably on Thursday, May 2, 1811, Thomas felt it necessary for each member of the Christian Association to give some indication of his awareness of the way of salvation, so he asked each publicly, "What is the meritorious cause of the sinner's acceptance with God?" While the answers were not recorded, Thomas was satisfied with the responses, except for those of two individuals, whose membership was postponed, then later denied on other grounds. (Neither their unsatisfactory answers nor the "other grounds" were recorded.)[43]

It is somewhat incredible that Thomas Campbell, having written in Proposition III of the *Declaration and Address* that "nothing ought to be inculcated upon Christians as articles of faith; nor required of them as

[41]*Ibid.*, pp. 361-365.
[42]*Ibid.*, pp. 365-366.
[43]*Ibid.*, pp. 366-367.

terms of communion, but what is expressly taught and enjoined upon them in the word of God," should now use a test question to indicate whether people are worthy of becoming members of a local church. Nowhere does the Word of God authorize such a procedure. This is simply one additional example of how far the Campbells' practice lagged behind their principles. The test question was never used again, but the surprising thing is that it was used at all.

Two days later, on Saturday, May 4, the Christian Association met and formally organized themselves into a church. Thomas was chosen as the elder (the only one), four men were selected as deacons, and Alexander was licensed to preach. (Even the licensing procedure was a carryover from Presbyterian practices.) The following day, May 5, was Sunday, and the church held its first communion service. Alexander preached on John 6:48, "I am the bread of life," and Thomas also preached. Weekly communion became a normal part of the worship of this congregation.[44]

Focus on Baptism

But it was noticed that three of the brand-new members of the congregation did not partake, including Abraham Altars. When they were asked why, they replied that they did not feel it appropriate to take communion since they had never been baptized, not even sprinkled. They now wished to receive baptism, and they specified it be immersion. Thomas Campbell was willing to perform such baptisms, even though the ceremony was not done until July 4, two months after the issue first came up.[45]

But Thomas had never witnessed an immersion before and was somewhat unsure exactly how it was done. In addition, there was some concern about his entering the water with those receiving immersion since he himself had never immersed. Thus Thomas got them into a deep pool in Buffalo Creek where the water came up to their shoulders. This pool was also near the bank, so Thomas stood on the roots of a tree, repeated the baptismal formula over each one and then shoved their heads under water.[46] It was at least total immersion, though Thomas later learned there were more decorous ways of performing the ceremony.

This incident focused the eyes of the Campbells on the subject of baptism, which had been receiving a good deal of attention for some time. Certainly up to 1809, neither of the Campbells had any reservations

---

[44]*Ibid.*, pp. 367-370.
[45]*Ibid.*, pp. 371-372.
[46]*Ibid.*, p. 373.

about the acceptability of the practice of infant sprinkling. Their Presbyterian background made infant sprinkling seem a normal and legitimate form of baptism. Shortly after the meeting in the summer of 1809, which resulted in the adoption of the principle "Where the Scriptures speak, we speak, and where the Scriptures are silent, we are silent," James Foster talked to Thomas Campbell about the lack of spiritual authority for infant baptism. For the sake of Christian union, Thomas was willing to leave this issue to private judgment as belonging to the class of "non-essentials." Foster remarked to Thomas, "Father Campbell, how could you, in the absence of any authority in the Word of God, baptize a child in the name of the Father, and of the Son, and of the Holy Spirit?" Campbell reddened, grew irritated, and in an offended tone simply replied, "Sir, you are the most intractable person I ever met."[47]

Shortly after the galley proof pages of the *Declaration and Address* came off the press, Alexander was discussing with a Presbyterian minister, Rev. Riddle, the principle of demanding a "Thus saith the Lord" for everything required as a matter of faith and duty. Riddle pointed out that if this principle were followed out, Campbell would have to become a Baptist. Campbell asked, "Is there in the Scriptures no express precept nor precedent for infant baptism?" "Not one," replied the minister. Startled, Alexander immediately went to the local bookseller to purchase all books in favor of infant baptism. Disappointed, he found not one Scriptural reference and reluctantly came to the conclusion that it was a human invention.[48]

Thomas agreed that there was neither express terms nor precedent to authorize the practice. "But," he said,

> as for those who are already members of the Church, and participants of the Lord's Supper, I can see no propriety, even if the scriptural evidence for infant baptism be found deficient, in their unchurching or paganizing themselves, nor in putting off Christ, merely for the sake of making a new profession; thus going out of the Church merely for the sake of coming in again.[49]

When pressed by Alexander for some scriptural precept or precedent for infant baptism, Thomas simply acknowledged that "it was merely inferential."[50]

One night when Alexander was courting Margaret Brown, a Baptist preacher stopped by the Brown household and the discussion turned to

---

[47]*Ibid.*, pp. 239-240.
[48]*Ibid.*, pp. 250-251.
[49]*Ibid.*, p. 251.
[50]A. Campbell, *Memoirs of Thomas Campbell*, pp. 23-24.

baptism. Alexander defended infant sprinkling, which the Baptist challenged by direct quotation of Scripture. Alexander felt uncomfortable in not being able to quote Scripture directly on the issue, but lamely replied that infant baptism should be treated as circumcision in the early church, that is, left as a matter of forebearance.[51]

Both in 1810 and 1811, when preaching on Christ's commission to the disciples in Mark 16:15-16, Alexander referred to baptism by simply stating, "As I am sure it is unscriptural to make this matter a term of communion, I let it *slip*. I wish to think and let think on these matters."[52] But later reflection led him to believe that in light of Mark 16:16, baptism might not be in the category of unimportant matters of opinion which could be allowed to "slip." It was not just a matter of rejecting infant baptism as a human invention, but of omitting believers' baptism, that was divinely commanded.[53]

Much of this interest was spurred by the birth, on March 13, 1812, of Alexander's first child, a daughter, named Jane after Alexander's mother. After all the concern over infant baptism for the past three years, it would have been difficult for Alexander to consent to baptizing this child. But the situation raised a further question. If no biblical authority existed for the practice of infant baptism, had he himself received proper Christian baptism? Alexander concluded that infant sprinkling was wholly unauthorized in Scripture and that he therefore was an unbaptized person. He also concluded that he could hardly preach baptism to others when he had failed to conform to it himself.[54] Thus he decided to be immersed.

He decided to ask Matthias Luce, a Baptist preacher friend, to perform the service for him, but first went to talk to Thomas about it. Thomas did not object, saying simply, "You must please yourself." The arrangements were made with Luce for Alexander and his wife to be baptized on June 12, at the same pool where Thomas had immersed the three people the previous year. Announcement was made to the Brush Run church for them to attend as well. Yet when the people gathered, Thomas and his wife showed up with a change of clothing; they also would be immersed. So, too, would Dorothea Campbell, Alexander's sister. So, too, would another couple of the Brush Run congregation. So instead of two baptisms, there were seven.

Prior to the actual immersions, however, Thomas felt it necessary to

---

[51]Richardson, vol. 1, p. 362.
[52]*Ibid.*, p. 392; italics in original.
[53]*Ibid.*, p. 394.
[54]*Ibid.*, pp. 391-395.

explain his change of thinking resulting in his submission to this practice. Alexander also spoke, explaining his understanding of Acts 2:38 and baptism in general. Then the immersions took place. Alexander had specified to Luce when he first made the arrangements that they would be baptized on the simple confession that "Jesus is the Son of God," with no recital of a religious experience. Luce at first objected since this was contrary to usual Baptist practice. But he finally consented, believing that Alexander was right, and he would run the risk of Baptist censure for his part in the ceremony.[55]

Certainly from this point onward, Alexander appeared as the leading spirit in the movement, Thomas moving more into the background. On the following Sunday, there were now ten immersed members of the Brush Run church. Soon thirteen others requested immersion, including James Foster. Thomas baptized these, plus a few others who came in succeeding weeks. The result was that this congregation became virtually one of adult immersed believers. Those who did not desire baptism began to drop out of the active life of the congregation, including Thomas Acheson.[56]

With the Baptists

This then made the Brush Run church look like a Baptist church, since the Baptists were the major group on the American frontier who practiced adult believers' immersion. Because both Thomas and Alexander were developing good reputations as pulpitmen, the Baptists now began to court the church at Brush Run. For one thing, their adoption of immersion without overt Baptist influence made the Baptists look good; for another thing, it would be a feather in the Baptist cap to gain the pulpit services of the two Campbells.[57]

Alexander, however, did not have a high opinion of the Baptist ministers he had met. He considered them "narrow, contracted, illiberal, and uneducated men." The ministers of the Redstone Baptist Association were

little men in a big office. The office did not fit them. They had a wrong idea, too, of what was wanting. They seemed to think that a change of apparel—a black coat instead of a drab—a broad rim on their hat instead of a narrow one—a prolongation of the face, and a fictitious gravity—a longer and a more

55*Ibid.*, pp. 395-398.
56*Ibid.*, pp. 402-403.
57*Ibid.*, pp. 436-440.

emphatic pronunciation of certain words, rather than scriptural knowledge, humility, spirituality, zeal, and Christian affection, with great emotion and great philanthropy, were the grand desiderata.[58]

But Campbell was impressed with the Baptist people. "They read the Bible, and seemed to care but little for any thing else in religion than *'conversion'* and *'Bible doctrine.'*" Baptists often asked him to come and preach in their churches, and "on acquaintance, liked the people more and the preachers less." Feeling that his prejudice against the Baptist ministers might be unwarranted, however, Campbell visited the Redstone Baptist Association meeting at Uniontown, Pennsylvania, in the fall of 1812. He was invited to preach, but declined, except once in a private setting. He came away, however, with his feelings reinforced, not intending ever again to visit another Baptist association meeting.[59]

But along the way home, he discovered that many of the Baptists themselves did not appreciate the style of the sermons delivered at the meeting, thinking the sermons were too Calvinistic in the matter of predestination. Baptists continued to urge Campbell to come preach for them, and he often did, up to sixty miles away. Many such churches urged Campbell to join the Redstone Baptist Association.[60]

Influenced by such requests, Campbell laid the issue before the Brush Run church for full discussion.[61] They decided to make an overture to the Redstone Baptist Association, but at the same time they presented a document of some eight to ten large pages detailing their dissatisfactions

---

[58]*Millennial Harbinger*, 1848, p. 345.

[59]*Ibid.*, p. 347. He states the meeting as being at Uniontown; the 1812 minutes place it at Big Redstone (*Minutes of the Redstone Baptist Association*, 1812, p. 1). The meeting at Uniontown was in 1814 (*Minutes*, 1814, p. 1).

[60]*Millennial Harbinger*, 1848, p. 347.

[61]There is some difficulty with the date to be assigned here. In his later references to this event, Campbell places their admission into the Redstone Baptist Association as the fall of 1813. (See his references in *Christian Baptist*, vol. 2, no. 2 [September, 1824; reprinted by Gospel Advocate Company, 1955], p. 37 as well as *Millennial Harbinger*, 1848, p. 346). Robert Richardson picked up that date and perpetuated it (Richardson, vol. 1, pp. 440, 458.) From there it has worked its way into most histories of the movement (Murch, p. 61; Garrison and DeGroot, p. 161; West, vol. 1, p. 61; Hailey, p. 67; Garrett, p. 177). Even Baptist histories continue the date (H. Leon McBeth, *The Baptist Heritage* [Nashville: The Broadman Press, 1987], p. 378). Unfortunately, however, the reprinting of the *Minutes of the Redstone Baptist Association*, which M. F. Cottrell of Denver, Colorado made available about 1960, clearly indicates that this date is erroneous. The minutes for 1813 contain absolutely no reference to Brush Run or the Campbells. The minutes for 1815, however, contain these comments:

with human creeds as bonds of union or tests of communion as well as their commitment to work with the Association "provided only, and always, that we should be allowed to preach and teach whatever we learned from the Holy Scriptures."[62] Their proposal was discussed at the Association and, "after much debate, was decided by a considerable majority in favor of our being received." But there was a minority voice that was opposed to the admission of the Brush Run church and the Campbell leadership. John Pritchard of Cross Creek, Virginia, and William Brownfield of Uniontown, Pennsylvania, were among that dissenting group.[63] They would be heard from again. Nevertheless, from this date in 1815, the Campbells were counted among the Baptists.

Joining with the Baptists did not mean that the Campbells (actually only Alexander, since Thomas had moved to eastern Ohio about a hundred miles away by this time; but he approved of the decision to join Redstone) had abandoned their concerns. Working with the Baptists gave the Brush Run church the opportunity to demonstrate their commitment to Christian unity. They had not compromised their position. They still insisted on following the Bible alone. They refused to be tied to the Philadelphia Confession of Faith, the normal creed of the Baptists. Instead of losing anything by joining the Baptists, the Campbells now had an open entry into every Baptist church in the tristate area of Pennsylvania, Ohio, and Virginia (West Virginia was not a separate state until 1863). Through this Baptist medium the Campbells hoped to influence a much larger group of people toward a return to New Testament Christianity. They had formed the Brush Run church because

---

"5. A letter from a Church in Washington was read, requesting union to this Association, which was unanimously granted.

"6. Likewise a letter was received, making a similar request from a church at Brush Run;—which was also granted."

Therefore, there is no doubt that the appropriate date for this admission is 1815, not 1813. McAllister and Tucker in their history do give the appropriate date (p. 120). It is ironic that while Campbell and Richardson got the date wrong, W. K. Pendleton got it right in the 1867 *Millennial Harbinger* (p. 42).

Campbell stated he attended the Uniontown meeting one year and that Brush Run joined Redstone Baptist Association the next. But he makes this 1812 and 1813. Perhaps both are wrong. The Uniontown meeting was in 1814 and Brush Run joined Redstone in 1815. If he attended the meeting in 1812, it was not Uniontown; if he attended the meeting at Uniontown, it was not 1812. Perhaps he got the interval right (Uniontown one year, membership the next), but the years wrong. It fits into place better if he attended Uniontown in 1814. His 1824 recollection in the *Christian Baptist* is obviously faulty.

[62]*Millennial Harbinger*, 1848, p. 346.

[63]*Ibid.*, p. 347.

the neighboring denominations would not recognize their efforts. Now they could concentrate their efforts through one of the existing denominations and hope it would be open to reform along the lines of the New Testament.

Brush Run was counted as a Baptist church, but in actuality it was not. There were, in fact, several differences between the typical position of Brush Run and the Campbells on the one hand and the Baptists on the other. Not all of these were crystal clear in 1815; some became obvious only later. But this is why Pritchard, Brownfield, and others voted against their admission at the very beginning.

These differences included the following:[64] (1) Brush Run administered baptism on a simple confession of faith in Christ, and this automatically brought admission into the church. Baptist practice was for the candidate to relate his saving experience before the church, after which the church then voted on whether to accept him. Baptism came later. (2) It was standard practice for Baptist churches to state their acceptance of the Philadelphia Confession of Faith as a prerequisite for admission into a Baptist association. Allowing Brush Run in without this was very much an exception. (3) The Campbells were still in the process of understanding the nature of "saving faith." Baptists were typically Calvinist on this matter, believing that faith was a gift of God through the Holy Spirit in the process of regeneration. The Campbells were influenced by Sandeman's understanding that faith was belief in testimony, much more of an intellectual process than a simply spiritual one. This later led to acrimonious charges between the two groups of "head religion" against "heart religion," although neither charge is entirely accurate. (4) Brush Run observed the Lord's Supper every week; Baptists usually observed it quarterly. This was obvious at the time and well known, and it is surprising that this particular item did not cause more controversy. (5) The Campbells were already making a major distinction between the authority of the two Testaments. Thomas, in Proposition IV of the *Declaration*, first voiced this. Alexander soon made some applications of it that inflamed the Baptist clergy. The Baptists depended upon Mosaic authority for some of their practices, and these Alexander soon challenged. (6) The status of the clergy was a controversial point. The

---

[64]This listing is borrowed from Garrison and DeGroot, pp. 162-163. In a somewhat different, shorter list, McBeth lists: (1) the nature of saving faith; (2) baptism as completing the process of salvation; (3) the Old Testament not authoritative; and (4) creeds (McBeth, pp. 378-379). McBeth, however, seems to seriously underestimate the Redstone Baptist Association's use of the Philadelphia Confession as a test of orthodoxy.

DIFFERENCES BETWEEN CAMPBELL AND THE BAPTISTS

1. Baptism—based on confession or experience?
2. Acceptance of the Philadelphia Confession
3. Nature of "saving faith"
4. Frequency of the Lord's Supper
5. Distinction between Old and New Testaments
6. Status of clergy

Baptists did not restrict preaching as the Presbyterians did; Baptists allowed lay exhorters and had no education requirements. But they did limit the practices of baptism and officiating at the Lord's Supper to ordained clergy. In this regard, the Campbells had an even lower concept of clergy. They abandoned the distinction between clergy and laity, allowing anyone to baptize, pray publicly, preach or exhort, and even preside at a communion service, although this would normally be done by the elders of a local congregation, whether ordained or not. Alexander in particular attacked Baptist clergy for their special pride of position. This only increased the bitterness between the two groups.

About the end of 1815, Alexander helped plant a new church in Wellsburg. There was no church in the town at all, in spite of its being the county seat. There was a Baptist church about three miles north of town, the Cross Creek church, ministered to by John Pritchard. For three or four months Campbell traveled to the east, visiting Philadelphia, New York City, and Washington, D. C., raising money for this new church building, and came up with about $1000 in contributions. But Pritchard did not take kindly to this new congregation so near his own flock.[65]

This tour to the east produced another interesting development. In New York City and Philadelphia, he was urged by a Baptist deacon in each place to settle there. Campbell declined, saying he did not believe that the church in either place was interested in submitting to the government of Jesus Christ or to the primitive order of things. Asking what that order was, Campbell explained it to them. Neither objected to it. The deacon from New York said the church there followed part of that, and he in fact preferred it. Campbell's reply was that however well this one deacon might accept it, he was convinced the majority of the members of the church would not, "and rather than produce divisions among

---

[65]Richardson, vol. 1, pp. 464-469; *Millennial Harbinger,* 1848, p. 347.

them, or adopt the order of things then fashionable in the city, I would live and die in the backwoods."[66]

As it turned out, the 1816 annual meeting of the Redstone Baptist Association was held at the Cross Creek church. By now Thomas Campbell had left Cambridge, Ohio, where he had taught school and started a church, and had gone to Pittsburgh, where he again began a school and a church. It was from here that he attended the 1816 meeting of the Association. He also brought with him a petition from his new congregation in Pittsburgh requesting admission to the Association. Since the petition was not presented "according to the constitution of this Association, the request cannot be granted."[67] In spite of this, however, Thomas was invited to take a seat in the Association. Apparently this was a seat with voting privileges, rather than just a seat among the visitors. This probably indicates that although the Association was leery of allowing another maverick church in (Brush Run had just been admitted the previous year), they still respected Thomas and accepted him as an individual. This is further evidenced by the fact that he wrote the official circular letter for the Association that was attached to the 1816 minutes and sent to all the churches. This was on the assigned subject of the Trinity. He wrote a fifteen-page essay on the topic, without using the word. "Bible names for Bible things" was already a concept of the Campbells, and although the concept of the Trinity was acceptable to the Campbells, the term was unbiblical and they refused to endorse it. Regardless, the Association approved the letter without amendment and attached it to the official minutes.[68] A committee was appointed to investigate Campbell's church in Pittsburgh, though no report is ever recorded.

Several people requested Alexander Campbell to speak on Sunday, but the host minister demurred, saying that it would be more proper to allow a speaker from some distance to be heard; the people present could always hear Campbell since he was so close.[69] Thus a speaker from Ohio was chosen. But when Sunday morning arrived, the speaker was indisposed. As Campbell put it, "He providentially was suddenly seized by sickness, and I was unexpectedly called upon" to preach, with about two hours notice. The sermon was rather extemporaneous, later gathered together from a few notes and put into writing.[70] It was probably Campbell's most famous sermon.

---

[66]*Christian Baptist*, vol. 7, no. 12 (July, 1830), p. 307.
[67]*Minutes of the Redstone Baptist Association*, 1816, p. 5.
[68]*Ibid.* The letter itself runs from p. 7 to p. 22.
[69]*Millennial Harbinger*, 1848, pp. 347-348.
[70]*Millennial Harbinger*, 1846, p. 494.

In it he pointed out what the phrase "the Law" meant in Scripture, what things the Law could not accomplish, why not, and how God remedied this. In the process he argued that Christianity differed radically from the Mosaic law. With the coming of Christ, the entire law was done away—not just the ceremonial part. The immutable principles of morality were still in effect (the Ten Commandments) because they had been refined in the New Testament (the Sermon on the Mount). Campbell concluded that there was an essential difference between the law and the gospel. It was not necessary to preach the law to prepare men for the gospel. Most significantly, the Old Testament had no authority for practices expected of Christians—such as infant baptism, fast days prior to observing the Lord's Supper, keeping the Sabbath, or paying tithes.

> All reasons and motives borrowed from the Jewish law, to excite the disciples of Christ to a compliance with or an imitation of Jewish customs, are inconclusive, repugnant to Christianity, and fall ineffectual to the ground; not being enjoined or countenanced by the authority of Jesus Christ.[71]

This Sermon on the Law created quite a furor. The Baptist people loved it, because they saw it as breaking the shackles of legalism and bondage by which they had been enslaved by the clergy. By the same token, many of the clergy resented Campbell's sermon because it lessened their authority and command over the people. In fact, early in the sermon Pritchard himself disturbed the assembly enough to request some clergy to join him outside, where he proposed to have Campbell formally condemned and his discourse repudiated as "not Baptist doctrine." One man questioned, however, whether it might be "Bible doctrine."[72]

When the annual Redstone Baptist Association meeting for 1817 came around, Alexander Campbell was chosen clerk. This would indicate that at least some of the people trusted him, for this made him the second in charge, after the moderator. Known renegades are not usually given such an official position. Thomas was again present and invited to a seat in the assembly. The circular letter for this year was written by Alexander Campbell on the topic, "The Purpose of God in Creating Angels and Men." Consisting of about twelve pages, it also was read and accepted without amendment.

---

[71]*Ibid.*, p. 520. The entire Sermon on the Law is reprinted here, pp. 493-521, as well as in Charles A. Young, pp. 217-288; and other places. A summary can be found in Richardson, vol. 1, pp. 472-479.

[72]*Millennial Harbinger,* 1848, pp. 348-349; 1846, p. 494.

Then things got sticky. The minutes record that several charges and complaints had been lodged against the Brush Run church, and particularly against Alexander Campbell and the "Sermon on the Law" he had preached at the previous Association meeting. The official decision of the Association, however, was recorded thus:

> Resolved that having heard a written declaration of their [Brush Run] faith as well as verbal explanations relative to the charges made against him, we are fully satisfied with the declarations of said Church.[73]

It is obvious that some people were trying to discredit Campbell, but it is also clear that the Association officially was not willing to take a position against him. In spite of some of the clergy, many of the Baptist laity supported him.

The next year things were even more tense. Alexander was again selected as clerk of the meeting. In addition, he was chosen to give the opening sermon. He was chosen to sit on official committees to meet with other neighboring Associations, and assigned to supply preach at some Baptist churches of the Association that lacked ministers. The minutes also record:

> 23. Whereas, the resolve contained in the 11th item of the minutes of the association for 1817 [the one quoted above], has been construed to amount to an approbation of a sermon preached by brother A. Campbell, referred to in said minute.
>
> Resolved, That it was not the sense of this association in the above resolve to pass a sentence of approbation or disapprobation on the sermon above referred to.
>
> 24. Resolved, that as the church of Cross creek has not availed itself of any opportunity to come to a good understanding with the church of Brush Run, with whom they have declared a non-fellowship, this association cannot grant them a letter of dismission.[74]

It appears that when Cross Creek's attempts in 1817 to discredit Campbell proved unavailing, they disfellowshipped the Brush Run church on their own and decided to leave the Redstone Baptist Association. But because it was not allowable for one congregation to disfellowship another (only the Association could do that), the Cross Creek church was no longer in good standing officially with the Association, and therefore could not receive an honorable letter of dismissal. This is simply a case of

---

[73]*Minutes of the Redstone Baptist Association*, 1817, p. 5.
[74]*Ibid.*, 1818, p. 4.

the machinery of the Baptist association being neutral on the judgment against Campbell, when Pritchard and others wanted to use it against him. Two other churches received dismissal letters in 1818, for unspecified reasons, but not Cross Creek.

Thus as this decade came to a close, it was obvious that Campbell was having his difficulties with the Baptists. Some people were trying to discredit him. Officially, however, he was still in good standing with them, used on committees and preaching assignments. In 1819 he was again chosen clerk of the annual meeting,[75] and then in 1820 made moderator.[76] How long this could go on, however, was problematic. Campbell still considered himself a Baptist and wished to continue working with this body in the effort to reform the church according to the New Testament.

At about this same time, Alexander Campbell became involved in his first American experiment in education. He had helped his father back in Ireland and had been responsible for the education of his brothers and sisters when he first arrived in Pennsylvania. But in 1818 he began the Buffalo Seminary in his own home.[77] He enlarged the building to accommodate the sleeping and teaching arrangements, just about doubling the size of the house. Two classrooms were erected on the first floor and sleeping rooms were on the second.

Campbell hoped to increase the educational level of the neighborhood and also to enlist some young men for the ministry. Some girls from the neighborhood also came, merely desiring to obtain a good English education. The school flourished for a few years but never accomplished what Campbell had fully desired. Although apparently several dozen students passed through the halls in the four and a half years of the school's existence, only two went into the ministry, and one of these had been preaching before he came. Therefore, Campbell could look upon over four years of work as recruiting only one young man for the ministry. By 1822 his health was being undermined by the constant confinement of classes indoors, and other requests for his time were intruding. The result was that by the fall of 1822, he disbanded the school.[78] But he never gave up his ideals for education. These continued to ferment for almost two decades and come to fruition later in Bethany College in 1840.

---

[75]*Ibid.*, 1819, p. 4.
[76]*Ibid.*, 1820, p. 3.
[77]Richardson, vol. 1, p. 491.
[78]*Ibid.*, vol. 2, p. 48.

1818	Walter Scott arrives in America
1820	Alexander Campbell debates John Walker Mahoning Baptist Association formed Campbell's followers called "Reformed Baptists"
1823	Alexander begins *Christian Baptist* Alexander debates W.L. Maccalla
1824	Redstone Association disfellowships Brush Run church
1826	Redstone Association drops four more churches
1827	Scott becomes evangelist for Mahoning Association
1828	Aylette Raines given freedom of opinion
1829	Beaver Baptist Anathema
1830	Baptists in Kentucky remove followers of Campbell Mahoning Association dissolves

Chapter 6

A Vision Lifted

THE YEAR 1820 began a significant year in the Campbell Movement. Alexander Campbell rose from local notice among the Baptists to having a larger audience because of his debate with John Walker. By the time the decade was over, his relationships with the Baptists had in fact been severed because of the outgrowths from this one momentous year.

Walker Debate

John Walker was a Seceder Presbyterian minister at Mount Pleasant, Ohio, about twenty-three miles west of Campbell's home. In the fall of 1819, there had been a Baptist revival going on around Mount Pleasant led by John Birch, a Baptist preacher from nearby Flat Rock. Walker and Birch got into a dispute, which led Walker to challenge Birch, or any other Baptist preacher in good standing, to a debate on baptism. Birch accepted the challenge and immediately urged Campbell to undertake the debate.[1]

Campbell did not enter this debate willingly. In fact, he delayed an answer to Birch's first appeal until Birch sent a second letter, and then a third. But Campbell had no confidence in the value of such debates. Debating "seemed to me to be rather carnal than spiritual, and better calculated to excite bad passions then to allay them."[2] "I did not like controversy so well as many have since thought I did; and I was doubtful of the effects it might have upon society."[3] Finally, after about six

---

[1]Richardson, vol. 2, pp. 14-16; see also *Millennial Harbinger,* 1848, p. 522.
[2]*Millennial Harbinger,* 1848, p. 522.
[3]*Christian Baptist,* vol. 7, no. 12 (July, 1830), p. 308.

123

months of this, Campbell consented to meet Walker.[4]

Each man appointed a moderator to keep order and keep the debate on the topic. This debate between Walker and Campbell was on the subject and mode of baptism. Walker argued the subject could include infants; Campbell restricted it to believers. Walker argued for sprinkling, Campbell for immersion. They also agreed that the debate would continue from day to day until either the people in attendance were satisfied, or the moderators thought enough had been said.[5]

Early on the Monday morning of June 19, 1820, Alexander, his father, and a few friends travelled to Mount Pleasant. Since Walker had given the challenge, he was to speak first; Campbell, as the respondent, would have the last word. Each speaker was to take forty minutes, and then speak in rotation. Walker started off, but gave only a short address. Basically he made no argument, simply gave his position in one paragraph. In the printed form of the debate, it consists of only thirteen lines.

> My friends—I don't intend to speak long at one time, perhaps not more than five or ten minutes, and will therefore come to the point at once: I maintain that Baptism came in the room of Circumcision—That the covenant on which the Jewish Church was built, and to which Circumcision is the seal, is the same with the covenant on which the Christian Church is built, and to which Baptism is the seal—That the Jews and the Christians are the same body politic, under the same lawgiver and husband; hence the Jews were called the congregation of the Lord—and the bridegroom of the Church says, "My love, my undefiled is one"—consequently the infants of believers have a right to Baptism.[6]

---

[4]Two books available on Campbell's debates are J. J. Haley, *Debates That Made History: The Story of Alexander Campbell's Debates with Rev. John Walker, Rev. W. L. McCalla, Mr. Robert Owens, Bishop Purcell, and Rev. Nathan L. Rice* (n.p., n.p. [1920, reprinted by College Press in their "Restoration Reprint Library" Series]); and Bill J. Humble, *Campbell and Controversy: The Story of Alexander Campbell's Great Debates with Skepticism, Catholicism, and Presbyterianism* (n.p., Old Paths Book Club, 1952). Of these two, the Humble book is by far the best. Haley's book is filled with invective, partisan shots, ridiculous generalizations, and a private agenda. For instance he calls Campbell's debates "the greatest in the English language, perhaps the greatest in any language" (p. 21). His comments on Robert Owens are filled with references to the Bolsheviks. Owens was a socialist, but to tar him with the same brush as the Communists who took over Russia just three years previous to Haley's writing is to use him unfairly as a whipping boy. Humble's book was a doctoral dissertation done at the University of Colorado and is a good piece of writing and balanced scholarship.
[5]Alexander Campbell, *Debate on Christian Baptism Between Mr. John A. Walker, A Minister of the Secession, and Alexander Campbell*, Second Edition Enlarged (Pittsburgh: Eichbaum and Johnston, 1822 [reprinted by Old Paths Book Club]), p. 4.
[6]*Ibid.*, p. 9.

Walker's beginning took only a minute or two, but it gave Campbell enough to work on all day. He first attacked the identity of circumcision and baptism, enumerating seven areas of difference between the two. Some of these are: (1) Circumcision is done only to males; baptism is done to both males and females. (2) Circumcision was done religiously on the eighth day after birth; baptism has no time requirements. (3) Circumcision required carnal descent from Abraham; baptism requires no such physical genealogy. (4) Parents, relatives, or civil officials performed circumcision; no such restrictions apply to baptism. (5) A different part of the body is used. Infant baptism is normally done to the face; circumcision is not.[7]

Campbell further pointed out, "If Baptism came in the room of circumcision, why were so many thousands of the Jews baptized who had previously been circumcised?"[8] Walker had argued that the two covenants were the same. Campbell argued they were different, based on Hebrews 8. He was willing to grant the use of the word "church" to Israel (Stephen used the word *ekklesia* to refer to them in Acts 7), but he denied that the apostles ever called the Jewish nation "the church of Christ."[9]

By the second day, Walker had given up arguing the identity of the covenants and argued the cases of household baptism. He suggested there must have been infants in these households, and they were baptized on the faith of the parents, which made their situation quite analogous to circumcision.[10]

Campbell's reply to this argument became one of his classics. He pointed out there are only four instances of household baptism in the New Testament—three in the book of Acts, and one in 1 Corinthians. First of all, to argue infant baptism from them is an argument from silence—the text says nothing about infants at all. Secondly, in every instance the text does say something that necessarily *excludes* infants. In Acts 10:2 Cornelius and his entire family are called "God-fearing." In Acts 16:34, the Philippian jailer's household "believed." In Acts 16:40, the household of Lydia is "comforted" by Paul's words. In 1 Corinthians 16:15, the house of Stephanas are said to be "addicted to the ministry of the saints."[11] In each of these instances, obviously things are required of the members of the household that disqualify infants. Infants cannot believe, fear God, be comforted by the words of a preacher, or be addicted to ministry. Through the remainder of the debate, Walker never brought up the subject of household baptism again.

---

[7]*Ibid.*, pp. 12-13.
[8]*Ibid.*, p. 19.
[9]*Ibid.*, pp. 40-43.
[10]*Ibid.*, p. 67.
[11]*Ibid.*, pp. 70-71.

For several hours the debate continued on the fact of whether infants had been baptized in the apostolic or early church. Arguing from Origen, Tertullian, Cyprian, Justin Martyr, and others, Campbell declared that there was no proof for the practice. He concluded one speech by repeating some words reminiscent of his father's *Declaration and Address:* "My conviction is, that nothing is to be admitted into the faith, doctrine, or discipline, of the Christian Church, that is not as old as the New Testament; nay that is not expressly revealed in the Bible."[12]

By Tuesday afternoon, they finally moved from discussing the *subject* of baptism to the *mode.* In addition, Walker's moderator suggested limiting the discussion to one speech on each side and then adjourning. Campbell was surprised, since the rules had stated the discussion would go on from day to day until either the people or the moderators were satisfied. But Campbell could get nothing more than the agreement to two more rounds of speeches.

In preparing to defend immersion as the only biblical baptism, Campbell brought a stack of concordances and lexicons with him to the stand. Walker chided him for bringing his "bundle of Greek," but said he would simply "stick to my Bible." He then proceeded to argue that in the Scriptures, sprinkling is God's plan for cleansing. Under the Law, blood was sprinkled for this purpose. God also said he would "sprinkle many nations."[13]

Campbell, of course, went to the Greek to argue for immersion. He argued the meaning of the Greek words, but added four facts to his argument: (1) King James prohibited his translators to use the word "immersion" instead of the word "baptism," thus creating the later confusion over the term. (2) The Westminster Assembly approved sprinkling over immersion by a 26-25 vote. (3) The Greek church, which ought to know the Greek language, has always immersed. (4) Even some of the early Latin fathers considered sprinkling, used only as an emergency measure, unworthy of the name of "baptism."[14]

When Campbell came to winding up his final speech of this tedious debate, he urged his hearers to go home and read their Bibles.

Amongst the clergy of different denominations I charitably think there are a few good men: but as a body of men—"they have taken away the key of knowledge from the people." And *how,* do you say? By teaching you to look up to them for instruction, as children to a father—by preventing you from

---

[12]*Ibid.*, p. 121.
[13]*Ibid.*, p. 121.
[14]*Ibid.*, pp. 128-130.

judging for yourselves; through an impression that you are not competent to judge for yourselves. This is a prevailing opinion with many. Of what use, then is the Bible to the bulk of mankind, if you are not to presume to examine it for yourselves or to think yourselves capable of judging it? This is to make you the dupes of haughty leaders who will cause you to err. To attempt directly or indirectly to dissuade you from thinking and examining for yourselves, by putting creeds already framed into your hands, or the works of men instead of the pure word, is, in my opinion, so far depriving you of the key of knowledge. I do not say that all the clergy are doing so, but I am sure that a vast majority of them are doing so.[15]

Feeling that the debate had gone quite well from his standpoint, Campbell concluded his remarks with the challenge to meet any other paedo-baptist for a further debate on the topic, "Infant sprinkling is a human tradition and injurious to the well being of society, religious and political."[16]

The debate was published, but since there were no actual stenographical reporters present, it had to be reconstructed to be put into print. In his "Introduction" to the Old Paths reprint edition, John Allen Hudson says that Campbell brought Salathiel Curtis, a reporter, to the debate.[17] In his preface to the printed debate, Campbell simply says he used notes taken by Salathiel Curtis, Thomas Campbell, and his own from Walker's arguments. He then used these documents, "together with his own recollection, . . . to present to the public a correct and satisfactory detail of the whole proceeding."[18] Obviously, then, this printed work does not propose to be a verbal, literal transcript. In fact in places Campbell even editorializes and says he has conflated two different speeches into one,[19] or has omitted material that is repetitious.[20] On the other hand, sometimes he included material that was not in the original discussion but which he now felt was helpful to the full flavor of the arguments.[21]

Campbell had one thousand copies of the debate printed at Steubenville, Ohio, that fall, and they sold out "after some months." In 1822 a second edition of 3000 copies was printed in Pittsburgh, which included Campbell's replies to another Presbyterian, Samuel Ralston, who had

---

[15]*Ibid.*, p. 140.

[16]*Ibid.*, p. 141.

[17]*Ibid.*, "Introduction," the seventh page, though they are unnumbered.

[18]*Ibid.*, p. 5.

[19]See, for instance, *ibid.*, p. 23.

[20]*Ibid.*, p. 63.

[21]See, for instance, *ibid.*, p. 116, and footnote on p. 97.

published some comments on the debate.[22] This debate, particularly its printed version, changed Campbell's life.

From the vantage point of 1830, he remarked that soon after his arrival in America, his father's unsuccessful efforts to reform the Presbyterians

> made me despair of reformation. I gave it up as a hopeless effort: but did not give up speaking in public assemblies upon the great articles of christian faith and practice. In the hope, the humble hope, of erecting a single congregation with which I could enjoy the social institutions, I labored. I had not the remotest idea of being able to do more than this; and, therefore, I betook myself to the occupation of a farmer, and for a number of years attended to this profession as a means of subsistence, and labored every Lord's day to separate the truth from the traditions of men, and to persuade men to give up their fables for the truth—with but little success I labored.[23]

But then the Walker Debate occurred, and copies of the printed version began to sell like hotcakes. Seeing the effects of this debate, "I began to hope that something might be done to rouse this generation from its supineness and spiritual lethargy."[24] It was this that encouraged Campbell to consider the possibility of printing a regular magazine to get reading material in the hands of people and influence their thinking toward reform. This resulted in the beginning of the *Christian Baptist* in 1823. Before that time, however, more immediate results of the Walker debate began to occur.

The printed version of the debate had not been in circulation long before Campbell began to receive numerous calls from a variety of places requesting visits and discourses on the subjects covered in the debate and its appendix. One such contact led to his meeting with Adamson Bentley. Bentley was a leading Baptist preacher in the Western Reserve district of northern Ohio. Bentley had also encouraged these Baptist churches to hold annual "ministers' meetings" to discuss religious topics as well as criticize each others' sermons with a view toward improvement. In August of 1820, he also convinced these churches to form the Mahoning Baptist Association. Then in the spring of 1821, Bentley obtained a copy of the Walker Debate.

That summer he visited Campbell himself, bringing with him another young Baptist preacher, Sidney Rigdon. Bentley wished to discuss with

---

[22]Richardson, vol. 2, p. 34; also *Christian Baptist,* vol. 2, no. 2 (September, 1824), p. 37.

[23]*Christian Baptist,* vol. 7, no. 12 (July, 1830), p. 307.

[24]*Ibid.*, p. 308.

Campbell some of the ideas presented in the debate. That evening after dinner, they began with baptism, and covered the covenants and the Gospel, "but especially the ancient order of things and the modern." The conversation lasted until the next morning. When the men left to go back home, Rigdon candidly commented that "if he had, within the last year, taught and promulgated from the pulpit one error, he had a thousand." The two men left, urgently inviting Campbell to come to the Western Reserve. In the process of the next year, they prepared the entire Mahoning Baptist Association to be receptive to Campbell's positions.[25] As we will see, the later effect of this was extremely significant for the entire Campbell Movement.

Christian Baptist

Before the long-range effects of the Campbell influence on the Mahoning Baptist Association became evident, however, another development was under way that also stemmed directly from the Walker debate. This was the development of his first monthly magazine, the *Christian Baptist*. Campbell himself states, "In 1823 I commenced editing the *Christian Baptist*."[26] In another place, Campbell states that it was the Walker debate that enabled him to see that "something might be done to rouse this generation from its supineness and spiritual lethargy. About two years afterwards I conceived the plan of [the *Christian Baptist*]."[27] As Robert Richardson put it, "Having realized in publishing the Debate with Mr. Walker the power of the press to disseminate his views, . . . he began to think of issuing, in monthly parts, a work specially devoted to the interests of the proposed Reformation."[28]

Campbell intended to entitle the paper, "The Christian," but it was Walter Scott (1796-1861) who suggested an alternative. Since Campbell intended the paper to circulate among the Baptists, Scott thought it would be helpful if the title of the paper carried the word "Baptist" to solicit Baptist support and identity. Campbell followed the suggestion, and the paper emerged as the *Christian Baptist*.[29]

Having introduced the name of Scott, it is necessary to say more about

---

[25]*Millennial Harbinger,* 1848, pp. 522-524.

[26]*Christian Baptist,* vol. 2, no. 2 (September, 1824), p. 37.

[27]*Christian Baptist,* vol. 7, no. 12 (July, 1830), p. 308.

[28]Richardson, vol. 2, p. 48.

[29]At least this is the standard understanding of how the name was chosen. See *The Evangelist,* New Series, vol. 1, no. 12 (December, 1838), p. 269; William Baxter, *Life of Elder Walter Scott* (Nashville: Gospel Advocate Company, n.d.

him because he had a significant role in the development of the *Christian Baptist* as well as in the events of the 1820s.[30] Scott was born in Scotland and educated at the University of Edinburgh, graduating in 1818. At that time he came to America, settling with an uncle on Long Island and teaching school for a year in New York City. But he did not feel permanent there. He heard glowing reports of the west and determined to see it for himself. With a companion, he walked to Pittsburgh, taking about a month for the journey, and arriving there in May of 1819.

Looking for work, he found a teaching position in a school operated by George Forrester (1782-1820), a fellow Scot immigrant. Scott also discovered that Forrester was a deeply religious man, but a man of independent thinking, intent upon making the Bible alone his authority and guide in religious matters. The two often got involved in religious discussions after school and stayed up far into the night examining the Scriptures. Under this tutelage, Scott was not long in discovering that infant baptism was without scriptural warrant, and further discovery brought him to the conclusion that sprinkling and pouring were human substitutes for the biblical practice of immersion. Under this conviction, Forrester then immersed Scott, and he became a member of a small body of believers that Forrester had gathered in Pittsburgh.[31]

In the winter of 1819-1820, George Forrester gave up his school, and Scott became the principal of it, using his creative and innovative

---

[reprint]), p. 73; and Richardson, vol. 2, p. 50. Alexander Campbell himself later demurred from this. His own comment is:

"When we drew up our Prospectus for our first publication, we headed it 'The Christian,' and had it not been that we found ourselves anticipated we should have adhered to the title. I hesitated between the title 'Baptist Christian' and 'Christian Baptist,' and on suggesting my embarrassment to a friend, who has since given himself due credit for the hint, as an original idea; he thought the latter was a better passport into favor than either of the others. We never fully approved, but from expediency adopted it." (*Millennial Harbinger,* 1839, p. 338)

This appears, however, to have a strident anti-Scott note to it. It must be kept in mind that from 1838 to about 1844, Scott and Campbell had a sharp dispute going on that put a significant strain upon their friendship. It is understandable that at the time, Campbell would not like to admit that he was beholden to Scott for the name. The exact provenance of the name may never be known.

[30]The best biographies of Scott are the Baxter work just referred to, as well as Dwight E. Stevenson, *Walter Scott, Voice of the Golden Oracle: A Biography* (Joplin, Missouri: College Press, n.d. [reprint]). Stevenson, originally published in 1946, the sesquicentennial of Scott's birth, has some new material, but he relies heavily on Baxter. A More recent treatment is William A. Gerrard III, *A Biographical Study of Walter Scott, American Frontier Evangelist* (Joplin, Missouri: College Press Publishing Company, 1992).

[31]Baxter, pp. 37-38.

qualities of teaching to gain a good reputation for his own abilities in education.[32] Unfortunately, a few months later, Forrester went to the Allegheny River to bathe, waded out, stepped off into deep water, and drowned.[33] Scott comforted the widow and also took the oversight of the little congregation of believers. The work of ministry and evangelism now began to appeal to him more than the classroom.[34]

In the spring of 1821 Mrs. Forrester gave to Scott a pamphlet printed by a Haldanean church of New York City the previous year, written by one of its elders, Henry Errett.[35] The pamphlet was on baptism, but it went beyond just talking about immersion. It laid emphasis on the purpose for baptism—the remission of sins. The same pamphlet came from Mrs. Forrester to Alexander Campbell in the fall of 1821.[36] Thus both men became acquainted with this doctrine the same year, through the same medium.

Young Robert Richardson (1806-1876) had once been a student under Thomas Campbell when Campbell had a school in Pittsburgh.[37] More recently, Richardson had been a student under Walter Scott.[38] The Campbell family maintained its friendship with the Richardson family, and when Alexander was once in Pittsburgh visiting the Richardsons, he met Scott.[39] The two men formed a strong acquaintance immediately and a deep friendship that lasted almost forty years. Campbell talked over with Scott his plans for beginning a magazine and, as we have seen, it was probably Scott that proposed the name *Christian Baptist.*

This monthly magazine changed Campbell's life, as well as the direction of the Restoration Movement. The prospectus for the new magazine was issued on July 4, 1823. The date was not at all accidental. Campbell probably intended this to serve as a declaration of religious independence. The first paragraph of the prospectus declared the editor's intentions.

> The "Christian Baptist" shall espouse the cause of no religious sect, excepting that ancient sect called "Christians first at Antioch." Its sole object shall be the eviction of truth, and the exposure of error in doctrine and practice. The editor acknowledging no standard of religious faith or works, other than the Old

---

[32]*Ibid.,* p. 41.
[33]Richardson, vol. 1, p. 507.
[34]Baxter, pp. 45-46.
[35]*The Evangelist,* 1838, p. 286. See also Baxter, p. 47, and Stevenson, p. 27.
[36]*The Evangelist,* 1838, pp. 286-287.
[37]Richardson, vol. 1, p. 463.
[38]*Ibid.,* p. 504.
[39]Baxter, p. 64; Stevenson, p. 37.

and New Testaments, and the latter as the only standard of the religion of Jesus Christ, will, intentionally at least, oppose nothing which it contains, and recommend nothing which it does not enjoin.[40]

The first full issue of the paper appeared on August 4, 1823, and was issued on the first Monday of every month for the next seven years. The last issue came from the press on July 5, 1830, by which time the magazine had been supplanted by Campbell's new paper, the *Millennial Harbinger,* which began on January 4, 1830, and appeared on the first Monday of every month thereafter through 1870.

Garrison and DeGroot, in their history of the movement, specify three innovations of the churches of the 1820s that the *Christian Baptist* specifically addressed in order to expose and correct: the pretensions of the clergy, the use of creeds, and unauthorized organizations.[41]

Campbell loved to attack the exalted self-esteem of the clergy. Ever since his days in Glasgow, he had resented the superior airs of the clergy, and his early days with Presbyterian clergy in western Pennsylvania did nothing to remove his prejudices. The very first issue of the *Christian Baptist* carried a satirical article, "A Sermon Upon Goats," in which Campbell suggested the clergy were fleecing the non-members of the church for support. This article was immediately followed by one on "The Origin of the 'Christian Clergy,' Splendid Meeting Houses, and Fixed Salaries, Exhibited from Ecclesiastical History." It is significant, however, that the article is introduced with the *nota bene,* "In our remarks upon the 'Christian Clergy,' we never include the Elders or Deacons of a Christian Assembly, or those in the New Testament called the Overseers and Servants of the Christian Church."[42] About a year later Campbell made another distinction: "Amongst the Baptists it is to be hoped there are but few clergy; and would to God there were none! The grand and distinguishing views of the Baptists must be grossly perverted before they could tolerate one such creature."[43] Throughout his writings, however,

---

[40]*Christian Baptist,* vol. 1 (1823), Preface, p. iv.

[41]Garrison and DeGroot, p. 176; they borrow this outline from Errett Gates, *The Early History of Relation and Separation of Baptists and Disciples* (Chicago: The Christian Century Company, 1904), pp. 43-46. This study is Gates' Ph.D. dissertation from the University of Chicago. An excellent introduction to the *Christian Baptist* can be found in Gary L. Lee, "Background of the *Christian Baptist,*" in College Press' 1983 reprint of the one-volume Burnet edition of the magazine done in 1835. Lee's article (pp. 1-36) was his 1981 M.A. thesis from Lincoln Christian Seminary.

[42]*Christian Baptist,* vol. 1, no. 1 (August, 1823), p. 20.

[43]*Ibid.,* vol. 2, no. 3 (October, 1824), p. 45.

Campbell had scathing things to say about the "hireling priests," a favorite appellation of his for the clergy. Campbell was often attacked for his censorious spirit, and Garrison-DeGroot assert that "this furious assault upon the clergy doubtless provoked more ill will in return than any other feature of Mr. Campbell's program."[44]

Campbell's attack on creeds was not a new issue. His father had called for their elimination in the *Declaration and Address* fourteen years earlier, and the Stone Movement had rejected them even earlier than that. But Alexander's ire against them was no less for that. His experiences with the Presbyterians and the Westminster Confession, and now with the Baptists and their Philadelphia Confession of Faith led him to issue numerous broadsides against any humanly devised test of orthodoxy. Perhaps his best-known article here was his "Parable of the Iron Bedstead," which originally appeared as part of an article simply called "A New Association." Here Campbell reworked an old fable from Aesop and likened Catholic, Lutheran, and Calvinistic creeds to iron bedsteads that were equipped to make everybody the same size, either by cutting them down or stretching them out.[45]

Campbell's attack on unauthorized organizations of the churches was the application of some of his earlier principles to a growing problem that he saw. The earlier experience of the Campbells had discouraged them with regard to such things as the Chartiers Presbytery, the Synod of Pittsburgh, and even the Redstone Baptist Association. Campbell came to see these organizations as threats to the independent life of the local church and its freedom in the gospel. In the very first issue of the *Christian Baptist*, the very first article was entitled "The Christian Religion," and it contained these comments on the early apostolic churches:

> Their churches were not fractured into missionary societies, Bible societies, education societies; nor did they dream of organizing such in the world. . . . They dare not transfer to a missionary society, or Bible society, or education society, *a cent or a prayer*, lest in so doing they should rob the church of its glory and exalt the inventions of men above the wisdom of God. *In their church capacity alone they moved.*[46]

This led to some friction within the Baptists, as Campbell's denunciation included the various associations that were the backbone of Baptist organization.

---

[44]Garrison and DeGroot, p. 177.

[45]*Christian Baptist*, vol. 4, no. 2 (October, 1826), pp. 59-61.

[46]*Ibid.*, vol. 1, no. 1 (August, 1823), pp. 14-15; italics in original.

Probably the most significant series of articles Campbell wrote in the *Christian Baptist* was that on "The Restoration of the Ancient Order of Things." This ran to thirty-two articles, spread over four and a half years, running from February of 1825 to the final installment in June, 1829. The series included articles on creeds, nomenclature, order of worship, the loaf (four articles), fellowship, foot washing, the bishop's office (three articles), deacon's office, singing (two articles), discipline (eight articles), and various other topics. In this series, Campbell was trying to demonstrate the *order* of the ancient church—its organization, worship, and congregational life. This emphasis on the "pattern" of the New Testament Church marked the Campbell Movement for some time to come.

In the very first article of this series, Campbell called for a return to the New Testament order, making a distinction between a restoration and a reformation. He called a reformation inadequate since it simply took the existing substance and put it into a different form. What was needed, he said, was not just reformation, but a restoring of the ancient apostolic order—a restoration movement, although he himself never used that phrase. Also in this first article he included a provocative statement that indicated his thinking about the movement he was leading: "Just in so far as the ancient order of things, or the religion of the New Testament, is restored, just so far has the Millennium commenced."[47] This post-millennial expression seemed to indicate that Campbell saw the Restoration Movement as the harbinger of the millennium. That concept became the name of his next magazine in 1830.

Campbell did not, of course, write all the copy for the magazine himself. He included numerous articles from other pens, including those of his father, Walter Scott, and others. Many of the articles were signed with a pseudonym, such as Amicus, Amos, Aquila, Barnabas, Beneglius, a Berean, and Biblicus, to name a few. The identity of most of these writers is unknown, although at one point the pen name "Philip" is identified with Walter Scott.[48]

Probably the most significant series of articles Scott did for the *Christian Baptist* appeared in the first volume; it was four articles under the heading "On Teaching Christianity." Here he developed the theme that Christianity consisted of one grand truth, "Jesus is the Christ," and that

---

[47]*Christian Baptist,* vol. 2, no. 7 (February, 1825), p. 136.

[48]Alexander Campbell so identifies him in *Christian Baptist,* vol. 4, no. 11 (June, 1827), p. 240. Stevenson points out that Scott "was conscious of being on the threshold of a new religious reformation, in which movement he thought of his friend Alexander Campbell as the Luther and himself the Melanchthon" (Stevenson, pp. 42-43).

this was the core of apostolic teaching.[49] Since this was a matter-of-fact statement, apostolic preaching produced the evidence to substantiate the claim of Jesus' messiahship and then warned people of the result of rejecting such evidence.[50] This issue, Scott maintained, was one that any person with normal intelligence could accept. Herein lay the influence of earlier Haldanean thinking as well as the seeds of his own success as an evangelist on the Western Reserve a few years later.

Further Relations with Baptists

While not all the implications of the *Christian Baptist* were immediately clear, some of the direction of the magazine was obvious in its first issue. That, coupled with Campbell's maverick ways ever since his "Sermon on the Law" in 1816, caused some individuals within the Redstone Baptist Association to eliminate his thorny presence among them. They chose to make their move in 1823.

As Richardson tells the story, Campbell's opponents made the rounds of some of the churches of the Redstone Baptist Association, influencing them to appoint as their annual delegates members who would be un-friendly to Campbell. Their intention was to discredit Campbell and his ideas and destroy his influence among them. Apparently Campbell was unmoved by this threat, except that he was to enter another debate in October with a Presbyterian in Kentucky. To go into the debate discred-ited among the Baptists might have a negative influence on the debate itself, and Campbell wished to avoid this. Consequently, a week before the Association's annual meeting he and about thirty other members left the Brush Run church and established a new church at Wellsburg, [West] Virginia, about five miles north of Campbell's home. In 1824 the new church joined the Mahoning Baptist Association of Ohio.[51] Therefore the move to discredit Campbell came to nothing since he was no longer a member of the Redstone Baptist Association. Significant, however, is the fact that the Association decided to have its constitution reprinted and attached to the minutes of the 1823 meeting. That constitution stipulates that every church of the association is to agree with "the Regular Baptist Confession of Faith."[52] This provided the background for the troubles of the next couple of years.

---

[49]*Christian Baptist*, vol. 1, no. 2 (September, 1823), pp. 29-32.

[50]*Ibid.*, vol. 1, no. 7 (February, 1824), pp. 133-137.

[51]Richardson, vol. 2, pp. 68-69, 100.

[52]*Minutes of the Redstone Baptist Association*, 1823, p. 7.

Meanwhile Campbell was preparing for his debate with W. L. Maccalla[53] of Augusta, Kentucky. In May of 1823, Maccalla sent Campbell a letter responding to his challenge at the end of the Walker debate. Unfortunately, several exchanges of letters were necessary before the debate could get under way, and in these letters both men demonstrated petty peevishness about agreeing to the details of the debate. Ultimately, however, the debate occurred in Washington, Kentucky, just outside Maysville, running October 15-22, and lasting seven days, since Sunday was not used. Campbell rode a horse the three hundred miles to Washington, accompanied by Sidney Rigdon, who took notes of the discussion that formed the basis for the printed version of the debate. For the first two days, the debate took place in the open, using a Methodist camping ground. By the third day, however, the weather turned colder and the debate moved into a nearby Baptist church building.

The debate was to consider the same topics as in the Walker debate: the mode and subject of baptism. Campbell was still interested in this topic, because he saw infant sprinkling as a major barrier to his heart's desire—the unity of Christians.

> We ardently desire the union of all christians on the one foundation; we believe infant sprinkling to be a barrier, a stumbling block in the way, and therefore we wish to see it removed, that those who believe and love the truth may walk in the fellowship of it.[54]

Maccalla promised that in the debate he would produce a divine command for infant baptism, *probable* evidence of apostolic practice of infant baptism, and *positive* evidence for the apostolic practice of infant baptism.[55] His basic line of reasoning was that God had sanctioned circumcision, infant baptism is in place of circumcision, and God has never rescinded his mandate for circumcision; therefore, this constitutes divine warrant for infant baptism.

To develop this entire argument, Maccalla had gone to some length in writing out a lengthy manuscript, which he proceeded to read during the debate. While Campbell spent time rebutting Maccalla's comments, the latter usually ignored most of Campbell's arguments and just proceeded

---

[53]The name is spelled various ways. "Maccalla" is the most consistent spelling in the original sources. Other variants appear as "MacCalla" and "McCalla."

[54]A. Campbell, *A Public Debate on Christian Baptism, Between the Rev. W. L. Maccalla, a Presbyterian Teacher, and Alexander Campbell* (London: Simpkin and Marshall, 1842 [Old Paths Book Club reprint, 1948]), p. 38.

[55]*Ibid.*, p. 42.

to read his prepared manuscript. Campbell complained to the moderators that Maccalla was not debating. The moderators split on the decision, but a majority gave Maccalla the freedom to proceed as he wanted.[56] This left Campbell frustrated and with little to say. Much of what Maccalla was saying had to do with the covenant of circumcision with Abraham. Campbell agreed completely with what Maccalla was saying about it, but he contended it had nothing to do with baptism and therefore was off the subject.[57]

Having exhausted most of his material on the subject and mode of baptism, and having little to respond to while Maccalla continued reading, Campbell then began to explore what he called the design, or purpose, of baptism. Here he urged that baptism was for the remission of sins. Little had been said on this topic, although it was briefly intimated in the Walker debate; Campbell had since examined the pamphlet from Henry Errett that he had received from Mrs. Forrester. But now in the Maccalla debate, Campbell developed this topic.

He argued that baptism must take place in the presence of faith; that was why infant baptism made no sense—infants could not believe. Looking at Acts 22:16, Campbell noticed that Saul/Paul was told to "arise, be baptized, washing away your sins." Thus he concluded that

> his sins were *now* washed away in some sense that they were not before. . . .
> Now we confess that the blood of Jesus Christ alone *cleanses* us from all sins.
> Even this, however, is a metaphorical expression. . . . The blood of Christ,
> then, *really* cleanses us who believe from all sin. Behold the goodness of God
> in giving us a *formal* proof and token of it, by ordaining a baptism expressly
> *"for the remission of sins!"* The water of baptism, then, *formally*, washes way our
> sins. Paul's sins were *really pardoned* when he believed, yet he had no solemn
> *pledge* of the fact, no *formal* acquital [sic], no *formal* purgation of his sins, until
> he washed them away in the water of baptism.[58]

Although the Baptists were delighted that Campbell was championing their cause for believer's immersion, they were not at all happy with this emphasis on remission of sins. Baptist thinking does not normally connect baptism with this purpose. Realizing this, Campbell noted,

> My Baptist brethren, as well as the Pedobaptist brotherhood, I humbly con-
> ceive, require to be admonished on this point. You have been, some of you no
> doubt, too diffident in asserting this grand import of baptism, in urging an

---

[56]*Ibid.*, pp. 55, 68, 73, and 123.

[57]*Ibid.*, pp. 79, 92.

[58]*Ibid.*, p. 116; italics in original.

immediate submission to this sacred and gracious ordinance, lest your brethren should say that you make every thing of baptism; that you make it essential to salvation. Tell them that you make nothing essential to salvation but the blood of Christ, but that God has made baptism essential to their *formal* forgiveness in this life, to their admission into his kingdom on earth. Tell them that God has made it essential to their happiness that they should have a pledge on his part in this life, an *assurance* in the name of the Father, and of the Son, and of the Holy Spirit, of their actual pardon, of the remission of all their sins, and that this assurance is baptism.[59]

This whole idea, introduced here in the Maccalla debate, becomes a complex one. On the one hand, Campbell asserts that the purpose of baptism is remission of sins; on the other hand, he asserts that it is a "formal" forgiveness only. Some of the implications of this come back in the Lunenburg Letter.

Some of the Baptists may have been glad to have Campbell championing their position against the paedobaptist Maccalla, but it was obvious that numerous other Baptists wanted to now distance themselves from Campbell and his followers. One indication of that came in the annual meeting of the Redstone Baptist Association in 1824. The constitution of the Association, reprinted in 1823, spelled out that each church each year was to send a letter to the Association stipulating its adherence to the Philadelphia Confession of Faith. In 1824 the letters from twelve churches were questioned because of their "informality." Such "informality" undoubtedly meant the churches had failed to indicate their adherence to the Philadelphia Confession. "After hearing satisfactory reasons why there was such informality," eleven of these churches were acquitted.[60]

The very next item in the minutes records: "The representatives of the church at Brush Run [Thomas Campbell and James Foster], not being able to give satisfactory reasons for the informality in their letter, were objected to." This was Saturday afternoon. That evening, the first item of the minutes records, "Resolved, that this Association have no fellowship with the Brush Run church."[61] The Association had tried to discredit Alexander Campbell in 1823, but he moved out of their jurisdiction; the very next year, however, they got rid of the maverick church that had been plaguing them for nine years.

The immediately succeeding item in the minutes is: "Resolved, that the 11th item of business in the Minutes of 1816, be null and void."[62]

---

[59]*Ibid.*, p. 125.
[60]*Minutes of the Redstone Baptist Association*, 1824, p. 3.
[61]*Ibid.*, p. 4.
[62]*Ibid.*

This was the acceptance of Thomas Campbell's circular letter on the Trinity in which he refused to use the word. No question had been made about his letter at the time, but now they apparently felt the need to remove any acceptance of Thomas on their books as well. There may be some irony in the fact that on Sunday morning, the Association had worship services and the two sermons were based on the texts of Isaiah 40:1 ("Comfort ye, comfort ye, my people") and 1 Thessalonians 5:19 ("Quench not the spirit").[63] The anti-Campbell faction certainly needed comforting, and they were certainly trying to quench the spirit of reform.

In 1825 the Redstone Baptist Association was obviously feeling the pressure of Campbell's position, probably due to the increasing circulation of the *Christian Baptist*. An inquiry was made into the doctrines held by the church in Washington, Pennsylvania, but a decision was deferred until the next year. However, the Association apparently felt the need to defend themselves concerning the very existence of their association. They adopted a resolution giving six reasons in favor of such meetings:

> 1st. To gain acquaintance with, and knowledge of one another. 2nd. To preserve uniformity in faith and practice. 3d. To detect and discountenance heresies. 4th. To afford assistance and advice in all difficult cases. 5th. To contribute pecuniary aid where necessary. 6th. To afford supplies for destitute churches, & every way advance & secure the interest of religion, and strengthen and draw closer the bonds of union and fellowship.[64]

It is obvious that Campbell's attacks on the unauthorized organizations of the churches were having an effect.

By 1826 the Redstone Baptist Association's members were ready to move even more strongly against the followers of Campbell. In 1823 they tried to discredit Campbell but failed. In 1824 they got rid of the Brush Run Church. Now in 1826 they eliminated several more churches.

Inquiry was made into the doctrines held by the church at Washington, Pennsylvania. After a full investigation, the church and its minister were found to be "heterodox"[65] and were excluded from the Association's fellowship. The brethren of the church at Maple Creek sent a letter that the Association judged to be an unsatisfactory explanation of their faith. The minister (Henry Spears) was requested to state the cause, but his statement was likewise judged unsatisfactory, and the Maple Creek church was denied a seat in the assembly. The church at Pigeon Creek

---

[63]*Ibid.*, p. 5.

[64]*Ibid.*, 1825, p. 3.

[65]*Heterodox* is a nicer word than *heretical,* but the result is much the same.

(Matthias Luce, minister) was unable to give a satisfactory explanation of their faith, and they were excluded from the fellowship. Inquiry was made into the doctrine held by the church at Somerset, and the investigation found them heterodox. They were also excluded from the fellowship.[66]

Further, the Circular Letter for that year was a nine-page indictment of "a couple of THEOLOGICAL ADVENTURERS" who had come into the Association several years previously by a bare majority of votes, disguised as Baptists. These men (unnamed, of course) soon professed their "intention to *revolutionize* the Regular Baptist Church" and soon introduced "the most pernicious heresies." The letter went on to single out "the junior of these two *adventurers*" as using "the genius of RIBALDRY" in "written and oral philippick [sic] against the association," picturing them as old-fashioned, bigoted, grossly ignorant, tyrannous, and inquisitorial.[67] Much of the rest of the letter was a defense of the special work of the Holy Spirit in the process of conversion, a significant Calvinist hallmark.[68]

The general pattern of Baptist activity becomes clear when examining the membership statistics for the Redstone Baptist Association. In 1824 the Association numbered 28 churches. By eliminating Brush Run, they were down to 27 the next two years. They added 2 new churches in 1826 but also eliminated 4, leaving them at 25 churches. By 1829 they were left with only 17 churches.[69]

In spite of these difficulties, however, Alexander Campbell still considered himself a Baptist in good standing. Late in the year 1825, Campbell received a letter from a man in Missouri wondering if he were a Baptist, an Arian, or a Unitarian. As part of his response, Campbell said,

> I and the church with which I am connected are in "full communion" with the Mahoning Baptist Association, Ohio; and through them, with the whole Baptist society in the United States; and I do intend to continue in connexion with this people so long as they will permit me to say what I believe, to teach what I am assured of, and to censure what is amiss in their views or practices. I have no idea of adding to the catalogue of new sects. This game has been played too long. I labor to see sectarianism abolished, and all christians of every name united upon the one foundation on which the apostolic church was founded.[70]

---

[66]*Minutes of the Redstone Baptist Association,* 1826, p. 3.
[67]*Ibid.*, p. 5; Italics and capitals are in the original.
[68]*Ibid.*, pp. 6-13.
[69]*Ibid.*, 1829, p. 3.
[70]*Christian Baptist,* vol. 3, no. 7 (February, 1826), p. 146.

Even while the Baptists were cleaning out the Campbellite churches from within the Redstone Baptist Association, Campbell still had a vision of Christian unity. Although he could not agree with everything the Baptists stood for, he was willing to be identified with them to make the point that he did not want to establish a new religious group. In fact, he was willing to acknowledge numerous peoples in Christian fellowship for the sake of Christian unity. When an "Independent Baptist" questioned Campbell regarding his statement about "full communion" with the Baptists, Campbell replied that this did not mean to include "full union in the common worship, doctrine, and institutions of any church or denomination." Instead, "it means no more than joint participation in a certain act or acts."[71]

> I have tried the pharisaic plan, the monastic. I was once so straight, that, like the Indian's tree, I leaned a little the other way. . . . I was once so strict a Separatist that I would neither pray nor sing praises with any one who was not as perfect as I supposed myself. In this most unpopular course I persisted until I discovered the mistake, and saw that on the principle embraced in my conduct, there never could be a congregation or church upon the earth.
>
> As to "the purblind Pharisee who strains out a gnat and swallows a camel," because he will not have full communion with all the evangelical sects in the mass, I have to remark, that it is not optional with me or you whether we would have christian communion with them. They have something to say upon that subject; and here once for all, it must be noted, that my having communion with any society, Baptist or Paido-Baptist, depends just as much upon them as upon myself. Some Baptist congregations would not receive me into their communion, and if any Paido-Baptist society would, it is time enough to show that I am *inconsistent* with my own principles when any "evangelical sect or congregation" shall have welcomed me to their communion, and I have refused it. At the same time, I frankly own, that my full conviction is, that there are many Paido-Baptist congregations, of whose christianity, or of whose profession of christianity, I think as highly, as of most Baptist congregations, and with whom I could wish to be on the very same terms of christian communion on which I stand with the whole Baptist society.[72]

> The Baptist society exhibits a greater variety than any other society in christendom. . . . But so long as they will bear reproof, suffer exhortation, and allow us to declare our sentiments without restraint; so long as they manifest a *willingness* to know the whole truth, and any disposition to obey it; so long as they will hear us and cordially have fellowship with us, we will have fellowship

---

[71]*Ibid.*, (May, 1826), p. 202.
[72]*Ibid.*, p. 203.

with them, we will thus labor for their good, and endeavor to correct what appears to be amiss—commending when praise is due, and censuring when it becomes necessary.[73]

Campbell thus continued to work for the combination of two goals— the continuing sensitivity toward a meaningful Christian union, while at the same time he desired all churches to see the Bible only as the basis for church teaching and practice. Differences in *practice* were not necessarily a barrier for Campbell, as long as people manifested a *willingness* to know the truth and a *disposition* to obey it.

The continuing nature of the difference between the Campbells and the Baptists is indicated in a statement from the 1830 minutes of the Redstone Baptist Association:

> Whereas the items of business of the association, contained in the Minutes for the year 1824 . . . concerning the exclusion of the Church at Brush Run, (of which Thos. Campbell and his son Alexander were members,) are indefinite as to the reason for the exclusion: And this Association having received some communications from a distance, requesting more specific information as to the cause of their exclusion: Therefore, unanimously resolved, that for the satisfaction of all concerned, we now farther state, that their exclusion was on account of being erroneous in doctrine, maintaining, namely, the essential derivation and inferiority of the true and proper Deity of Christ and the Spirit: that faith in Christ is only a belief of historical facts, recorded in the Scriptures, rejecting and deriding what is commonly called christian experience; that there is no operation of the Spirit on the hearts of men, since the days of penticost [sic], &c.[74]

Thus Campbell's differences with the Baptists were because they insisted on bringing Calvinist presuppositions into their doctrine and making such presuppositions a test of fellowship with others. When Campbell resisted their views of Holy Spirit operation and pointed to the sole sufficiency of the Scriptures, the Baptists felt they had no recourse but to break fellowship. Campbell did not necessarily agree, but as he said, fellowship had to be a two-way street.

Walter Scott

In 1826 Walter Scott moved from Pittsburgh to Steubenville, Ohio, where he found three churches "struggling to restore original christian-

---

[73]*Ibid.*, p. 205.
[74]*Minutes of the Redstone Baptist Association*, 1830, p. 5.

ity,"[75] a Haldanean church, a Christian church of the Stone Movement, and a Reformed Baptist church of the Campbell Movement. Scott identified with the Haldanean church. But that same year Alexander Campbell, on his way to the annual meeting of the Mahoning Baptist Association, stopped off to see Scott. Campbell invited Scott to go with him to the meeting and Scott accepted. He was cordially received by the Mahoning Baptist Association and was invited to preach on Sunday morning. His text was from Matthew 11. His sermon made a deep impression on many in the audience, many even supposing it was Alexander Campbell that they had heard preach.[76]

The next year Campbell again swung through Steubenville on his way to the annual Mahoning meeting and invited Scott to accompany him. Scott did but was reluctant to do so, since he was not a member of the Mahoning Baptist Association and thought he might be wearing out his welcome. It turned out to be a momentous occasion for both Scott and the Association. For some time, the membership statistics for the Association had not been encouraging. For instance, in 1827 there were 16 member churches of the Association, but only 12 of them sent membership statistics. These indicate that in the previous year, there were 34 persons added by baptism, 14 added by letter, 14 dismissed (probably by letter, that is, transferred out), 13 excommunicated, and 4 who died, leaving a total membership for these 12 churches of 492.[77] This also meant that in the preceding year, these 12 churches had a total net growth of 16. This is not what could be called rampant church growth! In addition, 2 churches (Wellsburg and Hiram[78]), accounted for 20 of the baptisms, 5 of the "added by letter," but only 5 of the subtractions. This meant for the other 10 churches of the Association, there was a total net gain of -4. This is even worse church growth!

It was probably because of this situation that the Braceville church officially requested the Association "for an evangelical preacher to be employed to travel and teach among the churches." A committee was appointed to look into this request, and they recommended Walter Scott for the position.[79] To say the least, Scott was surprised by this

---

[75]The phrase is Walter Scott's, in *The Evangelist,* vol. 2, no. 4 (April, 1833), p. 93.

[76]Baxter, pp. 82-83.

[77]These statistics from the minutes of the Mahoning Baptist Association for 1827 can be found in several places, including A. S. Hayden's *Early History of the Disciples in the Western Reserve* (n.p., n.p.; originally published, 1875), p. 56.

[78]Garrison and DeGroot call these "the two churches that had gone farthest in 'reform,'" p. 187.

[79]Baxter, pp. 84-86.

appointment, but he did not object. He had just vacated the school he had begun in Steubenville in order to publish a magazine named *The Millennial Herald,* for which he already had a goodly number of subscribers. He now "immediately cut all other connections, abandoned my projected Editorship, disolved [sic] my academy; left my Church, left my family," and began evangelistic preaching.[80]

His first sermon he considered a failure. He preached it outside the bounds of the Association and got not a single response.[81] His message was new, different from the orthodoxy of the day. The people regarded him as a deluded enthusiast. Some people responded with pity, some with wonder, others with scorn. But Scott's convictions became even stronger that he was on the right path.[82]

Under these circumstances Scott came to New Lisbon on Sunday, November 18, 1827. He preached on the Good Confession of Peter from Matthew 16:16, "Thou art the Christ, the Son of the living God." Developing the Messiahship of Christ, he moved on to Peter's sermon on Pentecost and urged people to respond the same way three thousand of them did then—repent and be baptized for the remission of sins. One man in the back of the audience, William Amend, had come late to the service. In fact, he had missed most of the sermon, catching only the summary that Scott gave at the end. But it was enough to convince Amend. He came down the aisle and was baptized that same night.

Later Amend was asked about the circumstances of his response. He related that his Bible studying had convinced him that infant baptism was wrong and that proper New Testament baptism was by immersion. He had asked his Presbyterian pastor for immersion. The Presbyterian tried to talk him out of it but finally agreed to immerse him privately so as not to upset the remainder of the Presbyterian congregation. This was not good enough for Amend, who became convinced that immersion was for the remission of sins. Just a couple of days before he heard Scott preach, he had remarked to his wife that if he ever heard anyone give the invitation Peter gave in Acts 2:38, that was the invitation he would accept.[83] Scott preached it, Amend accepted it, and Scott got enough encouragement from it to continue the same method.

Scott soon developed a formula for the "plan of salvation." There are, he asserted, three things people must do, and three things that God has

---

[80]*The Evangelist,* vol. 1, no. 4 (April, 1832), p. 94.

[81]Stevenson suggests that this first sermon took place in Steubenville (p. 65), though he admits (footnote #7, p. 226) that this is only speculation on his part.

[82]Baxter, p. 103.

[83]*Ibid.,* pp. 106, 112-113.

already said he has done. A person: (1) believe on the evidence that Jesus is the Messiah; (2) repent of his sins and vow to sin no more; and (3) be baptized. God has already promised He will then: (1) remit sins; (2) give the gift of the Holy Spirit; and (3) bestow the gift of eternal life.[84] These last two suggested each other and often became bound up together. This brought the total to five elements, and they became Scott's famous "five-finger exercise."

One of Scott's favorite applications of this exercise was to ride into a village near the close of the day when the school was about to let out. When the students came streaming out, Scott would gather several together and teach them the "five-finger exercise"—the plan of salvation represented in faith, repentance, baptism, remission of sins, and the gift of the Holy Spirit and eternal life. Drilling this into the students, he sent them home to tell their parents that a man would be speaking at the schoolhouse that night on the five-finger plan of salvation. No one on the frontier had ever heard the message of salvation made that simple. So people came to hear the strange message from the unorthodox preacher. They brought their Bibles to prove him wrong. But Scott's sermon provided biblical reinforcement of every point, and the people, with their Bibles open before them, could not argue with the points made by the preacher. The result was that Scott was soon baptizing scores of people throughout northeastern Ohio.

When word reached the Campbells that Scott was baptizing so many, the Campbells reacted with concern about the rumors of this "hitherto unheard-of and soul-destroying heresy." Since Alexander had more or less "sponsored" Scott into the Mahoning Baptist Association, he felt responsible for Scott's teaching. He feared that perhaps Scott's zeal had gotten ahead of his knowledge, and that Scott in the process was perverting the gospel. Alexander sent Thomas over to northeastern Ohio in the spring of 1828 to check up on Scott. On April 9, 1828, Thomas wrote to his son indicating his approval and pleasure at what Scott had been accomplishing. He stated that he and his son had "spoken and published many things *correctly* concerning the ancient gospel" but that it was only now in the preaching of Scott that he saw "the direct exhibition and application of it."[85] Someone later made the observation that it was Thomas Campbell who restored the ancient authority; it was Alexander who restored the ancient order of things; but it was Scott who restored the ancient preaching.

---

[84]Garrison and DeGroot, pp. 187-188.
[85]Richardson, vol. 2, p. 219.

But not everyone was pleased with the new procedures. In Sharon, just across the state line in Pennsylvania, some of the Baptists could find no objections to what others were calling heresy. John McCleary and his son Hugh fellowshipped with some of these "Reformed Baptists," and soon heard themselves denounced as "Campbellites." To gain a full hearing of the new doctrines, Scott himself was invited to preach in the area; he came, preaching every night for three weeks. Numerous converts confessed their faith in the Savior and were immersed.

But when Scott left, the local Baptist church discovered that these new converts had failed to conform to the usages of the Baptists. They had not appeared before a church meeting and had not given a saving experience. The church decided these individuals could not become members of the church. But other Baptists were already members of the church and had accepted the new position. The regular Baptists attempted to drive out the new position. As a last resort, they sent for Thomas Campbell to try to alleviate the difficulties. For three weeks he tried to reconcile the two groups, but all in vain. The result was the creation of a new congregation in Sharon, soon numbering over 100 persons.[86]

When the Mahoning Baptist Association gathered for its annual meeting in 1828, it was an entirely different story from the previous year. Five new churches had been established in the Association, although four churches had left, apparently over disagreement with the doctrines of Scott/Campbell.[87] Some churches had doubled their membership. In 1827 the total membership for the association registered 492. In 1828 it registered 1004—it had increased by 512 in one year! The older churches in the Association had 307 baptisms, the new churches had 284, for a total of 591. The moderator of the meeting also mentioned that there had been at least that many more baptisms of individuals who did not come into Baptist churches of the Mahoning Baptist Association. Scott's arrangement to travel was continued for another year, and William Hayden was added as a second evangelist. Scott commented, "Give me my Bible, my head, and Bro. William Hayden and we will go out and convert the world."[88]

Further Troubles With Baptists

But there were increasing troubles with the regular Baptists. As already mentioned, the Redstone Baptist Association had tried to discredit

---

[86]Baxter, pp. 163-164; Stevenson, pp. 96-98.
[87]Stevenson, p. 98.
[88]*Ibid.*, pp. 98-102; Baxter, p. 174.

Campbell in 1823 but failed. However, they got rid of the Brush Run church in 1824, and four other churches in 1826. By 1829 they had halved their membership in the attempt to exorcise the Campbellite influence. Even within the Mahoning Baptist Association there was dissatisfaction. Four churches left because of the new evangelistic message of Walter Scott.

What the followers of Campbell had been experiencing within the Redstone and Mahoning Baptist Associations was matched by other followers in Kentucky. The well-known preacher, Raccoon John Smith, had charges presented against him in 1827 in the Franklin Association. Similar animosities were developing against Jacob Creath in the Elkhorn Association in the next year or so. Associations throughout Kentucky were ready to expunge the Campbellites.[89]

Other Baptists were beginning to pull together in the common cause against the new position. In 1829 the Beaver Baptist Association of Pennsylvania anathematized the entire Mahoning Baptist Association for their acceptance of the new position.[90] They said that "the Mahoning Association disbelieve and deny many of the doctrines of the Holy Scriptures."[91] This was made even more bitter by the fact that the four churches that had left Mahoning had joined the Beaver Baptist Association[92] and were the catalyst for much of this animosity.

Walter Scott, however, pointed out that some of this was simply sour grapes. The churches themselves seem to be mostly "rump" churches. For instance, the Baptist church in Youngstown was in decline when Scott visited it in 1828. For three weeks he worked among them, and then preached the "ancient gospel" and gathered a church together of about 150. But about sixteen of the old members of the church refused to accept the new members. Instead, they called themselves the Church of Youngstown and joined the Beaver Baptist Association. The same thing happened at Palmyra. Scott and William Hayden preached and built the church up to about 100 individuals. Then some broke off—Scott said somewhere between 11 and 20—reinstituted creeds and monthly meetings, and joined the Beaver Association.[93]

---

[89]Alonzo Willard Fortune, *The Disciples in Kentucky* (n.p.: The Christian Churches in Kentucky, 1932), pp. 79-94; John Augustus Williams, *Life of Elder John Smith* (Cincinnati: R. W. Carroll, 1870), pp. 199-350; P. Donan, *Memoir of Jacob Creath, Jr.* (Indianapolis: Religious Book Service., n.d.), pp. 88-91.

[90]*Christian Baptist*, vol. 7, no. 8 (March, 1830), p. 198.

[91]*Ibid.*, p. 200.

[92]*Minutes of the Redstone Baptist Association,* 1829, p. 3.

[93]*Christian Baptist,* vol. 7, no. 12 (Jul, 1830) p. 292ff.

The "Beaver Anathema" was adopted by numerous other associations as well. The Franklin Association in Kentucky adopted its sentiments, and before 1830 was out, so did most of the other Baptist associations in the state, including Boone's Creek, Bracken, Elkhorn, North District, Tate's Creek, Sulphur Fork, Goshen, and Long Run. Thus the Baptists continued to "clean house."

This raised the question again of Christian union, or—at least this time—the lack of it. Campbell took the offensive on this. He was not willing to sit back and absorb the accusations silently. In his typical bristling style, he wrote:

Who is making divisions and schisms? who is rending the peace of the churches? who are creating factions, swellings, and tumults? We who are willing to bear and forbear; or they who are anathematizing and attempting to excommunicate. Let the umpires decide the question. For my own part I am morally certain they who oppose us are unable to meet us on the Bible; they are unable to meet us before the public; and this I say, not as respects their talents, acquirements or general abilities, but as respects their systems. Thousands are convinced of this, and they might as well bark at the moon as to oppose us by bulls or anathemas. If there be a division, gentlemen, you will make it, not I; and the more you oppose us with the weights of your censure, like the palm tree, we will grow the faster. I am for peace, for union, for harmony, for co-operation with all good men. But I fear you not, if you will fling firebrands, arrows, and discords into the army of the faith you will repent it—not we. You will lose influence—not we. We court not persecution, but we disregard it—we fear nothing but error, and should you proceed to make divisions you will find that they will reach much farther than you are aware, and that the time is past when an anathema, from an association, will produce any other effect than contempt from some, and a smile from others.[94]

Thus Campbell has raised anew the question that has come up several times previously—how does one maintain unity in the face of division? Campbell at least is asserting that if there is division, it is because people are separating from *him*—not the other way around. Campbell thus maintains his commitment toward unity, whether others join him or not.

But it was becoming obvious by the end of the 1820s that the Baptists had gone beyond the point of tolerating the Campbellites. Redstone had excluded some; Beaver had excluded others; and now other Baptist associations throughout the country were joining ranks against Campbell. The identification of his followers with the Baptists was becoming

---

[94]*Ibid.*, vol. 7, no. 8, (March, 1830), p. 203.

increasingly tenuous. This became even more problematic as a result of the dissolution of the Mahoning Baptist Association.

Because of the Beaver Anathema and other such declarations against them, many members of the Mahoning Baptist Association brought up the question of the scripturality of such organizations. Campbell and others thought such associations were useful as long as they did not become church tribunals; since Mahoning had laid aside human standards of faith and practice, they saw no danger in its continued existence. But a majority of those present at the annual meeting in Austintown in 1830 were opposed to the continuance of the Association completely. John Henry offered the motion that "the Mahoning Association, as an advisory council, or an ecclesiastical tribunal, should cease to exist."[95]

Campbell did not agree. He was about to speak in favor of the Association when Walter Scott came over to him and begged him not to oppose the motion. He yielded and the motion passed unanimously.[96] Campbell later remarked that he

> was alarmed at the impassioned and hasty manner in which the association was, in a few minutes, dissolved. I then, and since contemplated that scene as a striking proof of the power of enthusiasm and of excitement, and as dangerous, too, even in ecclesiastical as well as in political affairs. Counsel and caution, argument and remonstrance were wholly in vain in such a crisis of affairs.—It would have been an imprudent sacrifice of influence to have done more than make a single remonstrance. But that remonstrance was quashed by the previous question, and the Regular Baptist Mahoning Association died of a moral apoplexy, in less than a quarter of an hour.[97]

Campbell did not oppose the motion,[98] but immediately thereafter he suggested that the brethren continue to meet annually for preaching, for mutual edification, and for hearing reports about the progress of the gospel. This also was unanimously approved.[99]

---

[95]Baxter, pp. 216-217.

[96]*Ibid.*, p. 217.

[97]*Millennial Harbinger,* (1849) p. 272.

[98]Campbell did not oppose the motion, but he obviously was not pleased with the decision. However, his comments at the time in the *Millennial Harbinger* put the best face on the situation. He stated that the first day of the meeting was spent praising God for the wonderful reports of the progress of the ancient gospel. Then "the next day, finding no business to transact, no queries to answer, nothing to do but to 'love, and wonder, and adore,' it was *unanimously* agreed that the Mahoning Association as 'an advisory council,' as 'an ecclesiastical tribunal,' exercising any supervision or jurisdiction over particular congregations, should never meet again" (*Millennial Harbinger, 1830, p. 415*).

[99]Hayden, p. 296; *Millennial Harbinger,* 1830, p. 415.

The decision to dissolve the Mahoning Baptist Association removed one of the remaining links between the Baptists and the followers of Campbell. As long as Mahoning existed, they could at least claim to be Baptists, whether other Baptists claimed them or not. Now, however, that could no longer be the case. Even when they were Baptists, these people were often called "Campbellites," or even "Scottites." Now, they were increasingly called "Disciples of Christ."[100]

Another challenge to the unity aspects of the movement came a couple of years earlier, at the 1828 meeting of the Mahoning Baptist Association. This had to do with Aylette Raines (1788-1881). Raines was born in Virginia, but he emigrated with his parents into Kentucky about 1811. He later moved into Indiana where he was converted to Universalism, the doctrine that everyone in the universe ultimately would be saved. According to this position, there might be a temporary hell, but not an eternal one. People might spend some time in torment until they were purged of their sins, but there would be no eternal torment. God was a loving Father and would not do that to any of His children. This doctrine was also known as "Restorationism," since it taught that ultimately everyone would be "restored" to God.

In 1828 Raines travelled to the Western Reserve and heard of Scott's preaching. Hearing a corrupted version of Scott's message, Raines decided to hear Scott for himself. He then simply concluded that Scott was preaching the plain biblical gospel. On the fourth hearing, Raines yielded to the invitation. He was still convinced that all men would eventually be saved. But Scott called this a *philosophy,* not part of original Christianity. Raines was still free to believe it, which he did.[101]

That same year, Raines attended the annual meeting of the Mahoning Baptist Association. During this session Alexander Campbell preached a sermon distinguishing knowledge, faith, and opinions. Knowledge, said Campbell, is based on personal experience; faith is acceptance of other people's experiences; and opinions are things that nobody has experienced. Campbell's point was that biblical faith was based on the preaching of the apostles, and we can all have unity on that faith. Opinions are private views held in the absence of biblical testimony. This way, there could be unity in faith while still having freedom of opinions.[102]

A test case for this soon came up in the person of Aylette Raines. One of the Baptist preachers present asked Raines if he still believed in

---

[100]Baxter, p. 217.

[101]Hayden, pp. 151-154.

[102]*Ibid.*, pp. 163-166. A. Campbell later developed this distinction in an article in the *Millennial Harbinger,* 1837, pp. 439-445.

Universalism. Some members of the Association intended to disfellowship him if he did.

> Rains [sic] arose, and in a very clear and forcible manner, and with all deference, declared that, when he obeyed the gospel, he had, as he thought, virtually renounced sectarianism, and did not expect that the disciples of Christ were to judge him for his private opinions. It was true, he said, that many of his former opinions remained. These opinions he did not wish to inculcate; but if he were asked to avow his private opinions concerning his former peculiarity, he must confess that he was substantially of the same opinion still.[103]

When the case was brought up for general discussion, Thomas Campbell defended Raines by saying he himself was still a Calvinist but he held it as an opinion, and he would not condemn Raines for his opinion of universalism. Alexander Campbell summarized again his views on the difference between faith and opinions, asserting Raines' views were his opinion. As long as Raines held them as his private property, he was in harmony with the principles of the reformation they were pleading. Campbell also asserted that if Raines were free to hold them as private opinions, he was sure Raines would give up such opinions in a short time. Walter Scott also spoke in Raines' defense. Then Alexander had Raines explain his views of the gospel. Raines stated "My Restorationism was a philosophy. . . . I would neither preach it nor contend for it, but would preach the whole gospel, and teach the whole truth of Christianity." When Campbell then asked if there was any law of Christ by which Raines could be condemned, the vote was in the negative by an overwhelming majority.[104]

The case of Raines is an interesting study in the context of harmonizing biblical faith with Christian unity. Raines held views about universal salvation that many thought to be contrary to biblical teaching. Could he be acknowledged as a Christian brother? Many felt he could not. But the views of the Campbells won the day. As matters turned out, it worked well. Raines himself stated, "I became a day and night preacher of the gospel, and my mind becoming absorbed in this vast work, the opinion faded, and in ten months was numbered with all my former errors."[105]

About a year and a half after the incident, Raines wrote Alexander Campbell an informative letter.

---

[103]*Millennial Harbinger,* 1830, p. 148.
[104]Hayden, pp. 168-169; Richardson, vol. 2, p. 245.
[105]Hayden, pp. 169-170.

I wish to inform you that my "Restorationist" sentiments have been slowly and imperceptibly erased from my mind, by the ministry of Paul and Peter, and some other illustrious preachers, with whose discourses and writing, I need not tell you, you seem to be intimately acquainted. After my immersion, I brought my mind, as much as I possibly could, like a blank surface, to the ministry of the New Institution—and by this means, I think, many characters of truth have been imprinted in my mind, which did not formerly exist there. I also consider myself as growing in grace, and in the knowledge of Jesus Christ, every day—and as I give myself wholly to the work of an evangelist, I have, within the last twelve months, been instrumental in disseminating the truth extensively, and in removing from many minds, some heavy masses of sectarian rubbish. The facts of the New Testament will conquer the world. They have conquered me, and are now conquering thousands of others. The reformation is progressing in almost all parts of the Western Country through which I have travelled, beyond my most sanguine expectations.

My former associates persecute me, I would say, most cruelly. I hope you will not permit them to prejudice your mind against me. I shall have many difficulties to encounter, in consequence of the evil circumstances of having once been a Universalist. I however, hope to rise above the opposition of my quondam brethren, and during the remainder of my days, to devote my energies, not to the building up of sectarian systems, but to the teaching of *the word.*[106]

Thus the principle of liberty in opinions not only saved a brother for the work, but it also allowed him the freedom to mature above his opinions. Unfortunately, the Restoration Movement would not always work out so positively. Sometimes the freedom was not extended; at other times the freedom did not lead to the abandonment of troublesome opinions.

---

[106]*Millennial Harbinger,* 1830, pp. 148-149.

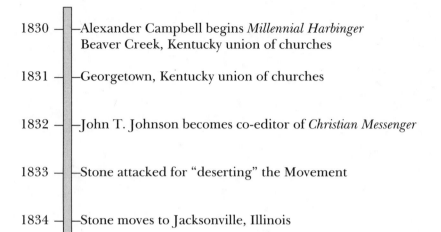

1830 — —Alexander Campbell begins *Millennial Harbinger*
Beaver Creek, Kentucky union of churches

1831 — —Georgetown, Kentucky union of churches

1832 — —John T. Johnson becomes co-editor of *Christian Messenger*

1833 — —Stone attacked for "deserting" the Movement

1834 — —Stone moves to Jacksonville, Illinois

Chapter 7

A Brotherhood United

The successful developments of the Stone and Campbell movements in the 1820s paved the way for the even more impressive accomplishments of the 1830s. The decade of the 1820s saw the Stone movement continue to expand, make contact with the Smith-Jones movement of the east, and number about 15,000 members. The same decade saw the Campbell movement grow among the Baptists and ultimately be evicted—but not before it had brought thousands of members out of a Baptist identity into a new awareness of reform.

Movement Toward Union

For Alexander Campbell in particular, the decade of the 1820s represented the *Christian Baptist,* a hard-hitting, iconoclastic paper. But by 1830, he no longer needed to circulate within a Baptist context. The Baptists had virtually disfellowshipped him, and there was no longer any value in having the term "Baptist" in the title of his paper. In addition, efforts were under way to designate Campbell's followers as "Christian Baptists," and he was unwilling for that kind of sectarian label to stick.[1] So he discontinued the first paper and began a second, the *Millennial Harbinger.*

The *Harbinger* was to be his major medium for the remainder of his life. It was a larger paper than the *Christian Baptist,* normally forty-eight pages per issue rather than the earlier twenty-four. In many ways it was the same Campbell—hard hitting, vitriolic, aggressive. But in other ways

---

[1]*Christian Baptist,* vol. 7, no. 12 (July, 1830), p. 309; see also *Millennial Harbinger,* 1839, p. 338.

it was a milder Campbell. Earlier Campbell had been an iconoclast, tearing down the traditions of denominationalism and pointing back to the purity of the apostolic church. Now, however, Campbell was in the process of building a movement, and this called for a more positive approach, a more positive paper. The title also reflected Campbell's optimism that the Restoration Movement would usher in the millennium.

Circulation figures are not available on the *Harbinger*, but it was undoubtedly the most significant of all the magazines published in the Movement in the nineteenth century. Through its pages Campbell continued to publish his viewpoints. In addition, it also became a medium of information. Numerous individuals wrote to Campbell reporting on the progress of the ideas of reformation in their individual localities. As a result, the pages of the *Harbinger* are filled with countless reports on churches established, revivals conducted, converts made, and local successes (and resistance) in particular areas. All this was simply one more reason why 1830 is such a significant year. Campbell and his followers had broken with the Baptists and were forging ahead on their own.

But if there was separation from the Baptists, there were overtures toward union in other directions. The followers of Stone and the followers of Campbell were beginning to become acquainted. Campbell and Stone first met in 1824 when Campbell made a swing through Kentucky following up contacts he had made the previous year in the Maccalla debate. Along the way Campbell stopped off in Georgetown and there met Stone. The two men immediately respected each other and became fast friends, though never as close as Campbell and Scott became. Nothing immediately came of this meeting, though it was a beginning contact.

Elsewhere, things happened more quickly, particularly in Ohio. There were Christians of the Stone movement in the Western Reserve within the boundaries of the Mahoning Baptist Association. In fact, three Christian Church ministers were present at the annual meeting in 1827 when Scott was hired as full-time evangelist. These three were all welcomed officially to the sittings of the Association and were appointed to the committee to discuss the selection of an evangelist.[2] When they learned of Scott's revolutionary but successful method of preaching, they also adopted it. One of these was Joseph Gaston.

Gaston was at Salem, Ohio, when Scott arrived to preach at the Baptist church there. The two had a face-off on open/closed communion, but Scott ignored the issue, saying it was silly and unprofitable. He instead

---

[2]Hayden, p. 56.

expounded the terms of the ancient gospel as he had arranged them, and Gaston responded with delight, taking him to another Christian minister in the area who also accepted Scott's methods. As Scott wrote, "Brother Gaston was the very first Christian minister who received the gospel after its restoration and who argued for the remission of sins by baptism."[3]

Scott's methods were raising concern not only among the Baptists, but also among the Christians, for the Stone movement had not become known for tying together baptism and remission of sins. Thus Elder J. E. Church of New Lisbon, Ohio, wrote to Stone on July 28, 1828:

> With Elder Walter Scott I fell in company a few days ago, at Fairfield, O. He has made an unusual number of disciples the past year. His method and manner are somewhat novel to me; but in consequence of his extraordinary success in reforming mankind, I feel no disposition at present to pronounce him heretical. He seems to suppose the Apostolical Gospel to consist of the five following particulars, viz: faith, repentance, baptism for the remission of sins, the gift of the Holy Ghost, and eternal life. Thus you see he baptizes the subject previous to the remission of his sins, or the receiving of the Holy Spirit. I would like to have your views upon the subject, either through the medium of the Christian Messenger, or by a private letter.

Stone immediately replied:

> Dear Bro:—You wish me to give my views on the manner of bro: Scott's baptizing the believing subjects prior to the remission of his sins, and of his receiving the Holy Spirit. I am sorry that I have not the back Nos. of the Messenger to send you, in which this subject is particularly treated. We have for some time since practised [sic] in this way throughout our country. Many of the most successful Baptists pursue the same course. I have no doubt but that it will become the universal practice, though vehemently opposed.[4]

Stone's acceptance of immersion for the remission of sins was a gradual thing. Immersion he had accepted as early as 1807. But tying the practice in with remission came later. In his autobiography, he tells of an incident where those mourning for their sins came down to the stand for

---

[3]*The Evangelist*, vol. 4, no. 2 (February, 1835), pp. 46-47. Scott's reference to Gaston as the *first* Christian minister to argue for remission of sins by baptism may have to be revised since this event obviously must have occurred no earlier than the fall of 1827. B. F. Hall relates that in the spring of 1826 he discovered this principle by reading Campbell's debate with Maccalla. See John I. Rogers (ed.), *Autobiography of Elder Samuel Rogers*, Fourth Edition (Cincinnati: The Standard Publishing Company, 1909), pp. 58-59. For this instance, see p. 158 of the present chapter.

[4]*Christian Messenger*, vol. 2, no. 11 (September, 1828), pp. 261-262.

prayer, but none seemed to be comforted. He was wondering why when he thought of the words of Peter at Pentecost—"Repent and be baptized for the remission of sins, and you shall receive the gift of the Holy Ghost." He arose, addressed the people in the same language and urged them to comply.[5]

Stone left his own account hanging there, but Sam Rogers describes a virtually identical incident about 1821. He added,

> When Brother Stone sat down, we were all completely confounded; and, for my part, though I said nothing, I thought our dear old brother was beside himself. The speech was a perfect damper upon the meeting; the people knew not what to make of it. On a few other occasions, Brother Stone repeated about the same language, with the same effect. At length, he concluded that the people were by no means prepared for this doctrine, and gave it up.[6]

Rogers also tells the story of B. F. Hall in a meeting in the fall of 1825 when numerous mourners could find no comfort. He concluded there was something wrong; they must not be preaching in the way the apostles and first evangelists did because the Scriptures do not tell of people who were convicted by the preaching but went away uncomforted. The next spring he was perusing a friend's library when he saw a copy of Campbell's debate with Maccalla. Leafing through, he came to Campbell's argument on the design of baptism.

> "I read it carefully from beginning to end; and I had scarcely concluded his masterly argument on that subject when I sprang to my feet, dropped the book on the floor, clapped my hands repeatedly together, and exclaimed: *'Eureka! Eureka!!* I have found it!! I have found it!!' And, thanks be to God, I had found it! I had found the keystone of the arch. It had been lost a long time. I had never seen it before—strange that I had not. But I had seen the vacant space in the arch a hundred times, and had some idea of the size and shape of it; and when I saw baptism as Mr. Campbell had presented it, I knew it would exactly fit and fill the vacant space. . . . From that day to this, I have never doubted that baptism is for the remission of sins. . . . Every brother I met on my way from Line Creek home I told of the grand discovery. . . .
>
> "In the summer of 1826, I met Elder B. W. Stone, and spoke of the idea to him. He told me that he had preached it early in the present century, and that it was like ice-water thrown on the audience; it chilled them, and came very near driving vital religion out of the church; and that, in consequence of its chilling effect, he had abandoned it altogether."[7]

---

[5]Rogers, *Biography of Stone*, p. 61.
[6]Rogers, *Autobiography of Samuel Rogers*, pp. 55-56.
[7]*Ibid.*, pp. 57-59.

The idea was soon spreading rapidly through the Stone movement. In 1829 James E. Matthews had a series of articles in the *Christian Messenger* on "The Gospel Plan of Saving Sinners." In the first article he stated:

> It is my design to prove, that the *ordinary* practice of the Apostles was to baptize a repenting sinner, in order to the remission of his sins, and to the receiving of the Holy Ghost; and as they were under the guidance of the Spirit, they doubtless acted correctly. The plan on which they acted, must therefore be the plan of Heaven; and their *example* is certainly a sufficient warrant for our *practice*.[8]

So many similarities were becoming known between the Christians and the Disciples that people began to ask some hard questions. Stone relates one that came to him in 1829:

> Not many days ago I was asked by a worthy Baptist brother this important question: Why do not you, as a people, and the New Testament Baptists unite as one people? By the *New Testament Baptists*, he meant those who reject all human creeds as authoritative, and who are generally disposed to receive the name *Christian* to the rejection of all others. I answered briefly his question, but promised to give him a full answer in the Messenger. This pledge I will now redeem.
>
> Ans.—I know of no reason, according to the Scripture, why all *Christians* of every name should not unite as one people. The New Testament enjoins it upon all in the most solemn and express terms. . . . They may differ in opinion of some of the truths of God; but where these opinions do not lead to irreligion, we are to exercise the grace of forbearance. . . .
>
> The New Testament reformers among the Baptists have generally acted the part which we approve. They have rejected all party names and have taken the denomination, *Christian;* so have we. They allow each other to read the Bible, and judge of its meaning for themselves; so do we. They will not bind each other to believe certain dogmas as terms of fellowship; nor do we. In fact, if there is a difference between us, we know it not. We have nothing in us to prevent a union and if they have nothing in them in opposition to it, we are in spirit one. May God strengthen the cords of Christian union.[9]

Similarities and Differences

Stone had said that he knew of no difference between his followers and those of Campbell. In fact, there were differences, and he did know of them. What he meant was that there were no significant differences

---

[8]*Christian Messenger*, vol. 3, no. 6 (April, 1829), p. 126. Italics in original.
[9]*Ibid.*, no. 11 (September, 1829), pp. 261-262.

and none such as to prevent a union between the two groups. Some of the significant similarities would include the following:[10]

(1) Both groups were committed to the ideal of Christian union. The "Imprimis" of *The Last Will and Testament* and Proposition I of the *Declaration and Address* both underline how much each group was desirous of the unity of all Christians in the one body of Christ.

(2) Both groups accepted the Scriptures alone as the authoritative source of church doctrine and practice. This emphasis on "primitivism" pointed them back to the New Testament and its picture of the church. They constantly looked back to the New Testament as the only guide to faith and practice.

(3) Both groups held that Christ alone was the object of faith. Stone's dislike of the Westminster Confession, and the Campbells' views toward the Philadelphia Confession of Faith were well known. Both sides abandoned creeds and confessions, allowing significant liberty in the area of nonessentials.

(4) Although both Stone and the Campbells had come through a strong Calvinism, both had rejected the major Calvinistic emphases—predestination; limited atonement; and irresistible grace with its presupposition of the special, miraculous work of the Holy Spirit on the unregenerate heart of the unbeliever.

(5) Similarly, both groups preached a gospel that all men were free to believe. Although Stone had not had the background of Sandemanian thought regarding the nature of faith, he still had similar views. Both groups believed that God had already prepared the way for salvation, and it was up to the unbeliever to respond to the gospel message. The evangelistic methodology was different, but both groups believed that man had the free will to respond.

(6) Both practiced baptism by immersion. Furthermore, both groups accepted that it was for the remission of sins, although Stone's followers were not as firm on this as were the Campbells'.

(7) Both groups were opposed to the use of unscriptural and sectarian names as labels for their people. Stone's followers had been known as "Christians" ever since 1804. Campbell's followers had been called

---

[10]These similarities do not include a number of things that virtually all Christian groups would have—such things as the existence of God, the deity of Christ, the inspiration of Scripture, the virgin birth of Jesus, etc. All evangelical Christians believed these. But the list that follows isolates elements that the followers of Stone and Campbell had in common, even though these elements separated them from most other evangelical Christians. This list is strongly dependent upon Garrison and DeGroot, pp. 208-212.

Reformed Baptists, but increasingly were known as "Disciples of Christ," or simply "Disciples." The terms "Stoneite" and "Campbellite" were heard, but only from their opponents.

These similarities were significant, but there were also some significant differences. At the moment they did not carry great weight, although some of them became more troublesome in later years. The union sentiment, however, normally overcame most difficulties.

(1) Both groups were committed to the combined goals of Christian union and biblical authority, but each group had a slight emphasis on different parts. The Christian Churches tended to emphasize unity rather than biblical primitivism; the followers of Campbell were more emphatic on restoring the nature and order of the New Testament church than they were on restoring a larger measure of Christian unity. These twin goals are not necessarily mutually exclusive; but putting an emphasis on one rather than the other or even an equal emphasis made for some nuances of difference that came out in later developments. Indeed, this difference alone caused some of the other tensions.

(2) For instance, both groups wound up believing that baptism by immersion for remission of sins was the biblical pattern. But the Stone movement was never as insistent upon this as were the Campbells. In 1830 Stone commented on the Reformed Baptists:

> Their reformation, it is hoped, will eventuate in good to the world. They have rejected all creeds as authoritative but the Bible. Their great aim, professedly, is to unite the children of God in one body. The doctrine preached by them, and the object they profess to have in view, which is to unite all Christians in the spirit and truth of the New Testament, are, as far as we can judge, the very same that we have constantly preached and defended for nearly thirty years, and for which we have suffered reproach, persecution, and the loss of worldly goods. To the subject of baptism they appear to attach more importance than some of us are willing to admit; yet baptism, in order to the remission of sins and the gift of the Holy Spirit, when well guarded, has long been advocated, by some of us, as the truth. Yet none of us are disposed to make our notions of baptism, however well founded, a bar of christian fellowship. We acknowledge all to be brethren, who believe and obey the Saviour, and, who walking in the Spirit, bear his holy image; yet, in the meekness of Christ, we labor to convince such of their duty in submitting to every ordinance of the Lord. . . . I entertain no doubt, but that, in coming years, immersion, on the profession of faith, will universally obtain in the church of Christ on earth.[11]

---

[11]*Christian Messenger*, vol. 4, no. 9 (August, 1830), pp. 200-201.

Yet Campbell chided Stone for contending for the *theory* of immersion for the remission of sins, while giving it up in *practice*.[12] Stone admitted his

> inconsistency, in receiving into the kingdom by immersion, and yet admitting the unimmersed, to the blessings of the kingdom. This we have long felt, and acknowledge it a difficulty, we are unable to solve to our satisfaction. When we consult our former experience, and the experience of thousands, our present feelings towards the pious unimmersed, the force of education and example, we are strongly impelled to acknowledge them brethren, and admit them with us, to the blessings of the kingdom. But when we are asked for our divine authority, from the New Testament, we have none that can fully satisfy our own minds. In this state our minds have labored, and are yet laboring.[13]

The question of baptism and various ancillary applications continued to disturb the movement for a long time into the future.

(3) The Christians had more of a sense of clergy than did the Reformed Baptists. References to their leaders always distinguished between "elders" (which meant ordained ministers) and "unordained preachers." The Campbell movement made no such distinction either in terms of function or of authority.

(4) The evangelism of the Christians was rooted in the revivalism of the frontier camp meetings. For a long time, the Stone Movement still used the method of the "anxious seat," or the "mourning bench"—having people come down to the front of the congregation and pray for their sins, with others kneeling around them, helping them to "pray through" to an experience of conversion and being forgiven. The Campbell Movement, particularly after the development of Scott's "five finger exercise," had a much more rational approach both to preaching and the conversion process. For them, conversion was more of an intellectual process—accepting the evidence about Christ, believing in Him, and then mentally deciding for Him. There was less emotionalism, more appeal to rational thought processes.

The two movements had much the same content, but the methodology was quite different. Unfortunately, the method of the Christians seemed to continue frontier Calvinism and its need for a conversion experience. The method of the Reformed Baptists tended to make conversion seem like simply an intellectual exercise, purely rational, without any Spirit-filled joy. Adding Scott's presentation of baptism by immersion for remission of sins convinced many outsiders that the followers of

---

[12]*Millennial Harbinger*, 1830, p. 372.
[13]*Christian Messenger*, vol. 4, no. 12 (December, 1830), p. 275.

Campbell had a materialistic, unspiritual, prayerless religion, centered in a mechanical dunking in water. This was an unfair criticism, although many of the Campbell movement preached in such a way as to support this observation. That is why later so many will conclude that Campbell and his group believed in "water regeneration," or "baptismal regeneration."

(5) Ever since the Brush Run church was organized in May of 1811, the Campbells had observed weekly communion. The Stone Movement did not insist upon weekly communion, although they were moving in this direction by the decade of the 1830s. In addition, the Stone movement had always practiced open communion, making communion available to all who wished to partake. The Reformed Baptists, reflecting their Baptist background, tended to be closed communion—making it available only to their church members. By 1843, in his debate with N. L. Rice, Alexander Campbell commented that by that time the practice of closed communion among his followers was very much on the way out, although some churches were still in it. These differences in communion practice between the two could have caused some difficult disagreement, but they never became bones of contention. In time, harmony and uniformity eliminated any problems.

(6) Stone still had trouble with the Trinity. Beginning with his studies for his preaching license back in North Carolina, Stone was unable to accept the classical view of the Trinity as stated in the Westminster Confession of Faith. Although he denied he was a Unitarian, an Arian, or a Socinian, he did in fact have a subordinationist view of Christ. He believed that Christ was not God, but the Son of God. He denied Arianism because it seemed that Arius denied the divinity of Christ. He accepted the divinity of Christ, but not His deity—that is, Christ is divine, but not God. He rejected the terms "eternal Son" and "eternally begotten" because he could not find them in the Bible. He believed in the pre-existence of Christ, but, like Arius, he thought Christ had a beginning.[14] Although Campbell also disliked the term "Trinity" because it was unscriptural, Campbell did accept the idea; Campbell was strictly Trinitarian in his thinking, though not orthodox in his vocabulary.

(7) Stone also had doubts about the orthodox understanding of the atonement. He refused to accept the idea of the death of Christ as a substitutionary sacrifice—that Jesus died in man's place. He believed that God's mercy, grace, and forgiveness were such that He did not need to be

---

[14]A good treatment of Stone's views on this topic is found in West, pp. 83-87.

satisfied with a blood sacrifice in order to forgive men.[15] He denied that the blood of Christ had any effect upon God.[16] His views are much more in line with what is called the "moral influence theory"—Christ's death has an effect on us because it demonstrates His great love for us.[17] Stone understood the word "atonement" to mean "reconciliation," in that "atone" means "at one," or "reconcile."[18] Campbell's views, again, are much more along the standard orthodox understanding of a vicarious, or substitutionary atonement.[19] Stone regretted much of this controversy over atonement because so much of it was speculation. He pointed out that so much of the vocabulary used in the controversy consisted of unbiblical words. Stone wanted to use only the words of Scripture, and asked others to do the same, with neither using the issue as a bar to fellowship.

> I have learned to my astonishment, that I am accused of speculating again on the doctrine of atonement, in my letters to brother T. Campbell, as published in the Messenger. I must be blind, if speculation be found there; and I am tempted to say that the man is shrouded in the clouds of unauthorized tradition, who can find it there. Is it speculation, because it does not accord with preconceived opinions? Is it of such a serious nature, as to authorize any to refuse the hand of fellowship? If this be a good cause, where shall we end? I confess myself unspeakably ashamed to see men pleading for reformation, and the ancient gospel, yet going in direct opposition to the very first principles of them, by making opinions the cause of disunion, and non-fellowship. Such men I cannot but view as sectarians in disguise.[20]

(8) A further cause of disagreement was the name by which the various people were called. Ever since the appearance of Rice Haggard in Kentucky, the Stone Movement had been called "Christians." But Alexander Campbell did not like the term. Because the Smith-Jones Movement also used the same term, and because the Smith-Jones Movement was tinged with a good deal of Unitarianism, Campbell was convinced the term was tainted. He first wrote in 1830:

> As to the name *Christian*, I have always, since I knew any thing of christianity, given it the appropriation of my heart. It is a name which we can legitimately

---

[15]*Christian Messenger,* vol. 8, no. 7 (July, 1834), p. 209.

[16]*Ibid.,* vol. 8, no. 8 (August, 1833), p. 230.

[17]*Ibid.,* vol. 10, no. 4 (April, 1836), p. 50.

[18]*Ibid.,* vol. 6, no. 7 (July, 1832), p. 211.

[19]In 1840 Stone and Alexander Campbell carried on a lengthy discussion on the atonement through the pages of the *Christian Messenger* and the *Millennial Harbinger.*

[20]*Christian Messenger,* vol. 8, no. 8 (August, 1834), pp. 239-240.

assume. But unfortunately some have assumed it as a *name* only. Suppose, for example, that these reforming Baptists who contend for the ancient gospel and the ancient order of things, should assume to be called *Christians*, how would they be distinguished from those who call themselves *Christians*, who neither immerse for the remission of sins, show forth the Lord's death weekly, nor keep the institutions, manners, and customs of those called *"Christians first at Antioch?"* If our friends [the Smith-Jones Movement] who assume this good name, never had gone into a crusade in favor of opinions, nor had *views* of the Deity, and other abstractions which I need not name; and if they had given to their churches the institutions of christians, we should have rejoiced that the name *Christian* did not now designate a *sect*, instead of the body of Christ. As it is, however, we choose the name *Christian*, with all its abuses, and have not for many years ever called the particular congregations to which we belong by another name than *the Church of Christ*. But if any one shall suppose that the term *"Christian"* denotes a Unitarian, or Trinitarian, in its appropriated sense, we shall choose the *older* name, *"disciple;"* and recommend to all the brotherhood to be called not *"Christians,"* but *"the disciples of Christ."*[21]

In 1839 Campbell published in the *Millennial Harbinger* an article simply entitled, "Our Name," in which he teasingly went through a variety of possible names, but ended up with a choice between "Disciples" and "Christians."[22] A later article under the same name elicited four reasons why "Disciples" was a better name than "Christians." (1) It is more ancient. That is, the term "Christian" first comes in Acts 11:26; the earlier label is "disciples." (2) It is more descriptive. A stranger or alien might imagine that the term "Christian" might be a geographical reference like American, Canadian, Russian. "Disciple of Christ" is therefore more descriptive and definite. (3) It is more scriptural. The term "Christian" appears only twice in the book of Acts, and never does a disciple speak of himself or his brethren under that name. Yet the term "disciple" is often used in such a way. Therefore, this term is more scriptural and a more authoritative and divine designation. (4) It is more unappropriated. In referring to the Smith-Jones people in New York and New England, Campbell stated, "Unitarians, Arians, and sundry other newly risen sects abroad, are zealous for the name *Christian;* while we are the only people on earth fairly and indisputably in the use of the title *Disciples of Christ.*"[23]

This matter of the difference on the name, again, did not create any great difficulty at the time, although it has remained a troublesome and confusing matter ever since. Stone obviously preferred the name

---

[21]*Millennial Harbinger*, 1830, pp. 372-373. Italics in original.

[22]*Ibid.*, 1839, pp. 337-339.

[23]*Ibid.*, pp. 401-403.

STONE—CAMPBELL MOVEMENTS

A. Similarities
1. Committed to Christian unity
2. Accept the Scriptures alone as authoritative
3. Christ alone is the object of faith
4. Reject Calvinism
5. Man has free will
6. Baptism by immersion
7. Scriptural names

B. Differences
1. Difference in emphasis between unity/authority
2. Insistence on baptism for the remission of sins
3. Sense of clergy
4. Methodology of evangelism
5. Frequency of the Lord's Supper
6. Views of Trinity
7. Views of Atonement
8. Name

"Christian." Apparently, Thomas Campbell did the same.[24] But there was no doubt that in the mid-nineteenth century, the voice of Alexander Campbell was the largest single influence within the Restoration Movement. Campbell preferred the term "Disciples of Christ," and thus this name came to have equal use with the term "Christian." In terms of the nineteenth century, the terms "Christian Church," "Church of Christ," and "Disciples of Christ" are all equally interchangeable. In the late twentieth century, the terms all have significant nuances and distinctive applications, but it is inappropriate to read these modern nuances back into the nineteenth century.

Union Achieved

In spite of all the differences and because of all the similarities, it was perhaps inevitable that the two groups get together. Both were motivated by a desire for Christian unity on the basis of biblical teaching.

Instances of harmony and cooperation abounded even in the late

---

[24]Richardson, vol. 2, p. 371.

1820s. Christian Church ministers such as Joseph Gaston and James G. Mitchell travelled with Walter Scott in Ohio as they preached together. Ultimately congregations of the two groups also united, although the dating of this (late 1820s or early 1830s) is somewhat uncertain. Hayden refers to Gaston and Scott as having

> labored together with great zeal and overwhelming success; whole churches of the "New Lights" and of the Baptists, in Salem, New Lisbon, East Fairfield, Green, New Garden, Hanover, and Minerva, unloading the ship of the contraband wares of human tradition, became one people in the Lord and in his word.[25]

Further encouragement came from a letter dated November 25, 1830, from J. D. White of Georgetown, Ohio. He wrote Stone about the growth of the church in Georgetown, and also the dwindling spirit of sectarianism.

> We have the satisfaction of seeing some of our brethren and sisters of different denominations, (particularly the Reformed Baptists) commune with us. O that Christians would lay aside their creeds, disciplines, &c, and unite on the *broad* and *sure* foundation of the gospel. I believe there is as great a union of sentiment, and as much brotherly love and affection existing among us as any other people on earth; we have no creed to contract our love, bound our desires, or teach us to hate one another. But taking the New Testament for our rule of faith and practice; which (like its Divine Author) breathes nothing but universal love and benevolence, our minds, hearts, and souls, are made to expand, and our love to God and our fellow creatures pervades the whole earth.
>
> Christian Union is the burthen [sic] of almost every prayer, the theme of conversation, it is mingled in their songs of praise, and the subject of frequent meditation with the members of the church of Christ, with whom I am acquainted in this state. O that all Christians would assert their right of loving and uniting with each other, and that preachers would no longer labor to divide and separate those for whose union our Saviour when on earth prayed. I believe that the Christians, and the Reformers among the Baptist brethren, would unite in many places were it not for the preachers.[26]

A similar encouragement came from Rush County, Indiana from John Longley, dated December 24, 1831. "The Reforming Baptists and we,

---

[25]Hayden, p. 85. Dean Mills, *Union on the King's Highway: The Campbell-Stone Heritage of Unity* (Joplin, Missouri: College Press Publishing Company, 1987) in pp. 78 ff. refers to a number of such union efforts. His research and documentation on the topic of union in the context of the 1820s and 1830s in the Movement makes this book a treasure trove of information and detail. It is a rich and useful compilation on the topic.

[26]*Christian Messenger*, vol. 5, no. 1 (January, 1831), pp. 22-23.

are all one here, and we hope that the dispute between you and Brother Campbell about names and priority will forever cease, and that you go on united to reform the world."[27]

This reference to a dispute between Stone and Campbell on names and priority has to do with some editorial exchanges between the *Christian Messenger* and the *Millennial Harbinger* that developed in the fall of 1830. It was begun by Stone with an editorial entitled "Union."

> The question is going the round of society, and is often proposed to us, Why are not you and the Reformed Baptists, one people? or, Why are you not united? We have uniformly answered; In spirit we are united, and that no reason existed on our side to prevent the union in form.[28]

Stone went on to point out that two problems had developed: the Reformed Baptists objected that the Stone Christians had fellowship and communed with unimmersed persons, and Campbell had raised questions about the use of the name "Christian," preferring instead the label, "disciple of Christ." Stone observed that he and his followers had been fighting sectarianism for thirty years; this is the basis for the sniping about "priority."

In reply Alexander Campbell quoted Stone's entire editorial, followed by a seven-page response of his own. In it Campbell observed that it was not sufficient to attack sects, creeds, confessions, councils, and human dogmas. Many persons both in Europe and America had done the same over the previous two centuries and even before Luther. What was important, Campbell insisted, was "the ancient gospel and the ancient order of things," for this is what distinguished his reformation from all other causes in both Europe and America since the great apostasy.

> We might be honored much by a union formal and public, with a society so large and so respectable as the Christian denomination; but if our union with them, though so advantageous to us, would merge "the ancient gospel and the ancient order of things" in the long vexed question of simple anti-trinitarianism, anti-creedism, or anti-sectarianism, I should be ashamed of myself in the presence of him whose *"well done, good and faithful servant,"* is worth the universe to me.[29]

In spite of this distinction, however, Campbell stated:

---

[27]*Ibid.*, vol. 6, no. 1 (January, 1832), pp. 28-29.
[28]*Ibid.*, vol. 5, no. 8 (August, 1831), p. 180. The entire editorial continues to p. 185.
[29]*Millennial Harbinger*, 1831, p. 391.

We have very high respect for him [Stone] and the brethren who are with him. Many of them with whom we are acquainted we love as brethren; and we can, in all good conscience, unite with them, in spirit and form, in public or in private, in all acts of social worship.[30]

Stone then quoted all of Campbell's remarks in the *Christian Messenger,* and added eight pages of response of his own. He confessed his uncertainty as to the distinction Campbell was trying to make between his [Campbell's] cause and Stone's.

As to the ancient order of things, both we and the Reformers have agreed that sectarianism, authoritative creeds, and ecclesiastical councils, composed of uninspired men, are contrary to this order, and therefore rejected, at least in word, by us both, as not being divinely warranted.—We both immerse penitent believers.—Some, not all, of both classes contend for, and practise [sic] weekly communion.—They differ from us in rejecting from communion the unimmersed, and in the ordination of elders or bishops. To what particular order brother C. may refer, as plead by the Reformers *alone,* I should be glad to know; and if indeed it is proved to be the ancient order, nothing shall prevent me from falling into it.[31]

Yet earlier in his comments, Stone observed:

I confess I have sincerely wished that the Christians and Reformers, who are united in spirit, should also be united in form. I know of neighborhoods where some of each class reside, who remain scattered and disunited, and who from their local circumstances and paucity of numbers, could not form two respectable congregations, yet united could be a respectable church. I have thought it better that they *formally* unite, and worship together as a congregation of brethren.[32]

Campbell replied by observing that there were some "unkind insinuations" in Stone's remarks that prevented his full reply. Yet he also observed that in Kentucky and the Southwest generally

many of the congregations called "Christians" are just as sound in the faith of Jesus as the only begotten son of God, in the plain import of these terms, as any congregations with which I am acquainted. With all such, I as an individual, am united, and would rejoice in seeing all the immersed disciples of the Son of God, called "Christians," and walking in all the commandments of the Lord and Saviour. We plead for the union, communion, and co-operation of

---

[30]*Ibid.,* p. 395.

[31]*Christian Messenger,* vol. 5, no. 11 (November, 1831), p. 251. Stone's comments run from p. 248 to p. 257.

[32]*Ibid.,* p. 249.

all such; and wherever there are in any vicinity a remnant of those who keep the commandments of Jesus, whatever may have been their former designation, they ought to rally under Jesus and the Apostles, and bury all dissensions about such unprofitable questions as those long vexed questions about trinity, atonement, depravity, election, effectual calling, &c. If it had not been for this most unreasonable war about Arian or Unitarian orthodoxy, the name *Christian* would not have been traduced in the land as it has been, and much might have been done to promote the union of all who love our Lord Jesus Christ sincerely. With all such I am united in heart and in hand, and with all such I will, with the help of God, co-operate in any measure which can conduce to the furtherance of the gospel of Christ. Indeed, I feel myself as an individual (for here I only speak for myself) at perfect liberty to unite in every act of religious worship with any sect of Baptists in America—not as a *sect*, but as disciples of Jesus Christ, if their moral and christian behaviour be compatible with the gospel, irrespective of all their speculations upon the untaught questions in their creeds.[33]

Through all of this exchange, it is obvious that although Stone and Campbell had some reservations about some nuances of closed communion and the name "Christian," they were still breathing much the same air of concern for Christian unity and charity. Specifically, it was Campbell's concern that the New England Christians (Smith-Jones Movement) had identified the label "Christian" with Unitarianism that gave him pause. Were this not a factor, he seemed to have no objection with the sentiments of Stone toward union. He specifically mentioned that the Christians in Kentucky were advancing in the Christian Scriptures and losing sectarian peculiarities; but those in New York and New England were not. He regretted that these Eastern Christians invested the name "Christian" with these speculations about the *modus* of the divine existence—Unitarianism.[34]

In spite of the sparring between Stone and Campbell, the continuing cooperation between their followers inevitably led to more than just unity in effort. The first consolidated congregation apparently formed late in the year 1830. In a letter dated Monticello, Kentucky, December 16, 1830, Elder Adam Vickrey reported:

A union has been lately formed between the separate Baptist Church and the Christian Church, at the Beaver Creek Meeting-house. The former have taken the name *Christian*; they have united on the word of God, and agreed to have no other rule but what is found written in that Book.[35]

---

[33]*Millennial Harbinger*, 1831, p. 558.
[34]*Ibid.*, pp. 557-558.
[35]*Ibid.*, 1831, p. 37.

In his history of the Disciples in Kentucky, A. W. Fortune called attention to the Millersburg Christian Church, which was organized on the fourth Lord's Day in April, 1831, by the union of the local Christian Church and the Church of the Reformers. According to the church's early record book, to which Fortune had access, B. W. Stone had constituted a church in Millersburg in 1820 and a church of the "Reformers" had been formed by Robert M. Baston. According to the record book,

> It was the practice of the brethren forming the two congregations to commune together at their several meetings, and finally, finding themselves to be one so far as faith and practice were concerned, they agreed to meet together without regard to difference of opinion, acknowledging no name but that of Christian, and no creed but the Bible. The result of these joint meetings was a union into one congregation in the year 1831, at which meeting they pledged themselves to each other not to indulge in speculations to the wounding of each other, but to regard the gospel as the power of God for salvation to all who believe and obey it.[36]

The record went on to say, "This was the first union so far as we know or believe that had taken place between the 'Christians' and those called at that time 'Reformers.'"[37] Obviously this is not true in light of the experience at Beaver Creek several months previously.

Although priority of time must therefore go to this Beaver Creek church, the priority of significance centers in Georgetown, Kentucky. It was here that two churches came together representing the larger pattern that emerged within the Stone and Campbell Movements. A central figure is that of John T. Johnson.[38] He was born near Georgetown in 1788 of Baptist parents. He served in the War of 1812, was elected several times to the Kentucky legislature, and in 1820 was elected to Congress. His brother, Richard M. Johnson, was Vice President of the United States under President Martin Van Buren. In 1829 he began to examine the teachings of Campbell and was soon convinced.

However, this brought consternation into his home church at Great Crossings, just outside Georgetown, so he withdrew in February 1831 with two others and formed a new church. Their first meeting led to three more added by baptism, and Johnson quit his lucrative law practice to preach

---

[36]Fortune, *The Disciples in Kentucky*, pp. 115-116.

[37]*Ibid.*, p. 116.

[38]The classic biography is John Rogers, *The Biography of Elder J. T. Johnson* (Cincinnati: Published for the Author, 1861). A useful brief sketch is in John W. Wade (ed.), *Pioneers of the Restoration Movement* (Cincinnati: The Standard Publishing Company, 1966), pp. 44-48.

the gospel.[39] Raccoon John Smith came over in November to preach a meeting. By that time, the congregation numbered forty members.[40]

It was also through this time period that Johnson became well acquainted with neighboring B. W. Stone, preaching and editing his magazine in Georgetown, just a couple of miles away. In the fall of 1831 (in January of 1832, the editors of the *Christian Messenger* referred to it as "a few months ago"), the Reforming Baptists and the Christians in and around Georgetown agreed to meet and worship together. They agreed to have a four-day meeting at Georgetown on Christmas, and a similar meeting in Lexington over New Year's. These meetings changed the history of the Campbell and Stone Movements.

The meeting at Georgetown was first, obviously, but it was the meeting at Lexington a week later that received more historical attention.[41] On Saturday, December 31, 1831, a multitude of Disciples and Christians came together at the Hill Street Christian Church in Lexington. It was arranged that one man from each group should deliver an address, plainly setting forth, from his own perspective, the scriptural ground of union among the people of Christ. Raccoon John Smith was selected by the Disciples, Stone by the Christians. Stone suggested that Smith go first, and Smith then delivered the most significant sermon of his life.

He pointed out that God had only one people on earth. He had given them only one Book, and in it He exhorted them to be one family. A union, then, of God's people on the one Book must be practicable. It was God's will that His people be united; such a union, then, must be desirable.

But, Smith acknowledged, there could never be union on abstruse or speculative matters. He encouraged people to speak on such topics only in the language of inspiration. Therefore a person could quote "My Father is greater than I" without speculating on the inferiority of the Son. He could also quote, "Being in the form of God, he thought it not robbery to be equal with God," without speculating on the consubstantial nature of the Father and the Son. The Gospel is a system of facts, commands, and promises; the deductions and inferences from them are not a part of the ancient Gospel.

There is only one faith, Smith contended, but there may be ten thousand opinions. If Christians are to be united, they must be one in faith, not in opinion. He closed his message by stating,

---

[39]Rogers, *The Biography of Elder J. T. Johnson,* p. 22.

[40]*Millennial Harbinger,* 1832, p. 29.

[41]The account following is drawn largely from the classic biography of Raccoon John Smith, Williams, *Life of Elder John Smith,* pp. 369-378.

Let us, then, my brethren, be no longer Campbellites or Stoneites, New Lights or Old Lights, or any other kind of *lights*, but let us all come to the Bible, and to the Bible alone, as the only book in the world that can give us all the Light we need.[42]

Stone then came to the front and acknowledged that the continual existence of controversies in the church proves that Christians can never be one in their speculations. He also admitted that he had once engaged in numerous speculations, but he now affirmed that such speculations should never be taken into the pulpit.

> When compelled to speak of them at all, we should do so in the words of inspiration.
>
> I have not one objection to the ground laid down by him [Smith] as the true scriptural basis of union among the people of God; and I am willing to give him, now and here, my hand.[43]

He then turned to Smith extending his hand. Smith grasped it "full of the honest pledges of fellowship, and the union was virtually accomplished!" They proposed to the others in the building that any who felt willing to unite on these principles should express that willingness by giving one another the hand of fellowship. Hands and hearts were thus joined in mutual accord; a song was taken up, confirming the union. Next day, Sunday, they broke bread together and again pledged brotherly love to one another.[44]

Williams insists that this union of Christians and Disciples was not a surrender of one party to the other.

> It was an equal and mutual pledge and resolution to meet on the Bible as on common ground, and to preach the Gospel rather than to propagate opinions. The brethren of Stone did not join Alexander Campbell as their leader, nor did the brethren of Campbell join Barton W. Stone as their leader; but each, having already taken Jesus the Christ as their only Leader, in love and liberty became one body; not Stoneites, or Campbellites; nor Christians, or Disciples, distinctively as such; but Christians, Disciples, saints, brethren, and children of the same Father, who is God over all, and in all.[45]

---

[42]Williams, pp. 372-373.

[43]Ibid, p. 373.

[44]*Ibid.* Another contemporary account of the union meeting and its result is a letter written by George W. Elley, from Nicholasville, Kentucky, dated January 17, 1832, printed in Walter Scott's new magazine printed in Cincinnati, *The Evangelist,* vol. 1, no. 2 (February, 1832), pp. 30-31.

[45]Williams, p. 374.

Several things happened as a direct result of these two unity meetings in Georgetown and Lexington. For one thing, the congregations in Georgetown did in fact unite. A couple of years later, Stone recorded this experience.

> In Georgetown, (Ky.) and its vicinity, there was a large church of *Christians* to whom I was minister.—In the neighborhood was also a church of those, called *Reformers*. Of which church John T. Johnson was the minister. We worshipped separately for some time, till we became better acquainted. We then found that we stood on the same foundation, the Bible alone, and were aiming at the same end, the salvation of our souls, and of the souls of others. They had imbibed the popular prejudices against us, and we had indulged in the same against them. We began to worship together; this produced love; love destroyed our prejudices; and union was the result.[46]

A second result was that Stone took Johnson on as a coeditor of his monthly magazine, the *Christian Messenger*.[47] The leading editorial of the January, 1832, issue of the magazine was written by Johnson. This was followed by a two-page article signed simply "Editors," reporting on the Georgetown and Lexington meetings. Significantly, the article is entitled, "Union of Christians." For the next three years, Johnson coedited the *Christian Messenger*, until Stone left Kentucky and moved to Illinois.

In his initial editorial, Johnson pledged

> the exertion of my humble powers in clearing away the cob-webs of speculation—in suppressing conjecture—in discarding from religion all the traditions and philosophy of men—and in enforcing the indispensable necessity of an immediate return to the word of God.[48]

---

[46]*Christian Messenger*, vol. 9, no. 2 (February, 1835), p. 43. Italics in original.

[47]Since the unity meeting took place at Georgetown on December 24-28, and at Lexington December 31-January 3, and since Johnson was installed as the co-editor of the *Christian Messenger* by January, it is hard to believe that the decision to add Johnson was not made until or after these meetings. It is almost automatic that for this to be in place by the January issue, the decision was made even before the unity meetings occurred. This supposition is reinforced by a comment in John Rogers' autobiography, "This arrangement was made in the close of 1831" [John Rogers, *The Life and Times of John Rogers, 1800-1867, of Carlisle, Kentucky*, transcribed by Virginia M. Bell and abridged by Roscoe M. Pierson and Richard L. Harrison, Jr. (Lexington: Lexington Theological Seminary, 1984) (actually this is vol. 19, nos. 1 and 2 of *Lexington Theological Quarterly*, January-April, 1984), p. 84]. It is still possible that "in the close of 1831" could be in the last several days, but this seems unlikely.

[48]*Christian Messenger*, vol. 6, no. 1 (January, 1832), p. 4.

Johnson pleaded for the union of truth and practice, as did Christ in his intercessory prayer so that the world might believe.

> Let it be engraven on every Christian's mind, that he who does most to unite the followers of Jesus, favors most the conversion of the world—and he who does most in opposition to such union, does most in opposition to the will of the king, and against the conversion of the world.[49]

A third result of the unity meetings was that two men were designated to travel among the churches urging similar union on the grassroots level.

> To increase and consolidate this union, and to convince all of our sincerity, we, the Elders and brethren, have separated two Elders, John Smith and John Rogers, the first known, *formerly*, by the name of Reformer, the latter by the name Christian. These brethren are to ride together through all the churches, and to be equally supported by the united contributions of the churches of both descriptions; which contributions are to be deposited together with brother John T. Johnson, as treasurer and distributor.[50]

John Smith, however, had some initial difficulty. When he returned from the unity meetings, the elders from the Mount Sterling church came to his home to question him about uniting with the Christians. After a lengthy explanation, the congregation acquitted him of censure and cordially went with him into the union. The three other churches where he preached did the same thing.[51] Smith then felt free to travel with Rogers, which he did, covering a good deal of central Kentucky, from the Tennessee line up to the Ohio River. Rogers himself reported that "Bro. Smith & I occupied the evangelical field for *three successive years;* & I look back upon those years as among the happiest & most successful of my life."[52]

Apparently the congregations at Georgetown united with no difficulty, as did other congregations elsewhere. But the two churches at Lexington had more difficulty. In February H. C. Coon wrote to Alexander Campbell that things had broken down in the city. After several friendly interviews from committees of both congregations, they had decided on February 12 that on February 26 they would unite on the New Testament and take that alone as the guide in matters of faith and practice. Since

---

[49]*Ibid.*, p. 6.

[50]*Ibid.*, p. 7.

[51]Williams, pp. 379-380.

[52]Rogers, *The Life and Times of John Rogers, 1800-1867, of Carlisle, Kentucky* (Lexington: Lexington Theological Seminary, 1984), p. 84.

the Reformers did not have a building,[53] they met with the Christians on February 19 for worship and breaking bread. But instead of a harmonious unified act of worship, the meeting led to a breakup.

The problem had to do with choosing an elder for the combined congregations. It appeared that there was not a single individual in either congregation that met the divine directions for being an elder. Believing that no one but an ordained elder (by which they meant a minister) could administer the ordinances, the Christians wanted to hire an elder from a sister church to administer them. The Reformers considered this an indication of a hireling system, a matter of clerical authority, for it meant that one eldership was exercising authority over two or more churches; they simply would not countenance it. Thus on February 25, the two congregations agreed to dissolve their pledge of uniting on the 26th.[54]

Alexander Campbell agreed with their demurral, commenting that the New Testament never heard of one bishop over two or four churches. He chastised the Christians in Lexington for believing they could not receive "the emblems and memorials of the great sacrifice, unless consecrated and presented by the hands of one ordained by men to minister at the altar." He stated, "The New Testament, indeed, could not be a bond of union to those thus traditionized; for it knows no such usages."[55]

Thus the two bodies continued separately for a while longer. In July of 1835, T. M. Allen, preaching for the Christian Church in Lexington, proposed that they unite with the Disciples. The congregation "waived all prejudice and differences of opinion on the subject of order and clerical privilege—if indeed any such differences still remained—and not only consented to the union, but nobly presented it to the Disciples."[56] That fall B. F. Hall, holding a meeting for the church in the city, reported a brightening prospect and concluded, "The difficulties between the two parties are settled *finally.*"[57]

Yet not entirely. Two years later, there were still some problems about church order, specifically selection of an evangelist and the election of officers. Alexander Campbell himself happened to be in town in the spring of 1839 and formulated a compromise whereby the congregation would accept the decision of a majority of those present at announced congregational meetings.[58] Thus, *finally,* the congregations in Lexington

---

[53]Fortune, *The Disciples in Kentucky,* p. 120.
[54]*Millennial Harbinger,* 1832, pp. 191-192.
[55]*Ibid.,* pp. 193-194.
[56]Williams, p. 378.
[57]*Millennial Harbinger,* 1835, p. 567.
[58]*Ibid.,* 1839, pp. 378-379.

united peacefully and became the seedbed for the future growth of the Restoration Movement in that city.

It is obvious that B. W. Stone held this whole issue of unity with the Disciples as a grand achievement. On the last page of his autobiography he wrote, "This union, irrespective of reproach, I view as the noblest act of my life."[59] Alexander Campbell was not so enthusiastic about it. His first awareness of the union seems to be in reflections upon information received from Fredericksburg, Virginia, that "the 'Campbellites' in Georgetown have united with the Arians." After making some pointed comments about the labels used, Campbell observed, "At all events, if they have united, it is upon this principle, that neither Campbell nor Arius shall be the bond of union nor the masters of their faith." Further,

> I can vouch for the fact, that in the case alluded to, those stigmatized 'Campbellites' have surrendered nothing, not a single truth that they either believed or taught; and they who have united with us from all parties have met us upon the ancient gospel and the ancient order of things.[60]

However, even Campbell's chief biographer commented that at first Campbell felt that the union "was prematurely effected."[61] In 1830 he was pleased to announce that Stone, editing the *Christian Messenger,* was directing his readers to the ancient order of things. He noted that Stone was advocating weekly communion and even seemed to endorse immersion for the remission of sins, though not as univocally as Campbell would have liked. He also noted, however, that many of the Christian preachers had in fact come out for immersion for the remission of sins. Further, "I was informed the other day, that in the commonwealth of Ohio, alone, there were 72 of those called Christian preachers who proclaim immersion for remission, and only 11 who opposed it."[62] It is possible that Campbell, seeing the Ohio Christian preachers adopt his viewpoints so readily, was hoping that in time the entire Christian movement would do the same. Having the union develop now might stop that process before the Christians had fully accepted Campbell's view of the ancient order of things. Thus he might view the Georgetown-Lexington development as "premature."

On the basis of a letter received from Georgetown dated November 13, 1831—that is, before the union meetings—Campbell commented about the congregation there under John T. Johnson's leadership:

---

[59]Rogers, *Biography of Stone,* p. 79.

[60]*Millennial Harbinger,* 1832, p. 36.

[61]Richardson, vol. 2, p. 387.

[62]*Millennial Harbinger,* 1830, pp. 473-474.

We rejoice to hear that the utmost harmony and christian love prevail, not only amongst the disciples composing this congregation, but between them and the disciples meeting under the *Christian* name in connexion [sic] with brother Stone in Georgetown, notwithstanding the sparrings between us editors. These brethren are endeavoring every Lord's day to keep the ordinances as they were delivered to them by the Holy Apostles. Hence they commemorate the Lord's death as often as his resurrection.[63]

A few months later, when Campbell received word of the union meetings and the appointment of Smith and Rogers as a travelling evangelistic team, he gave them his full endorsement.

With these two brethren we are well acquainted. They have both been preaching the ancient institutions for some years, and are very much devoted to the truth. They have both been very successful preachers. . . . We most cordially bid them God speed in their conjoint labors under the present arrangement.[64]

Referring to the union meeting itself, Campbell added.

From numerous letters received from Kentucky, we were pleased to learn that brethren Smith, Stone, Rogers, and others, at a public meeting in Lexington, Ky, on New-Year's day, renounced their former speculations, declaring that they were not conscious of having effected good, but rather evil, in their debates, preachings, writings, &c. about trinity, calvinism, arminianism, unitarianism, &c. and that they now go for the apostolic institutions. I say, then, from the present aspect of things, we have reason to thank God and take courage, and to bid these brethren God speed.[65]

Thus for all practical purposes, Campbell endorsed the union. There was some opposition to it, but most of the Christian Churches in Kentucky joined with the followers of Campbell. A few did not, and they seem to have been influenced by Christians in southwestern Ohio who were quite cool toward Campbell—namely Matthew Gardner and David Purviance. But in most other states, the union proceeded fairly well.

When B. W. Stone moved to Jacksonville, Illinois, in 1834, he discovered two churches—a Christian Church and a Reformers' church—worshipping in separate places. They each requested his involvement with their particular congregation, but he refused to join either of them until they united. He personally worked to accomplish it, and it was soon done.[66]

---

[63]*Ibid.*, 1832, p. 29.
[64]*Ibid.*, p. 138.
[65]*Ibid.*, p. 139.
[66]Rogers, *Biography of Stone*, p. 79.

Resistance

But if the union between the followers of Stone and Campbell went well in Kentucky, it was disastrous in Ohio. There were some accomplishments, of course, but except in northeastern Ohio where the immediate influence of Campbell and Scott was strong, the Christians and the Disciples usually did not get along.

The major sticking point was baptism—not immersion, for this the Christians in general accepted, but immersion for the remission of sins. David Purviance, the dean of Christian preachers in Ohio, never accepted this doctrine. Purviance's biographer, Levi Purviance, states, "He never believed in the doctrine of baptism, for the remission of sins, as published by A. Campbell, and others."[67] David Purviance himself stated that based on Acts 2:38, there were grounds for accepting this doctrine, but he believed this was insufficient because it was not the pattern in the household of Cornelius. "I conclude that if the design of baptism had been for remission, it would be found so expressed in the New Testament after the day of Pentecost, and more especially at the opening of the gospel to the Gentiles."[68]

Because of Campbell's strong identification with baptism for remission of sins, many of the Christians thought he believed in "baptismal regeneration," that it was the water itself that saved. They deplored this mechanical view of salvation and fought the "Campbellites" as a result. One man in Tazewell County, Illinois, reported, "We have many good brethren in Illinois. Campbellism they cannot swallow—they cannot drink so much water."[69]

Stone early faced the accusation that he had deserted his fellow Christians to join the Disciples. He and others hotly contended the rest of their lives that it was not a case of one faction "joining" the other, but a case of two streams blending into one, with neither left superior, or "having gone over to" or "become" the other. But it was a semantic problem that plagued Stone the remainder of his life. Exactly a year after the union meeting at Georgetown, a man wrote Stone:

Brother Stone:—I wish you to discontinue my No. of the Messenger. . . .
Brother Stone; I think the Messenger has forsaken the christian church, and I must withdraw my support. It appears to favor the errors of the Reformers who are splitting and destroying our churches, and it has left us to contend alone.

---

[67]Purviance, pp. 80-81.
[68]*Ibid.*, p. 130.
[69]*Christian Palladium,* vol. 6 (Nov. 15, 1837), p. 220.

Dear Brother; when McNemar and others left us, you stood by us; and when Marshall and Thompson turned to be our enemies, you pleaded our cause; but now, I fear, you are going to forsake us. May the Lord lead us into truth. Farewell.[70]

In a three-page reply, Stone asked how it was that he had left the Christian Church. He asked if he had ceased to advocate any of the elements that originally brought the body into being more than twenty-five years previously. He showed he preached even baptism for remission of sins almost twenty years earlier. He denied that he barred unimmersed persons from the Lord's table. The charge of admitting no unimmersed into the church he admitted, but he defended it on a New Testament basis, thus arguing it was part of their original commitment. Finally, he put the right accusation in the mouth of his discontinuing subscriber:

Ah! But you favor the errors of the Reformers, "who are splitting and destroying the churches, and you have left us to contend alone." This is the hardest rub, I suspect. Pray, brother, tell me what errors of the Reformers I favor; I really wish to know. I would prefer death to such a practice. The Reformers have, doubtless, errors, as fallible men—no doubt, we have also; and who, but his infallibility, can plead exemption from them? Your charge is too indefinite for my conviction. You may think I have seceded from the C. Church, because the Reformers and we, being on the same foundation, and agreeing to take the same name *Christian*, have united as one people. Is not this the very principle we have been pleading from the beginning? Is uniting with any people in this manner seceding from the church? In thus uniting, do we agree to unite with all the opinions and errors of each other? Have we not always had in our church, Calvinists, Arminians, Trinitarians and Unitarians? Have we by such union agreed to receive all their errors? No. In the great leading principles, or facts of the New Testament we agree, and cheerfully let each other have his opinions as private property. In vain may we expect a union on any system of opinions devised by the wisdom of man.

My dear brother, if a division ever take place among us, one part must secede from those principles on which we constituted. It would be worth attention to inquire, how do the Reformers split and destroy the Christian Church? Do they oppose the principles of our constitution, and the unity of the church? If so, they are wrong. It may be that you and others wrongfully oppose them. Let us my dear brother, examine this matter, and as an humble christian learn at the feet of Jesus.[71]

The New England Christians as a group felt the same way toward

[70]*Christian Messenger,* vol. 7, no. 1 (January, 1833), p. 3.
[71]*Ibid.,* p. 6.

Stone as did the brother quoted just earlier. They felt Stone had rejected them to go off and join the Campbellites. They believed that Campbell had made baptism to be the *sine qua non* of Christianity, and this they rejected.[72]

Some time later, Stone wrote again to the *Christian Palladium*, now edited by Joseph Marsh.

> I am grieved, Br. Marsh, at the course you and the Reformers (better known by you as the Campbellites) have taken, one against the other. Blame equally attaches to both parties. Had you both cultivated more of forbearance, and charity, the wide gulph between you might have disappeared. Christian union is my polar star. Here I stand as unmoved as the Allegany [sic] mountains, nor can any thing drive me hence. I have suggested the propriety of a convention of the eastern and western Christians, to meet at some middle point, and converse as brethren on the subjects of disunion. If we were to meet in a Christian spirit, I should not despair of union on the Bible. The Reformers are a precious people, but they have their failings like you and all. They are on some things too precise and dogmatic; and are rather disposed to urge measures too positively.[73]

When Stone a year later raised again the issue of union, Marsh replied that there could be no union because the western Christians had joined with the Disciples who practiced closed communion:

> Hence we are debarred from their communion. You being *one* with them we cannot of course unite with you unless we leave our *old ground*, follow your steps, and become *'Disciples,'* according to the rule laid down by Mr. Campbell. This we cannot do.[74]

At great length Stone replied and tried to reason away Marsh's fears. He pointed out that they had not "joined" the Disciples; they simply united with them on the basis of the Bible. Stone denied that there was any debarring from communion. He denied that he or any other western Christian had left "the old ground." "The old ground," Stone contended, was to stand for unity on the Bible, and this they still stood for, and they refused to move. They simply discovered some other people standing on the same ground. He also denied that they followed the rules of Campbell or anyone else. "My dear sir, we are not consummate blockheads to

---

[72]See the comments by Joseph Badger in *Christian Palladium*, vol. 6 (March 15, 1838), pp. 344-345.

[73]*Christian Palladium*, vol. 8 (January 15, 1840), p. 286.

[74]*Ibid.*, vol. 10 (May 1, 1841), pp. 9-10. Italics in original.

leave the word of God for rules laid down by brother Campbell or any other man."[75]

The results of this editorial exchange, however, were unsatisfactory. The eastern Christians continued to belabor the point that Campbell was a closed communionist, and if Stone was united with Campbell, he could not be united with them. Stone denied this repeatedly, but the conversations continued to go nowhere. The eastern Christians continued to contend that, by uniting with Campbell, Stone had deserted them.

The only good thing that emerged from this exchange was that the east finally admitted their disappointment over the lack of results of Badger's second visit in October of 1826.[76] Stone explained their discomfiture with Badger's presumption in calling for the conference to be in Cincinnati, as well as their reluctance to appoint delegates to union conferences that passed resolutions, etc.

The conversations pretty much died here, leaving hurt feelings all around. Basically Campbell wanted nothing to do with the eastern Christians because they seemed to be Unitarians. They wanted nothing to do with him because he seemed to be a water regenerationist. Actually he was not, but they refused to believe he was not. One also wonders why Campbell accepted union with Stone, even though Stone's view of Christ was not measurably different from the views of the eastern Christians. One wonders whether abrasive personalities were not more to blame than the alleged doctrinal issues.

But the result was to create significant difficulty for the Christians in Ohio. Many of the Ohio Christians preferred their connections with the eastern Christians and refused any involvement with the followers of Campbell. The eastern Christians certainly encouraged them in this.

The two leaders of the resistance in Ohio were David Purviance and Matthew Gardner. Purviance had been with Stone since the beginning difficulties with the Kentucky Presbyterians, but he felt he could not accept the emphasis on baptism represented in the Campbells. Gardner was probably the leading spokesman for the Ohio resistance to the union between the Christians and the Disciples. In Georgetown, Ohio, Gardner initiated an opposition to the Disciples' attempts to get the church there established "into a primitive order." A controversy over the selection of elders ultimately led to a splitting of the Georgetown congregation.[77]

---

[75]*Christian Messenger*, vol. 11, no. 10 (June, 1841), pp. 338-342.
[76]Discussed above, toward the end of Chapter Three, pp. 63-69.
[77]Mills, pp. 147-148.

Gardner had the reputation of being somewhat pugnacious and vituperative on the subject of Campbell and his Reformers. On the basis of several charges against him, Campbell questioned Gardner's moral character and referred to his trial before a packed ecclesiastical jury on September 5, 1835. Campbell claimed to have the documents in his possession and stated that "any honest and intelligent man" would not be satisfied with this trial and acquittal. He concluded by commenting, "I have nothing to say *of* him that is honorable."[78]

The bitterness of the contest led to several debates in Ohio. On June 9-10, 1839, in Jamestown, Matthew Gardner of the Christians and J. B. Lucas of the Disciples met on the proposition, "Faith, repentance and baptism precede the remission of sins under the gospel dispensation." Lucas affirmed and Gardner denied. The two men debated again in Lebanon in October, 1840. The next year, 1841, W. Belding of the Disciples and James Hayes of the Christians debated at Guilford and Hanover.[79]

Things were so bad in the Ohio Southern Conference (Gardner's home conference), that only Gardner and one other remained preachers in good standing by 1836. By 1837 a majority of the preachers had gone over to the Disciples, taking numerous churches with them. Both Georgetown and Bethel churches split, and only nine churches remained in the Conference.[80]

A similar story could be told of the Miami Conference, north of Cincinnati, the home conference of Purviance.[81] The Ohio Central Conference seemed to have the least problems. Only two counties on the edges reported problems with the Disciples. The Ohio Eastern Conference reported problems; geographically they were closer to Campbell and the Mahoning territory.[82]

The difficulties in Ohio led to bitter feelings. Many of the Ohio Christians felt Stone had deserted them; the eastern Christians encouraged this disaffection and polarization. David Purviance disagreed with Stone's decisions in this whole matter, but he concluded,

> I verily believe if all the preachers had been endued with as much of the wisdom that cometh from above as he possessed, a separation could not have been made. I have differed from him on some points, but while I have a spark

---

[78]*Millennial Harbinger,* 1835, pp. 571-572.
[79]Mills, p. 150.
[80]*Ibid.,* 152.
[81]*Ibid.,* p. 153.
[82]*Ibid.,* pp. 154-156.

of true religion, I cannot be separated in heart, from as good a man as Barton W. Stone.[83]

Stone was even more pointed in his comments on this unfortunate development. He acknowledged that there were differences between the Christians and the Disciples. He believed that Campbell

> was not sufficiently explicit on the influences of the Spirit, which led many honest Christians to think he denied them. Had he been as explicit then, as since, many honest souls would have been still with us, and would have greatly aided the good cause.[84]

Stone blamed "some irresponsible zealots among the Reformers" for publicly and zealously contending that sinners ought not to pray, nor even that professing Christians should pray for them (because, from the Reformers' viewpoint, this would seem to indicate that the Spirit could save such people before they came to have faith—a Calvinist position they strenuously resisted). They even rejected the idea that preachers should pray that God would help them in declaring the truth. Again, this seemed to ask for God to change the sinners' unregenerate mind rather than having the sinners' able intelligence apprehend the truth of the Word and then respond to it. The result was that many of the eastern Christians concluded that the Reformers' religious views were a "spirit-less, prayerless religion, and dangerous to the souls of men."

Stone's heart was breaking as he acknowledged these misunderstandings.

> I blame not the Christians for opposing such doctrines; but I do blame the more intelligent among them, that they did not labor to allay those prejudices of the people by teaching them the truth, and not to cherish them, as many of them did in their periodicals, and public preaching. Nor were they only blameable; some of the Reformers are equally worthy of blame, by rejecting the name *Christian*, as a family name, because the old Christians had taken it before them. At this, posterity will wonder, when they know that the sentiment was published in one of our most popular periodicals, and by one in the highest standing among us.[85]

In spite of disagreements with Campbell, however, Stone was agreed to disagree.

---

[83]Rogers, *Biography of Stone*, p. 129.
[84]*Ibid.*, p. 76.
[85]*Ibid.*, p. 78.

I will not say, there are no faults in brother Campbell; but that there are fewer, perhaps in him, than any man I know on earth; and over these few my love would throw a veil, and hide them from view forever. I am constrained, and willingly constrained to acknowledge him the greatest promoter of this reformation of any man living.[86]

Stone grieved over the misunderstandings and gave one of his strongest statements ever in print when he concluded:

This union, I have no doubt, would have been as easily effected in other States, as in Kentucky, had there not been a few ignorant, headstrong bigots on both sides, who were more influenced to retain and augment their party, than to save the world by uniting according to the prayer of Jesus.[87]

Stone concluded with the simple observation, "This union, irrespective of reproach, I view as the noblest act of my life."[88]

Indeed, this union represented the best intents of what the Restoration Movement is all about. Campbell and Stone were both committed to the authority of Scripture as well as the passion for unity within the body of Christ on earth. They had some differences in understanding several biblical issues, but none of the issues undermined the authority of Scripture. Instead, the passion for union overcame their differences and led to a lasting union. The members of the eastern Christians preferred their isolation rather than surrendering their differences, and so they never joined this union. Their choosing this sectarian response indicates their lesser priorities toward unity and biblical teachings. As Stone states so poignantly, "What could we do" when they found others also standing on the platform of biblical teaching? They united. History is grateful for this act of humility.

---

[86]*Ibid.*, p. 76.
[87]*Ibid.*, p. 78.
[88]*Ibid.*, p. 79.

1810	John Wright forms a Free-Will Baptist Church
1819	Wright and followers become just "Christians"
1826	Joseph Hostetler converts most of Dunkard association
1827	Absalom Littell converts majority of Silver Creek Baptist Association John Wright and Dunkards unite
1828	Wright unites with "New Light" Christians
1830	Sidney Rigdon joins Mormons
1836	Bacon College begun
1837	Campbell denounces John Thomas "Lunenburg Letter" in the *Millennial Harbinger*
1839	Indiana state meeting
1840	Bethany College begun
1841	Union meeting in Lexington
1845	American Christian Bible Society organized in Cincinnati
1849	General Convention held in Cincinnati American Christian Missionary Society organized
1850	James T. Barclay goes out as first missionary
1852	Jesse B. Ferguson defends "post mortem" gospel
1855	Tolbert Fanning and William Lipscomb begin *Gospel Advocate*
1859	Midway, Kentucky church uses musical instrument to aid congregational singing

Chapter 8

Unity Challenged

The union between the followers of Stone and Campbell seemed to represent the best of what the Restoration Movement stood for—the unity of Christians standing solely on the basis of biblical teaching. One result was to stimulate further growth of the Movement. Statistics are often difficult to come by for the early nineteenth century, but Joseph Badger on his trip east in 1826 reported that the Stone Movement numbered about 15,000. Historians Garrison and DeGroot have estimated that the Campbell Movement, about the time of its separation from the Baptists (that is, about 1830), numbered about 12,000-20,000.[1] It must also be remembered that about half of the Stone Movement remained in connection with the eastern Christians and did not merge into the union with the Campbell Movement. This means that approximately 8,000-10,000 followers of Stone united with the followers of Campbell, making a total of somewhere around 20,000-30,000.

Growth

The Movement continued to make steady growth throughout the nineteenth century. Part of this growth was the addition of several additional small movements. Dr. Chester Bullard, a Methodist medical doctor in Virginia, was stimulated by some of Campbell's writings in the *Christian Baptist* to request immersion from his church. Discouraged from immersion by the Methodists, Bullard left this congregation to form a new one. He did not identify fully with the Reformed Baptists because he was averse to what he saw of Campbell's negative personality. In the next

---

[1]Garrison and DeGroot, p. 325.

decade or so, however, Dr. Bullard had established about six or seven churches in Virginia and even into North Carolina. It was also in the 1830s that he learned that the Campbell of the *Millennial Harbinger* was not the irascible person he had assumed earlier. At a statewide meeting in Charlottesville in 1840, report was made of fifty-six churches in the state, with about 3,000 members. Campbell and Bullard first met at this conference, and the "Bullardites" blended with the Campbell Movement from this time on.[2]

Significant developments also occurred in southern Indiana. There several smaller movements came together, again representing the ideals of the Restoration Movement. In 1810 John Wright (1785-1851) organized a Free-Will Baptist Church near Salem, Indiana. He, his brother Peter, and his father Amos organized several others, forming an association of ten churches known as the Blue River Baptist Association. Then in 1819 the original Blue River Baptist Church became simply the Church of Christ at Blue River. The members preferred to be known as "Friends," "Disciples," "or just "Christians." The association in 1821 disbanded itself and became simply an annual meeting.[3]

Joseph Hostetler (1797-1870) was a German Baptist, or Dunkard, also in southern Indiana. He had tried unsuccessfully to persuade his Dunkard Association not to set up governing rules for the body. By 1826 he was receiving Campbell's *Christian Baptist*. It encouraged him to take such a stance against creeds that his Dunkard Association scheduled him for a heresy trial the next year. He defended himself so well, however, that the majority of the Association adopted his views and even dissolved their Association.[4]

In southern Indiana just north of Louisville, Separatist Baptists had located. They adhered to the Philadelphia Confession of Faith, but, reflecting their Separatist background, only reluctantly. Absalom Littell, a leader in the Silver Creek church and the Silver Creek Association, began receiving the *Christian Baptist* in the 1820s. Because of continued growth, the Association was subdivided in 1827, leaving Littell and other supporters of Campbell's views in the majority. By 1829 the Silver Creek

---

[2]Information on Bullard can be found in Frederick D. Power, *Sketches of Our Pioneers* (Chicago: Fleming H. Revell Company, 1898), pp. 133-136. The 1840 meeting in Charlottesville is also in Garrison and DeGroot, p. 273.

[3]Henry K. Shaw, *Hoosier Disciples: A Comprehensive History of the Christian Churches (Disciples of Christ) in Indiana* (n.p.: The Bethany Press, 1966), pp. 48-49.

[4]Shaw, *Hoosier Disciples*, pp. 50-51. Note also that this dissolution took place three years before the Mahoning Baptist Association dissolved itself in northeastern Ohio.

church voted to be governed by the Word of God rather than the traditional articles of faith. In 1836 the entire Association dropped the Articles of Faith. The next year they dissolved the Association and became only an annual meeting for fellowship and preaching.[5]

In addition to these developments among various groups of Indiana Baptists, the followers of Stone were also moving into southern Indiana in large numbers. Because of their revivalistic emphasis, they were often called "New Lights." Since the new Baptist developments were strongly influenced by the views of Campbell, obviously they also had numerous similarities to the New Light Christians.

Meanwhile, when John Wright heard of the reformation the neighboring Dunkard churches were going through in 1827, he suggested the two groups unite, face their problems together, and call themselves "Christians." His proposal was immediately implemented.[6]

With this encouraging beginning, Wright looked for other groups with whom to form similar unions. Because of the similarities with the New Light Christians, he and several others came to their annual conference at Edinburg, Bartholomew County, in July, 1828. They were cordially welcomed and in a report sent to Stone, the names of John and Peter Wright were included among the New Light preachers with no distinction. Furthermore, both John and Peter Wright were appointed as official delegates to the Christian Conference to be held in Harrison County the following September. John Wright was also appointed one of four men to participate in the ordination of a new preacher.[7]

Another of the preachers present sent a letter to Stone describing the meeting and drew particular attention to the arrival of the Wright brothers.

> The Bros. Wrights, [sic] whose names you will see in the minutes, have been formerly denominated "Depending Baptists;" but lately have laid that name aside, and now call themselves "the church of Christ." I judge there are six or eight Elders [ordained preachers] among them, and many churches. When we met in conference together, we could find nothing to separate us asunder.[8]

For all practical purposes, this Edinburg meeting represented a fusion between the followers of Stone and those of Campbell in parts of southern Indiana. Campbell had never made an appearance in Indiana as of yet,

---

[5]*Ibid.*, pp. 52-55.
[6]*Ibid.*, pp. 78-79.
[7]*Ibid.*, pp. 79-80; *Christian Messenger*, vol. 2, no. 11 (September, 1828), p. 259.
[8]*Christian Messenger*, vol. 2, no. 11 (September, 1828), p. 260.

and his followers were such only because of reading the *Christian Baptist*, but the effect was the same. It is significant also that this was more than three years prior to the meetings in Georgetown and Lexington. These latter two meetings are probably more significant because of the participation of Stone and other well-known leaders, and it was these meetings that focused attention on the unity developments. Yet this Indiana development is also important because it also represents a grassroots development, a spontaneous unity that lasted. It prepared the way in Indiana for the turn of events after the Georgetown-Lexington meetings.

Problems

What all of this represents is further growth of the Restoration Movement. As the decade of the 1830s rolled on, the Movement became even more successful in establishing new followers and churches in the Midwest. Yet the developments of this decade were not entirely favorable. Two negative factors deserve special notice.

One was Sidney Rigdon. Rigdon (1793-1876) was a young Baptist minister within the Mahoning Baptist Association in 1821 when he came under the influence of Alexander Campbell's ideas. He was also a brother-in-law of Adamson Bentley, one of the original leaders of the Mahoning Baptist Association. In 1822 Campbell persuaded Rigdon to assume the ministry of the Baptist church in Pittsburgh, apparently the congregation Campbell's father had established some years previously.[9] In 1824 this congregation merged with the congregation under Walter Scott's leadership.[10] When Campbell traveled to Washington, Kentucky, for his debate with Maccalla in 1823, Rigdon went along, taking notes of the event. Along with Campbell's own notes, these formed the basis of the printed Maccalla Debate.[11]

Yet in 1830 Rigdon left the Movement and joined Joseph Smith in the early stages of Mormonism. Richardson argues that Rigdon got possession of Solomon Spaulding's manuscript, which he transformed into the *Book of Mormon*.[12] (One of Smith's chief biographers, however, Fawn Brodie, argues against this thesis.[13]) Campbell called attention to

---

[9]Richardson, vol. 2, p. 47.

[10]*Ibid.*, p. 99.

[11]*Ibid.*, p. 95.

[12]*Ibid.*, pp. 344-345.

[13]See the discussion in Garrett, p. 384. Garrett also points out the more modern defenders of this "Spaulding thesis." Brodie was a Mormon who wrote a highly acclaimed biography of Smith, which led to her being thrown out of the

Rigdon's defection and attributed it to "a peculiar mental and corporeal malady" to which he had been subject for some years. It produced fits of melancholy, fits of enthusiasm, nervous spasms, and swoonings, which Rigdon interpreted into the agency of the Holy Spirit.[14] Richardson, writing in 1869, denigrated Rigdon's character by saying,

> In private he had been found petulant, unreliable and ungovernable in his passions, and his wayward temper, his extravagant stories and his habit of self-assertion had prevented him from attaining influence as a religious teacher among the disciples. He was ambitious of distinction, without the energy and industry necessary to secure it, and jealous of the reputation of others, without the ability to compete with them. Floating upon the tide of popular excitement, he was disposed to catch at anything which, without demanding labor, might serve for his advancement, and was naturally led to seek in deception the success which he found denied to indolence.[15]

At the time of the Mormon appearance, Rigdon was preaching for the church in Kirtland, Ohio. His speculative views of millennialism, communitarianism, and the restoration of supernatural gifts and miracles prepared the way for Smith's Mormonism. About one half of the Kirtland church went into the Mormon fold.[16] Receiving little support in Palmyra, New York, Smith himself soon moved to Kirtland and set up the headquarters for his Church of Jesus Christ of Latter Day Saints. A satellite growth of Mormons was also begun in Hiram, about thirty miles to the southeast, but when some of the early converts learned that communitarianism would deprive them of their property, they rousted Rigdon and Smith out of bed one night, tarred and feathered them, and sent them back to Kirtland.[17]

The defection of Rigdon to the Mormons affected the Campbell Movement in much the same way as the loss of Marshall and Thompson had affected the Stone Movement. It was embarrassing, and opponents of the Movement took it as proof that the Movement was ill-founded. "Mr. Sedwick of Zanesville, and Messrs. Noel and the Chronicle, club of Kentucky, represented this defection as the legitimate result of their phantom 'Campbellism.'" Yet Campbell contended that such was poor

---

Mormon church. See Fawn Brodie, *No Man Knows My History: The Life of Joseph Smith the Mormon Prophet* (New York: Alfred P. Knopf, 1945). Her treatment of the Spaulding-Rigdon theory is on pp. 143-144 plus Appendix B, pp. 419-433.

[14]*Millennial Harbinger,* 1831, p. 100.

[15]Richardson, vol. 2, p. 344.

[16]*Ibid.*, pp. 345-347.

[17]Hayden, p. 221.

reasoning. "Every person who receives the book of Mormon is an apostate from all that he ever professed, if, indeed, he ever professed to receive or value any thing we have ever spoken or written on the subject of christianity."[18]

The loss of half of one congregation, even accompanied by the loss of such a promising leader as Rigdon, was a small loss, but it represented the difficulty in maintaining the unity of the Movement under the doctrinal challenge of Mormonism. A second problem that developed in this decade centered on Dr. John Thomas of Virginia.

Dr. Thomas (1805-1874) was born in London and immigrated to the United States in 1832.[19] He came to Cincinnati where he heard Walter Scott and was immersed by him. He soon located in Virginia where he became active as a preacher and editor of the _Apostolic Advocate_ in 1834. Initially Campbell was very lavish in his praise of Thomas' abilities and his dedication to the gospel. When Thomas wrote a pamphlet against Roman Catholicism, Campbell referred to him as "our much esteemed brother."[20] By the next year, Campbell was talking about "our faithful fellow-soldier Dr. John Thomas,"[21] and when he announced Thomas' prospectus for the _Apostolic Advocate,_ he called him

> a talented, devoted, and zealous disciple of the Messiah . . . an honorable and independent advocate of the truth, . . . [who] through his veneration and affection for the apostolic institution, sacrificed his temporal and professional interests and honors.[22]

Later, Campbell's assessment changed dramatically.

Two issues in particular became Thomas' hobby horses. One was the doctrine of reimmersion for all people who did not understand the precise purpose of baptism at the time they were baptized, particularly Baptists. This first came out in a letter from a woman in Virginia dated August 1, 1835, in which she brought Thomas' practices to Campbell's attention. In his reply, Campbell sternly disagreed with the view of reimmersion, saying it becomes a circular doctrine of repeated baptisms.[23]

---

[18]_Millennial Harbinger,_ 1831, p. 101.

[19]A good discussion of the entire Thomas episode is in Garrett, pp. 388-399. Another good treatment is by Roderick Chestnut, "John Thomas and the Rebaptism Controversy (1835-1838)" in _Baptism and the Remission of Sins: An Historical Perspective,_ edited by David W. Fletcher (Joplin, Missouri: College Press Publishing Company, 1990), pp. 203-239.

[20]_Millennial Harbinger,_ 1833, p. 478.

[21]_Ibid.,_ 1834, p. 124.

[22]_Ibid.,_ p. 190.

[23]_Ibid.,_ 1835, pp. 417-420. See also pp. 565-567.

The continuing controversy prompted Campbell to an eight-page rejoinder in 1836. In the celebrated Lunenburg Letter, to which we shall return shortly, Campbell stated that his comments were prompted by "our brethren of Eastern Virginia,"[24] where John Thomas lived.

Thomas' second emphasis drew Campbell's attention in 1836 in an article called "Materialism."[25] Thomas believed the resurrection would be limited only to the righteous. All "infants, ideots [sic], Pagans, and modern Jews," being destitute of spiritual understanding, are only material. Therefore, they would never be raised, judged, justified, or condemned, but remain forever only unconscious dust.[26] In lengthy reviews, Campbell challenged and rebutted these views.[27]

The depth of Campbell's feelings can be gauged from the fact that in December of 1836, he denied that Thomas was a schismatic or factionist.[28] Yet within a year, the "Extra" of the *Millennial Harbinger* for 1837 dealt with Thomas' views, and in this context he referred to the schismatic character of the *Apostolic Advocate* and Thomas' "seeking to attach to himself a party."[29] In November of 1837, Campbell reached the point of declaring, "I can no longer regard him as a brother in the Lord."[30] Vituperative language from both men abounds in the discussions carried on in the *Harbinger* and the *Advocate*.

Campbell tried to focus on the central issues of the whole dispute in his "Extra" for 1837. Early in the article he stated, "The spirit and soul of all reformation is free discussion."[31] In his conclusion to the article, however, Campbell tried to distinguish between appropriate discussion of proper issues and sheer speculation of opinions. Campbell did not wish to encourage any discussion that held that the Spirit of God is only an attribute of God, or the Sabellian view of Christ.

> Liberty of speech and of the press is not with me licentious extravagance nor disregard for the opinions of others; nor is the proper use of our rights the sustaining of every restless demagogical spirit who will be conspicuous for something—for anything. On all Bible facts, precepts, promises, and declarations—on all its various documents, ordinances, and statutes, we go for free and full and satisfactory discussion; but we say that it is abhorrent to the reformation

---

[24]*Ibid.*, 1837, p. 566.
[25]*Ibid.*, 1836, pp. 396-403.
[26]*Ibid.*, p. 399.
[27]*Ibid.*, pp. 396-404, 451-457.
[28]*Ibid.*, p. 565.
[29]*Ibid.*, 1837, p. 587.
[30]*Ibid.*, p. 513.
[31]*Ibid.*, p. 575.

for which we plead, to propagate mere opinions and speculations; and that it is entirely off the ground we occupy to favor those who devote their tongues or their pens to build up any theory ancient or modern, original or borrowed.

The moment any one becomes a factionist, or even a dogmatist, to encourage him is to oppose the written law, and to summon every true citizen of Christ's kingdom to the walls of Zion to defend the city of our God. We are commanded to "mark them which cause divisions" and offences [sic] contrary to the Apostles' doctrine, and to avoid them, because they serve not our Master. . . . Opinionism must be put down, and kept down, or we have apostatized from the ground on which we commenced.[32]

A hoped-for resolution of the dispute occurred in the fall of 1838. Campbell was on a tour of the South, and he swung through eastern Virginia on the way. In the process, he stopped at Paineville, near where Dr. Thomas lived. In a meeting of three days and occupying ten hours, he discussed Dr. Thomas' views with him, in the midst of a group of twenty-three other brethren.[33] The entire group agreed to a resolution dated November 15, 1838, which stated that Thomas' views had given offense to many brethren and posed a potential division to the brotherhood. As a result, Thomas was to "discontinue the discussion of the same, *unless in his defense, when misrepresented.*"[34] According to the resolution, "all difficulties were adjusted, and perfect harmony and co-operation mutually agreed upon between them."[35]

Campbell left their meeting with the recommendation that Thomas write a statement of the meeting so as to put the interview on record, and he promised to have it published in the *Millennial Harbinger* without note or comment. This appeared in the February, 1839, issue.[36] But in the very announcement of the interview, Thomas reaffirmed his unshaken confidence in the truth of his own views. That is, in the very announcement of the resolution to discontinue the discussion, Thomas took the initiative to defend his views, thus renewing the discussion. Campbell resolved to take no notice of Thomas' initiative and let the whole thing die out.[37]

In the next few years, Dr. Thomas moved to Illinois where he managed to disturb the church in Chicago and gain a few converts. He also returned briefly to England, where he was first accepted and then

---

[32]*Ibid.*, p. 588.

[33]*Ibid.*, 1839, p. 9; see also "A Narrative of My Last Interview with Dr. John Thomas," 1843, pp. 225-230.

[34]*Ibid.*, 1843, p. 226. Italics in original.

[35]*Ibid.*

[36]*Ibid.*, 1839, pp. 72-75.

[37]*Ibid.*, 1843, pp. 227-228.

rejected by leaders of the Movement. He returned to the United States in 1844 and ultimately founded the Christadelphian denomination.[38]

It may be significant that in 1837, the apex of the Thomas episode, Campbell tried in a couple of ways to clarify the issues involved. One attempt was in a series of three articles in the *Millennial Harbinger* entitled "Opinionism."[39] The basic thrust of the series is found in the first article, in which he distinguishes between knowledge (our own experience), faith (our assurance of the experience of others), and opinion (our persuasion of the probability of a matter we neither know nor believe). By definition, therefore, opinions are in the realm of speculation. He also states that "opinionism" is *the liberty of propagating one's own opinions.* Although some claim this right is an essential part of Christian liberty, Campbell strongly denies it. *It is not the right of any one citizen of Christ's kingdom to propagate any opinion whatever, either in the public assembly or in private.*[40] Going back to the spirit of Thomas Campbell's *Declaration and Address,* Alexander Campbell here is stating that Christian teaching ought to be limited to Scriptural statements. Opinions are in the realm of human deductions, and for the sake of Christian unity, they should not be advocated. Obviously, since they are based on neither knowledge nor faith, there will be disagreements on the conclusions drawn, and therefore such opinions can only cause disruption in the Christian community. For the sake of unity, opinions should never be allowed to get beyond the level of privately held views.

This was the problem with the views of John Thomas. He had strong opinions about reimmersion and the nonresurrection of the unjust. But his advocating these views produced discord and strife. The 1838 agreement was that Thomas would discontinue their discussion. His failure to do so—that is, his continued defense of his opinions—produced the rupture in fellowship. Campbell's position is that unity could be maintained only by limiting teaching to clear Scriptural teaching. Teaching that went beyond the foundation of Biblical revelation was a threat to the unity of the Christian community.

The second attempt Campbell made in 1837 to deal with Thomas' views was the Lunenburg Letter and its attendant responses. It all began in the June issue of the *Millennial Harbinger* when Campbell wrote to

---

[38]For a brief statement of Christadelphian history and doctrines, see Frank S. Mead, *Handbook of Denominations in the United States* (New York: Abingdon-Cokesbury Press, 1951), pp. 48-49.

[39]These are found in the *Millennial Harbinger,* 1837, pp. 439-445; 481-485; and 549-555.

[40]*Ibid.*, pp. 439-441. Italics are in the original.

brethren in England and tried to describe some of the beliefs of the American movement. He talked about cooperating with other Christians in matters of social justice and observed, "We find in all Protestant parties Christians as exemplary as ourselves given their and our relative knowledge and opportunities."[41]

In July a sister in Lunenburg wrote to Campbell questioning him about this phrase, "we find in all Protestant parties Christians." She questioned whether it was appropriate to use the label "Christians" on people until they have believed, repented, and been immersed into the death of Christ.[42] This became the famous "Lunenburg Letter," and in answering it Campbell focused on the whole question of baptism, Christian labels, and the status of the "pious unimmersed."

Campbell initially replied to the letter by rhetorically asking, "But who is a Christian," and answered, "Every one that believes in his heart that Jesus of Nazareth is the Messiah, the Son of God; repents of his sins, and obeys him in all things according to his measure of knowledge of his will." Campbell acknowledges that this is a relative answer, but he insists that Christians can be imperfect in some respects without forfeiting total Christian state and character. He admits that he cannot

> make any one duty the standard of Christian state or character, not even immersion into the name of the Father, of the Son, and of the Holy Spirit, and in my heart regard all that have been sprinkled in infancy without their own knowledge and consent, as aliens from Christ and the well-grounded hope of heaven.[43]

He argued that to shun fellowship of spiritually minded and devout Paedobaptists was pure sectarianism and pharisaism. He admitted that obedience is the only way to determine whether someone loves the Master, but he would not substitute obedience to one commandment—immersion—for universal or general obedience.[44] He concluded that "there is no occasion, then, for making immersion, on a profession of the faith, absolutely essential to a Christian—though it may be greatly essential to his sanctification and comfort."[45]

These comments raised a storm of protest, and Campbell added a later response under the heading "Christians Among the Sects." He noted that

---

[41]*Ibid.*, p. 272.
[42]*Ibid.*, p. 411.
[43]*Ibid.*, p. 412.
[44]*Ibid.*
[45]*Ibid.*, p. 414.

Paul distinguished between the inward and outward Jews by noting that circumcision was a matter of the heart as well as of the flesh. Campbell concluded the same things of baptism. He then rhetorically asked whether a person who mistook the meaning of baptism but obeyed it as he understood it could have the inward baptism that made him acceptable toward God. He answered, "In my opinion, *it is possible.*"[46]

Campbell had a further response the next month because of all the heated letters he was receiving, all concerned that he had given up a crucial part of the gospel plan. Yet in this third response,[47] he argued first of all that he was not guilty of inconsistency, because he had said numerous times before that there were Christians in the sects.

Secondly, Campbell wanted to defend himself from a sectarian application of his comments. He was aware that many Paedobaptists now concluded that Campbell was saying that immersion was unimportant and easily ignored. Campbell disagreed by pointing out that he was limiting this application only to those people who were sincerely and involuntarily ignorant about proper baptism being immersion. Those people who were happy about Campbell's comments simply because they did not want to be immersed, Campbell dismissed as having a rebellious spirit and an unrepentant attitude.[48]

In the third place, however, Campbell gave some reasons for making such comments at all. He pointed out that too many people were denouncing the sects en masse as wholly alien from Christ and he felt constrained to rebuke them. He particularly attacked the brethren of eastern Virginia (the area where Dr. Thomas had most of his followers) for greatly and unreasonably abusing the sects and making Christianity turn more upon immersion than upon universal holiness.[49]

The result is that Campbell admits he has overstated his case just to counter Thomas and his followers for their overemphasis on proper Christian immersion for the right reasons. Twenty-five years later, W. K. Pendleton, then a coeditor of the *Millennial Harbinger*, points out that the lady from Lunenburg was in fact a follower of Thomas.[50]

An assessment of the Lunenburg Letter and Campbell's three responses leads to the conclusion that although Campbell firmly believed that proper New Testament baptism was by immersion for the remission of sins, he was warmly sympathetic to those who did not yet see it that way.

---

[46]*Ibid.*, p. 507. Italics in original.

[47]*Ibid.*, pp. 561-567.

[48]*Ibid.*, pp. 562-563.

[49]*Ibid.*, pp. 565-567.

[50]*Ibid.*, 1862, p. 132.

For these people—people who sincerely misunderstood immersion—
Campbell thought God would be gracious:

> There are many, in most Protestant parties, whose errors and mistakes I hope
> the Lord will forgive; and although they should not enter into all the blessings
> of the kingdom on earth, I do fondly expect they may participate in the resur-
> rection of the just.[51]

Thus Campbell was willing to advance his opinion (and it is interesting
that Campbell does so at the very time he was writing his series on
"Opinionism" and attacking Thomas for propounding his "opinions")
that as long as the pious unimmersed were pious and sincerely unaware
of the New Testament teaching on immersion, God would accept them.
This was one way Campbell harmonized his positions on unity and New
Testament teaching.

Thus the decade of the 1830s represented both growth of the
Restoration Movement and several challenges to that growth. Already
the Movement was facing difficulties as it confronted the difficult task of
delineating the parameters of the polar attractions of Christian unity and
biblical authority. The emphasis on biblical authority tended to restrict
by removing the foundations of the teachings of men such as Joseph
Smith and Sidney Rigdon as well as Dr. John Thomas. The emphasis on
Christian unity tried to include as many believers as possible leading to
an absorption of disparate though similar movements under men such as
Stone, Bullard, Wright, Hostetler, and Littell. In the Lunenburg Letter,
Campbell even charitably included the pious unimmersed, though not all
of his followers agreed with him. The inclusiveness of unity and the
exclusiveness of biblical authority were already creating tensions within
the Movement. Such continued as the Movement developed further.

An indication that concern for Christian unity was still a motivating
factor came in the 1840s when the leaders of the Movement around
Lexington called for and hosted a union meeting from April 2-5, 1841.
Alexander Campbell, John T. Johnson, and [Raccoon] John Smith were
present, as well as about a dozen other leaders. Baptist minister James
Fishback attended, but he was the only Baptist minister who took an active
part in the discussions. The assembly unanimously approved the resolution, "Christian union is practicable." Campbell spoke on Saturday from
10:00 A.M. until 4:30 P.M. (with a short break for dinner) on the proposition, "The union of Christians can be Scripturally effected by requiring a

---

[51]*Ibid.*, 1837, p. 567.

practical acknowledgement of such articles of belief, and such rules of piety and morality as are admitted by all Christian denominations." On Monday morning, Campbell's proposition was carried unanimously.[52]

A Baptist elder, W. F. Broddus, prohibited any Baptists from attending, and an old Methodist preacher denounced the meeting, identifying as heretics those who "sought the union of all good men."[53] Campbell expressed his delight at the meeting because it allowed him to talk genuine union in spite of the attack against him for "raising up and in leading a new sect."[54] Secondly, he pointed out that if schism still existed, he and his followers could not be held guilty.[55] Campbell felt good about the meeting.

> The terms of union discussed were equal, and equally honorable to all parties, requiring no greater concession from any one party in Christendom than from another. The adoption of the Bible, the whole Bible, and nothing else but the naked Book of God, as the expression of our faith, the guide of our worship, and the code of our morals. . . .

> Sects *never can unite*. It is impossible. . . . It is only on the Bible, the naked Bible, that good men in all parties can unite. The partizan [sic] features and attributes must be annihilated. Every thing that makes the Baptist, or the Presbyterian, or the Methodist, must be destroyed before the people now wearing these names can unite. Whatever makes the Baptist, the Methodist, and the Presbyterian is not of God, but of man. Immersion is of God; but immersion does not make a Baptist. Method is of God; but method does not make a Methodist. Elderships and presbyters are of God; but we have both, and are not Presbyterians. There are not a few who seem unable to learn this lesson.[56]

In retrospect, however, it seems the meeting accomplished nothing. The other groups assumed that union with the Disciples meant giving up their own valid agendas and simply accepting the Disciples' partisan one.

If there were gains in this period in the name of Christian unity, there were also disappointments. One of the most significant was a controversy that involved Alexander Campbell and Jesse B. Ferguson of Nashville, Tennessee.[57] Ferguson was a popular preacher among the Disciples in

---

[52]*Ibid.*, 1841, pp. 237, 258-260.

[53]*Ibid.*, p. 262.

[54]*Ibid.*, p. 261.

[55]*Ibid.*, p. 262.

[56]*Ibid.*

[57]For an excellent and detailed treatment of this whole issue, see Enos E. Dowling, *An Analysis and Index of the Christian Magazine, 1848-1853* (Lincoln, Illinois: Lincoln Bible Institute Press, 1958), pp. 192-230.

town, ministering with the Cherry Street church. He was also editor of the *Christian Magazine,* the unofficial state magazine of the Tennessee Christians.

In 1852 Ferguson wrote an article on 1 Peter 3:18-20, suggesting that while Jesus' body was in the tomb, he preached to the "spirits in prison," those who had been disobedient during and subsequent to Noah's time. This allowed them now an opportunity to respond to the gospel, what some called a "post-mortem gospel." In the *Millennial Harbinger,* Campbell called attention to Ferguson's argument and countered strongly. He accused Ferguson of heresy, called upon him to recant, and called upon the brotherhood to repudiate him. Under attack, Ferguson claimed to have communication with the spirits of certain dead people who affirmed his principle now under attack. As the controversy continued, the church in Nashville split, and Ferguson soon moved out of the fellowship of the Christian Churches.

Ferguson insisted he had only advanced an opinion, which he had every right to do. But Campbell denied the right and accused him of fomenting schism by propagating such an opinion. Ironically, when Aylette Raines held to the opinion of Universalism in 1828, Campbell advocated patience and tolerance.[58] But he now refused to grant Ferguson the same patience and tolerance. It is further ironic that just a decade earlier, in his debate with Nathan L. Rice in 1843, Campbell was still of his first mind. There he said:

> It is not the object of our efforts to make men think alike on a thousand themes. Let men think as they please on any matters of human opinion, and upon "doctrines of religion," provided only they hold THE HEAD Christ, and keep his commandments. I have learned, not only the theory, but the fact— that if you wish opinionism to cease or to subside, you must not call up and debate everything that men think or say. You may debate any thing into consequence, or you may, by a dignified silence, waste it into oblivion. I have known innumerable instances of persons outliving their opinions, and erroneous reasonings, and even sometimes forgetting the modes of reasoning by which they had embraced and maintained them. This was the natural result of the Philosophy of letting them alone. In this way, they came to be of one mind in all points in which unity of thought is desirable.[59]

This concept worked well with Raines; yet Campbell was unwilling to

---

[58]See above, Chapter Six, pp. 150-152.

[59]A. Campbell, *A Debate Between Rev. A. Campbell and Rev. N. L. Rice, on the Action, Subject, Design and Administrator of Christian Baptism* (Lexington: A. T. Skillman and Son, 1844), pp. 797-798.

follow it with Ferguson. It was but one indication that ideals often were ignored in the heat of debate and conflicting personalities.

Organizations

Another factor of the 1830s was the growing concern of leaders of the Movement for education. Throughout this decade, Campbell published several articles in the *Millennial Harbinger* dealing with education—theory, curriculum, and administration. The first significant school of the Restoration Movement (not counting Campbell's earlier Buffalo Seminary), was Bacon College, begun in 1836 in Georgetown, Kentucky. Walter Scott served for a year as the first president, followed quickly by D. S. Burnet. The school was first named "The Collegiate Institute and School for Civil Engineers," reflecting the need for surveyors on the frontier. But the name was soon changed to Bacon College, after Francis Bacon, the philosopher and scientist considered the father of empirical inquiry. Ultimately, the school was merged with Transylvania University in Lexington.[60]

Even more significant was the creation of Bethany College. Alexander Campbell had never completely given up his ideas on education after the closure of Buffalo Seminary in 1822. His plans finally materialized with the chartering of the school in 1840 and its opening for classes in 1841.[61] Campbell gave the plot of land for it and became its first president. It was the culmination of Alexander's long-cherished dream and he planned it to be the finale of his earthly projects.[62] For a number of years it was the flagship of higher education within the Restoration Movement. Other schools modeled themselves after it. Its alumni gave significant leadership to other schools and organizations over the next several decades.

Another area of tension arose out of the continuing growth of the Movement in the decade of the 1830s, and this was the factor of

---

[60]See Dwight E. Stevenson, "The Bacon College Story: 1836-1865," *The College of the Bible Quarterly*, vol. 29, no. 4 (October, 1962), pp. 10 ff., as referred to in McAllister and Tucker, pp. 162-163. For further information on Bacon College, see John D. Wright, Jr., *Transylvania: Tutor to the West* (Lexington: The University Press of Kentucky, 1980), pp. 190-193; also Dwight E. Stevenson, "Appendix IV, Bacon College and Kentucky University, 1836-1865," in *Lexington Theological Seminary, 1865-1965: The College of the Bible Century* (St. Louis: The Bethany Press, 1964), pp. 401-416.

[61]The Virginia statute authorizing the college is given in *Millennial Harbinger*, 1840, pp. 176-179.

[62]*Ibid.*, 1839, p. 446.

organizations developing beyond the level of the local congregation. These were not an entirely new element, for there were regional conferences in the Stone Movement prior to the union with the Campbells in 1831/1832. There were also organized Baptist associations within the Campbell Movement prior to their leaving the Baptists in 1830. However, the followers of Campbell normally dissolved their Baptist associations as they left the Baptist fold, and the Christian conferences of the Stone Movement seem not to have survived the union with the Campbells. Although there were a few annual meetings among former Baptists (the defunct Mahoning Baptist Association continued in this way for several years), the Restoration Movement had virtually no extra-congregational organizations by the early 1830s.

But continuing growth of the Movement seemed to inevitably suggest the need to get better organized. This posed an intriguing problem for the Movement. From the very earliest period, the Restoration Movement had been committed to congregational autonomy—as is seen in both the O'Kelly and Stone Movements. The O'Kelly Movement insisted that their annual conferences were advisory only; Jones left the Baptists for several reasons, one of which was their associations which threatened the independence of the churches. The Stone Movement left the Presbyterian organization in Kentucky, formed its own presbytery, and then dissolved it when they realized there was no New Testament authority for such organizations. When Joseph Badger came west in 1826 and talked about structures, the leaders of the Stone Movement shunned him on his second visit, leaving a residue of bitterness and ill feeling. In 1823 Alexander Campbell had insisted that there ought to be no religious organizations other than the local church—"in their church capacity alone" the apostolic church moved. In 1830 the Mahoning Baptist Association even dissolved itself, as had similar associations among Baptists earlier in Indiana. The early strands of the Restoration Movement thus showed a consistent and pervasive fear of ecclesiastical structure.

But by the decade of the 1830s, the Movement also began to realize the advantages of some organization. Alexander Campbell saw this immediately. In fact he was not in favor of the dissolution of the Mahoning Baptist Association. He was about to speak against the motion to dissolve when Scott stopped him. Further, in 1831 he wrote a series of four articles in the *Millennial Harbinger* on "The Co-operation of Churches." In the first article, Campbell argued that we are to use any means to reform the world. The mere fact that a means has been corrupted and perverted is not an argument against the use of it. He urged the churches of a district to cooperate against infidelity, atheism, and sensuality. "It is the duty of churches to co-operate in every thing beyond the individual achievements of a particular congregation." "A church can do what an individual disciple cannot, and so can a district of churches do what a single congregation cannot."[63] In the final article, Campbell pointed out that "the New Testament furnishes the principles which call forth our energies, but suggests no plan."

> The churches in every county, have from scripture and reason, all authority to bring their combined energies upon their own vicinity first, and when all is done at home, they may, and ought to co-operate with their weaker neighbors in the same state, and so on increasing the circle of their co-operations, as they fill up the interior, with all light and goodness, until the knowledge of the glory of the Lord cover the whole earth.[64]

Thus in 1831 the churches that had formerly made up the Mahoning Baptist Association met in New Lisbon and discussed a proposition to adopt some plan of cooperation among the churches to spread the gospel, even suggesting annual meetings of the churches in each county, though no church business was to be conducted.[65] In 1832 as the representative of the Bethany church, Campbell lent his support to the churches of Brooke County in sending out Henry Barton under cooperative support.[66] That same year Campbell endorsed the suggestion that brethren around Richmond cooperate in keeping Peter Ainslie in the field as an evangelist.[67]

The churches of Owen County, Indiana, planned a three-day meeting in October of 1833 to discuss the arrangements to be made for getting an evangelist in the field.[68] That same year John O'Kane became the evangelist of the Rush County Cooperation and organized the church in Indianapolis.[69] Through the decade of the 1830s, a number of county cooperations were set up. Brethren who saw many "unchurched" communities in their counties and nearby wished to respond to this need.[70] In Illinois a number of individuals met in Springfield, October 17-20, 1834, at which time the churches were encouraged to contribute to the support of one or more evangelists.

---

[63]*Ibid.*, 1831, p. 237.
[64]*Ibid.*, p. 437.
[65]*Ibid.*, pp. 445-446.
[66]Garrison and DeGroot, p. 236.
[67]*Millennial Harbinger,* 1832, pp. 597-598; see also p. 413.
[68]*Christian Messenger,* vol. 7, no. 8 (August, 1833), p. 247.
[69]Shaw, *Hoosier Disciples,* p. 85.
[70]*Ibid.*, p. 89.

Before the meeting was over, John Rigdon agreed to serve as the first evangelist for a term of six months.[71]

Matthias Winans of Ohio set the issue in proper focus when he wrote to Campbell early in 1835 to report that the churches of Clinton and Greene Counties met to select one or more evangelists and appropriate means for their support. He added that some of the brethren were opposed to the measure, fearing the churches would fall into the old sectarian tracks. Their mistake, he noted, is to think evangelists are to preach to the church rather than to the world.[72]

In response Campbell commented that he was glad to hear "the brethren in many places are waking up to a sense of their responsibility in reference to the conversion of the world." Acknowledging the concern over all these new agencies, Campbell insisted, "Co-operation among christian churches in all the affairs of the common salvation, is not only inscribed on every page of apostolic history, but is itself of the very essence of the christian institution." Campbell added, "There is too much squeamishness about the *manner* of co-operation."

> Some are looking for a model similar to that which Moses gave for building the tabernacle. These seem not to understand that this is as impossible as it would be incompatible with the genius of the gospel. A model for translating the Scriptures from Greek into Latin, and from Latin into the English, French, and Spanish tongues; a model for making types, paper, ink, and for printing the Bible, might be as rationally expected, as a model for the co-operation of churches on the banks of the Ohio for republishing the gospel in the valley of the Mississippi.[73]

Yet the very creation of these cooperative agencies alarmed some of the brethren. For years they had learned to quote Thomas Campbell's dictum, "Where the Scriptures speak, we speak; where the Scriptures are silent, we are silent." Fearful of sectarian authority, the brethren had earlier dismantled conferences, associations, and presbyteries. Now these extra-congregational organizations seemed to be coming back. What was the biblical authority for them? This was the key question. Certainly everyone wanted to see the conversion of the world. But the question was, should this conversion be conducted by unauthorized organizations of the churches? In 1823 Alexander Campbell had attacked such unauthorized agencies as Bible societies, mission societies, tract societies, saying the early Christians acted "in their

---

[71]*Millennial Harbinger*, 1834, pp. 599-600, 605.
[72]*Ibid.*, 1835, pp. 119-120.
[73]*Ibid.*, p. 121.

church capacity alone." Now he seemed to be endorsing these new agencies. This transition represented a crisis of conscience for many brethren who had grown up on Campbell's earlier statements; they now saw his shift as an abandonment of the previous commitment to biblical authority alone.

The fact is, however, that the new agencies were being created and serving useful purposes. County, district, even state meetings were being held. All of them insisted they had no authority over the churches. Most of these meetings were informal and unstructured, but they provided a platform for discussion of ways and means of evangelizing. A new milestone was achieved in 1839, however, with an Indiana state meeting. There had been state meetings previously, as witnessed by the Illinois assembly in 1834. But this Indiana meeting in 1839 was different in that it became a regular annual meeting with more continuity than previously. It was announced in advance in the *Millennial Harbinger*,[74] and then extensively reported afterwards.[75]

One of the most significant items in the record was a listing of the reported churches in the state, totaling 115 congregations with 7,701 members. The meeting also adopted some recommendations, relatively innocuous ones. One was to send out faithful and intelligent evangelists. Several had to do with education: that young and potential preachers get as much education as they can; that general education be encouraged; and that Indiana State University in Bloomington be patronized. In reprinting the details of this meeting, Campbell commended the Indiana meeting and stated that such an annual meeting in some central point of each state would promote the prosperity of the cause simply by gathering the statistics of the churches united in primitive Christianity. He concluded by observing, "Co-operation and combination of effort is the great secret of success."[76]

Not everyone, however, agreed with these later views of Campbell. The opposition, or resistance, showed itself quite early. In 1832 a writer to the *Millennial Harbinger* claimed, "There never was, and there never can be, any occasion for such a combination of 'the churches' to build up the Redeemer's kingdom." The explanation that cooperation produced more efficient evangelistic effort made no headway. "To convert the world is no part of their business; no object of their anxiety nor solicitude."[77]

In 1841 Campbell began a series of articles on church organization.

---

[74]*Ibid.*, 1839, p. 284.
[75]*Ibid.*, pp. 353-357.
[76]*Ibid.*, p. 253 [sic, should be 353].
[77]*Ibid.*, 1832, p. 201.

The following year he had an article entitled simply "Five Arguments for Church Organization."[78] These were: Bible distribution, home and foreign missions, improving and elevating the Christian ministry, protecting the church from irresponsible preachers, and using the total resources of the church. Campbell said none of these things could be done without cooperation. He pointed out the "great need of a more rational and scriptural organization," and "a more ample, extensive, and thorough church organization." He does not outline the details of this "more rational and scriptural organization," but it obviously would be something more than the currently existing loose affiliation of independent congregations. This certainly sounded quite differently from his comments in the 1823 *Christian Baptist*.

During the Campbell-Rice debate in Lexington in November of 1843, sixty-seven persons from eight states met "according to previous arrangement." John T. Johnson was chosen to preside over the discussions that were to be on church organization. Apparently there was an attempt to organize a missionary society, but Jacob Creath, Sr., argued strenuously against it and got the brethren to abandon the plan.[79] Because of the resistance encountered, McAllister concludes, "It is only reasonable to assume that some of the leaders may have felt it would be wise to meet quietly and discuss the issues before proceeding further toward national organization."[80]

At the request of churches in western Virginia (West Virginia) and some in Ohio, a meeting was held in Steubenville, Ohio, in October, 1844 for the purpose of a free exchange of views on the subjects of church organizations, church edification, and church cooperation. The result was to appoint a committee of five persons to draft and report some propositions for a general meeting to be held in Wellsburg, December 26, 1844. The propositions were discussed at length and the committee was urged to have them published prior to another meeting to be held at Wellsburg on April 1, 1845.[81] Included in the propositions were several strong statements on cooperation.

> It [is] the duty of all the congregations in any city or district to co-operate in accomplishing in that district, state, or nation, whatever they could not otherwise accomplish for the publication of the word and the edification of the church.

---

[78]*Ibid.*, 1842, p. 523.

[79]McAllister and Tucker, pp. 171-172, referring to the minutes of the meeting, now on deposit with the Disciples of Christ Historical Society.

[80]*Ibid.*, p. 172.

[81]*Millennial Harbinger*, 1845, p. 59.

To do this successfully, they must either occasionally meet together, by deputies, messengers, or representatives, and consult together for the better performance of their duties. These meetings, being voluntary expedients in matters of expediency, such persons have no authority to legislate in any matter of faith or moral duty, but to attend to the ways and means of successful co-operation in all the objects of duty before them.[82]

A further proposition provided for the control or correction of a wayward or schismatic congregation. In such a case neighboring churches were to form a committee to oversee the problem, and the wayward church was to submit to such a tribunal. If a schismatic faction refused such oversight, it was to be treated as "leprous persons were treated under the law—as separated or cut off from the congregation of the Lord."[83] This provision is certainly a far cry from the traditionally understood complete autonomy of each local congregation.

Up to this time, then, there had been regional organizations and state organizations, and even discussions of national associations, but in fact there had not yet been any national bodies organized. This changed in January, 1845, when D. S. Burnet and several other interested individuals from four churches in Cincinnati organized the American Christian Bible Society.[84]

Their desire was to distribute the Word of God both at home and abroad, translating and printing it into as many foreign languages as their means would allow. They acknowledged that the fact that other Bible societies were already doing this was a motive for the Christian Churches to do likewise without simply cooperating with those societies. "We can effect more in one year by the operations of the American Christian Bible Society, than can be accomplished during a century, by coalescing with any existing institution." Besides, having their own work would set forth to the world their commitment to the Word of God and secure the honors of their efforts "to that form of Christianity which we have considered as primitive."[85] D. S. Burnet was chosen president of the society, and there were nine vice presidents, including such luminaries as Walter Scott, John T. Johnson, John O'Kane, and Alexander Campbell.[86]

---

[82]*Ibid.*, pp. 66-67.

[83]*Ibid.*, p. 67.

[84]The best treatment of the life of Burnet is that of Noel L. Keith, *The Story of D. S. Burnet: Undeserved Obscurity* (St. Louis: The Bethany Press, 1954). The reference to four churches being involved is on p. 74, quoting the *Annual Proceedings of the American Christian Bible Society*, 1849, p. 49.

[85]*Millennial Harbinger*, 1845, pp. 370-371.

[86]Moore, *A Comprehensive History of the Disciples of Christ*, p. 420.

Most of the vice presidents, including Campbell, were not even present.

Many people questioned the appropriateness of this development. The American and Foreign [Baptist] Bible Society, organized in 1837, had taken the name "Baptist" out of their title and was publishing the Scriptures without note or comment. It had rescinded the clause that all officers were to be Baptists. It already had the plates, secured at great expense, to print the Bible in fifty-four languages; for the new Bible society to duplicate this effort by buying presses and redoing the plates would be a great waste of funds. Furthermore, such a separate society "savors of a sectarian feeling, or will appear to the world to do so." In light of the plea for Christian union, how could Christian churches refuse to cooperate with the Baptists in this Bible enterprise "without being able to complain of a single principle upon which the institution is founded, and while they are cordially inviting us to co-operate with them in the great and glorious work?"[87]

Alexander Campbell added his reservations as well. He seconded the encouragement that the churches ought to work with the [formerly Baptist] American and Foreign Bible Society, both out of financial considerations as well as the concern for Christian unity. Furthermore, he questioned

> the propriety of any institution being got up under the patronage of any society, and with its name upon it, without a general understanding some way obtained of the concurrence and support of the whole brotherhood in the scheme.[88]

This latter observation was a significant one, though in the short run it caused some embarrassment for Campbell as well.

D. S. Burnet, the president of the American Christian Bible Society, soon replied that Campbell's reservation ought to apply equally well to Bethany College. There was no general convention to call Bethany into being; it was begun by one man.[89] Campbell's response was that the cases were not parallel. If he had called his school "American Christian College," he might concede the point; or if Burnet had designated his group the Cincinnati Christian Bible Society or even the Cincinnati Bible Society, Campbell would admit his comments were uncalled for and unjustified.[90] Campbell's logic here seems a bit specious and less than candid, but he insisted that his remarks were not fully understood or placed in the proper context of his trust in the motives of the officers of the society.

---

[87]*Millennial Harbinger,* 1845, pp. 367-368.

[88]*Ibid.,* p. 372.

[89]*Ibid.,* p. 453.

[90]*Ibid.,* pp. 457-458.

In an editorial the next year Campbell came back to one of his original reservations.

> I never was opposed to any Bible Society in Cincinnati, New York, or London; but I am and was opposed, and I presume will always be opposed, to any Bible Society composed of a few individuals in Cincinnati or in any other city, who, without any notification, publication, or call upon the brethren outside their own city to participate with them in the affair, shall constitute themselves into a *continental association,* calling themselves the *"American Christian Bible Society,"* electing officers for the nation, appointing a treasurer from among themselves, &c. &c., and then calling upon the whole Christian community to form auxiliaries to them, and to send their funds to the management and disposal of their officers elect.[91]

The next year, the Corresponding Secretary of the American and Foreign Bible Society wrote to Campbell asking about his interest in their activities. In reply, Campbell stated that he was both a contributor and life director of the American Bible Society, and even more interested in the American and Foreign Bible Society. Referring to the group at Cincinnati who recently organized the "Cincinnati Bible Society," Campbell commented:

> I can neither approve the way of getting it up, nor see any necessity for it. To create an institution of this sort merely as a denominational affair, is, on our premises, in my judgment, wholly inexpedient.[92]

In fact Campbell was a contributor, member, and life director of both the American Bible Society and the American and Foreign Bible Society.[93]

Another unfortunate aspect of the American Christian Bible Society was its financial structure. Obviously it was necessary for the society to secure funds to accomplish its work. Similarly, they did not want people coming to their annual meetings and participating unless they were willing to shoulder the financial obligations of the society. Therefore, membership in the society was conditional upon financial support. A member paid one dollar a year. Contributing twenty-five dollars made one a life member. The payment of one hundred dollars made a person a life director.[94] Putting involvement in the society on this kind of financial basis may be understandable, but it had the unfortunate tendency of

---

[91]*Ibid.,* 1846, p. 296.

[92]*Ibid,* p. 564.

[93]Richardson, vol. 2, p. 497.

[94]The constitution of the ACBS is printed in Appendix VI of Keith, pp. 242-243, quoting the *Annual Proceedings* for 1849, pp. 49-50.

suggesting the whole arrangement was one of crass commercial concern and people had to buy their way in.

The American Christian Bible Society did not have a full, rich, and productive life. Individuals and churches of the Movement never supported it as much as its founders had hoped. Shortly after midcentury, the Baptists began plans for a new version of the Bible, translated in America. They formed a Bible Union to facilitate this, and the ACBS joined in. Alexander Campbell translated the book of Acts for the new version. But when the Baptists secured complete control over the Union, they redesigned the new version to conform to their theology. At that point the Christian Churches backed out of the project. By 1856 the ACBS was simply absorbed into the larger work of the American Christian Missionary Society.[95]

In 1846 Burnet also led in the creation of the Sunday School and Tract Society.[96] This group also came to be known as the Cincinnati Tract Society. A few years later it was enlarged to become the American Christian Publication Society.[97] This was a more ambitious organization, but its existence led to rivalry, criticism, and attack. It also was dissolved in 1856.

The ACBS was the first national organization of the Restoration Movement, and its appearance challenged the continuing unity within the Movement. At about the same time, an interesting, contrasting attraction of union came through the invitation of the Evangelical Alliance. This group was formed in 1846 by both American and European evangelicals desirous of forming a group in which denominational differences

---

[95]Keith, pp. 120-121, 152. According to Earl I. West, however, the Ohio State Convention agreed that year to terminate the Society and turn over all funds to the American Bible Union (Earl Irvin West, *The Search for the Ancient Order*, vol. 1, p. 165). Regrettably, West gives no documentation for this information. It is reinforced, however, by this statement in *The Life and Times of Benjamin Franklin* by Joseph Franklin and J. A. Headington (St. Louis: John Burns, Publisher, 1879), pp. 301-302: "The American Christian Bible Society at once turned to the American Bible Union, as the direction in which all its energies could best be expended. In 1856 the Bible Union was well-known among the Disciples, and was receiving very large direct contributions from them. The Bible Society was therefore dissolved." However, the same authors observe that in 1856 "the Bible and Publication Societies were dissolved, and their interests merged into the American Christian Missionary Society" (*ibid.*, p. 249). Perhaps the resolution of this is that the actual work of the ACBS was merged into that of the Missionary Society, but the interests of the Disciples in Bible translation work was transferred to the Bible Union. This will allow grains of truth in both positions presented.

[96]Keith, pp. 76-77, 203.

[97]Murch, p. 147.

would remain, while all Protestants agreed to a common creed and practiced intercommunion.[98]

Alexander Campbell was invited to attend the original meeting in London set for August, but he declined.[99] He considered it a union of sects rather than of spirits, Protestant (directed against Rome) rather than evangelical (directed toward the Lord Jesus). Yet he was encouraged to believe that it would focus attention on the desire to bring union and cooperation in the name of the church.[100] In his final notice of the Alliance he wished the union effort "God speed." Although he had significant reservations about the unbiblical language used in their doctrinal statements, he finished with a positive comment.

> I thank God and take courage from every effort, however imperfect it may be, to open the eyes of the community to the impotency and wickedness of schism, and to impress upon the conscientious and benevolent portion of the Christian profession the excellency, the beauty, and the importance of union and co-operation in the cause of Christ, as prerequisite to the diffusion of Christianity throughout the nations of the earth.[101]

The ACBS may have been the first national organization of the Christian Churches, but in 1849 its importance was superseded by another development that far overshadowed the ACBS's original significance. It was obvious by this time that there was a growing mood to develop some organization for the churches. Something similar had been discussed during the Rice debate, but abandoned.[102] Campbell began a new series of articles on "Church Organization" in February of 1849 with the statement, "There is now heard from the East and from the West, from the North and from the South, one general, if not universal, call for a more efficient organization of our churches."[103]

Alexander Hall, editor of the *Gospel Proclamation*, urged in March of 1849 that a general convention be held in the autumn. He seemed to sense that Cincinnati would be an acceptable location, and he suggested that Campbell set the date.[104] Campbell himself concurred in this

---

[98]R. R. Mathisen, "Evangelical Alliance," in *Dictionary of Christianity in America*, edited by Daniel G. Reid (Downers Grove, Illinois: InterVarsity Press, 1990), p. 408.

[99]*Millennial Harbinger*, 1846, pp. 232-235.

[100]*Ibid.*, p. 446.

[101]*Ibid.*, 1847, p. 253.

[102]See p. 200 of this chapter.

[103]*Millennial Harbinger*, 1849, p. 90.

[104]Garrison and DeGroot, p. 244.

call for a general meeting and suggested it take place in Cincinnati, Lexington, Louisville, or Pittsburgh.[105]

Realizing that there was still widespread resistance to the idea of such a meeting, Campbell continued his series of articles on church organization and defended the idea of the coming convention. Campbell was unwilling to accept the argument that such a meeting in the absence of explicit Scriptural authorization was compromising the nature of primitive Christianity.

> To ask for a *positive* precept for every thing in the details of duties growing out of the various and numerous exigencies of the Christian church and the world, would be quite as irrational and unscriptural as to ask for an immutable wardrobe or a uniform standard of apparel for all persons and ages in the Christian church.[106]

Furthermore, he argued, "In all things pertaining to public interest, not of Christian faith, piety, or morality, the church of Jesus Christ in its aggregate character, is left free and unshackled by any apostolic authority."[107] In another article, he continued, "Frequent conferences or conventions, sometimes called 'associations,' become expedient and necessary to give direction and energy to the instruments and means of social advancement."[108]

> It is not expedient, nor is it necessary, were we competent to the task, to go into a specification of all the objects that may legitimately and advantageously come before such meetings and conferences. The public press, evangelical missions, domestic and foreign bible translation, religious tracts, and moral agencies of every sort necessary or favorable to the prosperity of the churches of Christ and to the conversion of the world, Jew and Gentile, are probably the objects which might advantageously claim a sort of general superintendency.[109]

It is hard to reconcile this statement with Campbell's comment in 1823 about the apostolic church:

> They dare not transfer to a missionary society, or Bible society, or education society, *a cent or a prayer,* lest in so doing they should rob the church of its

---

[105]*Millennial Harbinger*, 1849, p. 273.
[106]*Ibid.*, pp. 269-270.
[107]*Ibid.*, p. 270.
[108]*Ibid.*, p. 271.
[109]*Ibid.*, pp. 272-273.

glory and exalt the inventions of men above the wisdom of God. *In their church capacity alone they moved.*[110]

Consequently, Campbell was often criticized by many of his brethren for now advocating and supporting such a convention and the rise of various societies. These brethren had become convinced of the rightness of Campbell's earlier position, and when he moved away from it, they did not accompany him. This created the first, serious widespread area of disagreement within the Restoration Movement.

Meanwhile preparations for the coming convention were moving along. Campbell gave it further encouragement by saying in August,

> I am of opinion that a Convention, or general meeting, of the churches of the Reformation is a very great desideratum. Nay, I will say further, that it is all important to the cause of reformation. I am also of opinion that Cincinnati is the proper place for holding such Convention. . . . [It should be] a Convention of messengers of churches, selected and constituted such by the churches—one from every church if possible, or if impossible, one from a district, or some definite number of churches. It is not to be composed of a few self-appointed messengers, or of messengers from one, two, or three districts, or States, but a *general* Convention. . . .
>
> The purposes of such a primary convention are already indicated by the general demand for a more efficient and Scriptural organization—for a more general and efficient co-operation in the Bible cause, in the Missionary cause, in the Education cause.[111]

Campbell went on to suggest that the proper time for such a meeting would be the following May, that is, May of 1850. However because the annual meeting of the American Christian Bible Society and the Tract Society took place in Cincinnati in October, many felt that since numerous brethren were already going to Cincinnati for this meeting, it would be appropriate to have the general convention assemble immediately thereafter, to save these many brethren an extra trip to Cincinnati. This was accordingly done, and the convention met in Cincinnati, October 23-28, 1849. Attendance was one hundred fifty-six, from over one hundred different churches, representing eleven states.[112]

Campbell wanted to be present, but before departure time he became ill and had to stay home. In his absence, however, he was elected president of the convention. W. K. Pendleton, Campbell's son-in-law, did

---

[110]*Christian Baptist,* vol. 1, no. 1 (August, 1823), p. 15. Italics in original.
[111]*Millennial Harbinger,* 1849, pp. 473-474.
[112]Garrison and DeGroot, p. 245.

attend and brought back to Bethany a full report. One of the first things the convention did was acknowledge that the ACBS was cooperating with the American and Foreign Bible Society, and recommend it to the support of the brethren. On the basis of this, Campbell immediately removed all objections to it.[113]

Campbell had recommended that delegates from the churches be sent, or at least delegates from each district. Some delegates did in fact arrive, but most of those who came were simply interested persons, not officially representing their churches. Thus early in the meeting, one man raised the question of what constituted a "delegate." Discussion of means of representation lasted most of one morning, but the question was left unresolved.[114]

Perhaps the most significant development to come out of the convention was the creation of a missionary society, soon called the American Christian Missionary Society, whose object was "to promote the spread of the Gospel in destitute places of our own and foreign lands." Alexander Campbell was chosen President, and D. S. Burnet was the First Vice President. There were provisions in the constitution for life members ($20 payment) and life directors ($100 payment); in the space of a few minutes, fifty-two paid for life memberships and eleven paid for life directorships, thus raising over two thousand dollars the first evening.[115] Unfortunately, the same criticisms that were earlier made about the mercenary character of the ACBS were now made about the ACMS.

James T. Barclay, a medical doctor from Virginia, was one of the regional vice presidents of the American Christian Missionary Society, but he also volunteered to go to the mission field. Approved by the Society, he sailed in 1850, arriving in Palestine in 1851. He had decided that the Movement must speak where the Bible speaks, and Jesus in Acts 1:8 charged His disciples to be His witnesses in Jerusalem, Judea, Samaria, and to the uttermost parts of the earth. Hence Barclay concluded that the Bible plan was to begin in Jerusalem. He was the first missionary sent out by the Society, and certainly the first foreign missionary. At that time, however, Jerusalem was mostly inhabited by Muslims, who are very difficult to convert to Christianity. Barclay stayed in Jerusalem ten years, until he was called home by the financial pressures of the Civil War. The Jerusalem mission dissolved, but it was at least the beginning of energetic missions endeavors for the Christian Churches.

---

[113]*Millennial Harbinger,* 1849, cf. pp. 692 and 694-695.
[114]Earl I. West, vol. 1, p. 174.
[115]*Millennial Harbinger,* 1849, pp. 690-691.

But the erection of the missionary society was not achieved without considerable criticism. The church in Connellsville, Pennsylvania adopted ten resolutions expressing their concern about the creation of the ACMS. Part of this concern was focused on the financial requirements for membership. They stated they could neither aid nor sanction any society that would exclude the apostles from membership, because as Peter said [Acts 3:6], "Silver and gold have we none"! They considered the church to be "the only scriptural organization on earth for the conversion of sinners and sanctification of believers." Therefore it is not *a* missionary society, but *the* missionary society—the only one authorized by Christ or sanctioned by the apostles. They considered the founding of the society dangerous because there is no "thus saith the Lord" for it, and the argument for expediency had already brought in such things as infant baptism, sprinkling, the papacy, and a thousand other evils. They regarded the society as heretical and schismatic because it would invariably divide the body of Christ by including some and excluding other members of the body of Christ.[116]

Campbell responded by focusing on their contention that the church is the only missionary society. He simply pointed out that the church at Connellsville is not *the church* of Christ. The church of Christ is not any particular congregation, but it is composed of all believers. Campbell contended that it is competent for "the church of Christ" to consult and cooperate with all individual communities [congregations] in her constituency.[117]

One of those who spoke out strongly against the convention and the missionary society was Jacob Creath, Sr., in a series of articles, most of which were quotations from William Ellery Channing. Channing warned against the potential despotism of such organizations encroaching on freedom of thought, or speech, and of the press.[118] Campbell simply replied, *"the abuse of any thing, is no reason, no argument against it."* [119] In a later installment, Creath pointed out the apparent discrepancy between Campbell's earlier position in the *Christian Baptist* and the position he is now taking defending the convention.

Permit me, my dear brother, to say to you in all kindness and candor, that your brethren who now oppose conventions and who have opposed them

---

[116]*Ibid.*, 1850, pp. 282-284.

[117]*Ibid.*, pp. 285-286.

[118]*Ibid.*, pp. 408-410. The additional articles in this series, and often Campbell's responses, are on pp. 469-471, 493-504, 614-617, and 637-641.

[119]*Ibid.*, p. 410. Italics in original.

since they entered this Reformation, are equally sorry to find you and others opposing conventions in the great platform you laid down for us in the Christian Baptist, and now to find you and them advocating conventions as zealously as you then opposed them. If you were right in the Christian Baptist, you are wrong now. If you are right now, you were wrong then. If you were right in the Christian Baptist, we are right now, in opposing conventions. We follow the first lessons you gave us on this subject. If we are wrong, Bro. Campbell taught us the wrong. Instead of denying this fact, and endeavoring to conceal it, and to throw the blame upon us, we believe it would be more *just* and Christian to confess the charge, and to acknowledge that the arguments you offered in the Christian Baptist, against conventions, are much more unanswerable than any that have been offered for them since that time. It is the desire of many brethren, who sincerely love and admire you, that you will reconcile the arguments in the Christian Baptist, offered against conventions, with those you now offer for them. We are unable to do this, and, therefore, we ask it as a favor of you to do it.[120]

Campbell's reply to this portion of Creath's comments is not a very candid or satisfying one. He said the "alledged [sic] antagonism between the Christian Baptist and the Millennial Harbinger" is disposed of by simply examining the definition of the word "convention," which "indicates merely a coming together for any purpose."

Hence a convention may be either scriptural or unscriptural, consistent or inconsistent with Christian law and precedent, good or evil, just as the end or object for which it is constituted, or for which it assembles. Paul and James have been, with as much reason and divine authority, arrayed against each other, as the Christian Baptist and Millennial Harbinger, on the subject of justification. . . . Bro. Creath can reconcile Paul and James. The same amount of perspicacity of mind and candor will, no doubt, enable him to see that in contrasting the Christian Baptist and the Millennial Harbinger, he is warring against a chimera.[121]

However, this denial of a contradiction does not really satisfy the disturbing awareness of an apparent contradiction.

One interesting attempt to explain Campbell's apparent change of position is that after the harsh experiences of 1847, he was a physically broken man, one who was now controlled by others, namely the organization-conscious D. S. Burnet. The year 1847 saw Campbell make an arduous trip to England, during which he received antislavery allegations, experienced a Scottish jail for alleged libel [from which he was

---

[120]*Ibid.*, p. 637.
[121]*Ibid.*, p. 638.

cleared], and suffered a bad chest cold and near-pneumonia. In addition, when he returned home, he learned that his ten-year-old son Wycliffe had drowned in his absence.

Tolbert Fanning went to see Campbell after the society was formed and reported that he was shocked to find Campbell's mind so shaken he could hardly keep it on any subject of discussion; he had to be prompted to keep up an ordinary conversation. David Lipscomb picked up this viewpoint from Fanning and continued to defend and popularize it.[122] For some time this remained the standard explanation for those who wanted to revere Campbell's memory yet who also wanted to reject his acceptance of the missionary society.

In the year of Campbell's death, his son-in-law, W. K. Pendleton, came back to the same issue in his address delivered at the eighteenth anniversary of the ACMS. Referring to the complaint that "we are departing from original ground. The Fathers of this Reformation were opposed to missionary Societies," Pendleton remarked that it was a case of appealing to human authority in the absence of biblical grounds. In a cutting assertion, he commented,

> There is a class among us, who have a sort of bibliolatry toward the Christian Baptist, and, as is usual in such cases, they imagine that it has uttered many oracles, which upon a more careful study it will be found are not to be discovered on its pages. This is especially the case, with reference to this subject of missions.[123]

Pendleton went on to observe that in his earliest writings, Campbell was fighting sectarianism,

> which as organizations, both in their theory and their practice, he was deeply convinced, were injurious to the highest interests of the church, and incumbrances upon the primitive power of the Gospel. As such he attacked them.[124]

Campbell was not, Pendleton insists, opposed to missionary work, but to the unauthorized plans and schemes. Yet this seems to concede the very point of those opposed to the ACMS.

In spite of such occasional bickering, the ACMS continued, supported by some, opposed by others. One of those who opposed for a long time into the future, and whose opposition crystallized a sizeable base of resistance to it, was Tolbert Fanning. In 1855 he and William Lipscomb

---

[122]Earl I. West, vol. 1, pp. 182-183.
[123]*Millennial Harbinger,* 1866, p. 497.
[124]*Ibid.,* pp. 497-498.

established the *Gospel Advocate* and hoped to provide a platform for discussion of such organizations.[125] Fanning was willing to provide the platform and listen to the arguments in favor of the ACMS, although he personally was not convinced that it was proper. Fanning attended the meeting in 1859 and addressed it, mostly for the purpose of presenting the means of direct congregational support for missions done by the church of which he was a member in Tennessee.[126]

Another result of this whole spate of organizing in the decade of the 1840s was to further the work of state societies. We have seen that Indiana gathered a state meeting in 1839. Indiana was also significant in that in 1849, barely three weeks ahead of the formation of the ACMS, the Indiana meeting organized itself under a constitution and bylaws as the Indiana Christian Missionary Society on October 6, 1849. Other states soon followed Indiana's lead and formed their own state societies. Kentucky had a state meeting in 1840 and organized the Kentucky Christian Missionary Society in 1850. The Ohio Christian Missionary Society came in 1852.[127] Virtually every state did the same, particularly in the heartland of the country. This pattern of state societies further reinforced the trend for the future.

Additional Problem Issues

Another issue that became troublesome about mid-century was that of full-time, located salaried ministers. In the early years of the movement, there were no full-time preachers. No church could have afforded one. Few denominations provided full-time salaries. B. W. Stone farmed in addition to serving his two churches in Kentucky. Even back in Ireland, Thomas Campbell had taught school to supplement his salary as a minister. Most Baptist preachers on the frontier farmed for a living and preached on the side.

In most of the early congregations of the Movement, the elders did the preaching, usually on an unpaid basis. The elders might take turns preaching, or an ordained minister might preach every other week or once a month on a regular basis. Many preachers went off on evangelistic tours of several months; what little financial compensation they received barely covered their expenses. Wife and children maintained the farm back home as a means of providing for their needs.

---

[125]Earl I. West, vol. 1, p. 20.
[126]*Ibid.*, p. 210.
[127]McAllister and Tucker, p. 179. See also Garrison and DeGroot, pp. 234 ff.

The end result of all this was that early preachers were not full-time salaried individuals; no church could have afforded that. Alexander Campbell had early on taken a position against preaching for pay; although he changed that position after several years, many of his followers still maintained that principle. Even as late as 1831, Campbell still maintained, "To employ men to preach the gospel in a christian congregation is a satire upon that congregation which employs them."[128]

By midcentury, however, the situation had begun to change, particularly in towns. In the cities, many people were paid cash in their jobs—as opposed to the countryside where farmers grew their own food, made their own clothing, and had only a negligible cash crop. Their support of the church was often in terms of produce or livestock. But workers in towns received cash for their labor, and this cash was easily given to the church where it could be used much more liquidly.

The result was that, by this time, many churches had a financial income that allowed the salary of a minister. Such a full-time, settled minister spending all his time with just one church and being paid for it was often called a "pastor." This was also often referred to as a "one-man system." Apparently the first church to do this was the church at Eighth and Walnut, Cincinnati, with D. S. Burnet as the minister. Isaac Errett in Warren, Ohio, may have been the second. Both of these occurred in the 1850s.[129]

There are three issues involved here. One is that the arrangement is an innovation. Such a situation had not existed in the earlier days of the Movement. The mere fact of its newness made it suspicious in the minds of many. A second issue was that of church polity. A church under such a one-man system seemed to place the preacher over the elders. This raised significant questions about proper church structure. In addition, it brought to mind the concerns of Alexander Campbell and the early days of the *Christian Baptist* where he was attacking the pretensions of the clergy. Having a full-time salaried preacher seemed like the return of the hireling system of clergy that the Restoration Fathers had attacked so strongly in the pioneer days.

A third issue takes its precedent from Thomas Campbell, who had coined the slogan, "Where the Scriptures speak, we speak." Where does the Bible speak about such a one-man ministry? The Bible talks about apostles; that office has ceased. The Bible talks about prophets; that office has ceased. The Bible talks about evangelists; those seem to be

---

[128]*Millennial Harbinger,* 1831, p. 237.
[129]McAllister and Tucker, p. 243.

traveling evangelists, not located. The Bible talks about pastors and
teachers; those seem to be the local elders. Where exactly does the Bible
talk about a full-time, located, salaried *preacher?* Because there is no
explicit Scriptural verse, many saw the whole arrangement not only as an
innovation, but a going beyond biblical authority, just as much as was the
missionary society.

Tolbert Fanning could not accept the idea of salaried ministers or the
arrangement that located preachers were pastors. For him,

> The logical teachers, and overseers of the church were the elders. The elders
> were but the elderly men in the church. They "kept house for the Lord," and
> edified the saints. All the teaching was done by this group. They had no office,
> but each elder (old man) in accordance with his ability, taught and edified the
> church. The evangelists went from place to place, preaching the gospel, estab-
> lishing churches, and encouraging them to meet regularly.[130]

In 1856, he wrote in the *Gospel Advocate,* "The brethren who advocate
the salary system lose sight of the fact that we professed in years past to
adopt the Scripture as our only rule of faith and practice." When D. S.
Burnet recommended "that each church be supplied with a resident
evangelist as pastor of the flock," Fanning replied, "There is not a word
in the Scriptures favoring such views; the brethren have adopted their
views and practices from the sectarian influences that surround
them."[131] Concerned over clerical hierarchy, Benjamin Franklin
opposed "the building up of a new or older order of *clergy,* as a class, distinct from other members of the Church" as well as "clerical conventions
. . . or associations for their own government . . . or any other purpose
not taught in Scripture."[132]

One of the factors that must be acknowledged here is the basic matur-
ing of the movement as well as the context of the times. Arrangements
that were adequate for the churches in the early days of the movement in
a pioneer frontier setting were one thing. However, the country was now
developing large cities in the Midwest, with churches numbering membership in the hundreds. Urban life was becoming more complex and
polished. With all due respect to the attacks on hireling clergy in the
1820s, by midcentury, a professional, trained ministry was proving to
have advantages in terms of ministering to people's needs and organizing
local congregations for evangelism, worship, and edification. Those who

---

[130]Earl I. West, vol. 1, p. 342.
[131]Garrison and DeGroot, p. 342.
[132]Quoted from the *American Christian Review,* in McAllister and Tucker, p. 243.

argued against located salaried ministers used the traditional arguments demanding biblical precedents. But a more accurate understanding of their situation may be to see them as a group of people looking back with nostalgia upon "the good old days" because they did not feel comfortable with the significant cultural transitions that were going on all around them.

Another issue that developed around midcentury became the most controversial issue of this entire period. This was the use of musical instruments in worship. On the original frontier, no musical instruments were used for worship. Part of the reason for this was simply economic—pianos and organs were much too expensive for the average church to have one. Other instruments that were easily available on the frontier—violins, for instance, commonly called "fiddles"—were associated with dancing and were therefore considered worldly and inappropriate for religious services.

But as the Midwest moved from the frontier period to midcentury, the standard of living rose as well, particularly in the cities. This meant that city families were more likely to have musical instruments in their homes. By the same token, they were more likely to be agreeable to having such instruments in their churches. As we have already seen with regard to the issue of salaried ministers,[133] city churches had more cash available. The same congregations that were likely to have a salaried minister were likely to use musical instruments in church; economics was a factor in both situations.

This issue was not limited to the Stone-Campbell Movements. Any group that held a conviction about the New Testament as a model was liable to be disturbed by the introduction of musical instruments. At the beginning of the Protestant Reformation in the sixteenth century, both Calvin and Zwingli were opposed to the use of the organ in worship. In early nineteenth-century America, the use of instruments in worship played a part in such schisms as the Free Methodists, the Primitive Baptists, and the Reformed Presbyterians.[134] The eastern Christians adopted a resolution against the use of musical instruments in worship in 1827.[135]

Within the mainstream of the Restoration Movement, controversy broke out in the decade of the 1850s, apparently originating in Kentucky. A writer to the *Ecclesiastical Reformer* brought up the issue, commenting that the Christian Church was far behind the Protestants in the subject of church music. Associate editor J. B. Henshall replied by saying that the

---

[133]See supra, in this chapter, pp. 218-220.
[134]Murch, p. 160.
[135]Garrison and DeGroot, p. 343.

worldly minded need helps to their devotion and those in the dark need symbolic rites; but those "who live in the full light of the gospel privileges, and enjoy God's mercies and providence" do not.[136]

This and other articles, notably on the encouragement of dancing, led John Rogers to write to Campbell and request a thorough treatment and denunciation of these vices. He was obviously repulsed at the thought of instrumental music in the churches and put it in the same category as dancing, card playing, theater going, and circus going.[137]

Two months later, Campbell quoted two paragraphs from "G." that strongly supported the idea of using instruments in worship to enhance the solemnity of worship as well as excite the emotions of the hearers. Campbell replied that such an aid to worship would be natural for those who had no spiritual discernment, "no real devotion or spirituality." But, he concluded, "to all spiritually-minded Christians, such aids would be as a cow bell in a concert."[138]

Up to this point, however, the discussion had been fairly theoretical. In fact, no congregation within the Restoration Movement had instruments to accompany the singing. That changed, however, in 1859 when the church in Midway, Kentucky, brought in a melodeon. The minister there, L. L. Pinkerton, said that the singing had degenerated to such "screeching and brawling" as would "scare even the rats from worship." In an attempt to improve the congregational singing, the people gathered on Saturday night to practice the songs for the next morning. Then someone brought in a melodeon just to give the right pitch. Before long, one of the women was playing the melodeon to accompany the singing. People noticed this improved the singing significantly. The next step was to use the instrument on Sunday morning.

Not everyone approved of this development, however. Late one night an elder, Adam Hibler, pushed one of his slaves, Reuben, through a window. Reuben passed the detested melodeon through the window and Hibler took it home with him. But another melodeon was soon brought in, and instrumental music continued to be used in the Midway church.[139]

Early in 1860, Ben Franklin, editor of the *American Christian Review*, was asked his opinion of instrumental music in the worship service. He thought it would be appropriate under three conditions: (1) where a

---

[136]Quoted in Earl I. West, vol. 1, pp. 308-309.

[137]*Millennial Harbinger,* 1851, pp. 467-468.

[138]*Ibid.*, pp. 581-582.

[139]The original offending instrument was discovered in this century in a private home outside Midway. The melodeon was brought to Midway College, where it now rests on display in the library building. See Hailey, *Attitudes,* p. 201.

church had lost or never had the spirit of Christ; (2) where a preacher had lost or never had the spirit of Christ and cannot keep his audience's interest; or (3) if the church intends to be only a fashionable society, a place of amusement and secular entertainment and not a place of religion and worship.[140] Pinkerton himself soon replied:

> As far as known to me, or, I presume, to you, I am the only 'preacher' in Kentucky of our brotherhood who has publicly advocated the propriety of employing instrumental music in *some* churches, and that the church of God in Midway is the only church that has yet made a decided effort to introduce it.[141]

This issue of instruments in worship became probably the most sensitive and controversial of the century. The missionary society issue was a close second, but the "organ question" became dominant. Part of this was because people who resisted the societies could still worship with those who supported them. But the use or nonuse of the organ was more immediate. Once an organ was introduced into a congregation, those who were opposed to it could no longer worship there.

The organ issue grew slowly. Midway was the first congregation to adopt its use, but soon other churches—particularly in larger cities— were doing the same. It was not until after the Civil War that the practice spread and the issue grew in proportion.

It is important to realize, however, that neither the missionary society, nor the organ, nor the issue of salaried ministers is the real issue. These are all symptoms of the underlying issue, which is that of biblical authority and how it is applied. It was usually the case (there were exceptions, of course) that those who were in favor of societies were in favor of salaried ministers and were in favor of instrumental music. Those who were opposed to societies were usually opposed to instrumental music as well as salaried ministers. These three symptoms were correlatives in a larger pattern of how one viewed Scriptural authority for the church.

The two viewpoints can both be traced back to Thomas Campbell's motto, "Where the Scriptures speak, we speak; where they are silent, we are silent." There is basically no problem with the first half. "Where the Scriptures speak, we speak." On things the Bible clearly talks about, the church is committed to teaching these things: the existence of God, the deity of Christ, elders in local churches, baptism, etc.

---

[140]*American Christian Review*, vol. 3, no. 5 (January 31, 1860), p. 19, as quoted by Earl I. West, vol. 1, p. 311.

[141]*American Christian Review*, vol. 3, no. 9 (February 28, 1860), p. 34, as quoted in Earl I. West, vol. 1, p. 311.

But the problem comes in the second half of the phrase. "Where the Scriptures are silent, we are silent." What does it mean to be "biblically silent"? One viewpoint is to insist that the church can do nothing more than is authorized in Scripture. This means that the biblical silence becomes a prohibition. The Scriptures do not specifically authorize societies, musical instruments, or salaried ministers. Therefore such things are wrong and must be prohibited. The other viewpoint is to insist that biblical silence grants personal liberty. Thomas Campbell said in Proposition V of the *Declaration and Address*, "Where the Scriptures are silent, no human authority has the power to interfere." Human authority can interfere by demanding or by prohibiting. In Proposition XIII, Campbell had stated,

> If any circumstantials indispensably necessary to the observance of Divine ordinances be not found upon the page of express revelation, such, and such only, as are absolutely necessary for this purpose should be adopted under the title of human expedients.[142]

Granted, this proposition talks about things being *absolutely* necessary, but it still gives way for flexibility in the name of expediency.

These two viewpoints are almost exactly parallel to the two views that were adopted toward the United States Constitution immediately after its adoption in 1789. In American political history, these two views came to be known as "loose construction" and "strict construction." The strict constructionists insisted that the federal government could do only what was explicitly authorized for it to do in the Constitution. The loose constructionists insisted that as long as the federal government stayed within the guidelines of both the letter and spirit of the Constitution, it could do whatever was necessary to get the job done.

An early case in point was the question of the U.S. Bank. The Constitution granted to the federal government the authority to coin money and establish a national currency. The loose constructionists (Alexander Hamilton, particularly—the Secretary of the Treasury) argued that the right to coin money and establish a national currency must also include right to control the money supply; this meant a bank to act as a reservoir to control the amount of currency in circulation. The strict constructionists (Thomas Jefferson and others) argued that such a bank was outside the authority of the Constitution and was therefore an unauthorized invasion of state banking privileges.

---

[142]T. Campbell, p. 26.

Notice that in this argument there is no question as to what is the authority—both sides agree it is the Constitution. The argument is over how it is applied—loosely or strictly. The same applies to the arguments going on around midcentury within the Restoration Movement. There is no question as to the authority—it is the Bible. The question, however, is how the Bible is to be applied—loosely or strictly. One side argues that the Bible does not explicitly authorize societies, instruments, or salaried ministers. The other side argues that these are expedients to getting the job done—evangelism, worship, ministry. The question is how the authority of Scripture is to be applied.

This argument continued throughout the remainder of the century and beyond. The major issues that were the focus of the argument were already on the scene by the time the Civil War broke out, but the war itself put them all pretty well into the background. The Civil War dominated the country's thinking for several years, but as soon as the war was over (and in some cases, even during it), the issues came back to influence the next stages of historic development of the Restoration Movement.

1856	Ben Franklin begins the *American Christian Review*
1861	Civil War begins
1866	Alexander Campbell dies *Christian Standard* begun
1869	Louisville plan for funding the ACMS
1872	International Sunday School Uniform Lessons
1874	Christian Woman's Board of Missions organized
1875	Foreign Christian Missionary Society organized
1881	Young People's Society of Christian Endeavor
1882	J.R. Garrison publishes *Christian-Evangelist* in St. Louis
1889	Sand Creek "Address and Declaration"

Chapter 9

Unity Broken

The American Civil War was a disastrous time for the entire country. It has been seen as one of the major watersheds of American history, and it determined American politics for the next half century. In retrospect, it is easy to see that there were numerous signs along the way heralding the political division. At the time, however, most people thought the union could be preserved, in spite of the increasing tension over slavery. Division in the churches was one of the first indicators of how deeply this issue ran in the American consciousness.

Civil War

Several of the largest denominations in the country divided over slavery in the 1840s. In 1845 both the Southern Baptists and the Southern Methodists officially split off from the larger bodies. The Presbyterians had already divided between the New Side and Old Side groups, but both of these divided over the Civil War, with the result that New Side and Old Side North formed one group and the New Side/Old Side South formed another. The eastern Christians back in 1811 had merged with the followers of Guirey, and in 1841 had absorbed the followers of O'Kelly. But in 1854 the southern and northern Christians divided over the issue of slavery, not reuniting until 1890.

The mainstream of the Restoration Movement did not divide over Civil War issues, although there was certainly a good deal of debate over slavery. Shortly after the schism of the Baptists and Methodists, Alexander Campbell remarked, "We are the only religious community in the civilized world whose principles (unless we abandon them) can preserve us

227

from such an unfortunate predicament."[1] Three months later he stated:

> To preserve unity of spirit among Christians of the South and of the North is my grand object, and for that purpose I am endeavoring to show that the New Testament does not authorize any interference or legislation upon the relation of master and slave, nor does it either in letter or spirit authorize Christians to make it a term of communion. *While it prescribes the duties of both parties, masters and slaves, it sanctions the relation,* and only requires that these duties be faithfully discharged by the parties; making it the duty of all Christian churches to enforce these duties and to exact them under all the pains of Christian discipline, both from the master and from the slave—leaving it to the Lord to judge, correct, and avenge those that are without.[2]

Campbell was an emancipationist, but not an abolitionist. This means he desired freedom for the slaves, but granted gradually over a number of years and with compensation to the owners.

He himself set free two slaves he had purchased from a Methodist preacher just a few years before his second marriage. At the time of their purchase, they were 18 and 20, and Campbell promised them their freedom when they became 28. He did so, and the two men continued to work for Campbell for many years.[3] In 1845, Campbell stated that he emancipated several slaves, advised the emancipation of others that would have come to him by inheritance, and concluded by announcing, "I have set free from slavery every human being that came in any way under my influence or was my property."[4] Campbell did not wish immediate abolition of slavery, uncompensated.[5] This position cost him some support among abolitionist groups in the North.

B. W. Stone held similar positions regarding slavery. In 1829 he announced that for thirty years he had advocated the cause of liberty and opposed unmerited, hereditary slavery. All slaves in his possession he emancipated, and he did not send them out empty-handed. He admitted that a few slaves were still with him, but not under his control—they were entailed upon his children by the will of a deceased relative. He argued that it is not a question of whether slavery is right or wrong. "It is settled

---

[1]*Millennial Harbinger,* 1845, p. 51.

[2]*Ibid.,* p. 195. Italics in original.

[3]Selina Huntington Campbell, *Home Life and Reminiscences of Alexander Campbell* (St. Louis: John Burns, Publisher, 1882), p. 454.

[4]*Millennial Harbinger,* 1845, p. 259.

[5]A fuller treatment of Campbell's position on slavery is included in a chapter in Harold L. Lunger, *The Political Ethics of Alexander Campbell* (St. Louis: The Bethany Press, 1954), pp. 193-222.

in the nation, that it is wrong, both politically and morally."[6] On April 21, 1830, Stone chaired the organizational meeting of the Georgetown Colonization Society and was made its first president.[7] His move to Illinois in 1834 was to get his family away from marrying into slaveholding families in Kentucky.

In spite of Campbell's personal tolerance on the slavery issue, other individuals in the Movement were not as flexible. Within the Christian Churches, perhaps the most vocal supporter of slavery was James Shannon, an Irish immigrant who later became a professor at the University of Georgia and then president of the University of Missouri. In 1855, the year after Congress adopted the Kansas-Nebraska Act, Shannon declared that slavery was sanctioned by Nature, the Constitution, and the Bible, and any violation of the right to hold slaves was a just cause of war between the states.[8]

Probably the most aggressive on the other side of the issue was Pardee Butler. He moved from Indiana to Kansas in 1855 to evangelize and resist proslavery forces gathering in the territory. He started seven congregations, but he became more controversial on his other agenda item. In 1858 Butler requested funds from the American Christian Missionary Society to aid his efforts. When the ACMS refused to subsidize such a blatant political agitator, abolitionists in Indiana organized a rival missionary society to support Butler, led by Ovid Butler (no relation).

Thus the North Western Christian Missionary Society was formed in Indianapolis in the fall of 1859. It was to be similar to the American Christian Missionary Society, but its constituency was in the North, and therefore it was free to speak out on such subjects as slavery, which was forbidden in the ACMS because of the risk of alienating southern support. Dr. Barclay, the missionary in Jerusalem, was a Virginia slaveholder, and the abolitionists were disgusted with the ACMS as a result. The society was organized but never accomplished much. The Civil War started within a year and a half, and by that time the ACMS was led by northern men who, because of the war mood, were no longer willing to sympathize with slavery interests.[9]

In addition, there was the dispute between Bethany College and

---

[6]*Christian Messenger*, vol. 3, no. 8 (June, 1829), p. 198.

[7]*Ibid.*, vol. 4, no. 7 (June, 1830), pp. 163-164.

[8]David Edwin Harrell, Jr., *A Social History of the Disciples of Christ, Vol. 1, Quest for a Christian America: The Disciples of Christ and American Society to 1866* (Nashville: The Disciples of Christ Historical Society, 1966), p. 124. Harrell gives over several pages to Shannon's position and activities on the issue.

[9]Shaw, *Hoosier Disciples*, pp. 157-159.

Northwest Christian University in Indianapolis. This school opened in
1850, and one of its claims was to be located in a free state where students were not exposed to the habits and manners of slavery states. Since
Bethany was located in Virginia, the implications were obvious. In addition, in the fall of 1855 several abolitionist students were dismissed from
Bethany for agitating the issue. They transferred to Northwest Christian
University, where they explained that 80 percent of Bethany's students
were from the South, and thus the school dismissed the abolitionists
rather than risk southern support and recruitment. Campbell denied this
was the case, but it is easy to see how the slavery issue was causing severe
tensions within the Movement.[10]

Although the country was gearing up for armed conflict, many of the
leaders were committed pacifists. On the evening of May 11, 1848, on
the conclusion of the Mexican War, Alexander Campbell addressed the
Lyceum of Wheeling, [West] Virginia on the topic of war. His unsympa-
thetic remarks filled twenty-five pages of the *Millennial Harbinger*.[11] A
month and a half after the bombardment of Fort Sumter, Campbell
came out in an editorial calling war "the climax of all human inconsis-
tencies."[12] Similar views of pacifism were evident from B. W. Stone,
Benjamin Franklin, J. W. McGarvey, Moses E. Lard, and numerous others.[13] J. W. McGarvey wrote to Ben Franklin stating, "Whether I remain
a citizen of this Union, or become a citizen of a Southern Confederacy,
my feelings toward my brethren everywhere shall know no change." He
urged all brethren to avoid joining any military company or making war-
like preparations.[14] Ben Franklin himself, commenting on McGarvey's
letter, wrote, *"We will not take up arms against, fight and kill the brethren we
have labored for twenty-years to bring into the kingdom of God."*[15] Fourteen
ministers in Missouri signed a statement of neutrality, which had as its
first point the following:

> Whatever we may think of the propriety of bearing arms in extreme
> emergencies, we certainly cannot, by the New Testament, which is our only
> rule of discipline, justify ourselves in engaging in the fraternal strife now rag-
> ing in our beloved country.[16]

---

[10]The details of the issue are covered in Shaw, *Hoosier Disciples*, pp. 112-168.
Campbell's explanations on the situation at Bethany are in *Millennial Harbinger*,
1856, pp. 54-60, 111-117.
[11]*Millennial Harbinger*, 1848, pp. 361-386.
[12]*Ibid.*, 1861, p. 348.
[13]Garrison and DeGroot, p. 335; McAllister and Tucker, pp. 201-203.
[14]Franklin and Headington, pp. 286-287.
[15]*Ibid.*, p. 287. Italics in original.
[16]*Millennial Harbinger*, 1861, p. 584.

Yet not all leaders were inclined to be neutral. The *Christian Record,* published in Indianapolis by Elijah Goodwin, openly favored the Union cause and disagreed with Ben Franklin's neutral position in the *American Christian Review.*[17] W. T. Moore was preaching in Frankfort, Kentucky, when the state legislature was debating a resolution on "armed neutrality." As he remembered it later, the legislators were about evenly divided, with five or six members yet uncommitted—and all but one of the uncommitted were members of his congregation. He announced that he would preach the next Sunday on "The Duty of Christians in the Present Crisis," and this drew some forty or fifty legislators to the church service, including all the uncommitted. He upheld the sense of union so well that the uncommitted voted against "armed neutrality," thus saving Kentucky for the Union.[18]

When the shooting started, Christians of the Restoration Movement on both sides of the Mason-Dixon line acted just like their neighbors— they joined the armies of the blue or gray and tried to kill as many of the enemy as possible. The eldest son of Alexander Campbell married the heiress of a rice plantation in Louisiana and served in the war as a Confederate cavalry officer. Robert Richardson's son David served as a member of Morgan's Raiders, dying in 1864. W. H. Hopson (1823-1889) left his pastorate in Lexington, Kentucky, to become a chaplain under General Morgan.[19] Barton W. Stone, Jr. commanded the Sixth Texas Cavalry, most of one company composed of members of the Christian Church of Grayson County, Texas. The captain and first lieutenant of the company were elders of the church, the orderly sergeant was the senior deacon, and the preacher, B. F. Hall (1803-1873), was regimental chaplain.[20] Hall "rode a fine mule, carried a splendid rifle and stipulated expressly that when there was any chance of killing Yankees he must be allowed the privilege of bagging as many as possible."[21] Hall stated that his rifle could kill a deer at two hundred yards and would be just as good with a Yankee as the mark. William Baxter met with Hall once during the war and

---

[17]McAllister and Tucker, p. 203.

[18]Harrell, vol. 1, pp. 146-147, quoting W. T. Moore, "Reformation of the Nineteenth Century," *Christian-Evangelist,* 36 (May 18, 1889), p. 617. McAllister and Tucker, p. 203, document the same incident from W. T. Moore, "The Turbulent Period," in *The Reformation of the Nineteenth Century,* ed. by James H. Garrison (St. Louis: Christian Publishing Company, 1901), pp. 167-170.

[19]Garrison and DeGroot, p. 334.

[20]Harrell, vol. 1, p. 155.

[21]William Baxter, *Pea Ridge and Prairie Grove: or, Scenes and Incidents of the War in Arkansas* (Cincinnati: Poe and Hitchcock, 1866), pp. 114-116.

ventured to ask what were his views concerning his brethren with and for whom he had labored in other years in the North and West. He replied that they were no brethren of his, that the religionists on the other side of the line were all infidel, and that true religion was now only to be found in the South. . . . Once during the evening he wished that the people of the North were upon one vast platform, with a magazine of powder beneath, and that he might have the pleasure of applying the match to hurl them all into eternity.[22]

Thomas W. Caskey served as chaplain in the Eighteenth Mississippi Infantry. Other chaplains commented that it was difficult to keep him out of the fighting. Caskey himself stated that he did not think he killed anyone or broke any arms, but he tried to break as many Yankee legs as he could, because this took an additional two Yankees out of the battle to carry the immobile soldier off the field.[23]

On the other side, the most famous member of the Christian Churches to serve in the Union armies was James A. Garfield (1831-1881). He resigned as principal of Western Reserve Eclectic Institute (Hiram College) to become the colonel of the Forty-Second Ohio Infantry, later rising to the rank of major general, member of the U.S. House of Representatives, and ultimately President of the United States. James H. Garrison (1842-1931) enlisted in the Twenty-Fourth Missouri Infantry, but was wounded at Pea Ridge, Arkansas. Upon recovering, he enlisted in the Eighth Missouri Cavalry, rising to the rank of major at war's end. Dr. Lewis L. Pinkerton (1812-1875) became both surgeon and chaplain of the Eleventh Kentucky Cavalry.[24]

All of this was still unofficial involvement, of course. The Restoration Movement did not officially take sides during the conflict, mostly because there was no denominational machinery to state any policy. This came close, however, in a couple of actions of the American Christian Missionary Society and the General Conventions during the war.

In October, 1861 the American Christian Missionary Society met in Cincinnati. The war had been under way now for about six months, and no one could ignore it. A number of preachers were present in recently tailored Union uniforms, including Colonel James A. Garfield. Eight hundred Disciples were in attendance, with no leaders from the Deep South. A statement from the Missouri *Christian Pioneer* that every Disciples preacher "of note" was taking a neutral, antiwar position had

---

[22]Harrell, vol. 1, p. 156.

[23]McAllister and Tucker, p. 205, quoting *Caskey's Last Book*, edited by B. F. Manire (Nashville: The Messenger Publishing Co., 1896), p. 34.

[24]McAllister and Tucker, p. 204.

been reprinted in the Cincinnati papers and set a tense tone for the meeting. Isaac Errett presided for the aged president Alexander Campbell, who was in the audience. As the meeting progressed, John P. Robinson, a leader of the Bedford, Ohio, Christian Church and an influential member of the Ohio State Senate, introduced this resolution:

> *Resolved,* That we deeply sympathize with the loyal and patriotic in our country, in the present efforts to sustain the Government of the United States. And we feel it our duty as Christians, to ask our brethren everywhere to do all in their power to sustain the proper constitutional authorities of the Union.[25]

The resolution was seconded by Pinkerton, who joined the Union Army the next year. D. S. Burnet questioned whether such a resolution was in order since the second article of the society's constitution stated that the purpose of the Society was to promote the spread of the Gospel in destitute places.[26] Errett ruled the resolution was in order, but Raccoon John Smith appealed his decision. After a heated discussion, he withdrew his appeal, but it was reentered by Richard M. Bishop, a wealthy Cincinnati layman, at the time mayor of Cincinnati and an elder of the church at Eighth and Walnut. The appeal was sustained by majority vote. However, Pinkerton then called for a ten-minute recess in the convention. During this time, D. S. Burnet called the "mass meeting" to order during which Robinson's resolution was again introduced. Colonel Garfield gave a short speech on its behalf, and the resolution was adopted with only one dissenting vote. This stratagem preserved the "neutrality" of the Society since officially the society had not voted on the issue; the "mass meeting" was obviously a gathering of northern Disciples who had no authority except to speak for themselves.

Soon after the convention, the *Christian Pioneer* received a letter from one of the men whom it had listed as opposed to the war. The letter, anonymously signed only as "One of the Men," stated that it was the *Christian Pioneer*'s original statement that led to the introduction of the loyalty resolution.[27]

---

[25]Harrell, vol. 1, p. 159, quoting *Report of the Proceedings of the Thirteenth Anniversary Meeting of the American Christian Missionary Society* (Cincinnati: E. Morgan and Son, Printers, 1861), pp. 19-20. Harrell has the best coverage of this whole issue (pp. 157-164), although treatments can also be found in Murch, pp. 153-154; Webb, p. 203; Garrett, p. 505; Garrison and DeGroot, pp. 335-336; and McAllister and Tucker, pp. 206-207.

[26]Keith, p. 162; the original constitution is given in *Millennial Harbinger*, 1849, pp. 690-691.

[27]Harrell, vol. 1, pp. 159-160.

In 1862 the Indiana state meeting adopted a loyalty resolution that brought on a strong attack from Ben Franklin. His remarks brought an equally strong attack from Elijah Goodwin, commenting that if Franklin "determined to make a schism," it would be only a small one. At the 1862 meeting of the American Christian Missionary Society, Corresponding Secretary D. S. Burnet's report referred to the effects of the "rebellion." Kentucky pacifist and southern sympathizer J. W. McGarvey (1829-1911) wished the word "rebellion" to be replaced by "attempt at revolution," but his motion lost. He in turn caused some uproar when he submitted a report from the Kentucky state society that reprimanded the church leaders of that state who were participating in the war.[28]

Then in 1863 state societies in both Ohio and Pennsylvania passed loyalty resolutions. Burnet's report made his sympathies with the Union quite apparent. Then came a decisive series of loyalty resolutions.

> Whereas, "there is no power but of God," and "the powers that be are ordained of God;" and whereas, we are commanded in the Holy Scriptures to be subject to the powers that be, and "obey magistrates," and whereas an armed rebellion exists in our country, subversive of these divine injunctions; and whereas, reports have gone abroad that we, as a religious body, and particularly as a Missionary Society, are to a certain degree disloyal to the Government of the United States; therefore—
>
> *Resolved,* That we unqualifiedly declare our allegiance to said Government, and repudiate as false and slanderous any statements to the contrary.
>
> *Resolved,* That we tender our sympathies to our brave and noble soldiers in the fields, who are defending us from the attempts of armed traitors to overthrow our Government, and also to those bereaved, and rendered desolate by the ravages of war.
>
> *Resolved,* That we will earnestly and constantly pray to God to give our legislators and rulers, wisdom to enact, and power to execute, such laws are [as] will speedily bring to us the enjoyment of a peace that God will design and bless.[29]

The convention then went into turmoil. A motion to adjourn was defeated. Question was raised as to the appropriateness of the resolution. Errett, again in the presiding chair, ruled that on the basis of the decision two years previously, the resolutions were out of order, even though he publicly stated that he thought the earlier ruling was in error. An appeal was then made over the chair's decision, and the appeal was sustained. Another motion to adjourn was lost, as well as a motion to

---

[28]*Ibid.*, pp. 161-162.

[29]*Ibid.*, p. 163, quoting *Report of Proceedings of the Fifteenth Anniversary Meeting of the American Christian Missionary Society* (Cincinnati: E. Morgan and Sons, Printers, 1863), p. 13.

table the resolution. Then the convention voted on the resolutions and overwhelmingly passed them.[30]

McGarvey was furious. He decided that the ACMS should now go out of existence, and opposition to the Society spread throughout Kentucky.[31] Earl West reports that when the news of these resolutions reached the South, a sizeable number of members of the Christian Church went out and joined the Confederate Army.[32] Churches throughout the South became disgusted with the ACMS.

Technically, the statement Moses Lard made in 1866 is true: "We cannot divide."[33] But there is no doubt that the tensions engendered by the slavery controversy and the Civil War brought on a significant and long-standing tension within the Movement. The polarization created by the war and its causes was the dress rehearsal for a bitter division that shattered the Restoration Movement some forty years later. The geographical and ideological patterns set up in the earlier dispute were mirrored in the later one.

It may be significant to note, as Garrett does, that most of the tension was not so much North-South, as entirely within the North, with some involvement from border states.[34] The abolitionists within the Movement directed their most severe attack on the moderates, such as Franklin and Campbell, not on the editors or churches in the South. Most of the leadership was moderate and pacifist, but the adoption of the loyalty resolutions by the ACMS in 1863 was a major slap in the face to the southern Christians. There was no immediate division, but the seeds of division were watered heavily, and often openly.

The basic cause for the Restoration Movement was a disenchantment with denominational divisions as they existed on the early frontier. Thomas Campbell's major impulse was to tear down these denominational barriers to Christian unity. B. W. Stone felt the same way when the Synod of Kentucky discouraged the openness of the frontier revivals. It is tragic, therefore, when a movement that began with a commitment to unity itself began to nurture the seeds of division.

Garrett has a lengthy treatment of the question, "Did the Civil War Divide the Movement?"[35] He analyzes the viewpoint and assessment of

---

[30]Harrell, vol. 1, p. 163.

[31]*Ibid.*, p. 164.

[32]Earl I. West, *Life and Times of David Lipscomb* (Henderson, Tennessee: Religious Book Service, 1954), p. 82, as quoted by Garrett, p. 505.

[33]Garrison and DeGroot, p. 336, quoting *Lard's Quarterly.*

[34]Garrett, pp. 512-513.

[35]This is the title of the section that runs on pp. 520-529.

numerous scholars who have dealt with the issue and concludes that although the war worked havoc on the Movement, it did not cause division.[36] He cites David Lipscomb's remark in 1866 that Christian union would not allow the northern preachers to live in ease and plenty while southern brethren were destitute.[37] In 1868 W. K. Pendleton stated there was no "party," nor "any sign or fear of a division among us. There never was a more united and indissoluble people than we are."[38] Yet the seeds of dissolution were already deeply planted.

Transition of Leadership

While not directly related to the issue of the Civil War's divisiveness, the passing of the first generation of leadership within the Movement is marked by the war. Stone died in 1844, and Thomas Campbell in 1854. Walter Scott died in 1861 soon after learning the news of Fort Sumter. Alexander Campbell died in 1866, but he had already passed the reins of leadership over to others. As noticed, Campbell attended the annual meeting of the ACMS in 1861, but Isaac Errett presided on his behalf. By 1863 Campbell was becoming forgetful, often rambling, and confusing his daughter's letters from the Mediterranean with his own experiences.[39] On some occasions, Mrs. Campbell got him excused from speaking situations because of his "fatigue and debility."[40] In January of 1864, Campbell mentioned that he had begun the current issue of the *Millennial Harbinger* with great hope, but discovered that he had to discontinue his position as publisher. "The Harbinger, henceforth, will be conducted and published by my long and well-approved associate and co-laborer in many works, Prof. W. K. Pendleton,"[41] who was also his son-in-law (twice).

The *Millennial Harbinger* continued through 1870, but it was no longer the leading voice of the Movement. Part of this was the transition from Campbell to Pendleton; part of it was simply that the circulation figures for the magazine had dropped considerably. Some subscribers in the North had cancelled their subscriptions because Campbell would not condemn slavery; others in the South cancelled because, during the war, this magazine published in Union territory could not reach them.

---

[36]Garrett, pp. 527-528.

[37]Garrett, p. 525, quoting from the *Gospel Advocate,* 1866, p. 200.

[38]*Millennial Harbinger,* 1868, p. 152.

[39]Richardson, vol. 2, pp. 647-648.

[40]*Ibid.,* p. 654.

[41]*Millennial Harbinger,* 1864, p. 43.

Regardless of the combination of reasons, the *Millennial Harbinger* was but a shadow of its former self.

Instead, its place was now taken over by younger magazines, with younger editors. Benjamin Franklin (1812-1878), an Indiana preacher, started the *American Christian Review* as a monthly magazine in 1856 but changed it to a weekly in 1858. It became a leading paper, well-received throughout the brotherhood. When Franklin died in 1878, J. H. Garrison, editor of the *Christian*, said that in the late 1860s the *Review* "was regarded as *the* paper among us, by most brethren, and no doubt its patronage exceeded all the rest."[42] Franklin was a conservative and readily used his magazine as a platform from which either to defend or to attack various causes. At first he supported the missionary society, and in 1856-1857, he served as the Corresponding Secretary.[43] Even earlier, in 1845, when a writer to Franklin's *Reformer* questioned whether there ever was such "a Bible thing as co-operation," Franklin vehemently responded. He pointed to 2 Corinthians 8:18-19 and found instances of cooperation in the churches sending out a brother, and in the next chapter meeting the needs of other believers. Franklin then stoutly affirmed:

> This thing of churches acting jointly, in certain cases is a *"Bible Thing;"* and one which we had better *do,* than to stand still disputing about the "Bible Name" of it. As it respects the manner of doing it, it is principally left discretionary with the churches; and if one "experiment" does not act well, they are at liberty to try another. If a company of men can unite their means and establish a college, construct a canal or turnpike, and keep them in operation, guided only by the judgment which God has given them; what necessity can there be for a law in the Bible, specifying every particular as to how a contribution shall be raised, by several churches, and conveyed to the poor saints at any particular place, or how a brother shall be chosen by the churches and supported to preach the Gospel? All I have to say further at present is, that I am tired of hearing it plead that we must have a law specifying all the particulars in this matter, and calling for it to be pointed out, when there is no such law, and no need of any, and continuing year after year doing nothing.[44]

In 1866, however, Franklin changed his position completely on this issue. From that time on he opposed the missionary society. He supported the Louisville Plan[45] for a while, but soon opposed the society

---

[42]*Christian*, December 26, 1878, p. 4, quoted in McAllister and Tucker, p. 215.
[43]Earl I. West, *Ancient Order*, vol. 1, p. 106.
[44]Quoted in Franklin and Headington, p. 326.
[45]See below, p. 243.

consistently. He opposed musical instruments in worship consistently from the beginning. His paper was often called "Old Reliable" because of the predictability of his conservative viewpoint.

Another significant new paper was the *Gospel Advocate*, edited in Nashville. Actually it was not a new paper, but a revived one. There had been a *Gospel Advocate* begun in Nashville in 1855, edited by Tolbert Fanning and William Lipscomb.[46] The paper suspended publication during the war, and William's brother David resumed publication in 1866.[47] It was a weekly magazine and reflected Lipscomb's strong conservative stance. In addition, the paper was frankly sectional, and not just because of the loyalty resolutions adopted by the ACMS in 1863. Lipscomb opposed the Society, but it went beyond that. In the first year of publication, Lipscomb admitted,

> The fact that we had not a single paper known to us that Southern people could read without having their feelings wounded by political insinuations and slurs, had more to do with calling the *Advocate* into existence than all other circumstances combined.[48]

This attitude considerably aided the growth of the paper in the South, while at the same time it limited its spread in the North.[49] The result was a reinforcing of the paper's southern orientation. Lipscomb opposed instrumental worship as well as the missionary society and had serious misgivings about other cultural trends within the Movement. Lipscomb and his paper became the chief spokesman for the Movement in the South. It would be difficult to determine to what extent Lipscomb influenced the thinking of the South or to what extent he became simply the spokesman for a mindset already established.

A third new paper on the scene came about in response to the conservative voices in the immediate postwar period, particularly the *American Christian Review*. In December of 1865, a number of men, all northern, met to form the Christian Publishing Association, which began publishing the *Christian Standard* in April of 1866 with Isaac Errett (1820-1888)

---

[46]The best biography of Fanning is that by James R. Wilburn, *The Hazard of the Die: Tolbert Fanning and the Restoration Movement* (Austin, Texas: Sweet Publishing Co., 1969).

[47]Two good biographies on Lipscomb are Earl I. West, *Life and Times of David Lipscomb* (previously mentioned), and Robert E. Hooper, *Crying in the Wilderness: A Biography of David Lipscomb* (Nashville: David Lipscomb College, 1979).

[48]McAllister and Tucker, p. 216, quoting *Gospel Advocate*, May 1, 1866, p. 273.

[49]West, vol. 2, p. 15.

as editor.[50] The incorporators included James A. Garfield as well as the wealthy T. W. Phillips of Newcastle, Pennsylvania.

The new journal got off to a good start by purchasing the two thousand names on the subscription list from Elijah Goodwin's *Christian Record*. Within a year, Errett had built the circulation up to six thousand, but the paper was soon in serious financial difficulty.[51] So bad was the outlook that the incorporators wanted to cease publication at the end of 1867. Errett demurred, pleading for the life of the magazine. Not wanting to be saddled with further losses, the incorporators simply signed over their stock and the company's debts to Errett and gave him their blessing. Errett moved the paper from Cleveland to Alliance, Ohio, where he took the job as the president of Alliance College, editing the *Christian Standard* without any salary.

In 1869 W. T. Moore convinced Errett to transfer publication to Cincinnati, where the Quaker publisher R. W. Carroll, who had already published numerous books by Christian writers, agreed to take over the publishing duties if Errett would continue as editor. This arrangement worked out extremely well. By 1872 circulation had climbed to fifteen thousand and was rising steadily.[52] By the next year, the Standard Publishing Company was formed, with Carroll a stockholder and treasurer. The following year, Errett bought out Carroll and became sole owner of the company.[53]

Under Errett's leadership, the *Christian Standard* became a primary voice for the Movement. He was progressive in methodology but conservative in theology. He supported the missionary society; in 1867 he claimed that the *Christian Standard* "is the only weekly among us that advocates organized effort for missionary purposes."[54] He was a moderate on the instrument issue, asking both sides not to offend their brethren. Under his leadership, from the late 1870s (after the death of Ben Franklin) to the turn of the century, "the *Standard* was doubtless the most powerful weekly among the Disciples."[55] A. T. DeGroot praises Errett's statesmanlike qualities and concludes, "More than to any other journal and person, it was to the *Christian Standard* and Isaac Errett that the

---

[50]The classic biography of Errett is James Sanford Lamar, *Memoirs of Isaac Errett;* 2 vols. (Cincinnati: The Standard Publishing Company, 1893).

[51]Circulation figures come from Garrison and DeGroot, p. 357, and from McAllister and Tucker, p. 218.

[52]McAllister and Tucker, p. 219.

[53]Murch, p. 177.

[54]Quoted in Garrison and DeGroot, p. 356.

[55]McAllister and Tucker, p. 219.

Disciples were indebted for being saved from becoming a fissiparous sect of jangling legalists."[56]

The leadership of the *Christian Standard* were not the only ones concerned with the negative vibrations coming from Ben Franklin and the *American Christian Review*. For in December, 1866 Franklin had reversed his earlier support for the ACMS.[57] His son and biographer points out that this was a three-year transition since the adoption of the loyalty resolutions. Franklin had earlier supported the Society, but now it was a matter of maintaining the pure congregationalism of the Movement. For the next three years, the *American Christian Review* discussed the merits of the issue. Franklin took no part in the discussion, although his son was one of the most persistent opponents of the Society. But Franklin concluded that the Society had not accomplished what was expected of it, and it had assumed a prerogative as a representative assembly he could no longer support. So his sympathies now joined the opposition.[58]

It was to counter the voice of the *American Christian Review*, while at the same time not joining the voice of the progressive *Christian Standard*, that in 1869 J. W. McGarvey, Moses E. Lard (his *Lard's Quarterly* had ceased publication the previous year), Robert Graham, and W. H. Hopson began the *Apostolic Times*. This paper supported the missionary society, but opposed the use of the instrument. Its founders represented a formidable array of editorial and journalistic talent, but they represented a middle position of accepting one innovation while resisting another one. In spite of their moderate stance, there were not enough Disciples of similar split viewpoints to support the paper, and it died within a year.[59]

Another important paper in the period following the Civil War was the *Christian-Evangelist*. J. H. Garrison started his editorial career with the *Gospel Echo* in 1868.[60] Through several mergers and changes of name and place of publication, Garrison wound up in St. Louis in 1882 with the *Christian-Evangelist*. Within two years, his circulation list had grown from 16,000 to 25,000 where it stabilized until his retirement in 1912. At the turn of the century, it was second in circulation and influence only to the *Christian Standard*, but after the turn of the century it

---

[56]Garrison and DeGroot, p. 358.

[57]Garrison and DeGroot provide the date for the shift, p. 354.

[58]Franklin and Headington, pp. 343-344.

[59]Statements on the *Apostolic Times* can be found in Murch, pp. 170-171; Garrison and DeGroot, p. 355; and McAllister and Tucker, p. 222.

[60]The best biography on Garrison is by William E. Tucker, *J. H. Garrison and Disciples of Christ* (St Louis: The Bethany Press, 1964); also useful is Garrison's autobiographical *Memories and Experiences: A Brief Story of a Long Life* (St Louis: Christian Board of Publication, 1926).

surpassed its rival in Cincinnati.[61] Garrison's viewpoint was normally similar to that of Errett. He was progressive on the issues, yet conservative in his personal theology. In the two and a half decades after Errett's death, Garrison's editorial leadership was as significant as Errett's had been in the two decades after Campbell's death. Errett, Garrison, and Lipscomb were probably the three most significant leaders within the Restoration Movement in the latter part of the nineteenth century. W. T. Moore has been credited with the observation, "The Disciples do not have bishops; they have editors." The statement is probably true and nowhere better represented than in these three editors who played such a crucial role in the development of the Restoration Movement between the Civil War and World War I. Both the men and their magazines became spokesmen for crystallizing positions within the Movement.

Missions

Meanwhile, the ACMS was facing difficult times after the war. Because of the nature of the organization itself, as well as the added fact of the wartime loyalty resolutions, many individuals still spoke against the ACMS. Many claimed that it was wrong in and of itself because it was unscriptural and was a threat to the freedom of the local churches. In an address to the annual meeting of the ACMS in 1866, W. K. Pendleton spoke to these issues.

One of his lines of argument was to clarify the accusation that the ACMS was unscriptural. Pendleton conceded that there was no "express precept in the Scriptures commanding it." But he questioned whether it was proper to conclude that everything in this category was therefore wrong. Granting that there is Scriptural silence on the issue,

> we demand by what canon of interpretation does he make mere *silence* prohibitory? You reply, the canon which forbids anything as a rule of Christian faith or duty, for which there cannot be expressly produced a "Thus saith the Lord," "either in express terms or by approved precedent."[62]

Pendleton went on to wonder, "Whence came this canon? Does he find it in *express terms* in the Scriptures? He will not say so. Yet . . . in *adopting* the canon with his restricted interpretation, he *violates* his own canon." Pendleton hastened to add that he had no wish to depart from the rule of the Movement, "No rule without an express precept in the

---

[61]McAllister and Tucker, p. 221.
[62]*Millennial Harbinger*, 1866, p. 501. Italics in original.

Scriptures," but he does wish "to strip the rule of the false interpretation that has been put upon it, by those that pervert it to the hindrance of the Gospel."[63]

He acknowledged that the rule first came from Thomas Campbell in the *Declaration and Address*. Yet he notes that this same document set up a nonchurch organization, the Christian Association of Washington, set up officers for this organization, and even made financial contributions a condition of membership in the Association. Obviously Thomas Campbell did not intend by this rule to prohibit such organizations as the one he had just formed. Instead the rule was pointed against creeds and confessions of faith. He allowed that Thomas stipulated that where the Scriptures are silent, no human power had the authority to interfere (Proposition V), but also that where necessary, the church could adopt human expedients to accomplish the spread of the Gospel (Proposition XIII).[64] Looked at in this way, Thomas' rule was not a constraint upon organized church activity.

> Let it not be said, then, that the disciples of Christ are to take the silence of Scripture on a given subject as a positive rule of prohibition against all freedom of action or obligation of duty. No rule could be more productive of mischief than this.[65]

Furthermore, Pendleton pointed out that the word "church" may Scripturally refer to a local assembly, but it can also refer to the entire body of Christ. He observed,

> We fear that this large conception of the Church Universal is too little realized by many Christians of the present day. Their ideas of the church, and of the responsibilities and work of the church, circle too much within the limits of a single congregation. The *kingdom* of God is scarcely recognized as commensurate with the *people* of God, and the sphere of its co-operative as well as of its free individual effort, as being as wide as the Commission—"Go ye into all the world and preach the gospel to every creature."[66]

Pendleton concluded that what a local church could not do in sending out workers, the Church Universal could do cooperatively, and individual Christians were certainly free to support such endeavors so that the Gospel could be preached.[67]

---

[63]*Ibid.*, p. 502.
[64]*Ibid.*, pp. 502-504.
[65]*Ibid.*, p. 505.
[66]*Ibid.*, p. 507. Italics in original.
[67]*Ibid.*, p. 509.

In spite of Pendleton's defense, the opposition remained. Some thought the very organization was wrong. Others thought the operation of the ACMS was inefficient. In 1866 Lipscomb charged that from twenty-five to forty percent of the income of the ACMS went to pay Society employees rather than to mission work.[68] Still others opposed the work of the ACMS because membership was made contingent upon financial involvement, smacking of crass commercialism. When the ACMS changed its constitution in 1867 to drop the practice of selling life memberships and life directorships,[69] it entered a severe financial crisis, since selling these life positions had previously been its chief source of income. In 1868, Errett, Pendleton, and others were ready to enter a resolution to reinstitute the life positions in order to provide a constant source of income.[70] But the move was forestalled by other developments.

Instead, a committee of twenty was appointed to study the issue and come up with a plan that would be free of objection. Thus in 1869 the convention met in Louisville and considered the "Louisville Plan," presented and adopted that year. There were only two negative votes, and even Ben Franklin, who was on the committee of twenty, approved.[71] In hindsight, this Louisville Plan seems to be a highly structured, awkward, unwieldy idea that instituted a series of bureaucracies that would horrify most independent Christian Churches today, much less in 1869. It is hard to imagine that it was actually adopted.

The Louisville Plan called for local churches to appoint delegates to district conventions. In turn, the district conventions appointed delegates to the state convention. Each state convention appointed two delegates to the national convention, plus an additional delegate for each 5,000 members in the state. Financially, the churches were asked to subscribe a definite sum for mission work, paid to the district treasurer. He, in turn, was to use half of it for district work and forward the other half to the state. The state treasurer was to keep half of this for state work and send the remaining half to the national convention, now called the General Christian Missionary Convention, which replaced the ACMS.[72]

---

[68]Earl I. West, *Ancient Order,* vol. 2, p. 71, quoting *Gospel Advocate,* May 8, 1866, p. 292.

[69]McAllister and Tucker, p. 256.

[70]Earl I. West, *Ancient Order,* vol. 2, p. 94.

[71]Garrison and DeGroot, pp. 354-355.

[72]Because of the general failure of the Louisville Plan, as well as the rise of newer missionary agencies in the 1870s, the name American Christian Missionary Society was reinstituted in the 1880s. McAllister and Tucker, p. 268, give reference to it under the new/old name as early as 1883.

One of the appeals of the idea was that it would eliminate the special agents of the Society since elders of local churches were now responsible for the raising of missionary funds. But most churches were remiss in raising missionary dollars. J. W. McGarvey also requested that the churches be allowed to stipulate where they wanted their money spent (at least the one-fourth of it that got up to the national level). Because the churches requested that it be spent close to home, foreign missions ceased during this period.[73] Financially, the whole plan was a disaster. Previously, the ACMS had been operating with about $10,000 income each year; for the next decade, they averaged about $4,000 annually.[74] Most churches saw the plan as too highly bureaucratic and ignored it. Even though eleven state meetings and thirty-six district meetings approved the arrangements, they mostly ignored its details.[75] Within two years, Ben Franklin was opposed to it.[76] In 1871 the Corresponding Secretary noted that although the local churches had given $48,123.33 for missions, the General Convention received only $2,600; the rest had been diverted for local work. The received amount was barely enough to pay the Secretary's salary and certainly allowed nothing for foreign work.

But this is not to say that interest in missions totally waned during this period. The women in particular desired to accomplish something in this area. In the country in general, women were taking a more active role. This soon transferred itself to church work as well. From 1869 to 1874, women's missionary societies developed within the Baptist, Congregational, Episcopal, Methodist, and Presbyterian churches. Perhaps because of the flagging zeal of the ACMS, several of its leaders began to consider enlisting the support of the women. A "Committee on the Cooperation of Women in the Missionary Work" reported to the General Convention in 1870,[77] but no specifics came of it.

It was a minister's wife in Iowa City, Iowa, that became the catalyst. Mrs. Caroline Neville Pearre got the idea of a women's missionary group in April of 1874. Correspondence with Thomas Munnell, Corresponding Secretary of the General Convention, added his encouragement. In June Isaac Errett visited Iowa City, met with Mrs. Pearre, and wrote an editorial in the *Christian Standard*, "Help Those Women" [Philippians 4:3], which brought them national attention and encouragement.

During the General Convention for 1874, which met at the Richmond

---

73McAllister and Tucker, p. 258.
74Garrison and DeGroot, p. 356.
75McAllister and Tucker, p. 257.
76Earl I. West, *Ancient Order*, vol. 2, p. 97.
77McAllister and Tucker, p. 259.

Street Christian Church in Cincinnati, the women met in the basement on October 21. Using the form of the women's missionary society of the Congregational Church, the women organized the Christian Woman's Board of Missions, completely under women's control. It was an organization officered by women, organized by women, run by women, paid for by women, sending women (and men) to the mission field. By 1876, they sent out their first missionaries, to Jamaica. From here the work grew until they became one of the most nationally significant women's missionary groups in the country. By 1919 the CWBM alone accounted for forty percent of all organized missionary work done by the Restoration Movement.[78]

This was not the only significant achievement of the 1874 convention. During one session, Joseph King spoke on "The Importance of Foreign Missions,"[79] and commented, "We are the only people not obeying the [Great] Commission and not even trying to."[80] W. T. Moore left the session and went to the basement to give some thought and prayer to the situation. He then asked some others to meet him in the basement and at the suggested time about twenty-five or thirty men assembled. Moore urgently recommended beginning a society for foreign missions, not in competition with the General Society, but to cooperate with it, even holding the annual meeting at the same time and place.[81]

When the General Convention met in 1875 in Louisville, the proposed constitution of the Foreign Christian Missionary Society was put forward and adopted. Isaac Errett was selected as president, and life directorships, life memberships, and annual memberships were provided for.[82] Foreign work began slowly, but soon picked up significant momentum. Within a decade, the Foreign Christian Missionary Society was operating around the globe.

The creation of the two new societies did not undermine the work of the General Society, which now intentionally focused on home missions. The women's work often worked in collaboration with a work initiated by one of the other two—either at home or abroad—adding workers and taking on special projects. As the scope and financial strength of the two new missions organizations increased, so did that of the ACMS. By the end of the century, all three were healthy and active, expanding into new fields and taking on more responsibilities. Garrison and DeGroot call the

---

[78]Details on the founding of the CWBM can be found in McAllister and Tucker, pp. 259-263; Garrison and DeGroot, pp. 365-367; Murch, pp. 186-187; West, vol. 2, p. 102; and Webb, pp. 230-232.

[79]Moore, p. 618.

[80]Garrison and DeGroot, p. 367.

[81]Moore, pp. 618-619.

[82]Moore gives the constitution on pp. 620-621.

period 1874-1900 "Renaissance."[83] Indeed the last quarter of the nine-teenth century was the heyday of missions for the Restoration Movement, as it also was for most of the rest of the Christian world, Protestant or Catholic, evangelical or not.[84]

Tension and Division

Although this was a very positive time for missions in the Movement, some of the old discords were still present, unresolved. There was still dispute about the use of musical instruments in worship, the validity of such things as missionary organizations, and the place of salaried minis-ters engaged in full-time local work. In addition, there was also a signifi-cant pattern emerging with regard to these issues. The people who were opposed to any one of these were generally opposed to the others as well. On the other side, the people who were in favor of any one of these were generally in favor of the others as well. There were significant exceptions, of course—J. W. McGarvey and the others on the *Apostolic Times* were in favor of the missionary society but opposed to musical instruments. But generally where a person stood on one of the issues indicated a more general application as well. Nor is it surprising that generally—again, there are significant and major exceptions—the oppo-sition was located in the South.

It is also important to realize that these issues mentioned were not the real issue. Musical instruments, missionary organizations, and located preachers were the symbols that were fought over, but the real issue was the application of biblical authority. This takes us back to Thomas Campbell's significant and oft-repeated motto—"Where the Scriptures speak, we speak; where the Scriptures are silent, we are silent." There was no trouble with the first part. "Where the Scriptures speak, we speak." The Bible talks about baptism, and so the churches of the Movement emphasized baptism. The Bible talks about the deity of Jesus, so the churches emphasized the deity of Jesus. The Bible talks about elders and deacons for the local churches, and so the churches had elders and dea-cons. That part was no problem. The problem came, however, in the sec-ond part of the slogan—"Where the Scriptures are silent, we are silent." What does "silence" mean? Here two different interpretations developed.

---

[83]The title of a chapter, p. 359.

[84]In terms of world evangelism, the latter part of the nineteenth century was the greatest outpouring of missions activity in the history of the church. Missions historian Kenneth Scott LaTourette refers to the nineteenth as the "Great Century."

One side determined that the churches can do only what the Bible strictly authorizes; since the Bible does not strictly authorize missionary societies, salaried local preachers, or musical instruments in worship, these are all wrong. To adopt them is to do so without authority, and thus to go against biblical authority. The other side, however, determined that all of these were within the realm of expediency to get the work of the church done. Such things are not prohibited, they are for the good of the church, and therefore they are allowed. The issue is simply strict constructionism versus loose constructionism.

There is also a geographical pattern involved here. Most of the South was strict constructionist, dating from the influence of Thomas Jefferson and frontier resistance to centralized authority. The southern states were most concerned about states' rights. This underlay the Virginia and Kentucky Resolutions of 1793, the Nullification Crisis of 1832 (mostly dealing with South Carolina), and certainly the tensions that developed into the Civil War where states' rights even led to secession. The more northern states were more willing to accept federal authority over the tarriff, slavery, and the idea of an indissoluble union. That is, the mindset that explained the political tensions also underlay these religious tensions.

We have already talked about some of these issues of religious tension with the Movement. All of them preceded the Civil War, but even during the war that tension escalated, particularly with the musical instrument issue. In 1864 an anonymous writer asked the editors of the *Millennial Harbinger* about the practices of pew-renting and the use of organs and other instrumental music in worship. In a lengthy reply, W. K. Pendleton advised caution.

> We confess to a fondness for good music of all kinds; and find it no offence [sic] to our own feelings of piety or praise to hear the grand and majestic swell of the organ rolling forth, laden with the strains of our sacred music; yet, like Paul with respect to meats, I would rather never hear one again, than to have them interfering with the free, full, grateful, heartfelt singing of the whole congregation. Better the occasional discord of an untrained voice, and more acceptable to God, provided it bear the melody of a true and loving heart, than the sublimest swell of harmony ever uttered by the deep-throated organ.[85]

That same month, Moses Lard wrote on dancing and instrumental music. He stated very pointedly, "The day on which a church sets up an organ in its house, is the day on which it reaches the first station on the

---

[85]*Millennial Harbinger*, 1864, p. 127.

road to apostasy." He encouraged preachers to never enter a building
that housed an organ, he encouraged persons to never transfer membership to a congregation that used an organ, and he advised that if the
opponents of an organ could not keep it out of a congregation, they
should withdraw without even asking for a letter of transfer.[86] This, of
course, encouraged division.

Initially, of course, the use of musical instruments (instruments in general, but specifically the use of organs and pianos) was extremely infrequent. As mentioned previously, such instruments were expensive on the
frontier. Only as the standard of living went up from frontier basics did
such instruments begin to appear. In 1868 Ben Franklin estimated that
there were about ten thousand congregations within the Movement,[87]
but that instrumental music had been adopted in no more than fifty of
them.[88]

Isaac Errett allowed discussion of the issue in the *Christian Standard*,
but the paper reflected a fairly negative view in these early years. H. T.
Anderson stated,

> I am no advocate for instrumental music in churches. But the Doctor with his
> legalism cannot legislate it out of the churches. I might easily say to him,
> where there is no law, there is no transgression. There is no law against instru-
> mental music in churches, therefore, those who use it are not transgressors.[89]

Robert Richardson argued against him on the basis that even expediency needed authorization. His logic is question-begging, but it is significant that Alexander Campbell's close friend and biographer came out
against the use of music. After two years of the discussion, Isaac Errett
himself stated his position in 1870.

> We intend to counsel against the use of instrumental music in our churches.
> Our object is to persuade brethren who favor such use to hold their prefer-
> ences in abeyance for the sake of *harmony;* for as the love of harmony is that

---

[86]McAllister and Tucker, p. 246, quoting *Lard's Quarterly*, March, 1864, vol. 1,
pp. 332-333.

[87]This number seems extremely high. Indications are that the entire
Movement numbered about 225,000 adherents in 1870 (Howard E. Dentler,
"Statistical Profile of the Christian Church [Disciples of Christ], in *The Christian
Church [Disciples of Christ]: An Interpretative Examination in the Cultural Context*, edited by George G. Beazley, Jr. [n.p.: The Bethany Press, 1973], p. 308. This would
make an *average* of only 22.5 per church. Franklin's estimate of the number of
congregations needs to be cut in half, or perhaps even divided by three.

[88]Earl I. West, *Ancient Order*, vol. 2, p. 81.

[89]*Ibid.*, p. 90, quoting *Christian Standard*, June 12, 1869, p. 186.

which leads them to see that the deeper and more precious harmony of *soul* must not be sacrificed by the lovers of harmony to the inferior harmonies of sound. . . . It is a difference of opinion. It is wrong to make this difference a test of fellowship or an occasion of stumbling.[90]

Two points stand out in Errett's position. One is that it is a matter of opinion. Most of those who opposed the instrument did not agree; they saw it as a matter of faith, concluding that whatsoever was not of faith [biblical precept] was sin. Errett's other point is that those who favor it should yield out of deference to those who would stumble over it.

In the next couple of decades, there were numerous instances of animosity over the instrument issue. Some churches introduced the organ in spite of opposition. There is no doubt that many of these instances were done out of a lack of charity and concern for an offended brother. West details difficulties in St. Louis, Chicago, Akron, Memphis, and Cincinnati in the years 1867-1872.[91] In Cincinnati in 1872, Central Christian Church dedicated its new building, which cost $140,000, including an $8,000 organ. It is difficult to determine which offended David Lipscomb and the *Gospel Advocate* more—the cost of the building or the addition of the organ.[92]

It is difficult to filter out exactly what the issues were in such contests. Sometimes it was a political power play in certain congregations. Sometimes a majority of a city congregation thought an organ would elevate and dignify the worship service. Some brethren thought this amounted to a caving in to secular influences; others thought it was simply a matter of relating to the culture in a positive way. Thus the issue often broke down between those who argued expediency and those who argued apostasy.

But perhaps the most unhealthy development was the divisiveness these arguments spawned. Those who believed the issue was a matter of apostasy felt impelled to separate from those who worshipped with the instrument. This issue caused more divisions than the older Society issue because the Society was not as visible within the church building, nor as obvious during a worship service. It was possible for brethren to worship together in spite of differences on the Society question. It was impossible to do this on the organ question. The organ just could not be ignored.

The result was an increasing distinction between those who favored its

---

[90]Earl I. West, *Ancient Order*, vol. 2, pp. 87-88, quoting *Christian Standard*, May 7, 1870, p. 148.
[91]Earl I. West, *Ancient Order*, vol. 2, pp. 81-83.
[92]*Ibid.*, pp. 138-142.

use and those opposed to it. The significance of the editors was obvious. Certain journals accepted musical instruments—the *Christian Standard* and the *Christian-Evangelist*. Other journals sternly resisted them—the *Gospel Advocate* and the *American Christian Review* and its successors, particularly the *Octographic Review* under Daniel Sommer (1850-1940), beginning in 1887. Each of these magazines in turn created a constituency that tended not to fellowship with brethren on the other side of the issue.

A major milepost in this development occurred on August 18, 1889, when a mass meeting of about six thousand gathered at the Sand Creek Church of Christ in rural Shelby County, Illinois. Daniel Sommer was present and charged the "innovators" with all the problems in the church. Then one of the Sand Creek elders, P. P. Warren,[93] read the document that later became known as the Sand Creek Address and Declaration, or more commonly, the Sand Creek Declaration. The document stated the affirmation that "nothing should be taught, received or practiced, religiously, for which we could not produce a 'Thus saith the Lord.'" Furthermore, it acknowledged that "There are among us those who do teach and practice things not taught or found in the New Testament," and it specifically referred to church festival fund-raisers, instrumental music in worship, the select choir, "the man-made society for missionary work," and "the one-man, imported preacher pastor." "We cannot tolerate the things of which we complain," the Declaration stated, and it concluded by announcing,

> We are impelled from a sense of duty to say that all such as are guilty of teaching or allowing and practicing the many innovations and corruptions to which we have referred, after having had sufficient time for meditation and reflection, if they will not turn away from such abominations, that we can not and will not regard them as brethren.[94]

A similar gathering in 1892 at Sand Creek brought the recommendation that every church that purchased property should put a clause in the deed stating that no instrument of music or other innovation should ever be used on the premises.[95]

It was obvious as the churches neared the end of the nineteenth century that a major split had occurred. The Sand Creek Declaration of 1889

---

[93]*Ibid.*, p. 430, refers to "P.D." in his text, while using "P.P." when he quotes the document itself. There is no unanimity in the other textbooks either.

[94]*Ibid.*, pp. 430-432, quoting *Christian Leader*, September 10, 1889, p. 2.

[95]*Ibid.*, p. 434.

was not the cause of it; that document simply represented an attitude and viewpoint that had already developed. In fact it is difficult to put any date on this growing polarization since no state or national agency dealt with the issues. It was fairly much left up to individual local congregations. Daniel Sommer, editor of the Indianapolis-based *Octographic Review,* represented a general view of strict constructionism. At various times he was opposed to colleges and orphanages as well as the missionary societies and instrumental worship. "Sommerism" took over numerous churches in the North, particularly Indiana. According to Benjamin Franklin's son, there were two hundred to five hundred Sommerite churches in the North by 1895.[96]

The tenseness of the dispute was illustrated by a series of legal battles over church property. When factions within a church disagreed over the instrument, the question arose, "Who owns this church building?" Trials in McGregor, Texas (1898), and Henderson, Tennessee (1905), were both won by the organ faction, but they were hardly done in a Christian spirit.

A somewhat more tolerant variant of Sommer in the South was David Lipscomb, editor of the *Gospel Advocate.* Lipscomb did not have as long a list of "innovations" he was fighting, although he certainly did stand against the two most significant—the missionary society and instrumental music. It was also Lipscomb who provided a concrete date by which to determine that in fact a separation had occurred within the Movement.

In 1906, the director of the U.S. Bureau of the Census, S. N. D. North, was analyzing the religious census data when he discovered what appeared to be an overlapping of data for preachers listed either with the Christian Church or the Churches of Christ. He wrote to Lipscomb for clarification of the data, asking if the Churches of Christ were in fact separate from the Christian Church. Lipscomb wrote back that there was a definite difference, and this distinction has been observed in official U.S. statistics down to the present. For all practical purposes, therefore, the Movement had broken.

It is both ironic and tragic that a movement that began as a unity movement should so divide over the application of the principles that were supposed to bring unity. Thomas Campbell began by believing that Christian unity could only come through a restoration of the Bible alone as the unique guide to Christian faith and practice. Thomas was able to hold in tension the two principles of unity and biblical authority, trying to bring all denominations to unity through the unanimous acceptance of biblical principles. By the end of the century, however, many of his

---

[96]Garrett, p. 592, quoting *Christian Standard*, vol. 30 (1895), p. 923.

followers were insisting on such a rigid application of biblical authority that they were not interested in unity with anyone who disagreed with them on the application of these principles. Thus the division occurred.

It is important to note, however, that this division was not over whether the Bible was to be authoritative. Both sides agreed to that. The difference was in the application of biblical authority, particularly in the areas of biblical silence. This highlights the significant influence of "strict" and "loose" constructionism, the mental viewpoints that lay behind the various applications. West himself affirms that "the use or non-use of the instrument was symptomatic of an attitude toward the scriptures."[97] Another Church of Christ historian, Homer Hailey, agrees, stating, "The two bodies are separated today, not over instrumental music *per se,* nor over missionary societies, but as the result of an attitude toward the authority of the Scriptures."[98] It is this attitude on the one part of one group that allowed the emphasis on biblical authority to override the considerations for Christian unity.

Yet at the same time that tensions on one issue were reaching the breaking point, other demonstrations of Christian unity/cooperation were developing. When the International Sunday School Association initiated the Uniform Lessons concept in 1872, Disciples soon saw the value of such a cooperative project. Isaac Errett served on the Lesson Committee from 1884 until his death in 1888. He was replaced on the committee by Benjamin B. Tyler, who was elected president of the International Sunday School Association in 1902. Other Disciples personnel continued to serve in such interdenominational educational endeavors.[99]

A similar spurt of involvement occurred when the Young People's Society of Christian Endeavor was organized in 1881. Because of its commitment to the generic foundations of Christianity, Disciples found it easy to participate actively.[100]

Thus the Disciples continued to reflect their twin concerns—biblical authority and Christian unity—even though there was often a sore lack of consensus as to how the two should be dovetailed.

---

[97]Earl I. West, *Ancient Order,* vol. 2, p. 73.

[98]Hailey, p. 246.

[99]McAllister and Tucker, p. 279; William Clayton Bower and Roy G. Ross (eds.), *The Disciples and Religious Education* (St. Louis: Christian Board of Publication, 1936), pp. 102-103, 203-211.

[100]McAllister and Tucker, p. 279.

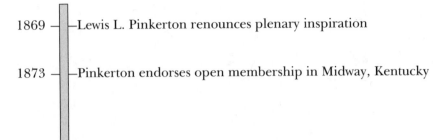

1869 — —Lewis L. Pinkerton renounces plenary inspiration

1873 — —Pinkerton endorses open membership in Midway, Kentucky

1883 — —Isaac Errett downplays the infallibility of Scripture

1885 — —W.T. Moore accepts open membership in London

1889 — —R.C. Cave preaches liberal sermon in St. Louis
1890 — —H.L. Willett and W.E. Garrison begin studies at Yale

1893 — —Bible chair begun at University of Michigan
         J.W. McGarvey begins column, "Biblical Criticism" in the
              Christian Standard
1894 — —Disciples Divinity House begun at the University of Chicago

1896 — —Campbell Institute begun

1898 — —Willett writes Sunday School column for *Christian-Evangelist*
1899 — —First Congress of the Disciples held
1900 — —*Christian Oracle* becomes *Christian Century*

1902 — —Willett gives lectureship in Kansas City
         Charges raised against Hiram van Kirk in Berkeley, California
1903 — —E.S. Ames begins open membership in Chicago

1906 — —Chicago Christian Missionary Society supports open member-
              ship at Austin
1908 — —Willett questions Old Testament miracles
         Willett appointed to program of Centennial Convention

Chapter 10

The Incursion of Liberalism

T
he Restoration Movement was changed dramatically by the events of the turn of the century. At no other time in its history has the Movement been so seriously threatened, not even by the frustrations and divisions represented by the Noninstrumentalist split covered in Chapter Nine. The arrival and acceptance of religious liberalism among the Disciples of Christ all but destroyed the Restoration Movement.

Beginnings of Liberalism

Liberalism itself is a somewhat difficult phenomenon to define. At its best, liberalism is an attitude of openness and toleration, a willingness to be free from encrusted traditions carried over from previous generations. Liberalism can be defined in terms of liberty and freedom; certainly no one wants to argue against liberty and freedom. In this sense, liberals throughout the history of the church have been at war with the enervating effects of restrictive institutionalism. From this perspective, the apostle Paul can be viewed as a liberal, and the Judaizers were the conservatives. It was the Judaizers who wanted to keep things as they were, with all converts to Christianity first having met the requirements of being good Jews. But Paul was not willing to accept their legalism and their restrictions. Under his inspired leadership, Christianity broke out from the Judaistic mold to become a message of love and grace.

In a similar way, Martin Luther was a liberal, as he battled the restrictions of the papacy and its salvation-by-works theology. Even more significantly, Thomas Campbell was a liberal in that he wanted to break out of the denominational shell of nonsensical Presbyterianism. Alexander

Campbell tried to liberalize the Baptists. Both Thomas and Alexander failed in their respective attempts to remain within their denominational identity and broaden their fellowship at the same time, but their desire to liberalize their environment must not be overlooked. By this definition, liberalism is a good attribute, a return to New Testament Christianity by broadening fellowship in the name of Jesus and making the Bible alone the guideline for the Church.

Unfortunately, however, in the latter half of the nineteenth century, the term "liberalism" takes on other connotations. Many people not only wanted to be broadminded and tolerant, they also wanted to be free from the restrictions of biblical dogma and traditional Christian doctrine. None of this development was begun as an intentional effort to subvert the faith; instead it was the natural development of the religious ideology of the nineteenth century. The development itself is much too complicated to be considered in detail here, although it will be helpful to note its four components.

First was the work of Friedrich Schleiermacher (1768-1834), who in 1799 wrote his little book, *On Religion: Speeches to Its Cultured Despisers,* in which he pointed out that the most important thing about religion was not doctrine or a pious lifestyle, but the "feeling of dependence upon the Infinite." His emphasis on feelings and conscientious intuition influenced theological thought so much that he is usually considered the father of modern theology. A concern for feeling and the guiding of conscience was a hallmark of much of liberal theology.

A second aspect of liberalism came through the work of Albrecht Ritschl (1822-1889). Ritschl is known as the father of the social gospel because of his emphasis on ethics. He defined the Church as "the community of the Redeemed" and insisted that the church comport itself as such responding to the social and economic needs of society. Indeed, a modern American religious historian notes that the two items that mark American liberal theology are "its concern for ethical results and its preoccupation with the empirical."[1]

The third important ingredient for the development of liberalism came through the work of Charles Darwin (1809-1882). Darwinian thought is more important than merely the biological evolution with which his name is most closely associated. Darwinism represents evolutionary development in society (Social Darwinism), political theory, and even in religion. Darwin's concepts fostered the idea among scholars that

---

[1]Jaroslav Pelikan, in the "Foreword" to Kenneth Cauthen, *The Impact of American Religious Liberalism* (New York: Harper & Row, Publishers, 1962), p. vii.

Judaism itself went through successive stages, reflecting the progress of the Jews from a nomadic tribe, to a pastoral people, to a people struggling with social injustices in the eighth century B.C., and finally, the latter-day prophet Jesus who broke out of the nationalistic mold and proclaimed an international gospel. One theologian identified liberal theology in terms of bringing Christian thought into organic unity with the evolutionary world view, movements for social reconstruction, and expectations of "a better world."[2] The world view of modern science questioned both the authority of Scripture and the possibility of miracles: in short, the traditional supernaturalism of Christian orthodoxy.[3]

Fourth, and perhaps most important, was the increasingly significant field of biblical criticism. Biblical criticism divides itself into two fields: "lower" and "higher." Lower criticism deals solely with the text of Scripture and seeks to recreate the original text as accurately as possible. Higher criticism is more concerned with the historical understanding of the document involved: who wrote it, why, to whom, when, and how does it coincide with other historical knowledge of the period? Higher criticism did not originate in the nineteenth century, but it was in this period that it became such a prolific field for scholarship. The goal of biblical study came to be historical objectivity—which often meant deliberately ignoring the internal testimony of the Christian tradition. Conservatives accused the biblical critics of undermining the integrity of the Bible and thus removing the only objective authority of religion. Some critics admitted this and pointed to the authority of religious feelings and ethics (the influence of Schleiermacher and Ritschl). Conservatives became even more outraged when the critics discounted the stories of the Old Testament patriarchs, the Creation, Joshua at Jericho, the crossing of the Red Sea, and Elijah's fiery chariot. Many critics reduced all miracles to the status of myths, including such central teachings as the virgin birth and physical resurrection of Christ.

Many of these ideas were already germinating in Europe by midcentury, but they did not begin to have much effect in America until after the Civil War. Then several denominations suffered severe controversies. David Swing, a Presbyterian minister in Chicago, was put on trial for heresy in 1874. He won acquittal, but when the case was appealed to a higher body, he resigned rather than face another trial. In 1878 Southern Methodist Alexander Winchell, a naturalist at Vanderbilt

---

[2]Daniel Day Williams, quoted in Lloyd J. Averill, *American Theology in the Liberal Tradition* (Philadelphia: The Westminster Press, 1967), pp. 22-23.

[3]Cauthen, p. 7.

University, published a book that contradicted the Genesis account of creation. When he refused to resign, the board of trustees abolished his position.[4] In 1879 Crawford H. Toy of the Southern Baptist Theological Seminary in Louisville resigned under pressure because of his liberal views.[5] Northern Baptist Ezra P. Gould was dismissed from Newton Theological Seminary in 1882. Probably the most famous of the trials, however, was that of Charles A. Briggs, Presbyterian, at Union Theological Seminary in New York City. When he denied verbal inspiration in 1891, a trial ensued. The local presbytery acquitted him, but the General Assembly overturned the judgment and vetoed his appointment as professor of biblical theology. As a result, Union simply broke with the parent denomination and kept Briggs on anyway.[6]

In spite of the trials and resistance, liberalism seemed to take over several of the major American denominations. Even though Gould was ousted from Newton in 1882 and Nathaniel Schmidt from Colgate in 1896, by the end of the century, all the Northern Baptist seminaries were firmly in the liberal camp. The same was true of the Congregational seminaries.[7] In the Restoration Movement the process took longer.

Perhaps the earliest liberal was Dr. Lewis L. Pinkerton.[8] Baptized by Alexander Campbell himself in 1830, Pinkerton became a medical doctor, but then gave up the medical practice to become a minister. He had a lengthy ministry at Midway, Kentucky, where he was the first minister to introduce mechanical musical instruments into worship service. This by itself labeled him a liberal in the most conservative circles. But his liberalism went beyond that. In his own little magazine, the *Independent Monthly*, in 1869[9] he openly renounced plenary inspiration, saying that

---

[4]See Kenneth K. Bailey, *Southern White Protestantism in the Twentieth Century* (New York: Harper & Row, Publishers, 1964), pp. 9-10.

[5]For a full discussion, see Pope A. Duncan, "Crawford Howell Toy: Heresy at Louisville," in George H. Shriver (ed.), *American Religious Heretics: Formal and Informal Trials* (Nashville: Abingdon Press, 1966), pp. 56-88.

[6]For the Briggs case, see Max Gray Rogers, "Charles Augustus Briggs: Heresy at Union" in Shriver, pp. 89-147.

[7]Winthrop S. Hudson and John Corrigan, *Religion in America: An Historical Account of the Development of American Religious Life*, Fifth Edition (New York: Macmillan Publishing Company, 1992), p. 269.

[8]The best source for Pinkerton is John Schackleford, Jr., *Life, Letters, and Addresses of Dr. L. L. Pinkerton* (Cincinnati: Chase & Hall, Publishers, 1876).

[9]Garrison and DeGroot on p. 149 refer this to 1868; however on p. 390, they affirm the paper itself lasted only from 1869—1870. This would make impossible an 1868 date. Shackleford, p. 112, ascribes the statement to 1869 as well. McAllister and Tucker state that Pinkerton questioned biblical inerrancy as early as 1849, but they provide no documentation; see their p. 227.

he could not believe that Psalm 137:9 was inspired. (This Psalm, a cry for vengeance against Israel's enemies, speaks of "Babylon, you devastator," and concludes: "Happy shall he be who takes your little ones and dashes them against the rock!") In addition, in articles in the *Christian Standard* in 1873, Pinkerton came out in favor of open membership,[10] that is, receiving a person into local church membership without baptism by immersion. Pinkerton went on to say that he did not believe that such a person was baptized, for he was convinced that baptism and immersion were the same. However, if such a person conscientiously disagreed, Pinkerton would not be judgmental. He would simply point the person to the New Testament and urge him, "take heed how you read."[11]

One of the significant things about Pinkerton and his liberalism was that he was such a lone wolf in his generation. Apparently no one else shared his views except his biographer, John Shackleford,[12] and even in Shackleford's biography of Pinkerton, he states,

> I do not propose in this chapter to discuss the truth or error of his alleged heresies, but as a matter of impartial history to allow him to state, in his own language and with his own illustrations, the opinions which many of his brethren believed to be heretical and of evil tendency.

To this note is appended: "The editor has not thought it necessary in this chapter to note specially either his dissent from Dr. Pinkerton or his agreement with him."[13]

A controversy with broader implications surfaced some years later around W. T. Moore (1832-1926). Moore was one of the founders of the Foreign Christian Missionary Society, and for a considerable time was minister with the Central Christian Church in downtown Cincinnati, "at that time the largest and most influential church among the Disciples."[14] In 1881 Moore became the minister of the West London Tabernacle, a congregation of the British Churches of Christ.[15] The congregation

---

[10]There are three articles in the series, "No Immersion—No Membership in a Church of the Reformation," *Christian Standard*, May 31, 1873, p. 170; June 7, 1873, p. 178; and June 28, 1873, p. 201.

[11]Shackleford, pp. 108-112; see also Samuel P. Freeman, "Trends of Disciple Preaching on Christian Unity" (Unpublished M. A. Thesis, University of Chicago Divinity School, Chicago, 1936), p. 15.

[12]W. E. Garrison, *An American Religious Movement* (St. Louis: Christian Board of Publication, 1945), p. 136.

[13]Shackleford, p. 106.

[14]Archibald McLean, *The History of the Foreign Christian Missionary Society* (New York: Fleming H. Revell Company, 1919), p. 39.

[15]*Ibid.*, pp. 54-55.

included both immersed and unimmersed. He himself practiced only immersion, but he did not see fit to challenge those members who had not been. When Frank Allen, a writer for the conservative *Old Paths Guide,* discovered the situation in 1885, he wrote a scathing rebuke, asserting "Moore is supported by the Foreign Christian Missionary Society and is not representing the cause he was sent to represent."[16] Significantly, Isaac Errett, president of the Foreign Christian Missionary Society and editor of the influential *Christian Standard,* came to Moore's defense. He urged that the magazines not get into an argument over adapting missionary policy to local needs in a foreign field and asked that the whole matter be left up to the executive committee of the Foreign Society. Under his advice, the matter was dropped, Moore continued unchastised, and conflict was avoided.[17] In light of the fact that similar situations tore the Movement apart thirty years later, the peaceful settlement of this earlier incident is somewhat amazing.

If the Moore issue in 1885 created only a ripple of controversy, the year 1889 witnessed an angry wave of protest among the Disciples. It also indicated some of the limits at which broad-minded Disciples would draw the line between toleration and heresy. R. C. Cave (1843-1923) was the eloquent preacher at St. Louis' Central Christian Church. In December, Cave preached on John 1:18—"No one has ever seen God; the only Son, who is in the bosom of the Father, he has made him known." Cave asserted that the Old Testament patriarchs, including Abraham and Moses, were grossly ignorant of God's true character. He went on to deny the virgin birth and physical resurrection of Jesus, described the Bible as an evolution rather than a revelation, and said there were no "conditions" to salvation.[18]

The sermon was printed in the *St. Louis Republic* for December 8, and it soon came to the attention of Disciples nationally. Numerous Disciples leaders were outraged that such a sermon should come from a minister identified with the Disciples. Many of them demanded that J. H. Garrison (1842-1931), editor of the St. Louis-based *Christian-Evangelist* and an elder in the Central Christian Church, do something to counter Cave's teaching. Garrison refused. He said the whole thing was Cave's opinion, and it was the Disciples' custom to allow liberty of opinion as long as the "faith which is essential to Christian character is held."[19]

---

[16]Quoted in Garrison and DeGroot, p. 391.
[17]*Ibid.*, pp. 391-392.
[18]*Ibid.*, pp. 386-387.
[19]*Christian-Evangelist*, December 12, 1889, p. 792.

Yet a week later, the situation dramatically changed. Cave presented a series of resolutions for a congregational vote. One of these resolutions stated: "The Christian Church makes nothing a test of fellowship but that which a man's own experience tells him is right or true."[20] This was more than Garrison could tolerate. He and his family requested letters of dismissal. Within a few months, however, Cave also left the congregation. At that point J. H. Garrison returned, to salvage the congregation and the church building.

Two results came from the Cave incident. One was J. H. Garrison's concern that perhaps too many young men had been insufficiently schooled in doctrinal orthodoxy. He launched a series of articles in the *Christian-Evangelist* written by some of the most conservative leaders in the brotherhood. These articles were later edited into the volume, *The Old Faith Restated*, printed in 1891.[21] The second result was the recognition that virtually no one defended Cave; he was just as much a lone wolf in 1889 as Pinkerton had been two decades previously. The *Christian Oracle* of Chicago dismissed the incident by simply remarking:

> The real fact appears to be that Bro. Cave has become an Infidel, with no faith in either the Old or New Testament as an authoritative revelation from God, or in the Supreme Lordship of Jesus of Nazareth, and wants to take the church for which he is preaching with him into the same faith.[22]

The same editorial referred to Cave's "broad-gauge Unitarianism," while the most eminent of Disciples historians has called it Cave's "Emersonian Liberalism."[23] Garrison and DeGroot in their official history of the Disciples even remark: "The new liberalism had a streak of dogmatism in it, too. It was not enough for the church to permit its pastor to believe that Moses made mistakes; the church also must believe it."[24]

---

[20]*Ibid.*, December 26, 1889, p. 825.

[21]Winfred Ernest Garrison, *Religion Follows the Frontier: A History of the Disciples of Christ* (New York: Harper & Row, Publishers, 1931), p. 269. J. H. Garrison's 450-page tome bore the complete title of *The Old Faith Restated: Being a Restatement, by Representative Men, of the Fundamental Truths and Essential Doctrines of Christianity as Held and Advocated by the Disciples of Christ in the Light of Experience and of Biblical Research* (St. Louis: Christian Publishing Company, 1891.)

[22]*Christian Oracle*, January 2, 1890, p. 1.

[23]Winfred Ernest Garrison, *Variations on a Theme: "God Saw That It Was Good"* (St. Louis: The Bethany Press, 1964), p. 81.

[24]Garrison and DeGroot, p. 388.

Biblical Criticism

Of the various issues of liberalism, it was a matter of biblical criticism that troubled the Disciples the most. In good part this was because of the nature of the restoration concept. The Restoration Movement was committed to the unity of all believers in the one body of Christ; it was also committed to the authority of Scripture. Yet the newer teachings of biblical criticism were often undercutting this very item, the integrity and authority of Scripture. Because the Restoration Movement was so keenly concerned with biblical authority, the new biblical criticism drew considerable attention from the Disciples, at least by the 1890s. Their mixed responses indicated both the potential impact of the discipline as well as the growing polarization within the brotherhood with respect to it.

A. W. Fortune has acknowledged the significant role that J. H. Garrison played in helping the Disciples face the issues of biblical criticism and the relation of science to religion.[25] In an article on "The Right Attitude for Biblical Criticism" in his *Christian-Evangelist*, Garrison stated there was nothing to fear from a critical study of the Bible undertaken in the right spirit, although one should be careful lest his conclusions jeopardize the faith of others.[26] In an article in the *New Christian Quarterly* in 1892, Garrison claimed that they were living in a time of inquiry, and friends of the Bible ought to welcome all honest and earnest inquiry into the nature and authority of the Bible.[27] In the same year in the *Christian-Evangelist*, Garrison continued, "We may challenge false methods and unauthorized conclusions; but we cannot deny the legitimacy of historical Biblical criticism without forfeiting our place and plea as religious reformers, hospitable to all truth."[28]

There is thus a confident note of support for biblical criticism in the view of Garrison. There is a note of caution about challenging false methods and unauthorized conclusions, but on the whole Garrison is sympathetic to the new field of biblical studies. Not everyone, however, shared his viewpoint. The *Christian Standard* in 1891 made the observation that higher criticism was only for the intelligent Christian—those still immature in the faith should not attempt it.[29] Although the *Christian*

---

[25]Alonzo Willard Fortune, *Adventuring with Disciple Pioneers* (St. Louis: The Bethany Press, 1942), p. 72.

[26]*Christian-Evangelist*, May 22, 1890, p. 322.

[27]*New Christian Quarterly*, vol. 1, no. 1 (1892), p. 118.

[28]*Christian-Evangelist*, July 7, 1892, p. 419.

[29]*Christian Standard*, August 9, 1891, p. 730.

Standard was not opposed to the biblical studies, it was much more reserved in encouraging the discipline.

This difference in approach between the two magazines toward biblical criticism was indicative of the changing stance of the two magazines in general. As long as Isaac Errett was alive, he and Garrison stood shoulder-to-shoulder on virtually every issue that was discussed in the periodicals of the brotherhood. Errett was known as a progressive thinker, tolerant in his sympathies toward a variety of viewpoints. These same qualities became known as liberalism in the generation following his death. This is not to say that Errett was a liberal—certainly he was not in his own theological convictions. However, he was certainly a liberal in the eyes of the Noninstrumentalists. This points out the basic difficulty in terminology, as discussed earlier. But Errett was certainly a broad-minded man. Upon his death in 1888, leadership of the Standard Publishing Company went into the hands of his son, Russell Errett. Russell was more conservative than his father, perhaps alarmed by the direction of drift he saw taking place in brotherhood thinking. The result was that in the 1890s, the *Christian Standard* and the *Christian-Evangelist* began to diverge in their editorial approaches to issues. The *Christian Standard* became more conservative; the *Christian-Evangelist* became more liberal. At first this increased liberalism in the *Christian-Evangelist* meant only a greater willingness to tolerate a variety of viewpoints; increasingly, however, this also meant more willingness to defend the newer ways of thought, and ultimately it meant that the magazine identified itself with the newer thinking. Toward the end of his life Garrison wrote to his son, "After Isaac Errett—great soul that he was—left us, I had almost to stand alone—so far as public agencies were concerned—against a strong legalistic and literalistic tendency in our brotherhood."[30]

As the discussions over biblical criticism continued in the 1890s, one figure in particular became the acknowledged spokesman for the conservative side of these questions. That was J. W. McGarvey.[31] He was a native Kentuckian who lived in Illinois for eight years of his youth. McGarvey graduated from Bethany College in 1850, having sat under the instruction of Alexander Campbell. He preached in Missouri for a while, but in 1862 he became the minister of the Main Street Church in

---

[30]Letter of James H. Garrison to Winfred E. Garrison, December 2, 1924, in the J. H. Garrison Papers, at the Disciples of Christ Historical Society, Nashville, Tennessee; quoted in McAllister and Tucker, p. 251.

[31]The best biography of McGarvey is that by W. C. Morro, *"Brother McGarvey": The Life of President J. W. McGarvey of The College of the Bible, Lexington, Kentucky* (St. Louis: The Bethany Press, 1940).

Lexington, Kentucky. He was one of the charter faculty members of the College of the Bible in 1865, although he continued various ministries for decades thereafter. In 1895, McGarvey became the president of the College of the Bible, which he remained until his death.

McGarvey was opposed to the use of instrumental music in worship, and after having been a member of the Broadway Church in Lexington, he moved his membership elsewhere when Broadway accepted the use of organ music in worship in 1902. Yet McGarvey never made the instrument question a test of fellowship or church membership.

His attitude toward biblical criticism, however, was far different. He believed firmly in biblical inerrancy and plenary inspiration and refused to acknowledge any doubts about either. He contended for his positions so strongly that people often misunderstood him. Herein lies the greatest tragedy about the character of McGarvey.

McGarvey had his enemies, but even they agreed that he was the epitome of southern charm and hospitality; his students regarded him as a gentleman in the fullest sense of the word. J. J. Haley ran afoul of McGarvey's views, but he could still say of him, "a kinder-hearted, sweeter-spirited man, one more devoted to the highest ideals of divine service and human living, it would have been hard to find."[32] Yet when McGarvey took up his pen to write, he often dipped it "in gall and vitriol."[33] When McGarvey criticized the writings of his opponents in the field of biblical criticism, he made no distinction between the man and his teaching. In one article he commented, "A man's personality and his teaching are so identified that it is next to an impossibility to keep them separate in thought."[34]

A sample of his caustic pen is the following:

> A writer in the *Christian-Evangelist,* commenting on the articles by Prof. Deweese and myself in review of J. J. Haley's *Quarterly* article, thus deposes: "The fact that *all* the evidence bearing on the date of Deuteronomy is not yet in, should prevent any of us from being dogmatic on such a question." He affirms that *all* the evidence is not yet in. In what? If he means that it is not in his own little knowledge-box, *he* ought to *know.* But the rest of us can not wait till all of it gets in *there.* We might die waiting. It is not always safe to judge of what is in another man's knowledge-box by what is not in your own.[35]

---

[32]J. J. Haley, *Makers and Molders of the Restoration Movement: A Study of Leading Men Among the Disciples of Christ* (St. Louis: Christian Board of Publication, 1914), p. 151.

[33]Morro, p. 187.

[34]*Ibid.,* pp. 185, 186, quoting the *Christian Standard,* August 28, 1897.

[35]*Christian Standard,* April 7, 1894, p. 347.

Because of his biting sarcasm and ridicule, many of his opponents claimed they had been totally misrepresented. Most Disciples journals gave him a rough time because he often quoted them and then subjected the quotations to ridicule. Even the patient and tolerant editor of the *Christian-Evangelist* exclaimed:

> The special criticism we would make upon his method of criticism is that he frequently does not give a fair hearing to the side which he criticises [sic]. An illustration of this is found in the *Christian Standard* of July 8th, in which the Professor criticises a recent editorial of ours entitled "Higher Criticism and the Supernatural." We venture to say that the readers of Prof. McGarvey's criticism will be wholly unable to learn from it the purposes of the editorial which he reviews, or the position which the editorial criticises.[36]

McGarvey acted as he did not to build up a coterie of followers but because he was convinced he was fighting for a righteous cause. With the credibility of the Scriptures at stake, no tactic seemed out of reason. He not only attacked infidelity where he found it, he attacked it where he even *suspected* it. When McGarvey suspected that G. W. Longan was not as sound as he should be, he systematically set about to undermine the latter's influence in Disciples circles. In 1890 Longan wrote to J. H. Garrison in a tone bordering on despair:

> McGarvey knows that in the vital things of Christianity I am as sound as he is—every whit—and I am sure that in the critical questions, about which we differ, I am right and he is wrong. But of this last, no matter. My soundness in things of the gospel he knows; of this I am sure. *But this is the painful side of the matter: he will seek to make the impression that I am not sound—rationalistic in fact, for the effect it will have in breaking down my influence, and that of others, with the younger preachers of this state, and other states, where the C. E. has carried my articles.* I know the man, I want you to understand, and he is just the man to do that thing, and to imagine he is thereby doing God service.[37]

McGarvey may have found fault with numerous journals and their editors, but one magazine with which he got on very well was the *Christian Standard*, particularly after the death of Isaac Errett. Famous and significant was the encounter between the two men during the Missouri Christian Lectures at Independence, Missouri, in 1883. Errett had lectured on "Inspiration," and had steadfastly held to the inspiration of the Scriptures. But he was unwilling to affirm that the Scriptures were

---

[36]*Christian-Evangelist*, July 20, 1893, p. 450.
[37]Quoted in Tucker, p. 85; italics in original.

free from error, nor was he willing to apply the word "infallible" to them.[38] In response McGarvey noted his disappointment at the presentation: "I was pained to hear from Bro. Errett the concession that the Scriptures are not infallible."[39]

But by the early 1890s, when the discussion of biblical criticism was becoming more intense, nowhere does McGarvey give any similar reservations about the policy of things at the *Christian Standard*, nor does he disclose any questions about its direction under the leadership of Russell Errett. Indeed the paper and the professor seem to be mutually self-supporting in every particular. In 1893, McGarvey began his weekly *Christian Standard* column "Biblical Criticism," which ran for the next eighteen years, until silenced by his death. In this column, McGarvey waged war against those who would compromise the uniqueness or authority of the Bible. Unfortunately, his methods of waging war often alienated individuals within the brotherhood who accepted McGarvey's theological and biblical positions but were offended at his tactics. This created a great deal of support for people whom McGarvey attacked, so that often McGarvey's methods became counter-productive.

But it was not through the discussion of biblical criticism in the papers that the discipline began to exert influence on the movement. It was through exposure to classroom teaching and liberalism that the seeds of future conflict were sown. The Disciples had always had a goodly number of colleges, but in the early 1890s they frankly could not be considered top-caliber schools.

In 1893, W. C. McCollough of Indiana compiled statistics that showed that Disciples colleges lagged behind state universities, denominational colleges, and even religious schools in such indices as number of professors, student enrollment, books in the library, and admission standards.[40] As a result, the bright young men of the Disciples often went to Disciples colleges, but then began to yearn for something more in the way of graduate education. Herbert Lockwood Willett (1864-1944) exemplifies this situation.

Willett was born in rural Michigan and in 1883 went to Bethany College. In reviewing his first year of college, Willett revealed how little the Disciples schools had been influenced by the newer ideas.

---

[38]*The Missouri Christian Lectures, Delivered at Independence, Mo., July, 1883* (St. Louis: John Burns, Publishers, 1883), p. 167.

[39]*Ibid.*, p. 183.

[40]See his figures in the *Christian Standard*, January 14, 1893, p. 25; January 18, 1893, p. 65; February 4, 1893, p. 89; February 11, 1893, p. 109; and April 22, 1893, p. 315.

The religious point of view at Bethany, both in classroom and pulpit was quite like that to which I had been accustomed at home. The Bible was accepted throughout as an inerrant book not only in its religious teachings but as well in its references to matters of history and science. If Biblical criticism or scientific subjects of controversial nature were ever mentioned it was in terms of positive and even mordant disapproval, and such a theme as the social implications of the gospel did not even suggest itself for consideration. This attitude met my entire approval, and in my letters home I was glad to assure my Father and Mother that they need have no fears regarding my intellectual and theological atmosphere. It was assumed by the faculty that there were no disturbing problems which needed discussion, or at least they were not likely to be introduced to the student body. Bethany was thoroughly sound.[41]

Willett completed his B.A. in 1886 and an M.A. in 1887. Before he left the school, a new administration had begun, and President Woolery advised the young men to enroll in graduate work in one of the larger universities if possible. Willett could not do so at the time but became instead the minister at Central Christian Church in Dayton, Ohio. After three years of the pastorate, Willett wanted to undertake more graduate work without further delay. He applied to Yale and was accepted. He studied for entrance exams, took them upon arrival in New Haven in September, and did well enough to be placed in the third year of the three-year B.D. program.[42]

But at Yale he came under the influence of Dr. William R. Harper, an outstanding Old Testament scholar, and Harper influenced Willett to abandon his plans for the B.D. degree, and instead begin a doctoral program in Old Testament studies. While Harper was also an evangelical, he was already well known as a liberal scholar.[43] Under his tutelage, Willett began to accommodate his own theological and biblical thinking to the liberal presuppositions. It was not a quick process, but it became a steady one over the next several decades.[44] Harper left Yale after Willett's first year, to become the president of the new University of Chicago. Without

---

[41]Herbert Lockwood Willett, "The Corridor of Years: An Autobiographical Record"; introduction and edited by Herbert Lockwood Willett III (Typed, photocopied, and bound, 1967; on file in the library of the Disciples Divinity House of the University of Chicago), p. 146.

[42]*Ibid.*, pp. 36-40.

[43]For an excellent biography of Harper, and a sensitive portrait of him as a biblical scholar concerned with the implications of liberalism for his faith, see Thomas Wakefield Goodspeed, *William Rainey Harper: First President of the University of Chicago* (Chicago: The University of Chicago Press, 1928).

[44]See the observations made by Tucker in comparing some of Willett's books, published respectively in 1899, 1917, and 1929, in Tucker, pp. 91-92.

Harper, Willett left Yale and returned to his pastorate in Dayton. But in the spring of 1893, he left Dayton to resume doctoral study under Harper at Chicago.

In 1890, but before Willett had gone to Yale, Miss Jane Errett, daughter of Isaac Errett and a voice in policy decisions in the Standard Publishing Company, asked him to conduct the Sunday School department of the *Christian Standard* and also edit its Sunday School quarterly. He did this for over two years, amid some protests from readers over some of his statements. After Willett's return from Yale, the editorial offices of the company began to grow uneasy with him, but when he moved to Chicago in 1893, they terminated their contract with him. As Willett commented later, "The arrangement was discontinued, and the Sunday School department was committed to 'safer' hands."[45]

Willett was not the only young Disciple getting exposed to liberalism and higher criticism. Edward Scribner Ames (1870—1958) was born into a Disciples parsonage, graduated from Drake University in 1889, and even stayed on for a year of graduate work. He later observed that at this period he was "controlled by very conservative attitudes."[46] In 1891 Ames went to Yale where he was soon exposed to the concept that religion itself was a developmental process. He noted that "the evolutionary conception of religion was making its way into all departments."[47]

Another example of early exposure to liberalism was the case of Winfred Ernest Garrison (1874-1969), son of J. H. Garrison. He graduated from high school at age sixteen, went to Bethany College for a semester, then to Eureka College in Illinois for a year, receiving his B.A. at age eighteen. He then went to Yale but had to do two years of makeup work before he could enroll in a graduate program. This indicates the lack of quality work available in the Disciples colleges at the time.

Garrison of course grew up in a conservative home. Years later he remembered that at age seven, he accurately recorded what he had been taught and also what he personally believed when he began a poem with the lines "The Bible is God's holy book,/And in it all is true."[48] Yet after he finished his B.A. at Yale in 1894, he enrolled in the Yale Divinity School and there became acquainted with the new higher criticism. He came to see the discipline as so natural and right that he adopted it as

---

[45]Willett, "Corridor," pp. 149-150.

[46]Van Meter Ames (ed.), *Beyond Theology: The Autobiography of Edward Scribner Ames* (Chicago: The University of Chicago Press, 1959), p. 20.

[47]*Ibid.*, pp. 28, 29.

[48]W. E. Garrison, *Variations,* pp. 177-178.

his own method.[49] His essay on Deborah reflected the view of higher criticism. When it appeared in his father's journal,[50] McGarvey attacked it as the worst case of destructive criticism he had yet seen among the Disciples of Christ.[51] As Garrison later observed, "The episode clearly revealed to me that I was on the liberal side in biblical matters, and I had got there by an entirely painless process."[52]

In general there seem to have been three attitudes toward biblical studies among the Disciples at the end of the nineteenth century. One saw the Bible in terms of inerrancy and infallibility; a second saw it as a reasonable revelation that accorded with man's best thinking and imagination; a third saw the Bible as "a written record of the experience of people in search of the highest and best values of life." McGarvey represented the first attitude; J. H. Garrison the second; while Willett, in his mature years, represented the third.[53]

Educational Concerns

Because Disciples schools did not figure in the top-ranking schools in the country, many Disciples became interested in what could be done to improve them. In 1892, during the General Convention in Nashville, a number of Disciples college presidents, professors, and others interested in ministerial education met to discuss the situation. Ultimately they appointed a committee to make recommendations. This committee included J. W. McGarvey, J. H. Garrison, H. L. Willett, and others. The committee itself soon began talk of erecting a "biblical seminary."[54]

Unfortunately this was soon confused by the discovery that the Christian Woman's Board of Missions was also discussing the plight of education among the Disciples youth. In 1892, they decided to establish a Bible Chair at a state university, namely the University of Michigan in Ann Arbor.[55] Since the two proposals surfaced the same year, many people thought the new biblical seminary would be in Ann Arbor, affiliated with the University of Michigan. The president of the Woman's Board, Mrs. O. A. Burgess, had to do a lot of explaining, but in the end the Ann

---

[49]*Ibid.*, p. 184.

[50]*New Christian Quarterly,* vol. 4, no. 2 (1895), pp. 51-70.

[51]*Christian Standard,* June 15, 1895, p. 567.

[52]W. E. Garrison, *Variations,* p. 184.

[53]Woodrow W. Wasson, "Approaches to the Understanding and Use of the Bible Among the Disciples of Christ," *Scroll,* vol. 57, no. 2 (1965), pp. 36-38.

[54]*Christian Standard,* December 17, 1892, p. 1059.

[55]Ida Withers Harrison, *Forty Years of Service: A History of the Christian Woman's Board of Missions, 1874-1914* (n.p., n.p., n.d.) pp. 72-75.

Arbor Bible Chair became a reality. Arrangements were completed in the summer of 1893, and that fall Clinton Lockhart and H. L. Willett began teaching classes. The idea of a Bible Chair caught on, with others soon established at the University of Virginia in 1898, the University of Kansas in 1901, the University of Texas in 1904, and the Tri-State College at Angola, Indiana, in 1908.[56]

But the establishment of Bible Chairs around the country was not sufficient to meet the need of improved Disciple ministerial education. There was still the matter of that "biblical seminary." In 1893, President Harper of the University of Chicago encouraged the Disciples to establish an educational center in Chicago in affiliation with the university's Divinity School. That way the Disciples could take advantage of the Divinity School's faculty, library, and general course offerings, while the Disciples could offer classes geared to Disciples interests and needs, particularly in Disciples history and theology. When the General Convention met in Chicago in September of 1893, Harper spoke to them about the possibility.[57]

Willett was already a student at the Divinity School, W. D. McClintock was a Disciples professor of English in the university, and these men enthusiastically supported the idea. The Chicago Board of City Missions of the Disciples of Christ endorsed the project in April of 1894, and in the same month the Board of the General Christian Missionary convention did likewise.[58] In May the General Board appointed fifteen men as trustees of the Disciples Divinity House, including seven men from Chicago, three from Cincinnati, and J. H. Garrison of St. Louis. The trustees met a week later and elected H. L. Willett the dean.[59] The classroom instruction of the new institution began that fall.

This development was not met with universal rejoicing among the Disciples. Some were enthusiastic, to be sure. Numerous others were uncomfortable with establishing an institution in cooperation with a Baptist school. Professor Deweese of Eureka College was only one individual of many who maintained this line of argument.[60] J. H. Garrison

---

[56]*Ibid.*, p. 74.

[57]*Christian-Evangelist*, September 28, 1893, p. 613. The full history of the school that became Disciples Divinity House is in Wm. Barnett Blakemore, *Quest for Intelligence in Ministry: The Story of the First Seventy Years of Disciples Divinity House of the University of Chicago* (Chicago: The Disciples Divinity House of the University of Chicago, 1970).

[58]*Christian Oracle*, June 28, 1894, p. 404.

[59]*Ibid.*

[60]*Christian-Evangelist*, August 2, 1894, p. 487.

ran most of the interference in defending the new school. He pointed out that since the Disciples did not have the financial resources to establish a school the equivalent of Harvard, Yale, or Chicago, then they must avail themselves of what these institutions could offer, adding "the necessary Biblical and theological instruction" to their curricula.[61] Garrison argued that it was not a case of luring students to Chicago; they were already there. Seven Disciples professors, eight preachers, "and others" were already at Chicago for the summer quarter in 1894. Thus the Disciples Divinity House was necessary to catch up with the students who were going to go to Chicago anyway.[62]

The *Christian Standard* ran a symposium for its readers to express themselves with regard to the new educational venture. Some gave guarded comments, asserting much depended upon the circumstances. Others centered their opposition on the idea of erecting a Disciples institution in connection with a "secular," "alien," or "denominational" school. One man asserted that the environment would not be right for proper biblical learning, and that within a generation Disciples students would have been converted to the hostile camp—hostile in the sense of accepting the liberalism of men such as President Harper.[63]

J. W. McGarvey was firmly in the camp of the opposition. He noted that a Baptist preacher and lecturer in Chicago reported that the University was "doing great injury to the young men who are under Dr. Harper's influence." Garrison had previously said that by keeping Disciples students in the Midwest near numerous preaching points, the chances of them becoming disaffected toward the brotherhood were less than if they went to the East Coast schools. McGarvey observed that this was an admission that going to Chicago was dangerous, only less so than going to the East.[64]

In spite of the attacks, there was never any doubt about whether the Disciples Divinity House would open for classes in the fall of 1894. It did so, and numerous Disciples students continued to come to the school. In the process, the Disciples House accomplished exactly what its detractors had feared. Numerous students were exposed to liberalism, became comfortable with it, and then carried it back to Disciples colleges and Disciples pulpits. Within a generation there was major controversy over the issues supported by the younger liberals, most of whom had received

---

[61]*Ibid.*, August 9, 1894, p. 498.
[62]*Ibid.*, August 30, 1894, p. 546.
[63]*Christian Standard*, September 8, 1894, p. 883.
[64]*Ibid.*, May 30, 1894, p. 687.

graduate instruction at Chicago. Unfortunately, this did not become clear until later on. At the time there was widespread support for the Disciples House, seeing it as a means of elevating Disciples educational standards. Those who were broadminded and tolerant trusted the institution to be an agent of good for the brotherhood. It also became a center of liberal influence within the movement. H. L. Willett came to the University in 1893 and earned his Ph.D. in 1896; E. S. Ames came in 1894 and earned his Ph.D. in 1895; W. E. Garrison came in 1895 and earned his Ph.D. in 1897.[65] These men became the cutting edge of much of the liberalism in the next two decades.

Meanwhile the issue of open membership again raised its head, this time in central Indiana. Hugh C. Garvin began to teach at Butler University in 1889. He had studied in Germany for a while where he became acquainted with biblical criticism and the current trends in theology. By 1896 he raised the question of the status of the pious unimmersed. Although the *Christian-Evangelist* had supported Garvin in some earlier disputes, pleading for tolerance on what it took to be a minor issue,[66] on this issue it chided him for emphasizing "how much one may leave undone" instead of conforming to the facts of the New Testament.[67]

When one of Garvin's students, George E. Hicks, introduced open membership into a church in Indianapolis, the little church split over the issue. Hicks' actions were blamed on "Garvinism," even the *Christian-Evangelist* blaming the professor for teaching views subversive to the biblical principles of the brotherhood.[68] In 1897, Garvin resigned from the school and retired to West Virginia.[69]

In 1895, open membership was also discovered in the Cedar Avenue church in Cleveland, Ohio.[70] When the Cedar Avenue church sent in its regular offering to the Foreign Christian Missionary Society, the *Christian Standard* complained that to receive such monies would amount to an endorsement of the church's open membership policies. Under pressure, F. M. Rains, secretary of the Foreign Society, returned the money.[71] The

---

[65]For these dates, see Blakemore, pp. 142-143, 147-148.

[66]*Christian-Evangelist*, April 26, 1894, p. 260; May 3, 1894, p. 276.

[67]*Ibid.*, January 23, 1896, pp. 50-51.

[68]*Ibid.*, March 26, 1894, p. 194.

[69]Shaw, *Hoosier Disciples*, pp. 265-270.

[70]Henry K. Shaw, *Buckeye Disciples: A History of the Disciples of Christ in Ohio* (St. Louis: Christian Board of Publication, 1952), pp. 288-290; see also Alfred Thomas DeGroot, "The Practice of Open Membership Among the Disciples of Christ" (Unpublished B.D. Thesis at the College of Religion, Butler University, Indianapolis, Indiana, 1929), p. 20.

[71]*Christian Standard*, January 18, 1896, p. 82; March 21, 1896, pp. 369-370.

implications of open membership within a Disciples' church were beginning to raise some difficult questions. In 1898 J. M. Philputt, preaching for a church in Harlem, New York began open membership, explaining that these people were members of the congregation, not members of the church. Not even J. H. Garrison could accept this distinction.[72] Philputt continued the practice until 1902, when he left the church to begin a new ministry in Buffalo.

Within a few years, numerous students had been exposed to the new learning at Chicago, Yale, Harvard, and Union. Some were more liberal than others, but most of them had enjoyed the challenge of intellectual enrichment. In the fall of 1893, five Disciples students at Yale gathered and began to talk of an organization of university-trained men among the Disciples. Stimulated by the powerful intellectual environment at Yale, they desired to nurture this environment more adequately among the Disciples. In the next three years, most of this group transferred their studies to the University of Chicago.[73]

On October 19, 1896, during the meeting of the General Convention in Springfield, Illinois, those interested in enriching the educational level among the Disciples met at the State House and established the Campbell Institute. W. E. Garrison was then only twenty-two years old, but he drafted the statement of purpose for the organization. Among two other goals, he enunciated the desire to encourage and keep alive a scholarly spirit among its members through a free discussion of vital problems.[74] The Campbell Institute was open only to those who had completed an undergraduate degree. This, coupled with the fact that new members' names had to be presented by an existing member and meet with unanimous approval, opened the Institute to charges of intellectual snobbery. By its very intent, the Campbell Institute was to represent the educational elite among the Disciples of Christ. Fourteen persons formed the charter membership, and fifteen more names were presented for membership in its first day of existence.[75]

---

[72]*Christian-Evangelist*, February 17, 1898, p. 103; see also Herbert Lockwood Willett and Lillian Reynolds Philputt (eds.), *"That They May All Be One": Autobiography and Memorial of James M. Philputt, Apostle of Christian Unity* (St. Louis: Christian Board of Publication, 1933), pp. 65-66.

[73]Herbert L. Willett, Orvis F. Jordan, and Charles M. Sharpe (eds.), *Progress: Anniversary Volume of the Campbell Institute on the Completion of Twenty Years of History* (Chicago: The Christian Century Press, 1917), pp. 35-36.

[74]"Campbell Institute Record, 1896-1921" (a bound volume of minutes and reports in the library of the Disciples Divinity House of the University of Chicago, Chicago, Illinois), p. 3.

[75]"Campbell Institute Record," p. 10.

Members of the Campbell Institute were leaders. They were already active in Disciples educational committee meetings; all the daily Bible study sessions at the Springfield convention were led by charter members of the Institute.[76] Since most of the members of the Institute were students at Chicago, that city became the site of its annual meetings. In 1897, J. D. Forrest acknowledged that the members of the Institute were discussing problems of great interest to the brotherhood, but that the mere discussion of some of these would create misunderstanding. Yet he warned that for conservatives to suppress this inquiry would only beget equally intolerant radicalism.[77] By 1898, the annual meetings of the Campbell Institute were closed to nonmembers. Members of the Institute felt that their meetings were already beyond the sympathetic understanding of most Disciples.[78] Years later, Alva W. Taylor remembered "those first days when those of us who joined took our professional lives in our hands."[79]

The Campbell Institute was so named because its members were convinced that Alexander Campbell would have endorsed their desire for knowledge and open discussion of religious ideas. Yet the conservatives soon grew extremely suspicious about this organization of Young Turks. Conservatives could only wonder what those young whippersnappers *were* discussing if they had to meet behind closed doors. Secrecy bred distrust, and it worked on both sides. The Campbell Institute was begun to foster a scholarly spirit and frank discussion about the new currents of thought among the Disciples. Yet by its very nature, it became a breeding ground for liberalism among the Disciples. At first the Institute was only a club of bright young men (and a very few women); soon, however, the young liberals were actively attempting to foster the spread of liberalism within the brotherhood.

Willett and the *Christian Century*

Increasingly, H. L. Willett became the representative liberal among the Disciples. He had been discharged from his writing duties with the *Christian Standard* in 1893 because of unfavorable readers' comments on

---

[76]*Christian Oracle,* May 7, 1896, p. 293; *Christian-Evangelist,* October 29, 1896, p. 690.

[77]*Christian-Evangelist,* August 5, 1897, pp. 488, 489.

[78]"Campbell Institute Record," p. 36.

[79]Letter of July 21, 1944 (in a loose-leaf notebook of letters from alumni in commemoration of the Fiftieth Anniversary of the Disciples Divinity House of the University of Chicago; currently in the Divinity House Library).

his Sunday School lessons. When he was made president of the Illinois Christian Missionary Society in 1897, there were vague grumblings about higher criticism, and efforts were launched to wrest control of the state convention away from those regarded as liberal.[80] More fuel was poured upon the fire late in 1897 when J. H. Garrison hired Willett to write the Sunday School commentary for the *Christian-Evangelist*.

In his very first column, Willett provoked a protest. He stated that baptism was used by the Jews prior to the Christian era in order to initiate proselytes into Judaism.[81] When Willett said some of the Psalms came from the second century B.C.,[82] McGarvey denounced him and said such teaching should not be given to the young people in the churches.[83] Two months later, Willett stated that Paul was so embarrassed about the cross of Christ when he appeared before the philosophers on Mars Hill, that he trimmed his message to fit the audience, omitted the crucifixion, and failed to preach the gospel.[84] Willett also attributed the book of Daniel to Maccabean authorship.[85] When told that Jesus attributed the book to Daniel, Willett replied that this was only a further illustration that Jesus accommodated himself to the popular views of the time.[86]

Numerous readers began to complain to J. H. Garrison and asked him to blue-pencil such comments out of his paper. Garrison refused, saying Willett was only describing the current state of biblical scholarship. But the stockholders of the Christian Publishing Company did not agree. A majority of the stockholders challenged Garrison's handling of the Willett crisis, and Garrison survived it only by buying some stockholders out and holding in his own hands controlling interest in the publishing corporation. Garrison contended he was fighting only for freedom of expression, and that the Disciples had nothing to fear from higher criticism. McGarvey replied that there must also be freedom to control outrageous editors and pernicious teachers.[87] Garrison tried to minimize the differences within the brotherhood, saying the brethren did not differ in essentials. McGarvey replied that the issues were essential ones— the divinity of Christ and the inspiration of Scripture. He concluded that

---

[80]Perry J. Rice, "The Disciples of Christ in Chicago and North-Eastern Illinois, 1839-1939." (Bound, typed manuscript, in the library of the Disciples Divinity House of the University of Chicago), p. 113.

[81]*Christian-Evangelist*, December 23, 1897, p. 816.

[82]*Ibid.*, March 10, 1898, p. 151.

[83]*Christian Standard*, April 2, 1898, p. 423.

[84]*Christian-Evangelist*, June 2, 1898, p. 342.

[85]*Ibid.*, July 6, 1899, p. 860.

[86]*Ibid.*, August 31, 1899, pp. 1099-1100.

[87]*Christian Standard*, November 11, 1899, p. 1441.

Garrison was trying to camouflage the insidious tendencies of higher criticism.[88]

When Garrison was in the midst of his stockholders' war, the Standard Publishing Company sent out a circular stating that Standard's Sunday School materials were free from the taint of infidelity and should be purchased by the churches. Garrison was outraged and called this an underhanded attack undertaken solely for the sake of increased sales and profits.[89]

Yet this was more than merely a newspaper war. The *Christian Standard* and *Christian-Evangelist* had polarized considerably since the days of Isaac Errett. Although they were agreed on opposing open membership, they disagreed on most other issues—attitudes toward higher criticism, Disciples attending eastern schools, Disciples Divinity House at Chicago, and whether a missionary society ought to receive money from an open membership church.

In effect there was a division among the minds of the Disciples and the two major papers simply reflected this division. They did not cause it, and they were not to blame for perpetuating it. It would have continued without or in spite of them. What was at stake was the basic question of whether the original plea and practices of the Disciples ought to be refined and adjusted by the principles of liberal Protestantism. The issues would not go away even if both papers had stopped talking about them. The development of a local Chicago paper into a major voice only increased the tensions. Chicago was becoming known for its cluster of liberal institutions.

The *Christian Oracle* was begun in 1884 as a voice for the Iowa Disciples. Yet its finances were never very stable, so in 1888 its editors moved it to Chicago to make it a state paper for both Illinois and Iowa. Its finances, however, remained rather shaky. In 1898, editor F. M. Kirkham wearied of the task and traded it to J. H. Garrison for a California paper, the *Pacific Christian*. The *Christian Oracle* had a reputation for being somewhat inclined toward a liberal position. It had attacked Cave's excesses,[90] although it defended President Harper's lectures on Genesis,[91] in spite of McGarvey's attacks on them.[92] The *Christian Oracle* defended the idea of the Bible Chair in Ann Arbor[93] and

---

[88]*Ibid.*, December 9, 1899, p. 1568.

[89]*Christian-Evangelist*, December 21, 1899, p. 1612.

[90]*Christian Oracle*, January 2, 1890, p. 1.

[91]*Ibid.*, February 15, 1894, p. 97.

[92]Beginning in the *Christian Standard*, February 17, 1894, p. 177.

[93]*Christian Oracle*, November 10, 1892, p. 709.

strongly endorsed the founding of Disciples Divinity House in Chicago.[94] The editor of the *Christian Oracle,* F. M. Kirkham, was the first president of the board of trustees of the Disciples Divinity House, serving from 1894 to 1897.[95] After Garrison took over the *Christian Oracle,* Willett became a contributing editor to it.[96]

Garrison had no better luck with the paper's finances. In addition, the *Christian-Evangelist* was also trying to serve Illinois' needs, and both he and other stockholders of the Oracle Publishing Company felt he was trying to serve two masters. Consequently, late in 1899, he sold his controlling interest in the Chicago operation to Charles A. Young, George A. Campbell, and Angus McKinnon.[97] Young became president of the company and Campbell the editor. Campbell, minister of the Austin Christian Church in a western suburb of Chicago, suggested that the twentieth century should be a *Christian* century, and he proposed that the paper be renamed the *Christian Century.*[98] This was done, and the first issue of the paper under its new management, on January 4, 1900, bore the new title.

New management did not immediately bring financial stability to the paper, but it did put the paper unmistakably in the hands of the young liberals. In May, Young became editor, with Willett soon a contributing editor.[99] Young, Campbell, and Willett were all charter members of the Campbell Institute. In its very first issue, the junior editor of the paper issued a mocking attack on McGarvey as a biblical critic.[100]

For some time, a number of Disciples had felt that some kind of forum was needed to discuss the issues of biblical criticism and theological developments as they affected the Disciples and their work. Such discussions would have been out of place at the annual General Convention, but as early as 1890, J. H. Garrison began to request some kind of a congress for the full discussion of such issues.[101] The Campbell Institute began discussing such a proposal in 1897.[102] The first Congress of the Disciples convened in 1899 with J. H. Garrison as general chairman.

[94]*Ibid.,* September 27, 1894, p. 562; see also March 14, 1895, pp. 161-162.
[95]Blakemore, p. 140.
[96]*Christian Oracle,* November 24, 1898, pp. 3-4.
[97]*Christian Century,* January 14, 1900, p. 9; *Christian-Evangelist,* February 1, 1900, p. 139.
[98]*Christian Century,* October 8, 1958, p. 1135.
[99]*Ibid.,* May 10, 1900, pp. 4, 6.
[100]*Ibid.,* January 4, 1900, pp. 3-4.
[101]*Christian-Evangelist,* May 1, 1890, p. 274.
[102]"Campbell Institute Record," p. 27.

Specific topics included city evangelization, college endowment, adjusting church organization to present needs, as well as more theological subjects. The second Congress in 1900 featured a frank discussion between Willett and McGarvey on the benefit of higher criticism.[103] Conservatives participated in the meetings for the first five years or so, but ultimately lost interest as the topics continued to reflect liberal interests. Liberals tried to recruit more conservative participation, but most conservatives were not willing to invest the time and effort to prepare scholarly papers. As a result, the Congress soon became virtually another liberal voice with personnel largely identical with the Campbell Institute. The absence of conservatives in the Congresses, which continued until 1926, was another indication of the increasing polarization within the brotherhood.[104]

Issues of Distrust

As we have seen repeatedly, one of the major goals of the Restoration Movement has always been to heal the rifts in the denominational world and restore unity to the body of Christ. With the erosion of biblical authority under liberalism, the liberals came to emphasize this aspect of the movement's *raison d'etre*. Thus the *Christian Century* in particular began to highlight the need for increased effort among Disciples to work for unity.

Contributing editor H. L. Willett ran a series of editorials that later appeared in a book entitled *Our Plea for Union and the Present Crisis,* a severe indictment of the sectarian spirit among the Disciples and a plea to return to the genuine desire for Christian unity. Willett said Disciples must learn that members of other denominations believed their opinions were Scripturally right too,[105] and he implied a hesitancy in insisting on immersion as an essential to unity.[106] Understandably the book was criticized by the *Christian Standard*[107] but reviewed sympathetically by the *Christian-Evangelist.*[108]

Willett's book certainly increased suspicion about him in the eyes of the

---

[103]*Christian-Evangelist,* April 5, 1900, pp. 421-422.

[104]See McAllister and Tucker, p. 376.

[105]Herbert L. Willett, *Our Plea for Union and the Present Crisis* (Chicago: The Christian Century Company, 1901), p. 81.

[106]*Ibid.,* pp. 45-46, 107-108.

[107]*Christian Standard,* November 9, 1901, pp. 1426-1428.

[108]*Christian-Evangelist,* November 14, 1901, p. 1445; December 5, 1901, pp. 1549-1550.

conservatives. He seemed to them to be arguing for an interdenominational recognition, soft-pedaling immersion in the process. When the *Christian Century* complained that the *Christian Standard* was trying to drive Willett out of the brotherhood, it simply replied that it had no desire to impugn his standing as a member of the church, but it did intend to nullify his teaching and repudiate him as a representative of the Disciples.[109]

When the Kansas City Disciples Ministerial Association invited Willett to give a series of addresses on the Old Testament in February of 1902, the conservatives were even more concerned about the recognition and stature this provided for Willett within the brotherhood. George W. Muckley, the full-time secretary of the Disciples Board of Church Extension, chaired the committee on local arrangements. Muckley used his official letterhead to invite ministers from the surrounding area to come to the lectures. The *Christian Standard* charged that this gave an official endorsement by one of the national Disciples agencies of Willett and all his teachings.[110]

If the Disciples were experiencing difficulty in achieving unity within their own ranks, it was even more difficult to achieve it with other Protestant groups across the country. In 1902, Dr. E. B. Sanford, a leader in the movement to establish the National Federation of Churches, spoke to the General Convention in Omaha, explaining the purposes of the Federation. J. H. Garrison offered a carefully worded resolution expressing approval of the effort to bring about closer cooperation and unite the followers of Christ. He was greatly surprised when J. A. Lord, editor of the *Christian Standard,* argued against the resolution on the grounds that it would mean recognizing the denominations. W. E. Garrison replied that the resolution did recognize denominations as facts, but did not recognize them as an "ideal, scriptural or permanent condition of things." The resolution was adopted, but a large minority voted against it.[111] For the next several years, the brotherhood continued to polarize on the issues of combining with the proposed Federal Council of Churches. Because the Disciples had no denominational machinery as such, they could not officially join the Federation. But a committee was appointed among the Disciples to discuss the issue, and it reported favorably. When the convention met in Norfolk, Virginia, in 1907, a public meeting was held extraneous to the sessions of the convention at which interested Disciples could voice themselves on the

---

[109]*Christian Standard,* January 25, 1902, p. 130.
[110]*Ibid.,* February 22, 1902, p. 278.
[111]*Christian-Evangelist,* October 30, 1902, p. 130.

matter. A resolution to seek membership on the Federal Council was approved by this group, which amounted to official membership in the Council when it organized in 1908. Still, many conservatives were unhappy with this effort to combine efforts with the "denominations," particularly because this meant having "fellowship" with numerous groups that were unimmersed.

It was becoming apparent that an unhealthy polarization was forming among the movement. On the one hand were those influenced by liberalism who no longer saw the Scripture as authoritative because of their acceptance of biblical criticism. These individuals, often identified with the Campbell Institute and the Disciples Divinity House, were emphasizing the goal of Christian unity in the movement. On the other hand were those who were still conservative in their view of Scripture, who saw liberalism as an insidious erosion of biblical authority. They were unable to look favorably upon efforts to implement union with people who did not accept the veracity of Scripture or even who did not follow its teachings with regard to believer's immersion, congregational autonomy, or other such applications that had long been venerated within the Restoration Movement. The people within the Restoration Movement who wished to protect the authority of Scripture even reached the point of believing that appeals for union were simply masks to shield people's infidelity with respect to biblical authority and integrity. It was often difficult to keep the focus on the real question at hand. It was so easy to jump to conclusions concerning the other person's motives and goals. People were being judged by the company they kept and the personalities they displayed, rather than by the more demanding question of whether they accepted the basic position of the Restoration Movement.

A classic case in point occurred in California beginning in 1902 concerning Hiram Van Kirk. Van Kirk was typical of the bright young men in the movement in the 1890s. He finished his B.A. at Hiram College in 1892, and a B.D. at Yale Divinity School in 1895. That same fall he began doctoral studies at the University of Chicago Divinity School.[112] He was one of the charter members of the Campbell Institute.[113] He completed his Ph.D. in Systematic Theology in 1900 and became the dean of Berkeley Bible Seminary, affiliated with the University of California at Berkeley.[114]

---

[112]*Annual Register of the University of Chicago* (Chicago: The University of Chicago Press, 1896), p. 310.

[113]"Campbell Institute Record," p. 10.

[114]W. E. Garrison, *Religion Follows the Frontier,* p. 262.

In the fall of 1902, J. W. McGarvey mentioned that a student from Berkeley left the Disciples to become a Unitarian minister because of views of higher criticism he had received from Van Kirk.[115] For the next six months, charges and countercharges flew back and forth. Relying upon evidence from individuals in California, the *Christian Standard* charged that Van Kirk denied the inspiration of Scripture, that he believed the gospel was an evolution from the Law, and that the New Testament was "an uninspired record gathered by uninspired writers."[116]

The board of trustees of Berkeley Bible Seminary entered the fray by issuing a report garnered from student questionnaires to the effect that Van Kirk's teaching was wholesome, not destructive. Van Kirk attacked the integrity of the *Christian Standard*'s witnesses charging they were troublemakers in the Oakland church;[117] the *Christian Century* simply said they were immoral men.[118] Documentation put out by the Seminary's board of trustees indicated that one of these witnesses was expelled from a church and stripped of teaching certification because of "gross immorality"; another witness was known as a habitual liar; others were cited for questionable morality or obvious conflict-of-interest in the case.[119]

Faced with this material, the *Christian Standard* only said it was waiting for a "promised communication from the brethren" in California.[120] Apparently that promised communication did not arrive. The *Christian Standard*'s difficulty was that Berkeley was two-thirds of a continent away from Cincinnati, and they did not know whom to trust at such long distance. It was not until they sent a representative to California in the summer of 1904 that they were able to sort through the issue. This resulted in the embarrassing notice on an editorial page to the effect that the witnesses they had relied upon were indeed untrustworthy; they regretted the unfortunate incident, but considered it closed.[121]

The Hiram Van Kirk case is a classic indicator of what was occurring in the brotherhood at the time. There is early evidence that the teaching of higher criticism was detrimental to the faith of young seminary students. Van Kirk, with a Ph.D. from Chicago, was the obvious source of the infection. In its determination to prove that Van Kirk was unreliable, the *Christian Standard* used witnesses who themselves were unreliable. In

---

[115]*Christian Standard*, November 29, 1902, p. 1660.
[116]*Ibid.*, February 21, 1903, pp. 254-258; May 9, 1903, p. 657.
[117]*Christian-Evangelist*, March 12, 1903, p. 210.
[118]*Christian Century*, May 14, 1903, p. 583.
[119]*Christian-Evangelist*, May 14, 1903, pp. 397-400.
[120]*Christian Standard*, May 30, 1903, p. 758.
[121]*Ibid.*, August 13, 1904, p. 1121.

the attempt to discredit Van Kirk and the kind of teaching he defended, the *Standard* itself was discredited. McGarvey himself had initiated the whole controversy but stood aside and allowed the *Standard* to finish the battle. As a result, many people felt that both McGarvey and the *Christian Standard* had been unfair. The tactics employed in this case convinced many that McGarvey and the *Standard* leaders were narrow-minded men who were opposed to honest and full investigation of the Scriptures. In attacking the field of higher criticism, they now appeared as uninformed bigots who were willing to rely on slanderous untruths to ruin the reputations of honest young scholars. Such instances only decreased peoples' credibility with regard to revelations and accusations made by the *Christian Standard*. It was much like the story of the young boy who cried "Wolf!" Later, when the wolf did appear, no one believed his urgent cries. Much the same happened in the Restoration Movement. Van Kirk was no wolf; when later wolves did appear, the conservatives' outcries often went unheeded. This was simply another tragedy of the Van Kirk incident.

Before the smoke had completely cleared from the Van Kirk episode, Chicago again became a focus of attention. Edward Scribner Ames became minister of the Disciples church in Hyde Park, the area in which the University of Chicago was located. He had received his Ph.D. in philosophy from the University in 1895, then taught at Butler University for three years. In 1903, now back in the University area, he introduced a form of open membership at the Hyde Park church. Ames was not just a liberal; he was, even in the estimation of a secular historian, a modernist.[122] One who knew Ames personally characterizes his religious thinking as "humanistic theism."[123] Ames denied that Disciples had ever rigidly believed that immersion was essential to salvation, though they had regarded it as essential to church membership. Thus for a while Ames practiced open membership, but called such people brought in under this form only "associate members." Within a few years he dropped even this designation. Ames admitted that the New Testament knew of no situation of a person claiming to be a Christian without immersion, but that there were numerous such people in the world today. Therefore, Ames concluded, we are faced with a situation for which there is no New Testament precedent, and he felt that open

---

[122]Gerald N. Grob and Robert N. Beck (eds.), *American Ideas: Source Readings in the Intellectual History of the United States; vol. 2: Dilemmas of Maturity (1865-1962)* (New York: The Free Press, 1963), p. 218.

[123]Wm. Barnett Blakemore, in the "Introduction" to the work edited by Van Meter Ames, *Prayers and Meditations of Edward Scribner Ames* (Disciples Divinity House of the University of Chicago, 1970), p. 13.

membership was an acceptable application of New Testament guide-lines.[124]

The Hyde Park Church was certainly not the first church to practice open membership, but it was the first church to begin it and never relinquish it. Other churches had always given it up within a few years, usually when the minister left who had inaugurated it. But Ames remained as the minister of Hyde Park (later called the University Christian Church) until 1940. By then the practice was deeply rooted. In addition, he was a leading liberal spokesman associated with the other liberal agencies in Chicago. As a result, Hyde Park's adoption of open membership became a *cause celebre* in the movement. Yet there were other implications of the issue.

In 1887, the Disciples in Chicago had organized the Board of City Missions to coordinate the effort to plant new churches in the city and its suburbs. In 1900, this was reorganized as the Chicago Christian Missionary Society. In the struggle to get sufficient funds, the Chicago Christian Missionary Society entered into an agreement with the American Christian Missionary Society to receive money from that body for the cause of mission work in the city.[125]

Then in 1904, the CCMS was disturbed because of a rumor that reached ACMS headquarters that open membership churches in Chicago were represented on the CCMS board, helping to decide how to spend the money from the ACMS, and also that some of the money was supporting mission churches practicing open membership. The rumor continued that the ACMS had decided to discontinue sending money directly to the CCMS, which would seriously curtail its activities. A delegation of men from the CCMS went to the ACMS headquarters in Cincinnati to explain that two of the accused churches were not in fact practicing open membership, that the Hyde Park church was receiving no money from the board, and that no member of the city board was in sympathy with the Hyde Park practice. The outcome was that the ACMS continued to channel its contributions for work in Chicago through the CCMS.[126]

Then in early 1906, the situation broke open again. A conservative minister in Chicago, Lloyd Darsie, reported that the church in Austin was receiving mission support and also was receiving the unimmersed

---

[124]Edward Scribner Ames, "Christian Union and the Disciples, A Sermon for the Hyde Park Church of the Disciples, Chicago, January 11, 1903" (n.p. n.d.), pp. 11-14.

[125]Chicago Christian Missionary Society Minutes (in the library of the Disciples Divinity House of the University of Chicago), May 31, 1906.

[126]*Christian Standard*, December 24, 1904, p. 1832.

into fellowship.[127] Darsie also attacked the CCMS for using students from the University of Chicago Divinity School to preach in various mission stations, and he condemned "certain teaching in vogue at the Chicago University" as destructive of the Christian faith.[128]

Six days later, the President and Superintendent of Evangelism of the ACMS came to Chicago to meet with the board of the CCMS to iron out this problem. Darsie was present and gave his complaints, after which the chairman of the CCMS Executive Board moved that the CCMS was not in violation of its 1904 agreement with the ACMS. Without any discussion the motion was seconded and approved unanimously. Just before the meeting ended, the Superintendent of Evangelism of the ACMS recommended that the money from the ACMS be used to pay the salary of the City Superintendent of Missions.[129] As long as the City Superintendent was orthodox, the ACMS did not feel responsible for what was done in mission churches the CCMS supported.

It is important to see in a connected view what had been occurring in Chicago. In 1903, the Hyde Park church became open membership. Because the Restoration Movement has always emphasized the autonomy of the local congregation, there was little that outside congregations, agencies, or influences could do about the situation. If Hyde Park, under its duly selected elders and minister, wanted to practice open membership, there was nothing the remainder of the brotherhood could do about it. But the situation at Austin was a different matter. Here was a mission-sponsored church. Being autonomous is one thing; receiving mission support from conservative churches and agencies is something else again. Those who opposed open membership could properly refuse to condone and financially support such activities. Here was a natural opportunity to impede the spread of open membership. But the ACMS was willing to wink at the practice, divert its support to the salary of the local evangelist, and then claim it was not responsible for open membership in Austin. In effect it was a tacit approval of open membership, and a tacit encouragement of the liberalism that had already struck deep roots in the Chicago context. The Austin situation did not receive wide publicity outside the immediate Chicago context, but the time soon came when conservatives—in Chicago as well as elsewhere—refused to allow such maneuvers. The covert acquiescence of the ACMS with the open membership situation at Austin caused many to begin to wonder about

---

[127]CCMS Minutes, n.d., p. 152.
[128]CCMS Minutes, February 26, 1906, p. 148.
[129]CCMS Minutes, March 4, 1906, pp. 153-154.

the integrity of missionary executives when it came down to liberal practices. Such an undermining of confidence was to have a serious effect in the next couple of decades.

In 1905, Errett Gates wrote the first scholarly history of the movement. Gates, a Ph.D. recipient in church history from the University of Chicago in 1902, was an instructor in the Disciples Divinity House. In his writing Gates developed the thought that Thomas Campbell had focused his thinking on the need for Christian union, but that Alexander Campbell had become wrapped up in the need for an authoritative pattern, which he found in the New Testament record of primitive Christianity. Gates acknowledged that both the principles of the authority of primitive Christianity and the obligation of Christian unity were present in Thomas. Both were equally binding, although the former was the means, the latter the end. Gates suggested that Thomas did not anticipate a condition where the principles would become mutually exclusive.[130] Gates contended that when Alexander began to make such a point of baptism, at that point the chief focus of the movement was shifted away from union.[131] Thus Gates and other liberals were now making the assertion that the emphasis on immersion was a compromise with the original single-minded plea for unity. The message was clear—the Disciples ought to be more accommodating on the issue of immersion.

In 1906, open membership began at another Chicago church, the Monroe Street Church of Christ under its minister, C. C. Morrison, later the influential editor of the *Christian Century*. The first announcement of Monroe Street's open membership was made through the Campbell Institute's monthly paper, the *Scroll*. This again drew attention to the CCMS and its relationship to the ACMS. The chairman of the Executive Board wrote to Cincinnati explaining the situation. He recalled the 1904 agreement that no one in sympathy with open membership was to be on the Chicago board, but it now had representatives from both Monroe Street and Hyde Park. Both of these churches practiced open membership—was this a violation of the agreement?[132] W. J. Wright, the Superintendent of Evangelism for the ACMS, wrote back stating that since the ACMS was not making any direct appropriation to the treasury of the city board (they paid the local city superintendent directly), the ACMS did not feel involved in the local controversy about Chicago

---

[130]Errett Gates, *The Disciples of Christ* (New York: The Baker & Taylor Co., 1905), pp. 60-61.

[131]*Ibid.*, pp. 94-95, 112-113.

[132]CCMS Minutes, n.d., p. 227.

churches practicing open membership.[133] It was becoming obvious that the ACMS would neither blow the whistle on practices in Chicago, nor cut off the funds.

In 1908, H. L. Willett again came in for a great deal of attention. In connection with his work in the Semitic Department at the University of Chicago, he delivered a series of public lectures on "Types of Old Testament Literature." In the process, he discussed the miracle narratives and classified them as follows: some were natural events that people who recorded them thought were supernatural; some miracles were merely figures of speech; some referred to cases of healing that were probably psychosomatic; and others referred to incidents of mythology common to various Semitic religions.[134]

These statements were sensationalized in the local papers and received national attention. McGarvey again denounced Willett as an infidel.[135] Willett tried to explain that all he was trying to say was that the Old Testament had similarities with other Semitic literature, but that this did not obviate the uniqueness of the religious and ethical teachings of that Testament.[136] But these explanations did not satisfy his accusers.

Z. T. Sweeney challenged Willett to a debate on miracles, but it got nowhere. Willett refused to define a miracle as an intervention of the supernatural into the natural order because it suggested a conflict between the two. He preferred to see a miracle as "the unusual but normal activity of a perfect life in the domain of nature." This allowed Christ to work miracles because His was the one perfect life in history.[137] Sweeney refused to accept this definition. When Willett asked Sweeney to come up with a workable definition, he demurred, saying he was not the one who had to do the explaining.[138] Communication broke off at that point and was not resumed.

Meanwhile, Willett was the center of another surge of controversy that followed immediately on the heels of the miracle incident. In the fall of 1908, the program committee for the great Centennial Convention that was being planned released the first tentative list of speakers for the Pittsburgh Convention—and on the list was H. L. Willett. The *Christian Standard* declared it was an insult to the brotherhood to put Willett on

---

[133]*Ibid.*, p. 228.
[134]Willett, "Corridor," pp. 107-108.
[135]*Christian Standard*, August 5, 1908, p. 1379.
[136]*Christian Century*, August 13, 1908, p. 415.
[137]*Ibid.*, September 3, 1908, pp. 463-464.
[138]*Ibid.*, June 3, 1909, p. 538.

the program since he was not at all representative of what the Disciples believed. A month earlier, it had also charged that the missionary societies were becoming the dupes of the Chicago contingent of liberals.[139] Now the *Christian Standard* demanded that the missionary leaders have Willett's name removed from the program.[140]

Willett felt that for him to resign would be construed as an admission that the charges against him were true, which he denied. The program committee refused to remove Willett, and he stayed on the program. But the *Christian Standard* was quick to point out that the majority of the committee were missionary executives, the salaries of the entire committee were being paid out of missionary funds, and obviously the missionary societies were both responsible for and in favor of the liberalizing trends, and this in spite of overwhelming opposition on the part of loyal Disciples.[141]

The missionary societies began to receive a significant amount of mail in opposition to Willett's appearance on the program—so much that the leaders of the societies became alarmed. Archibald McLean, president of the FCMS, wrote to Willett and begged him to resign. Yet W. J. Wright of the ACMS also wrote to Willett begging him *not* to resign. Dozens of others wrote the same thing, saying that to yield to the reactionaries would be a severe defeat to the cause of freedom of thought among the Disciples.[142] Willett himself was in a quandary. He did not personally want to remain the center of controversy, but at the same time he thought the principle of free thought was important enough to suffer for. He stayed on the program.[143]

Willett ultimately spoke at the Centennial Convention but said nothing controversial. Through the entire episode, however, conservatives could only continue to wonder about the continuing direction of their missionary society leadership. It was obvious that a deep loss of confidence was already setting in. The missionary societies were increasingly being seen as under the influence of the liberals from Chicago. It was only a question of time before the conservatives' loss of confidence reached the point where they would no longer financially support the societies. That would take another decade, but the hints of that step had already been indicated in the first decade of the twentieth century.

---

[139]*Christian Standard*, August 22, 1908, p. 1418.

[140]*Ibid.*, September 12, 1908, p. 1548.

[141]*Ibid.*, November 14, 1908, pp. 1950-1951.

[142]These letters are in the Willett Papers at the Disciples of Christ Historical Society in Nashville, Tennessee.

[143]Willett, "Corridor," p. 154.

1909	Centennial Convention in Pittsburgh
1911	Guy Sarvis sent to China
	C.B. Titus recalled from China
	McGarvey dies; R.H. Crossfield becomes president of College of the Bible in Lexington, Kentucky
1912	A.W. Fortune hired at College of the Bible
	Phillips Bible Institute begun
1914	CWBM approves comity agreement with Mexico
	Northern California convention refuses delegates from Berkeley church
1915	Conservative churches in Chicago form Chicago-Calumet Evangelistic Association
1917	Liberalism charged at College of the Bible
1919	Merger of missionary societies to form UCMS
1920	R.E. Elmore charges open membership in China
	Medbury Resolution at Convention
1921	China missionaries refuse Medbury Resolution
	Clarke Fund receives wider support
1922	Sweeney Resolution
	E.K. Higdon practices open membership in Manila
	Both Sweeney Resolution and Higdon Interpretation accepted at convention
1923	McGarvey Bible College and Cincinnati Bible Institute formed
1924	The Cincinnati Bible Seminary formed
	General convention acknowledges division
	Peace Committee appointed
1925	Clarke Fund becomes Christian Restoration Association
	Peace Resolution
1926	Orient Commission reports no open membership
	Conservatives defeated at Memphis Convention

Chapter 11

The Crisis of Confidence

The Centennial Convention in Pittsburgh in 1909 was a great celebration for the Restoration Movement. The year 1909 was one hundred years after Thomas Campbell had written his epochal Declaration and Address, which many people took to mark the birth of the Movement. The annual convention that year, therefore, was to be a big centennial birthday party. The planners wanted to have it in the very city where the Declaration and Address had first been printed, but Washington, Pennsylvania, did not have the facilities needed for such a large gathering. So the convention was held in Pittsburgh, not very far away, but having the rail connections, hotels, restaurants, and meeting rooms necessary.

Numerous chartered trains came from all over the country bringing Christians to the city. The sessions went on for ten days meeting in churches and auditorium halls all over the city, since there was no single building that could accommodate such a crowd. The accomplishments in new church planting as well as foreign missions were detailed and brought rejoicing in the spread of the message of simple, New Testament Christianity. Thirty thousand people gathered in Forbes Field on a Sunday afternoon to celebrate the Lord's supper. Statistics placed the membership of the Restoration Movement at approximately one and a quarter million people, and the future seemed bright and positive as continuing growth seemed assured.

Issues in Tension

Yet there were problems. For one thing, very few members of the Restoration Movement who chose to worship without musical instruments came to the Centennial Convention. For all practical purposes, they had separated from the remainder of the Movement and continued to go their own way for the next several decades.

Secondly, the advance of liberalism had brought severe tensions among the people that celebrated the Centennial Convention. The turmoil over whether Willett should speak had ended with his remaining on the program. He said nothing controversial during his address, but Walter Scott's grandson, Samuel Hardin Church, created a major controversy when he suggested that sprinkling and pouring should be allowed as optional modes of baptism among the Disciples. Interestingly enough, even the liberal *Christian Century* protested this as an inexcusable abandonment of New Testament teaching and practice.[1] When the Standard Publishing Company published the souvenir book of all the convention speeches, they refused to print Church's address and at the same time disclaimed any responsibility for the appearance of the names of H. L. Willett and Perry J. Rice, the president that year of the Campbell Institute.[2]

One of the highlights of the convention was the Veterans' Campfire, open only to those fifty years of age and older. After several addresses numerous beloved and elderly leaders came to the platform to make spontaneous remarks. Some made snide remarks about infidelity, which were greeted with applause; others pleaded for a more magnanimous spirit of humility, truth, and unity. Even among the aged preachers, the unsettling issues of liberalism could not be ignored.[3] Thus the Christian Churches came away from Pittsburgh pleased with the accomplishments of a century, but disturbed over the new issues that continued to threaten their harmony.

The issue of baptism simply would not remain in the background. Early in 1910, the *Christian Century* began a series of editorials analyzing baptism as part of the Disciples overall position. The general conclusion was that too much was being made of the *dogma* of immersion. The *Christian Century* preferred to present immersion as the basis for future unity without insisting that other forms were wrong. This meant open membership for now, so that all might practice immersion in the future.[4]

Errett Gates conceded the point that the "baptism conscience" of the

---

[1]*Christian Century*, November 11, 1909, p. 1113.

[2]*Centennial Convention Report: One Hundredth Anniversary of the Disciples of Christ, Pittsburgh, October 11-19, 1909* (Cincinnati: The Standard Publishing Company, 1909), p. 5.

[3]*Ibid.*, pp. 315-332.

[4]*Christian Century*, January 13, 1910, p. 27; January 20, 1910, p. 51.

Disciples pulled toward an exclusivist policy, but he argued that the "union conscience" must move toward a *rapprochement* with all children of God. He suggested that a united church was more pleasing to Christ than an immersed one.[5]

Perry Rice agreed, but he added his fears that an attempt to develop the "union conscience" would only agitate the "baptism conscience."[6] Here indeed was the dilemma of the Movement at the time. The twin concerns of the Movement were again becoming polarized. The concern for Christian union was pulling away from the concern for biblical authority, represented in the proper (biblical) practice of baptism.

J. H. Garrison disagreed with the *Christian Century* assessment. He contended that the original founders of the Disciples felt no antagonism between the practices of immersion and union. "They believed and taught that the only way to bring the unity of the church was to restore its original constitution—its faith, its ordinances, and its life." Immersion was simply a part of that original constitution.[7] A decade later F. D. Kershner, a prominent Disciples historian, heartily agreed with Garrison on this very point.[8]

Increasingly the geographical center of the liberalism within the Disciples was located in Chicago. The notable leaders were C. C. Morrison, editor of the *Christian Century*; E. S. Ames, minister at University Christian Church and professor of philosophy at the University; and H. L. Willett, professor of Old Testament at the University of Chicago Divinity School. All of them were involved in the Campbell Institute, recognized as a club of liberals. The Institute was also identified with Chicago since most of its early members were students at the University of Chicago and the Disciples Divinity House. Referring to Willett, Ames, Morrison, and W. E. Garrison, McAllister and Tucker call them "the intellectual center of the Disciples for many years. Brilliant and determined, they led the Stone-Campbell movement into and through the heyday of American liberal theology."[9]

Murch also acknowledges the significant impact of this Chicago cluster of liberal institutions, although he also includes the Disciples Congresses, which began in 1899. Originally these were to provide a

---

[5]*Ibid.*, February 24, 1910, pp. 178-179.

[6]*Ibid.*, p. 181.

[7]*Christian-Evangelist*, May 5, 1910, p. 638.

[8]Frederick D. Kershner, *The Restoration Handbook, Series IV; Studies in the History and Principles of the Movement to Restore New Testament Christianity* (Cincinnati: The Standard Publishing Company, 1920), p. 55.

[9]McAllister and Tucker, p. 374.

medium for scholarly discussion, but by 1912 the speakers were almost always liberals. That year Professor F. O. Norton of Drake argued that the texts in the gospels that have Jesus authorizing baptism were either interpolations or of questionable authenticity. The reviewer, Burris Jenkins, essentially agreed.[10] C. C. Morrison, reading a paper entitled "The Essential Plea of the Disciples in the Light of Their Origin and Aim," spun out the thesis that the adoption of immersion was an abandonment of the original aim of Thomas Campbell. J. H. Garrison disagreed, but O. F. Jordan wrote up Garrison's remarks in a condescending manner, remarking that the discussion had opened the minds of "scores of young men" who hitherto thought immersion a closed question.[11] The next year even Garrison's paper noted that the Congress was becoming a platform for the most radical ideas.[12] Murch even argues that the Campbell Institute was "the medium for the development of a liberal strategy for the capture of the schools and agencies of the Disciples."[13] Yet this "conspiracy thesis" raises some difficult questions. There is no doubt that many members of the Campbell Institute achieved leadership positions in the next couple of decades. Does this prove a conspiracy, however, or is it merely the natural rise of the more educated to positions of prominence in schools and agencies? The conservatives soon developed a "conspiracy paranoia," as early as Willett's appointment to the Centennial program. When John D. Rockefeller made financial gifts to the Foreign Christian Missionary Society, Murch saw it in sinister terms.

> Rockefeller, benefactor of the liberal University of Chicago, the very center of aggressive modernism, was making such gifts to the foreign boards of all the leading denominations. This was a part of the liberal strategy to obtain control of these boards.[14]

Such conspiracy theories are difficult to prove since the question of motive is difficult to determine. To say, without any proof, that Rockefeller gave money to foreign missions for purposes of a liberal takeover is not very convincing. Yet the Disciples conservatives continued to believe there was a liberal conspiracy to take over the agencies of the brotherhood.

---

[10]*Christian Century*, April 25, 1912, pp. 396-397.
[11]*Ibid.*, pp. 397, 403, 406-407.
[12]*Christian-Evangelist*, March 20, 1913, p. 395.
[13]Murch, p. 239.
[14]*Ibid.*, p. 245.

Another piece of evidence in the argument came in 1911 when the Foreign Christian Missionary Society appointed Guy Sarvis to China as a missionary educator. Sarvis had just completed his studies at the University of Chicago Divinity School and Disciples Divinity House; moreover, his last year he spent as the associate minister of the University Christian Church—the church under E. S. Ames that practiced open membership. The conservatives complained this marked Sarvis as a liberal, and it was wrong to send him to the mission field where he would plant more open membership.[15]

Another element in the arrangement was that Sarvis was being sent to Nanking, China, to teach in a Disciples college recently merged with Baptists, Presbyterians, and Methodists. Because C. B. Titus, a veteran missionary in Nanking, was opposed to this merger and its acceptance of the unimmersed, he was recalled. The *Christian Standard* labelled the whole thing a conspiracy, "a preconcerted and carefully worked out scheme" on the part of the Foreign Christian Missionary Society to replace a trusted conservative with a liberal, and thus further open membership and liberalism on the mission field.[16]

In spite of the furor, Sarvis sailed for China in September, 1911. The conservatives were convinced this was implicit conspiracy on the part of the Foreign Society. Add to this the disenchantment the conservatives had with the American Christian Missionary Society in 1906 over open membership in Austin, Illinois, and a pattern begins to emerge whereby the missionary societies were losing their credibility in the eyes of the conservatives. The *Christian Standard* concluded a "guilt by association" by graphically portraying in its pages a series of chain links labelled "Campbell Institute," "University Christian Church," "Guy Sarvis," "Foreign Society leadership," and finally, anyone who supported Sarvis or the FCMS.[17]

Some of the implications of this were not lost on the missionary society leadership. While the conservatives were suspicious of conspiracy and looking for witches in the closet, the liberals continued to support the missionary programs. The inevitable result was gradual and subtle, but the missionary societies were moving in a liberal direction. The conservatives sensed this, but they were unable to realize they were in fact pushing the societies in that direction. Their only explanation was additional charges of conspiracy. This in turn hastened the shift. In another dozen years, the situation passed the point of no return.

---

[15]Guy Sarvis, "A Perspective of Missions," in Winfred Ernst Garrison (ed.), *Faith of the Free* (Chicago: Willett, Clark & Company, 1940), p. 215.

[16]*Christian Standard*, May 20, 1211, p. 808.

[17]*Ibid.*, February 24, 1912, p. 305.

Organizations in Tension

The increasing conservative distrust was reflected in the controversy that began in the fall of 1911 with regard to the College of the Bible in Lexington, Kentucky. J. W. McGarvey had been one of the original faculty members of this institution which began in 1865. In 1895 McGarvey had become the president. McGarvey was without question the leading conservative biblical scholar among the Disciples. His attacks on higher criticism had become a staple in the diet of the conservative Disciples. His death in October of 1911 created a serious problem for the conservatives as well as for the administration of the College of the Bible. McGarvey was a teaching president, and his death left a vacuum both in the classroom as well as the president's office. The latter was filled when R. H. Crossfield, president of Transylvania University (on whose grounds the College of the Bible was located), was named president.

But that still left McGarvey's classrooms empty. The new administration thought they had that position filled with the announcement in the spring of 1912 that A. W. Fortune would teach New Testament Theology at COB beginning that fall. Fortune, an 1898 graduate of Hiram College, received an M.A. from there in 1901. He began studies at the University of Chicago Divinity School in 1904, receiving his B.D. degree in 1905, and ultimately completing his Ph.D. in 1915.[18] At the time of his appointment to COB, he was minister with the Walnut Hills Christian Church in Cincinnati.

With his background from the University of Chicago, his appointment was guaranteed to antagonize the conservatives, who were convinced he would import Chicago liberalism into the school that had heretofore been a bastion of conservativism. A conservative Kentuckian, John T. Brown, led a determined campaign against his appointment, challenging Fortune's views on immersion, miracles, and the inspiration of the New Testament.[19] Brown identified Fortune with the Campbell Institute and quoted extensively from Willett and the *Scroll* to indicate how unsound the Institute was, thus tarring Fortune with the same stick.[20] Yet when the college's Board of Trustees investigated the charges against Fortune, they discovered them to be grounded in insubstantial and inconclusive "hearsay" evidence and dismissed them.[21]

---

[18]Blakemore, pp. 142-143.
[19]*Christian Standard*, July 17, 1912, p. 1206.
[20]*Ibid.*, August 17, 1912, p. 1326.
[21]*Ibid.*, December 7, 1912, p. 2018.

Fortune himself soon won great popularity with his students, and a year and a half later the editor of the *Christian Standard* could report no irregularity with Fortune's teaching.[22]

At about the same time a new school developed in Canton, Ohio, to train men for ministry, particularly in rural churches, many of which were closing for lack of ministers. P. H. Welshimer was the guiding spirit behind this school, but it was financially supported by the wealthy Disciples layman, T. W. Phillips of nearby Newcastle, Pennsylvania. The school was even named after him, Phillips Bible Institute.

One of the concerns of the school, however, was how to keep "unsound" men such as Fortune off the faculty. There was no problem during the lifetime of the founders, but what about later—such as in the College of the Bible after the death of McGarvey. So the founders of the school wrote out a statement of belief to which all employees must subscribe in writing, a simple five-part statement of faith.[23] When both the *Christian-Evangelist* and the *Christian Century* shouted "Creed!" T. W. Phillips, Jr., replied that the statement was not a test of fellowship, merely a legal contract or a condition of employment.[24] Yet the tradition of the Campbells and Stone was so vehement against creeds that the statement of belief was never implemented.

This had no impact on the future of the Phillips Bible Institute, since that institution died within a few years and they never had to worry about the future employment of a figure such as Fortune. However, when another Disciples ministerial training school opened in Texas, Brite College of the Bible, affiliated with Texas Christian University, it also had a statement of beliefs to which all teachers were to subscribe.[25] This met the same criticism as had the statement of beliefs from Phillips, with the result that it was never implemented. In this case, however, Brite Divinity School survived and went on to become a respectable graduate Disciples seminary, still in connection with TCU. It still exists today and represents a liberal position.

It was in that same year, 1914, that another furor developed over liberalism and missions. The Christian Woman's Board of Missions had been involved in Monterrey, Mexico, since 1895. In 1914, however, a Mexican revolution forced all American missionaries out of the country because conditions were not safe for foreigners. With all missionaries out

---

[22]*Campbell Institute Bulletin*, vol. 9, no. 2 (1912), p. 12; *Christian Standard*, February 28, 1914, p. 347.

[23]*Christian Standard*, April 2, 1914, p. 426.

[24]*Ibid.*, April 25, 1914, p. 724.

[25]*Christian-Evangelist*, September 24, 1914, pp. 1226-1228.

of the country at the same time, several denominations thought it would be a good time to give some overall planning to Protestant mission work there. A conference held in Cincinnati in June brought about a large measure of goodwill between the various denominational mission boards. One of their agreements provided for a division of the country among the various boards, each denomination to receive an allotted part of the country (this is commonly called a "comity agreement"). To fit into the overall plan, the Disciples women relinquished to the Methodists their work around Monterrey in northern Mexico in exchange for a work in the central part of the country.[26]

The *Christian Century* later reported other decisions of the conference—a joint evangelical publishing house to be established in Mexico City; a proposed evangelical seminary, college, and series of high schools; and a uniform designation of all Protestant churches in Mexico as "The Evangelical Church of Mexico."[27] The *Christian Century* rejoiced in this development of interdenominational cooperation and unity, but the *Christian Standard* refused to condone or support it.[28] When the agreement was finally implemented in 1919 (it took five years for the revolution to end), with the CWBM pulling out of Monterrey, the conservatives convinced one of the missionaries, E. T. Westrup, to remain there and supported him directly, bypassing the missionary societies. This was a harbinger of increasingly common activities with regard to conservatives and missionary support.

The root issue involved in this dispute again was central to the basic understanding of the Restoration Movement. The development of the comity agreement in Mexico and the cooperation with other evangelical Protestant missionary societies in the country was an outgrowth of the Restoration Movement's commitment to practicing Christian unity. How better to practice such unity than cooperate in evangelism, form a national "Evangelical Church of Mexico," and swap mission territories in the name of expediency? But for the conservatives it meant abandoning the Restoration Movement's unique teaching on baptism by immersion for the remission of sins, accepting Methodist doctrine and practice, and abandoning local congregational autonomy with its pattern of authority vested in elders and deacons. The ideal of unity was again in conflict with the ideal of biblical authority.

---

[26]*Survey of Service: Organizations Represented in International Convention of Disciples of Christ* (St. Louis: Christian Board of Publication, 1928), pp. 450-451; Harrison, pp. 57-59, 106-107.

[27]*Christian Century*, July 23, 1914, p. 705.

[28]*Christian Standard*, November 7, 1914, p. 179.

Conservatives continued to be concerned about the spread of liberal ideas and practices, but given the principle of local church autonomy, there seemed to be little that other churches could do about a particular church that wanted to adopt liberalism. One response emerged in California, however, in 1914. The Christian Churches of northern California had an annual convention and even had official delegates appointed from the churches. The unusual thing that occurred this year was that the delegates from the church in Berkeley were refused seating, since that church had adopted open membership in 1911. The convention leaders explained that open membership had removed the Berkeley church from the fellowship of sister churches in California.[29]

Reactions to the incident varied. The *Christian Standard* rejoiced at the ouster of the Berkeley church and again remarked that the practice at Berkeley was part of a larger conspiracy supported by the *Christian Century*.[30] At the same time, however, it deplored the fact that the action was done by an unscriptural body called the "Christian Church of California" and represented an unsupportable ecclesiastical power over member churches.[31] The *Christian Standard* was certainly opposed to open membership, but it would not countenance ecclesiastical structures to excise it; the cure would be as bad as the disease.

Interestingly, at the time, the Disciples General Convention in 1914 was organized on a delegate basis. The *Christian Standard* complained that the machinery was available for the general convention to throw out an individual church, although the convention officials denied they had any such intention. The missionary societies, for their own protection, wanted a representative body (delegates from the churches) rather than a mass meeting that might change in flavor from year to year as the convention met in different cities. The *Christian Standard* took their choice for a delegate convention as further evidence of their desire for ecclesiasticism, their control by the Campbell Institute, and their infidelity to the tradition of congregational autonomy.[32]

About this time, another incident occurred in Chicago that further polarized the conservatives and liberals there. For some time the Chicago Christian Missionary Society had come under the increasing influence of the liberals associated with the Disciples Divinity House of the University of Chicago, the Campbell Institute, and the *Christian Century*. The

---

[29]*Christian-Evangelist*, August 12, 1915, p. 1023.

[30]*Christian Standard,* August 1, 1914, p. 1328; August 29, 1914, p. 1499.

[31]*Ibid.*, August 15, 1914, p. 1414; August 29, 1914, p. 1498.

[32]*Ibid.*, September 26, 1914, pp. 1660-1661; January 9, 1915, p. 488; *Christian-Evangelist*, March 11, 1915, pp. 291-92; Garrison and DeGroot, pp. 524-527.

conservatives in the city were becoming increasingly uncomfortable about the drift of things. This came to a crisis in the fall of 1913 over the planting of a new church in Morgan Park, a southern Chicago suburb.

One of the leading Christian Churches in the city was the Englewood church, located on the south side. Its minister, C. G. Kindred, noticed late in 1913 that several members of his church were driving in from Morgan Park, where there was no Disciples church. Taking the members of his own church as a nucleus, Kindred organized a new church in the suburb. The problem came because the Disciples, through their Chicago Christian Missionary Society, were members of an interdenominational group of missionary societies in Chicago, the Cooperative Council of City Missions.[33] To prevent the problem of one region of Chicago or its suburbs being overchurched while other areas were underchurched, the CCCM had set quotas on the number of churches to be allowed in various areas. They had decided on four churches in Morgan Park. The new Disciples church made five.

When the new Disciples church in Morgan Park appeared, the other denominations protested to the CCCM, which in turn asked the Disciples to either pull out or at least allow the CCCM to make a recommendation on the situation.[34] Kindred refused, unless he was given a guarantee in advance that the CCCM would sanction the new Disciples church. When they refused such an advance permission, he refused to consider pulling out. Again, the conflict here represented a clash between the ideal of unity with the ideal of planting churches true to a New Testament pattern. Many individuals thought the idea of asking some ecclesiastical organization for permission to start a new congregation smacked of ecclesiasticism. Word of the local dissatisfaction reached the Cincinnati offices of the American Christian Missionary Society, and its president even mentioned they might have to withdraw their financial support from the CCMS.[35] In the midst of the discussions, J. F. Futcher, minister of Ashland church on the south side of Chicago, made a telling comment.

> It is all summed up in one word, "theology." Not until we get together from a theological point of view, will we become one. These financial and church problems are going to continue to come upon us just as long as we are divided in our theology.[36]

---

[33]CCMS Files, "President's Report for the Year November 1907 to October 31, 1908," p. 7.

[34]CCMS Minutes, February 17, 1914.

[35]CCMS Minutes, March 29, 1915.

[36]*Ibid.*, May 3, 1915.

Futcher could not have put it any more succinctly. The problems in Chicago were rooted in theological disagreements over the tenets of liberalism. That is why in June of 1915 a number of conservative Disciples in Chicago withdrew from the CCMS and formed the Chicago-Calumet Evangelistic Association. In announcing their birth, they called attention to the need to be able "to preach the gospel and establish churches wherever possible . . . with entire freedom and unhampered nor embarrassed by any source." They also called attention to the decline of many Disciples mission churches in Chicago, which they attributed to "the modern, so-called scholasticism."[37] In effect, the churches in Chicago had split.

This development was two decades in coming, but it represented a pattern in Chicago that would be duplicated elsewhere. There were three causes and two results of these developments. First there was liberalism in the schools; in this instance, Disciples Divinity House. Then there was open membership in the churches; in this instance, University Christian Church under E. S. Ames. Finally there were comity agreements with regard to mission work; in this instance, CCMS and Morgan Park. The two results were an open split between the liberals and conservatives and the replacement with conservative institutions of those agencies that had gone liberal; in this instance, the C-CEA replacing the CCMS. Again, the whole dispute concerned where the ideals of Christian unity and biblical authority interacted.

The difficulties in Chicago were to have far-reaching implications. It was the first instance of the division that became more national within the next decade or more. The Chicago churches pretty much split down the middle. About the same number of churches were on either side, with a few churches straddling the fence for a while. The CCMS still exists today as the Chicago Disciples Union. The C-CEA still exists as the Chicago District Evangelistic Association (CDEA). Thus the events of 1915 are still the best tool for understanding the division of the Christian Churches in the Chicago area down to the present.

In 1916 the University Christian Church committed twenty-five dollars per month to be given through the CCMS to help the struggling Monroe Street Christian Church on the west side of town.[38] This church

---

[37]*Christian Standard*, July 17, 1915, pp. 1367-1368. A year later, J. H. O. Smith complained that the CCMS had become an employment agency for the Disciples Divinity House students at the University; they were more interested in their studies than in evangelism, so the mission churches where they preached died. *Christian Standard*, September 9, 1916, p. 1684.

[38]CCMS Minutes, March 14, 1916.

was practicing open membership. Knowing that open membership was involved, the CCMS approved the arrangement, as did the ACMS. In fact the twenty-five dollars per month was given by the University Church to the ACMS, which would send the money directly to the Monroe Street Christian Church.[39] Here was open evidence that both societies approved of open membership.

In 1916, the annual Disciples Congress met in Chicago. One of the papers was by Charles M. Sharpe, instructor at the Disciples Divinity House who had received his Ph.D. from Chicago in 1912. His paper, "Shall We Re-Construct Our Plea," contended that the goal of Disciples thought was the conversion of the world to Christianity; therefore, if another method could achieve that end better than the restoration of primitive Christianity, then the Disciples plea should be changed accordingly.[40] F. D. Kershner reviewed Sharpe's paper and simply stated that there was either a norm to Christianity or there was not. If there was not, then every man is his own god; if there is a norm, it can only be found in primitive Christianity, which becomes the authoritative standard.[41] Again, the liberals' passion for unity was undercutting any concern for biblical authority. (Frankly, they did not believe the Bible was authoritative.)

Then in 1917 came the most serious imbroglio to date, concerning the College of the Bible in Lexington, Kentucky.[42] We have already mentioned the replacement of McGarvey in the classroom with A. W. Fortune. Within the next few years, all the faculty at the school were replaced with younger men, all of whom reflected the new liberalism. E. E. Snoddy and G. W. Henry had both attended the University of Chicago Divinity School and Disciples Divinity House, while W. C. Bower graduated from Butler University where he was influenced by W. E. Garrison and E. S. Ames, both of whom were Chicago products. Thus, of the four new faculty at COB, all had contact with the Chicago liberalism. All of them had been added while R. H. Crossfield was president, and he himself later said that he had looked for "men of modern scholarship" to fill the positions needed at the school.[43]

In March of 1917, a student, Ben Battenfield, sent a letter to COB trustees and three hundred supporting churches, claiming that liberalism

[39]*Ibid.*, May 8, 1916.
[40]*Christian-Evangelist*, May 25, 1916, pp. 647-649, 660.
[41]*Ibid.*, June 1, 1916, pp. 679-681.
[42]Some irreverent wits later referred to it as "The Battle of Lexington."
[43]George W. Bushnell, "The Development of the College of the Bible Through Controversy" (Unpublished B.D. Thesis at the College of the Bible, Lexington, Kentucky, 1934), p. 47.

was in fact being taught at the school.[44] Soon the academic dean Hall Calhoun seconded the charges, announcing "For more than a year I have been fully convinced that destructive criticism was being taught in the College of the Bible."[45]

The Board of Trustees of the school held an investigation into the charges, but they insisted it was only a hearing, not a heresy trial. However, when the conduct of the board seemed overly sensitive to the faculty and very hostile to the students making the charges, Calhoun resigned from the school and the students refused to participate further.[46] Thus when the Board made its report it could only say that no faculty members were found to be out of harmony with fundamental Disciples convictions.[47] Two weeks after his resignation, Calhoun initiated a four-month series of articles in the *Christian Standard* detailing the charges against the four professors.[48]

Numerous churches in Kentucky even organized a "Christian Bible College League" in an attempt to return the college to conservative teaching, but without success. The school claimed that the administration and its professors were loyal to the traditions of Campbell and Stone and officially denied liberalism was taught there, contending only that the charges were made by uninformed or biased persons.

Yet because of the uncertainty of the charges, the new editor of the *Christian-Evangelist*, B. A. Abbott, came to Lexington in the fall of 1917 to carry on his own investigation. His conclusion was that the accused professors "were liberal, accepting the results of modern science and the methods and results of modern biblical scholarship, but thoroughly loyal, constructive, and dedicated."[49] The *Christian Standard* could have accepted the first conclusion, but not the second. From its perspective, to be liberal meant the men were disloyal to the Movement, for this meant rejecting the authority of the Scriptures as a standard. Most students at the College of the Bible accepted the "loyalty" of the professors; according to the liberal *Christian Century*, only seventeen students contributed to Calhoun's attacks while eighty-seven percent of

---

[44]Stevenson, Lexington Theological Seminary, has a whole chapter on the controversy, pp. 165-207.

[45]*Christian Standard*, March 31, 1917, pp. 764-765, 769.

[46]William Clayton Bower, *Through the Years: Personal Memoirs* (Lexington, Kentucky: Transylvania College Press, 1957), pp. 39-42; *Christian Standard*, May 19, 1917, pp. 968-969.

[47]*Christian-Evangelist*, May 24, 1917, p. 614.

[48]See *Christian Standard*, May 12, 1917, p. 948 and succeeding issues.

[49]Bower, pp. 43-44.

the student body of three hundred fifty backed the professors.[50] Most Disciples also accepted the loyalty of the professors, in spite of their higher criticism. Modern Disciples historians openly admit the liberalism involved,[51] but for the school to have done so in 1917 would have meant a loss of financial support among the churches. Thus the administration hid the liberalism behind such words as "loyal," "dedicated," "faithful," and "scholarship."

Focus on the Conventions

One result of the battles between liberals and conservatives over the past several decades was that now both groups felt the need to try to control the national convention. The issues up to this time had been fairly piecemeal; now the battleground became the national convention itself. At issue in the whole process was a crisis of confidence building within the Brotherhood. More and more conservatives felt they could no longer trust the leadership of many of the institutions: the schools, the missionary societies, and ultimately, the convention itself.

Early in 1918 the *Christian Century* urged "More Aggressive Progress," stopping the quarter century in which the Disciples national organizations had been forced to curry the favor of "the reactionary forces" in the Brotherhood. The *Century* went on to characterize this "progressive movement" within the Disciples as being sympathetic with modern scholarship, honoring the social service aspect of religion, and adopting an attitude toward other Christians more consistent with the ideal of Christian unity. Of the more than one million Disciples in the country, the *Century* supposed that ten percent were progressive, ten percent were "reactionary," while eighty percent were ignorant of the issues. Of the six thousand ministers, the *Century* considered 1,500 progressive, 1,500 "middle-of-the-road," while 3,000 belonged to the reaction.[52] The *Christian Standard* claimed that this editorial proved that there was a conspiracy on the part of those who wanted to control the organizational machinery of the Disciples, and that the center of this trickery was the Campbell Institute.[53] Meanwhile the *Christian Century* itself was undergoing some transition. For a long time the paper labelled itself as

---

[50]*Christian Century*, March 28, 1918, p. 16.

[51]Garrison and DeGroot refer to "the liberals" on the faculty in 1917 (p. 420), while McAllister and Tucker openly state, "All four of the new professors were theological liberals" (p. 369).

[52]*Christian Century*, February 21, 1918, pp. 1-6.

[53]*Christian Standard*, March 30, 1918, p. 828.

"published by the Disciples of Christ."[54] In 1917, the masthead claimed that the paper was "a free interpreter of the essential ideals of Christianity as held historically by the Disciples of Christ. Committed to Christian unity, published *by* Disciples, The Christian Century is not published *for* Disciples alone, but for the Christian world."[55] Read by more and more people outside the Disciples, in 1919 the paper launched an advertising campaign throughout the denominational press. By 1920, the masthead simply stated:

> The Christian Century is a free interpreter of essential Christianity. It is published not for any single denomination alone, but for the Christian world. It strives definitely to occupy a catholic point of view and its readers are in all communions.[56]

Six weeks later, the paper carried its last column of "News of the Disciples."[57] Although most of its editorial staff were still Disciples (and also members of the Campbell Institute), the *Christian Century* was now only marginally a Disciples paper. Its quest for unity had virtually taken it outside the Disciples.

If the liberals were calling in 1918 for a more aggressive progressivism, the other side was calling for a more aggressive conservatism. Part of their strategy was to call a Restoration Congress prior to the 1918 convention to inform the uninformed and marshall strength against the liberals. The *Christian Standard* claimed there was an open propaganda campaign to encourage unsound teaching in the colleges and influence the congregations toward open membership. It also charged that the International Convention itself was "in the hands of Campbell Institute men."[58] Both the president and the secretary of the 1918 convention were members of the Campbell Institute.[59]

The popular minister of First Christian Church in Canton, Ohio, P. H. Welshimer (1873-1957), was a leading figure among the conservatives. In underlining the urgency of the situation he announced that seven presidents and seven deans of Disciples college were members of the Campbell Institute, as were a majority of the executive committee of the Board of Education, and various trustees of the ACMS, the Foreign Christian

---

[54]*Christian Century*, October 2, 1913, p. 643.
[55]*Ibid.*, December 6, 1917, p. 5.
[56]*Ibid.*, March 4, 1920, p. 3.
[57]*Ibid.*, April 15, 1920, p. 20.
[58]*Christian Standard*, September 21, 1918, pp. 1523-1524.
[59]*Ibid.*, April 20, 1918, p. 925.

Missionary Society, the Boards of Church Extensions, Ministerial Relief, and American Temperance. Quoting the apostle Paul, who said to withdraw from those who pervert the gospel, Welshimer warned that the conservatives would withdraw from the organized work of the Disciples if the "rationalists" and open membership men continued to dominate it.[60]

As it turned out, however, there was no convention in 1918. Spanish influenza was sweeping the country in 1917-1918, and it hit St. Louis the week before the convention was to assemble there. By order of the health authorities, the convention was cancelled.

Since 1917, the annual Disciples convention was called the International Convention.[61] In 1919 it met in Cincinnati for a crucial consideration of whether to combine the various national agencies (missionary societies as well as other boards) into a United Christian Missionary Society for both financial as well as organizational efficiency. The conservatives feared such a consolidation because it represented to them a strong agency that could resemble denominational authority. Furthermore, such a united agency could easily be the target of a liberal takeover, and in one fell swoop the liberals would gain control over Disciple agencies. Conservative attempts to stop such a consolidation, however, were unsuccessful, and by 1920 the legal steps had been taken to combine many of the national Disciples agencies into the new UCMS.

Then the issues of the 1920 convention increased the tension and suspicion. In August R. E. Elmore, a former member of the Executive Committee of the Foreign Christian Missionary Society, released to the *Christian Standard* a number of letters from Frank Garrett, a Disciples missionary in China, suggesting that several of the China missionaries were sympathetic to open membership.[62] C. C. Morrison, editor of the *Christian Century*, confirmed that indeed open membership was being practiced in China, and he lauded the missionaries for their bold willingness to adapt to the modern needs of the mission field.[63] The Executive Committee of the Foreign Christian Missionary Society, however, stated flatly, "The China Mission is not practicing or advocating open membership and never has done so."[64]

The various papers presented an interesting picture that fall. The

---

[60]*Ibid.*, October 26, 1918, p. 76.

[61]For a discussion of this development, its reasons and results, see Garrison and DeGroot, pp. 526-527.

[62]*Christian Standard*, August 7, 1920, pp. 6-7.

[63]*Christian Century*, August 26, 1920, pp. 6-7.

[64]*Christian-Evangelist*, September 16, 1920, p. 929.

Christian Century said there was open membership in China, and it was a good thing. The *Christian Standard* said there was open membership in China, and it was a bad thing. The *Christian-Evangelist*, reflecting its status as the "official paper," said there was no open membership in China, and everyone ought to keep those dimes and dollars coming and loyally support the missionary societies. Because of the confusion over the apparently simple question of whether there was or was not open membership in China, many Disciples were losing confidence in the credibility of the leadership of their national societies.

The *Scroll* of the Campbell Institute called upon the liberals to organize themselves to present a united front at the St. Louis convention in October.[65] On the eve of the convention the *Christian Century* argued that the Disciples must choose between their two stools of unity and restoration, calling for an abandonment of the temporizing policy of the previous twenty years.[66]

Once the convention began, there was fervent debate over the China situation. Out of it emerged a resolution submitted by Charles S. Medbury, minister of Central Christian Church in Des Moines, which stated plainly that the Executive Committee of the Foreign Christian Missionary Society expected missionaries to act in consonance with usual Disciples practice in the United States. The resolution also specifically denied approval of open membership and called for missionaries to support this stand against open membership or else resign.[67]

During the debate on the Medbury Resolution, Morrison substantiated his charges of open membership in China by quoting from letters he had received from a Disciples missionary there, George B. Baird. One missionary society official, Abram Corey, claimed that Baird did not adequately represent the situation in China, but the effect of Morrison's disclosures was still overwhelming.[68] Official protestations that there had never been any open membership in China now appeared empty and deceitful. The convention could now easily believe that either the missionary societies were in a conspiracy to spread open membership or were so ignorant of the true situation on the mission field as to be incapable of their position of trust. Either way, the convention was eager to stamp out the detested practice; the Medbury Resolution passed easily.

---

[65]*Scroll*, vol. 17, no. 1 (1920), pp. 5-7.
[66]*Christian Century*, October 14, 1920, pp. 6-7.
[67]*Christian Standard*, October 30, 1920, p. 1433.
[68]*Ibid.*, November 6, 1920, pp. 1470-1473.

Conservatives had feared the merger of the various Disciples agencies into the United Christian Missionary Society because it might create an "ecclesiasticism"—a power-mad tyranny that would result in the loss of freedom and liberty enjoyed by autonomous churches and agencies. Substance for this fear appeared in two incidents, one an ouster of some independent agencies from the convention headquarters in 1920,[69] another in the spring of 1921 when the state secretary of the Ohio Disciples tried to expel a Toledo minister against the wishes of his congregation.[70] Those who remembered the history of Thomas Campbell and Barton W. Stone and their respective Presbyterian synods were not encouraged.

In the summer of 1921, the Disciples met for their annual convention on the shores of Winona Lake, Indiana. The most important question that hung in the air was how the Medbury Resolution had been applied. In its report, the Executive Committee of the UCMS reported that the China missionaries denied any practice of open membership; they could not accept the Medbury Resolution as binding them to *American* practices (it had demanded they act "in consonance" with usual American practices)—they must be free to find their authority in the Word of God. Frank Garrett was present at the convention and explained the position of the China Mission. He also stated that the China Mission would not practice open membership as long as the American Disciples did not want them to. One man in the audience then pointed out the inconsistency of refusing the Medbury Resolution because it bound them to American practices, while being willing to practice open membership if the American Disciples agreed.[71]

The end result was that the convention adopted by an overwhelming vote the report of the committee—a report that accepted the refusal of the China Mission to sign the Medbury Resolution. Conservatives were, of course, greatly displeased. R. E. Elmore found evidence to suggest that the Executive Committee had encouraged the reluctance of the China Mission by adopting phraseology borrowed from *Christian Century* editorials. This looked too much like collusion between Chicago heresy and United Christian Missionary Society procedures.[72] In response to the whole situation, a number of churches began to close their purses to the UCMS—exactly what Welshimer had warned three years previously.[73]

---

[69]*Christian Standard*, November 13, 1920, pp. 1496, 1499; December 11, 1920, p. 1605.

[70]*Ibid.*, May 21, 1921, p. 2263; June 4, 1921, p. 2311.

[71]*Ibid.*, September 17, 1921, pp. 2667-2670; September 24, 1921, p. 2695.

[72]*Ibid.*, October 1, 1921, p. 2721.

[73]Supra, pp. 303-304 of this chapter.

There is an interesting pattern that begins to emerge after this 1921 convention. Whenever the situation was simply open membership, the overwhelming majority of the Disciples voted strongly against it. The conservatives were able to make the argument convincing that an abandonment of immersion was an abandonment of New Testament teaching. Most Disciples would respond to a call to the ideal of biblical authority. Open membership as such was always voted down in these years. But when the convention or missionary society leadership reinterpreted the issue into terms of freedom or liberty, the middle of the road moderates and the uninformed followed this line of interpretation. Therefore, when the China missionaries were able to argue that the Medbury Resolution tied them to American practices rather than the New Testament, the overwhelming majority of those who attended Winona Lake in 1921 voted with the missionaries against the Medbury Resolution, which they had voted in overwhelmingly the previous year.

Conservatives held a meeting in Louisville in December to discuss means to combat "the inroads of open membership and destructive teaching." Both Frank Garrett and F. W. Burnham, president of the United Christian Missionary Society, were in attendance. In the process of the discussion, Burnham denied any open membership in China, saying Baird was using the phrase with a different meaning.[74]

The result of the questioning and testimony was to leave the conservatives no more satisfied than they had been at Winona Lake three months earlier.[75] The conservatives did not know what to believe about the China situation. The testimony was too conflicting. C. C. Morrison said there was open membership in China; the president of the UCMS denied it. Baird said open membership was rampant in China, but Garrett said Baird did not mean what that would mean in America. Burnham said that Baird did not need to be recalled because he was misunderstood; but Garrett said that Baird misrepresented the China situation. It was all somewhat confusing. But the conservatives could not shake the feeling that something fishy was going on in China and that the missionary officials were not being honest or candid about it. Until the conservatives got the answers they wanted, they would not condone the existing situation.[76] They passed a resolution suggesting that

---

[74]*Ibid.*, December 31, 1921, p. 3058.

[75]An interesting presentation of this issue is in Mark G. Toulouse, "Practical Concern and Theological Neglect: The UCMS and the Open Membership Controversy," in *A Case Study*, edited by Williams, pp. 194-235.

[76]Incidentally, the struggles recorded here were not unique to the Restoration Movement, nor do they indicate a basic flaw in their position. Virtually every

Disciples cut off funds to both the UCMS and the International Convention and that no missionary be sent out who was not in harmony with the historic position of the Disciples.[77]

In spite of all the attention that immersion was receiving, however, many conservatives realized that it was not the prime issue. L. A. Chapman of Johnstown, Pennsylvania, said that the difficulties among the Disciples were more deeply rooted than open membership or the truth of the China Mission situation; the real difficulty lay in a different understanding of the basics of New Testament teaching.[78] Though the conservative leaders knew this, they also knew the battle plan could not be switched. To make up a list of "basic New Testament teachings" would mean to construct a creed, which was anathema in Disciples circles. One "basic" about which they felt sure, however, was immersion—and so the battle was fought there. Nevertheless, the conservatives were forced to fight over the *symptom* of the underlying difficulty, rather than the *cause* itself.

In a statement from a few years later, P. H. Welshimer put the issue rather plainly.

> If you remove the authority of Jesus, you destroy the meaning of baptism. If you eliminate the inspiration and the all-sufficiency of the Scriptures, you take away the meaning and sacredness of baptism, and hence it would be of no importance to practice anything and call it baptism.

---

significant denomination in America was going through similar struggles during these decades. As mentioned earlier (supra, pp. 257-258 of Chapter Ten), the Methodists, Baptists, and Presbyterians had their heresy trials in the previous century. But the Northern Baptists were not through with them. In his book *A History of Conservative Baptists* (Wheaton, Illinois: Conservative Baptist Press, 1971), Bruce L. Shelley records the struggles the conservatives among the Northern Baptists experienced in the period 1900-1930. He details the same issues as the Disciples experienced (higher criticism, open membership, comity agreements, trustworthiness of missionary work) and the same results (a division, with the conservatives erecting new agencies to take the place of those gone liberal) in the very same time period as the Disciples were experiencing.

In a correlative work, Chester E. Tulga in *The Foreign Missions Controversy in the Northern Baptist Convention* (Chicago: Conservative Baptist Fellowship, 1950) details the missions situation. One statement in particular highlights what the Disciples were going through in the early 1920s as Tulga states, "an uninformed, deceived fundamentalist, will vote with the Convention leadership" (p. 105). This is exactly where the majority of Disciples were with regard to the College of the Bible controversy as well as the 1921 convention in Winona Lake. Other examples will continue the pattern. The uninformed, deceived conservatives tend to follow their convention leadership.

[77]*Ibid.*, December 17, 1921, p. 2997; *Christian-Evangelist*, January 26, 1922, p. 113.

[78]*Christian-Evangelist*, November 2, 1922, pp. 1396-97.

This is a fight for more than an ordinance. It is a fight for loyalty to Jesus Christ and for an appreciation of His authority, the inspiration of His word, and the compliance with stipulated conditions that remission of sins may be granted.[79]

Those churches and individuals cutting funds off from the United Christian Missionary Society found an outlet for them in the Clarke Fund. This fund originated in 1871 when Sidney S. Clarke of Cincinnati died and left $50,000 to the Richmond Street Church of Christ in Cincinnati. Terms of the fund stipulated that the principal could never be spent; only the interest could be allocated for missions. The elders of the Richmond Street church had been disbursing the fund since 1871, but in mid-1921 the *Christian Standard* (their offices were located only a couple of blocks from the Richmond Street church) called attention to this fund and suggested it would be a worthy recipient of missionary offerings.[80] The Clarke Fund quickly became the recipient of thousands of dollars in conservative missionary offerings, and the *Standard* gleefully pointed out that none of the money paid presidents, secretaries, or other usual "overhead" expenses of the UCMS. All the money generated went directly to missions.[81]

The disenchantment of the conservatives with the UCMS and the success of the Clarke Fund were so significant that within a few months, the financial stability of the UCMS was greatly shaken. The board of managers of the UCMS met in a special session in St. Louis in January, 1922, to discuss the emergency situation. The conservative members of the board pointed out that too many churches simply no longer trusted the Society with regard to open membership. As a result, Z. T. Sweeney of Columbus, Indiana, presented a resolution that was adopted by a 48-2 vote. Significantly, the two dissenters were full-time missionary executives. The Sweeney Resolution was straightforward.

In harmony with the teaching of the New Testament as understood by this board of managers, the United Christian Missionary Society is conducting its work everywhere on the principle of receiving into membership of the churches at home or abroad, by any of its missionaries, only those who are immersed, penitent believers in Christ.

Furthermore, it is believed by the board of managers that all of the missionaries and ministers appointed and supported by this board are in sincere accord with this policy, and certainly it will not appoint, and indeed it will

[79]*Christian Standard*, December 4, 1926, p. 655.
[80]*Christian Standard*, May 14, 1921, p. 239; Shaw, *Buckeye Disciples*, p. 378.
[81]*Christian Standard*, December 17, 1921, p. 3006.

not continue in its service, any one known by it to be not in such accord. It disclaims any right and disowns any desire to do otherwise.[82]

Immediately upon the release of the Sweeney Resolution, the *Christian Century* shouted, "Creed!" claiming that the resolution left no room for missionaries to hold a private contrary opinion since they were to accept the teaching of the New Testament "as understood by the board of managers." In spite of all official protestations to the contrary, and the various interpretations put upon Baird's statements, Morrison contended that open membership *was* being practiced in China, and that the Sweeney Resolution hampered efforts in China to practice Christian unity.[83] The *Christian-Evangelist*, however, joined the *Christian Standard* in insisting that the Sweeney Resolution was not a creed, but merely a statement of procedural principles the UCMS used in discharging its trust of missions.[84]

As the summer of 1922 rolled around, the big question was how the executive committee would interpret and apply the Sweeney Resolution. The convention met again in Winona Lake and was very interested in the report of John T. Brown, a Louisville minister who had just returned from a tour of mission stations in the Far East. He reported that open membership was being practiced not only in China, but also in the Philippines under E. K. Higdon, a missionary working under the UCMS in Manila.

Since open membership was in direct violation of the Sweeney Resolution, the United Christian Missionary Society's board of managers had to decide how to proceed. With regard to the China situation, several of the China missionaries were present and were able to help out. They explained that the Chinese were very hospitable people, and when they discovered that Brown had come to China expecting to find open membership, they gave him all the information he needed to support his preconceived belief. But, explained the missionaries, this simply reflected the Oriental philosophy of being kind to a guest in their country. The missionaries denied there was any open membership in the country, Brown's report notwithstanding.

With regard to the Philippine situation, the board of managers determined that the Sweeney Resolution phrase "in sincere accord" meant

---

[82]*Christian Century*, February 23, 1922, p. 243.

[83]*Christian Century*, February 9, 1922, pp. 166-168; February 23, 1922, pp. 243-244.

[84]*Christian-Evangelist*, March 2, 1922, p. 260; *Christian Standard*, February 18, 1922, pp. 3228-3229.

that a missionary should be willing to work in accord with UCMS procedures, though he need not sacrifice his personal opinion that open membership was a good thing. The board had no objection to missionaries'
believing in open membership just as long as they did not *practice* it. They
also explained that indeed there had been open membership in Manila
when Brown visited there in the spring, but there was none now, and
therefore Higdon was within the guidelines of the Sweeney Resolution.
This became known as the Higdon Interpretation of the Sweeney
Resolution. The conservatives felt the Higdon Interpretation weakened
considerably the force of the Sweeney Resolution, but the entire package
was presented to the convention as a single entity. There was no way to
vote for the Resolution without also voting for the Interpretation, or
rejecting the latter without also rejecting the former. Thus the convention overwhelmingly adopted the package, which included the Sweeney
Resolution against open membership and the Higdon Interpretation,
which effectively made it meaningless.[85] This was another cycle in the
pattern of adopting a resolution to control open membership, and then
adopting the official explanation that voided the resolution. As Tulga
said,[86] the deceived, uninformed conservatives normally followed the
convention leadership.

If the year 1922 was a stormy one for the Disciples (Sweeney
Resolution, Brown Report, official denials, Higdon Interpretation), the
year 1923 was a placid one. It seemed that the UCMS and convention
leadership tried hard to avoid all controversy. The *Christian Century*, however, two weeks prior to the convention called for a decision: would the
Disciples plead for the unity of the church, or would they attempt to
restore the church according to an apostolic mode? Until the question
was answered, continued the *Century*, there would never be agreement
about foreign missions policies.[87]

The convention did not mention the China situation, so it was a
peaceful gathering. As redoubtable a fighter as J. B. Briney published "A
Pre-Convention Address to the Brotherhood" in which he tearfully
pleaded for the end of strife. A staunch conservative himself, his remarks
against troublemakers could apply equally well to both conservatives and
liberals.[88] A month before the convention, the *Christian Century* printed
an article by George Lawrence Parker on "Liberal and Conservative,"

---

[85]*Christian Standard*, September 9, 1922, pp. 3946-3951; *Christian Century*,
September 14, 1922, pp. 1139-1140.

[86]Tulga, p. 33.

[87]*Christian Century*, August 23, 1923, p. 1063.

[88]*Christian-Evangelist*, August 16, 1923, p. 1033.

which argued that both liberal and conservative were needed.[89] A few months after the convention, the liberal Kansas City minister Burris A. Jenkins published "The Conservative and the Liberal Should Work and Pull Together."[90]

Yet the issues of 1922 had not been forgotten and could not long remain hidden. The first issue of the *Christian Century* for 1924 carried an editorial, "Fundamentalism and Modernism: Two Religions," which asserted that the issues involved were grave ones, not merely superficial ones as most liberals contended. At issue was the entire concept of religion. Fundamentalist and modernist definitions of Christianity were mutually exclusive, and the stage of mutual tolerance was fast passing.[91]

Indeed the conservatives had not been lulled into inaction by the apparent calm of 1923. That fall they launched two new schools, McGarvey Bible College in Louisville, and Cincinnati Bible Institute in Cincinnati, located only a block and a half from the Standard Publishing Company. Both schools were replacements for the College of the Bible, now considered lost to the liberals. The next year the two schools, backed by the Clarke Fund, merged to become The Cincinnati Bible Seminary.

One instance of the continued tensions had to do with Peter Ainslie. Ainslie was the minister of the Christian Temple in Baltimore, a second-generation Disciples minister. In 1910, when he was the president of the General Convention, he called upon the Disciples to return to their original commitment to Christian unity. He was a zealous proponent of the ecumenical movement, and he sought to present the Disciples' ideals of Christian union to other religious bodies.

To help in this line, he proposed the formation of an agency within the Disciples to lead in this endeavor. Approval was given, and the Council on Christian Union was formed, with Ainslie as its president. The name was changed to the Association for the Promotion of Christian Unity in 1913, and Ainslie remained its directing light until his death in 1934.[92] The Association met with the similar commissions of the Episcopalians, Congregationalists, and Presbyterians in 1911, and that same summer began a magazine, *Christian Union Quarterly*.

But it was in the year 1923 that Ainslie made an interesting statement about the rationale of open membership. The Christian Temple, where

---

[89]*Christian Century*, August 9, 1923, p. 1006.

[90]*Christian-Evangelist*, January 3, 1924, p. 10.

[91]*Christian Century*, January 3, 1924, pp. 5-6.

[92]Surveys of the work of the Association can be found in McAllister and Tucker, pp. 282-283; Garrison and DeGroot, pp. 566-567; Webb, p. 266; Murch, pp. 345-347.

he preached, was not only large and successful, but it also had ten branch churches. Two or three of these branches were "community churches" since they were located in areas where there was no other Protestant church; these churches practiced open membership. The other branches, and the Christian Temple itself, were located in areas among other Protestant churches, and for them open membership was thus unnecessary. Ainslie's position seemed to be that if unimmersed Christians had churches of their own handy, they should attend there; if not, a Disciples church should accept them in lieu of additional churches being established in the area.[93]

This perspective changed the next year, however, when the Christian Temple itself adopted open membership.[94] Since he was the president of the Association for the Promotion of Christian Unity and therefore answerable to the convention, he came in for censure at the 1924 convention, which met in Cleveland. Nothing was resolved here, but it is a measure of the growing frustration of the conservatives that they took this occasion to strike at Ainslie and the growing practice of open membership. In 1925, the *Christian-Evangelist* commented that Ainslie and his Association had become divisive elements in the Disciples—ironic for an agency designed to promote Christian unity.[95] Such ironies continued as some Disciples pushed the traditional ideal of Christian unity in opposition to the Disciples' other traditional ideal of biblical authority and the necessity of maintaining biblical teaching (namely, immersion).

Convention in Crisis

In the fall of 1924, the Disciples met in Cleveland for their annual convention. For perhaps the first time, the convention openly acknowledged the polarization that continued in the Brotherhood. The convention adopted a resolution calling attention to the serious misunderstandings that existed between the "organized agencies" and other brethren and churches that opposed these agencies. The resolution also formally called for a committee to completely review the disagreements and formulate constructive recommendations to remedy the situation by the next convention. This committee was duly appointed and soon became known as the Peace Committee.[96]

---

[93]*Christian Standard*, September 1, 1923, p. 1377.
[94]*Christian Century*, July 1, 1924, p. 895.
[95]*Christian-Evangelist*, February 26, 1925, p. 262.
[96]*Christian Standard*, November 1, 1924, p. 111.

Here finally was a healthy acknowledgment that there was a serious problem. Never previously had the convention admitted the growing polarization and the seriousness of the looming division. Now the convention not only admitted the issue, but appointed a committee to make realistic proposals to resolve the problem. An article in the *Christian-Evangelist*, the officially owned paper of the convention and the closest thing to a voice for the Brotherhood, openly stated that those practicing open membership and denying biblical miracles should not even be counted among the Disciples. If such were done, the apparent rift could be healed easily.[97] This is a surprising admission for the *Christian-Evangelist* to make, and indeed if such persons had been removed from the Disciples fellowship—particularly leadership of the agencies—the rift could have been healed. But such was not to be.

The conservatives had heard nice promises before, but they were not lulled into inaction by this one. Instead, they geared up for further activity. The Clarke Fund reorganized itself into a clearinghouse for independent missions (missionary, benevolent, and educational), under the name Christian Restoration Association. The new agency became a rival to the UCMS, but without the "ecclesiasticism" that the conservatives feared. Its obvious intent, however, was to supplant the UCMS as the missionary arm of the conservatives.[98] When the reorganization became official in July of 1925, sixteen independent agencies were already identified with the Christian Restoration Association, and a new periodical became its voice: the *Restoration Herald*.[99]

When the convention met in Oklahoma City in the fall of 1925, the most important item was the report of the Peace Committee. The heart of it became known as the Peace Resolution.

> It has become apparent to the Committee that, in a very large measure, the peace of our people is disturbed and the unity of effort by our forces broken by the conviction held by a considerable number of our brethren that the United Christian Missionary Society retains in its employment, as missionaries, brethren who are committed to the belief that it is proper and right to receive unimmersed persons into the membership of Churches of Christ. . . . We submit the following recommendations.
>
> 1. That no person be employed by the United Christian Missionary Society as its representative who has committed himself or herself to belief in, or

---

[97]*Christian-Evangelist*, November 13, 1924, p. 1465.

[98]*Christian Standard*, December 20, 1924, pp. 286-287; *Christian Century*, February 5, 1925, pp. 182-183.

[99]*Christian Standard*, July 18, 1925, p. 1001.

practice of, the reception of unimmersed persons into the membership of churches of Christ.

2. That if any person is now in the employment of the United Christian Missionary Society as representative who has committed himself or herself to belief in or practice of, the reception of unimmersed persons into the membership of churches of Christ, the relationship of that to the United Missionary Society be severed as employee.[100]

The Peace Resolution is honest in pointing to the fact that many people *believed* that the UCMS was involved in open membership. Yet it does not admit that the UCMS was in fact doing that; that would have brought an argument and an official denial. But no one could deny that people were convinced the UCMS was, so the Peace Resolution was designed to state policy, not to argue facts.

In the floor discussions of the proposal, most of the attention turned on whether the resolution was a creed. Claude Hill, the chairman of the Peace Committee, denied it set forth any creed, but several United Christian Missionary Society officials contended it did. C. H. Chilton, who had resigned from the board of managers because of the Sweeney Resolution, said that the recommendations, like the Medbury and Sweeney Resolutions, would rectify nothing; P. H. Welshimer replied that if the Medbury and Sweeney Resolutions had been enforced as originally intended, there would be no need for the recommendations then under discussion. Finally the issue came to a vote, and the convention approved the Peace Resolution by a wide margin.[101] Even the *Christian Century* said the vote was at least four to one, if not ten to one.[102]

The next question was how the resolution would be interpreted. The *Christian-Evangelist* called for the resolution to be interpreted in all fairness, without high pressure or abstruse logic.[103] The *Christian Standard* called the vote a victory for the conservatives and insisted that the resolution be enforced—not like the Medbury and Sweeney Resolutions.[104] The *Christian Century*, however, suggested that there was doubt as to what was meant by the phrase "committed to belief in."[105]

The board of managers of the UCMS met in December. After discussion, they released this announcement: "The Board of Managers interprets the expression 'committed to belief in' as not intended to invade

---

[100]*Christian-Evangelist*, October 15, 1925, p. 1336.
[101]*Ibid.*, pp. 1337-1338.
[102]*Christian Century*, October 22, 1925, p. 1315.
[103]*Christian-Evangelist*, October 15, 1925, p. 1318.
[104]*Christian Standard*, October 24, 1925, p. 239.
[105]*Christian Century*, October 22, 1925, p. 1322.

the right of private judgment, but only to apply to such an open agitation as would prove divisive."[106] The *Christian Century* admitted that the Peace Resolution "plainly calls for no less than" an "inquisition into the private beliefs of missionaries on the question of open membership," though the board now took that to mean a discharge of only those missionaries who believed in open membership so strongly that they insisted on its implementation, thus causing trouble in the field.[107] The *Christian-Evangelist* asked that the Resolution be "faithfully observed," though it accepted the board's interpretation.[108] The *Christian Standard* said that the decision not only destroyed the force of the Peace Resolution, but "insolently" reenacted the Higdon Interpretation.[109] Toulouse admits that "the interpretation obviously broke faith with the intent of the resolution."[110] The conservatives again felt betrayed.

An additional shock came the following summer. An official investigating commission to visit and report on missions in the Far East had been talked about ever since John T. Brown had made his revelations in 1922. That commission was now sent out in early 1926; it returned and released its report in late June. In sum it concluded that there was *no open membership* being practiced in the Orient. There had been some in Manila, but that situation had been corrected. Nor was there any in China—which Brown would have known if he had used a reliable and knowledgeable interpreter. Baird *had* practiced open membership, but he was no longer on the field, and he had miscalculated the sentiments of the other China missionaries when he said they supported the practice.[111]

Another complication involved Leslie Wolfe, a missionary in the Philippines. Just as the sending of Guy Sarvis to China was clouded by the recall of C. B. Titus, so now the report of the Orient Commission was clouded by the recall of Wolfe. The Orient Commission concurred in the recall of Wolfe, asserting that his manner alienated native workers, he was inefficient in evangelism, and he was completely unable to get along with other Disciples missionaries in the Philippines.[112] The UCMS insisted that there were no doctrinal issues involved.[113]

---

[106]*Christian-Evangelist*, December 10, 1925, p. 1599; *Christian Century*, December 17, 1925, p. 1582.

[107]*Christian Century*, December 17, 1925, pp. 1565-1566.

[108]*Christian-Evangelist*, December 10, 1925, p. 1582.

[109]*Christian Standard*, February 6, 1926, p. 129.

[110]Toulouse, in Williams, *A Case Study*, p. 218.

[111]*Christian-Evangelist*, July 22, 1926, pp. 905-912.

[112]*Christian-Evangelist*, July 22, 1926, p. 905.

[113]*Ibid.*, April 1, 1926, p. 408.

Wolfe's supporters, on the other hand, insisted that doctrinal difficulties underlay the entire situation—Wolfe had been fighting open membership in the Philippines since 1922. Wolfe charged that his "inability to get along" with other Disciples missionaries was because they were trying various forms of open membership in Manila.[114]

As the Disciples got ready for their 1926 convention in Memphis, things seemed to be heading for a breaking point. Conservatives were convinced there was a mounting array of evidence that indicated that the United Christian Missionary Society was determined to support open membership, at home and abroad, and was acting in utter defiance of clear resolutions that had been adopted to stop the practice. The credibility gap between the conservatives and the society leadership was now too great. The conservatives went to Memphis in 1926 determined to break the back of the UCMS, even dissolve it back into its various original societies.

The convention, however, decisively overruled them. The report from the Orient Commission was approved by an overwhelming majority.[115] Two days later, R. E. Elmore's resolution for the dissolution of the UCMS into its five constituent societies (home, foreign, woman's, benevolence, and church extension) failed by a large majority. The same session accepted the board of manager's interpretation of the Peace Resolution with a scarcely audible negative vote. The *Christian Century* explained that the vote in support of the board's interpretation was not a vote for liberal theology, but a vote for liberty of opinion.[116]

Here indeed was one of the dilemmas of understanding the Disciples thinking at the time. Most Disciples were adamantly opposed to open membership, but they were also keenly sensitive to any charge of encroaching on another man's conscience. Even though the Peace Resolution clearly stated that all missionaries who *believed* in open membership should be recalled, when the board of managers interpreted it in phraseology that defended Christian liberty, the convention could do nothing other than accept that interpretation. It was the third cycle of a resolution adopted but removed through interpretation. The people who voted for the Peace Resolution and also voted to accept the Board's interpretation thought they were being consistent both to the Disciple inheritance of claiming biblical authority as well as liberty against creeds.

---

[114]*Christian Standard*, April 3, 1926, pp. 313, 318-319; July 31 1926, p. 731.

[115]*Christian-Evangelist*, November 25, 1926, pp. 1490-91; *Christian Century*, November 25, 1926, p. 1461.

[116]*Christian Century*, November 25, 1926, p. 1462; *Christian-Evangelist*, November 25, 1926, p. 1495.

It was another instance of Tulga's observation that uninformed, deceived conservatives will vote with the convention leadership.

The 1926 International Convention in Memphis was the last time the conservatives mounted a serious challenge to the direction of the United Christian Missionary Society. They had lost faith in both the convention and the UCMS and no longer felt affiliated with these agencies. The *Christian Standard* came away from Memphis calling it "a convention of bad faith." Edwin R. Errett, the next editor of the paper, reviewed the meeting with savage bitterness and disdain.[117] Early the next year, the conservatives were planning a national rally of their own to be held in October, obviously intended as a counterpart and replacement of the International Convention.[118] By June the rally was being called the North American Christian Convention, to be held in Indianapolis.[119]

In effect, the Disciples had split, following the same rough outline of what had occurred earlier in Chicago. There was liberalism in the schools, open membership in the churches and agencies, and comity agreements with regard to mission work. This resulted in a split within the Movement, and the conservatives began to erect new agencies to replace the ones that went liberal—The Cincinnati Bible Seminary to replace College of the Bible, Christian Restoration Association to replace the United Christian Missionary Society, and the North American Christian Convention to replace the International Convention. It took several decades for this division to work its way down through other schools, state missionary societies, and other institutions, but for all practical purposes, after 1927 the two sides had already withdrawn from each other. It took a while for the uninformed and the middle-of-the-road moderates to polarize, but the events of Memphis in 1926 were irreversible.

Heretofore the Disciples as a whole had been fairly tolerant, but the majority were inclined to stay in the middle of the road. That is, Disciples generally were favorable to higher criticism, to interdenominational conversations looking toward Christian unity, and to an efficient organization of missionary, benevolent, and educational interests. Disciples were tolerant of both conservatives and liberals who wished to continue in the general Disciples tradition. With a few exceptions, Disciples also generally refused open membership. The paradox is that most Disciples refused it for themselves, but tolerated those few Disciples

---

[117]*Christian Standard*, November 27, 1926, p. 631.
[118]*Ibid.*, February 26, 1927, p. 193.
[119]*Ibid.*, June 4, 1927, p. 529.

who did practice it. Refusing to practice open membership for themselves, most Disciples still recognized the freedom of others to engage in it. If an autonomous congregation wanted to observe open membership, that was one thing. But missionaries were not autonomous agents. Autonomous churches were not subject to any higher control; but missionaries were subject to the missionary societies, which were in turn subject to their annual conventions and financial supporters. Missionaries, therefore, were forbidden to *practice* open membership. Yet even missionaries still enjoyed the right of free conscience and liberty of thought, even if they did not enjoy liberty of action.

It was precisely at this point that the conservatives balked. They were not willing to have missionaries in their employ who *believed* in open membership, even if they did not practice it. For the conservatives, doctrinal orthodoxy was more important than freedom of conscience. A person's conscience was limited by the New Testament, which committed him to believing in immersion. Conservative Disciples were not even willing to tolerate open membership churches, in spite of local autonomy. Deviation from the New Testament plan of baptism was heresy and could not be tolerated, intellectual trends of the twentieth century notwithstanding.

Both conservatives and liberals claimed to stand at the center of the historic position of the Disciples of Christ—the liberals standing for freedom of Christian conscience and a commitment to Christian unity, the conservatives standing for the historical practices of the early church as understood by the Campbells and their early followers. Ironically, however, liberal Disciples and conservative Disciples were not compatible with each other. The difference lay in a completely different view toward the New Testament (or the authority of early Christian precedents), the Campbells, and the modern world. Conservatives were convinced that the original pattern of the New Testament church should be duplicated in all ages. Liberals were convinced that within a very general framework of commitment to Christian ideals, each generation (and culture) could work out its own concepts of Christian identity.

One segment of the Disciples was unwilling to give up its commitment to biblical authority, while the other side had so accepted the liberal understanding of the Bible that it was no longer authoritative; Christian unity as evidenced by their inclinations toward open membership and comity agreements was their major goal.

The liberals often argued that the ideal of Christian unity demanded some softening of traditional doctrinal positions. They were simply trying to implement the traditional commitment to Christian unity. The conservatives observed, however, that in the name of Christian unity, the liberals were willing to separate from the conservatives. They concluded that the liberals desired Christian unity with the denominations more than they desired Christian unity with conservatives who adhered to biblical authority. It was not just a matter, then, of Christian unity versus biblical authority. It was a matter of Christian unity at what price and with whom? The liberals chose Christian unity at the expense of biblical authority and with the denominations. The conservatives chose Christian unity under biblical authority and with others who accepted a similar commitment to biblical authority. Once again, the two goals of the Restoration Movement had been separated and division was the result.

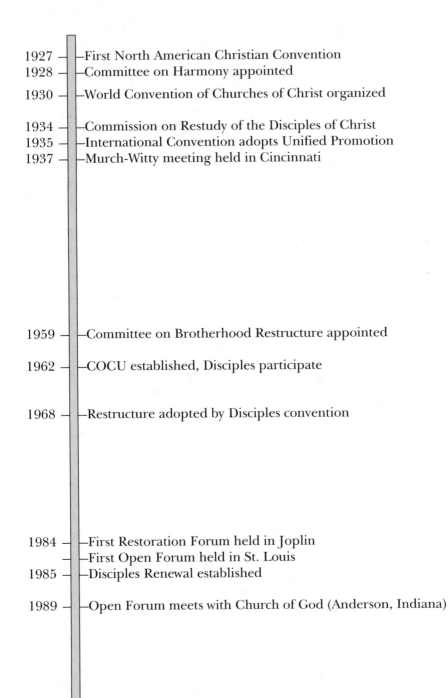

1927 — —First North American Christian Convention
1928 — —Committee on Harmony appointed

1930 — —World Convention of Churches of Christ organized

1934 — —Commission on Restudy of the Disciples of Christ
1935 — —International Convention adopts Unified Promotion
1937 — —Murch-Witty meeting held in Cincinnati

1959 — —Committee on Brotherhood Restructure appointed

1962 — —COCU established, Disciples participate

1968 — —Restructure adopted by Disciples convention

1984 — —First Restoration Forum held in Joplin
— —First Open Forum held in St. Louis
1985 — —Disciples Renewal established

1989 — —Open Forum meets with Church of God (Anderson, Indiana)

Chapter 12

A Brotherhood Divided

Ｗith the split over instrumental music and other issues made concrete in 1906, and the division between conservatives and liberals made inevitable in 1926, it is unfortunate that the Restoration Movement ever since has existed in three main branches. It is tragic that a movement that began with a commitment to Christian unity should itself fail to maintain a united existence.

Details of Division

One other point needs clarification, however. The significance of the dates 1906 and 1926 is clearer in hindsight than it was at the time. Many Noninstrumental churches were still listed among the Disciples in the period immediately after 1906. It was some time before the listings each side maintained were both accurate and mutually exclusive. Yet in terms of seeking a pinpoint date by which to chronicle the division, 1906 is probably the best. Some would suggest 1889, the date of the Sand Creek Address and Declaration, and there is some good rationale for choosing this date. But the 1906 date is probably better in terms of noting an irreversible division among erstwhile brethren.

But the date of the second division is a bit more controversial. Some historians, including this author, choose the date 1926-1927 as the significant date of division, for it was the combination of disillusionment at the Memphis Convention and the convening of the first North American Christian Convention a year later that made obvious the division that had already taken place.

Murch does not stipulate any particular date, although Leroy Garrett seems to think Murch favored a date in the 1940s when he says this decade "saw the decline of a significant number of organized efforts at reconciliation."[1] Murch does point to a "change in policy" in the *Christian Standard* in 1943 to become a "rallying center for all who believe implicitly in the authority of Christ as revealed to us in the divinely inspired New Testament Scriptures,"[2] and in 1944 he observes that the International Convention for the first time chose as its president an outspoken advocate of open membership.[3] In 1948 the Commission on Restudy made its last report and disbanded.[4] Yet it would be hard to argue that any of these events represents the key date for the break.

Other historians point to 1955 as the key date,[5] for it was at this time that the conservative churches, increasingly called "Independents" by the Disciples, first published a listing of their ministers and churches, *The Directory of the Ministry*, published annually ever since. Although this publication is significant in terms of self-identity, yet the listing it represents is simply making concrete the inevitable fallout of what had happened in 1926-1927. Therefore, the 1955 date is not as significant as the former.[6]

Some historians argue for 1968 being the key date for the separation. This is the date at which Restructure was accepted by the Disciples, which resulted in approximately 2,500 churches officially having their name taken from the *Disciples Year Book* listing of churches. Yet here again one can argue that this purging of names does not represent a new division, only cleaning up the paperwork of what had occurred back in 1926-1927.[7]

Still again, some historians argue for the importance of the date 1971, since this was the first time the "Independent" Christian Churches were listed separately in the *Yearbook of American Churches*, apparently at the

---

[1]Murch, p. 276; Garrett's reference is on p. 617.

[2]Murch, p. 276.

[3]*Ibid.*, p. 277.

[4]*Ibid.*

[5]A. T. DeGroot is in this category, with the publication of *Church of Christ Number Two* (Birmingham, England: Published by the author, 1956), pp. 1-4.

[6]Henry Webb does not favor any particular date, saying, "It is not possible to fix a precise date for this division" (Webb, p. 361), although he does refer to events in 1946 and then state, "Within the next few years, the body divided" (*Ibid.*). Therefore, he seems to favor a date around midcentury, but he does not specify a particular one. He does suggest as possibilities 1949, when the editor of the *Christian Standard* chided the centennial observance of the founding of the ACMS; 1950, when the North American Christian Convention decided to meet every year; and 1955, the publishing of the *Directory of the Ministry*.

[7]McAllister and Tucker admit the significance of 1968, but they also argue that what happened at this time was but the "completion of a process which had begun much earlier. . . . This was a formal acknowledgement of a division which had been in process since the formation of the North American Christian Convention in 1927." (McAllister and Tucker, pp. 446-447.)

initiative of the Independent churches.[8] Yet 1971 is much too late to date the beginning of the division. Surely what happened in this listing was again but an acknowledgment of what had really occurred decades earlier. So, although there were indeed numerous details to be worked out in the polarization of the Brotherhood, the best date for the beginning of the division seems to be that of 1926-1927.

If nothing else, what this controversy indicates is that the division was not a simple, immediate, obvious, and accomplished fact in 1927. The fallout resulting from the polarization took years, indeed decades, to find its way into the lives of individuals and churches scattered throughout the Brotherhood. Yes, in the view of hindsight there was a definite event in 1926-1927 that made division inevitable; but it still took a good while for this to manifest itself in numerous local situations.

In fact, for a while many within the Disciples saw the NACC as a healthy alternative to the International Convention. Let there be two conventions, they affirmed—one for the conduct of official business essential to the Disciples, the other for fellowship and the preaching of the great themes of the Restoration Movement. The editor of the *Christian-Evangelist* took this stance in 1928, emphasizing that each convention served its particular need.[9]

The Congresses were still a bone of contention. In 1927, F. D. Kershner in the *Christian-Evangelist* disdainfully mentioned that the Congresses had for some time been regarded as a platform for propagandist purposes rather than a forum for free and impartial discussion.[10] By 1930 the Disciples' Congress suffered a quiet and apparently unnoticed end, perhaps because its detractors were right. With the conservatives increasingly breaking way from the International Convention, a separate forum for scholarly discussion was not needed. The liberals no longer needed to "propagandize" their views—that was being done by most of the Disciples colleges, and the liberals now had almost unlimited and undisturbed access to the International Convention. The Congress was no longer worth the effort to maintain its separate existence.

The 1928 International Convention viewed its rival convention "with regret" and appointed a Commission on Harmony to meet with the disaffected conservatives in a hopeful attempt to preclude full division. The Commission met throughout the year and reported at the 1929

---

[8]Garrett, p. 616. He also seems to suggest that Tucker leans toward this date (see McAllister and Tucker, p. 386).

[9]*Christian-Evangelist*, September 13, 1928, pp. 1170-1171.

[10]*Ibid.*, May 26, 1927, p. 721.

International Convention in Seattle. Its recommendations were a pale imitation of those of the Peace Committee four years previously. Now it suggested little more than that the International Convention make plain its disinclination to be an ecclesiastical dictator and jealous wife—in other words, that the "independent agencies" be allowed to exist without coming under the jurisdiction of the International Convention.[11] This innocuous suggestion met with no objection during the convention; neither did it pave the way for widespread participation of the independent agencies in the convention itself. The issues that led to the 1926 departure were not resolved, so there was no progress in reversing the polarization between the two groups.

The *Christian Standard* recorded what seemed to it a "strange perversity" at the Seattle Convention. The convention voted on resolutions relative to military training, battleship construction, motion pictures, international relations, prohibition, the Y.M.C.A., and Philippine independence. Yet when someone suggested a resolution to the effect that the Disciples were not a sect and that Disciples sought to restore the church of the New Testament, the resolution was voted down as a "creedal statement."[12]

In discussing the presentation of the Commission on Harmony in Seattle in 1929, George A. Campbell remarked that there were two causes for the disturbances among the Disciples: one was theological and the other organizational.[13] The organizational cause was directly related to the United Christian Missionary Society and conservatives' fears that it would control policy for supposedly autonomous churches. For over a century, the Disciples had been afraid of ecclesiastical organization. Thomas Campbell and Barton W. Stone left the Presbyterians because of it. Alexander Campbell condemned it in 1823. When he changed his position in 1849, a number of conservatives attacked *him*. Twentieth-century conservatives were extremely reluctant to create any sort of agency that might later assume authority over churches and individuals. Conservatives counted their freedom more precious than organizational efficiency.

The other cause of Disciples disturbances was much more complex. Ostensibly the major disturber of Disciples conventions was the issue of open membership. Yet most knowledgeable leaders realized that open membership was but the symptom of theological divergence, as indicated by a *Christian Standard* editorial that proclaimed that open membership

---

[11]*Christian Standard*, August 24, 1929, p. 796.
[12]*Ibid.*, August 31, 1929, p. 821.
[13]*Christian Century*, August 28, 1929, p. 1071.

was but a screen for the array of "the liberalistic philosophy of religion." The real enemy was "the disposition to treat Christianity as an evolution rather than a revelation."[14] Seeing the Scriptures as a growing awareness of man's conscious seeking for God was a basic liberal position.[15] If the Scriptures are therefore an evolution rather than a revelation, then they are no longer authoritative. But ever since the Campbells and Stone, the Restoration Movement has hinged on the authority of Scripture—this is one of its two main emphases. To depart from the authority of Scripture is thus to depart from a traditional Disciples commitment.

George A. Campbell was therefore right in pointing to these two disturbances in 1929. Concern over the growing institutionalism and ecclesiasticism of the International Convention shook Disciples down to their frontier roots of autonomy and freedom. Concern over Scriptural authority shook them down to their original commitment to the Bible alone as the source of faith and practice for the church. These twin concerns were certainly enough to split the Brotherhood.

The impact of liberalism in Disciples higher education was pointed out in April 1930 when P. H. Welshimer called attention to the demise of Hiram College (his alma mater) as a Disciples school. The college had withdrawn from the Disciples Board of Higher Education; both the president and the professor of religious education were Baptists; and the chairman of the board of trustees attended a community church. The college no longer prepared men for the ministry. The *Christian Standard* concluded that the loss of Hiram was not occasioned by any of these things—"Hiram left this Restoration movement when it began to dally with modernism and to lose its passion for loyalty to the Scriptures."[16]

There was no North American Christian Convention held in 1930— even the conservatives joined in the great International Convention held in Washington, D.C., in honor of the nineteenth centennial of Pentecost in the spring. It was a moving event, and it was a good time to preach evangelism, something that had not been emphasized at the International Convention for years. Even so, the conservatives were restless. The dedication of National City Christian Church, a church in the national capital paid for by solicitations throughout the Brotherhood as a national monument to the Disciples, left many conservatives with an uneasy feeling of ecclesiasticism.[17] The next year the North American

---

[14]*Christian Standard*, October 5, 1929, p. 946.
[15]See *supra*, Chapter Ten, pp 255-257.
[16]*Christian Standard*, April 11, 1930, pp. 355, 359.
[17]*Ibid.*, February 25, 1928, p. 176.

Christian Convention met again, separately from the International Convention. Whatever camaraderie and unity had been attempted at Washington was unsuccessful.

Yet another event that coincided with the International Convention in 1930 has had a continuing institutional presence. This was the first gathering of the World Convention of Churches of Christ. Jesse M. Bader was a professional evangelist within the Christian Churches who was also sent as the first fraternal delegate to the annual conference of the British Churches of Christ in 1926. Since he knew of Disciples in at least thirty nations, he began to suggest the idea of a world gathering of Disciples. The first such meeting took place in Washington, D.C., in 1930 in connection with the International Convention. Since then the World Convention has met approximately every five years in various countries. Bader was appointed to the first full-time position in the World Convention in 1954, where he served until his death in 1963.[18]

Not only did the World Convention reflect continuing Disciples interest in Christian unity, but Disciples were also active in various ways in different interdenominational and ecumenical organizations. Some of these agencies were the World Council of Christian Education, Foreign Missions Conference of North America, Committee on Cooperation in Latin America, Faith and Order, Life and Work, World Conference of Christian Youth, and certainly the World Council of Churches.[19]

Further Polarization

Meanwhile the continuing polarization among the Disciples still had a long way to go. C. C. Morrison had indicated in 1918 that about 80 percent of the Disciples were ignorant of the issues.[20] Therefore, it took a good deal of time for awareness of the issues to filter down through the Brotherhood and for both sides to accept the inevitability of the split that had already occurred. Thus for the next couple of decades, the Disciples were still counted as one body, but the moderates in the middle of the road were increasingly moving either into the conservative orbit, or knowingly accepting the increasingly liberal direction of things coming from the UCMS and the International Convention leadership.

One of the more clear-cut indications of the growing chasm in the Brotherhood was the increasing number of Bible colleges that were

---

[18]McAllister and Tucker, pp. 327, 391-392.

[19] McAllister and Tucker, pp. 422-423.

[20]See *supra*, Chapter Eleven, p. 302; *Christian Century*, February 21, 1918, pp. 1-6.

begun to prepare a conservative ministry. They were replacement schools for the Disciples schools that had gone liberal. Most of the educational institutions already in existence prior to the national mobilization of the conservatives about 1919 were sooner or later taken over by the liberals. A few exceptions were Milligan College (1881) in northeastern Tennessee; A. S. Johnson's School of the Evangelists (1893; later Johnson Bible College) outside Knoxville, Tennessee; and International Bible College (1913; later Minnesota Bible College), in Minneapolis (later, Rochester, Minnesota). But these few schools were soon joined by dozens of others. Kentucky Christian College (1919) and The Cincinnati Bible Seminary (1924), each in their own way, were replacements for the College for the Bible. Pacific Christian College (1928) was a replacement for Chapman College in Los Angeles. Lincoln Christian College (1944) was a replacement for Eureka College. Numerous other schools were begun as evangelistic centers to lead the churches in certain areas in fresh efforts in evangelism.

To prevent these schools from falling into liberalism under a later generation of leadership (as happened at the College of the Bible after McGarvey's death), most of them adopted a statement of faith that all teachers had to sign as a condition of employment. These statements were not seen as creeds but as business arrangements between employer and employee. A sample statement, similar to most of the others, is that from Great Lakes Bible College (1949), Lansing, Michigan:

> Every trustee and teacher or other worker in any capacity must be a member of the church of Christ (undenominational) and must believe, without reservation, in the full and final inspiration of the Bible to the extent that it is to him the infallible Word of God, and therefore the all sufficient rule of faith and life; in the deity and supreme authority of Christ; obedience to the Gospel; the edification of the church; and the restoration of its unity on the New Testament basis.[21]

McAllister and Tucker quote this statement, adding,

> The unwavering opposition of Stone and the Campbells to creeds as tests of fellowship was lost in the strenuous effort to guarantee theological orthodoxy. It is obvious that the dissidents distorted the Disciples tradition when it served their purpose to do so.[22]

---

[21]McAllister and Tucker, p. 384, quoting Alfred T. DeGroot, *New Possibilities for Disciples and Independents* (St. Louis: The Bethany Press, 1963), pp. 65-66.
[22]McAllister and Tucker, p. 384.

Not only do these Disciples historians intentionally misinterpret the function of the statement, but their talk about distorting Disciples traditions is also very self-serving. They made no such observation when Ames used the Lunenburg Letter to defend open membership. McAllister and Tucker were not above distorting Disciples traditions themselves when it served their purpose to do so.

Again, it is tempting to look at the events of the 1920s and 1930s from the later viewpoint and talk of the later clear-cut polarization that was not yet fully in place. We have already referred to the Commission on Harmony, which the International Convention appointed in 1928. A similar but much more thorough job was begun in 1934 when the International Convention appointed a Commission on Restudy of the Disciples of Christ. The document that established this commission began by referring to the "passion for unity which gave birth to the brotherhood of the Disciples of Christ," and recommended a commission "to restudy the origin, history, slogans, methods, successes and failures of the movement of the Disciples of Christ, and with the purpose of a more effective and a more united program and a closer Christian fellowship among us." It also suggested a commission "composed of twenty members, proportionately representing the varied phases and schools of thought in the institutional life among us."[23]

This commission lasted for about fifteen years, and in the interim it was composed of many of the best-known names within the Brotherhood—liberal, conservative, and moderate. After interviewing scores of individuals from the whole spectrum of the Brotherhood, the Commission on Restudy prepared and submitted to the International Convention an official report in 1946. The Commission dissolved in 1949.[24]

The 1946 report from this Commission was a classic. Carefully written, but again striving to describe the current situation in neutralist terms, the report acknowledged that elements within the Brotherhood differed on a variety of viewpoints. Is the Disciples of Christ a denomination or a movement? Have the agencies threatened the autonomy of local churches? Does the New Testament contain the pattern for the church or just principles for its operation? Should the Brotherhood continue to hold the twin ideals of unity and restoration, or abandon restoration for a greater development of unity? Is open membership a betrayal of the Scriptural teaching on baptism? The report, unfortunately, "was largely

---

[23]Quoted in Murch, p. 263.
[24]McAllister and Tucker, p. 401; Murch, pp. 263-271; Webb, pp. 339-351. Both Murch and Webb give the entire text of the 1946 report; Webb also gives the substance of the further report in 1948.

ignored."[25] It may be significant that the two "Independent" histories, Murch and Webb, quote the entire report, while of the two Disciples histories, McAllister and Tucker deal with the Commission in one medium paragraph, while Garrison and DeGroot do not mention it at all. For all practical purposes, the work of this Commission was fruitless; one comes to wonder whether the International Convention even wanted anything to come from it at all.

Another indication of the growing separation in the Brotherhood was the missionary situation. Those Disciples still affiliated with the International Convention continued to support the United Christian Missionary Society and its various missionaries. The conservative Disciples, however, because of the unhappy experiences with the UCMS over the past decade or two, supported missionaries independently of the organized societies. In fact, this provided the common two labels within the Brotherhood for much of this period. Those Disciples supporting the UCMS were known as the "Cooperatives" while the others were known as the "Independents," or the "Non-Cooperatives."

The titles are somewhat misleading. The "Independents" did cooperate with other "Independents"; it is just that they did not wish to support the UCMS because to do so seemed to amount to a support of liberalism. Sometimes the Independent mission movement is referred to as "direct support," since the missionaries receive their financial support directly from the congregations (and individuals) rather than having the money processed through a missionary society.[26] Even today labels and titles are somewhat confusing. Those churches affiliated with the North American Christian Convention are still sometimes referred to as the "Independent Christian Church" to distinguish them from those Christian Churches that are identified with the organized work of the Disciples of Christ.

Regardless of labels, the independent missions work proliferated in the years after 1927. Early examples include W. D. Cunningham, but his case is rather unique. He was refused acceptance from the Foreign Christian Missionary Society for health reasons, but he went to Japan on his own in 1901 and established a flourishing mission station. His situation had nothing to do with the later theological tensions, but he was probably the first significant "independent" missionary.[27] We have

---

[25]Webb, p. 351.

[26]An excellent history of this whole development is in David Filbeck, *The First Fifty Years: A Brief History of the Direct-Support Missionary Movement* (Joplin, Missouri: College Press Publishing Company, 1980).

[27]The Cunningham situation is treated in Filbeck, pp. 137-150; and Webb, pp. 321-323.

already mentioned Enrique T. Westrup in Monterrey, Mexico (1914/ 1919), and Leslie Wolfe in the Philippines (1925). Additional missionaries went to Africa, Asia, and the Caribbean.

The real explosion, however, occurred after World War II. Many men who saw military service in foreign lands took up the challenge to return as Christian missionaries. The generous GI educational benefits helped many of them through college. Filbeck states that the number of independent missionaries in 1946 was less than 100; by 1976, that number had risen to nearly 2,000.[28]

Bridges and Failures

Yet there were some missionary developments that seemed to bridge the growing schism. The European Evangelistic Society was organized in 1943 and sent Earl Stuckenbruck to Germany in 1946.[29] For decades this agency has received official recognition from the Disciples organizations but also reception and support from Independents.

The Christian Missionary Fellowship was organized in 1949, basically to provide an organized missionary society for work supported by the conservative Disciples—the "Independents." The theology of the organizers was conservative, but they felt some organization, direction, and follow-up needed to be provided in supervising mission work on the field. They are a full missionary society, not just a regional cooperative of independent missionaries—as is true with such organizations as Central African Mission, South East Asia Evangelistic Association, and others. The Christian Missionary Fellowship has full-time paid leadership and office headquarters. Missionaries who serve under its banner pay a portion of their income to the CMF office for clerical services and general institutional operating expenses. The significant element is that for a long time, CMF received income from conservative churches that were still involved with the Disciples organizations.

Then there were significant individuals who still seemed to bridge the division between the organized Disciples and the Independents. James DeForest Murch was one such person. There was no doubt that he was conservative, and opposed to the direction of the Disciples organization. Yet he still attended the meetings of the International Convention, had numerous personal acquaintances within the organized institutions,

[28]Filbeck, p. 283.
[29]Garrison and DeGroot, p. 507.

served on the Commission on Restudy, and worked to reconcile the differences.[30]

Another such figure was P. H. Welshimer. Garrett makes a major point of observing how much he stood in both camps. Welshimer was certainly a theological conservative, but, in Garrett's words, he was "as irenic as forthright."[31] He was one of the first of those to withdraw funds from the UCMS because of the suspicions of open membership on the mission field, but he also put UCMS back into his church's budget for a couple of years before finally taking it out again. He was the first president of the North American Christian Convention, but he was also a member of the Commission on Restudy. He also served as vice-president of the International Convention.[32] In 1938 the International Convention selected him to represent the Disciples at the convention of the British churches.[33]

He had the respect of both groups, and in his presidential address to the NACC in 1940 he urged people "to disagree without being disagreeable."[34] As late as 1948 the editor of the Disciples' leading paper, the *Christian-Evangelist*, expressed hope for peace between the two conventions, still recognizing the NACC as "part of the brotherhood designated as Disciples of Christ."[35]

If there were still some shaky bridges between the Cooperatives and Independents, there were other attempts to build bridges between the Instrumental and Noninstrumental brethren.

One such effort came through the work of J. D. Murch. At one point in the mid-1930s, he was speaking in Toronto, where some Noninstrumental brethren were present. In his address, he expressed his desire to break

---

[30]Murch was a prolific author, and his writings are excellent sources for insights into this period. His book *Christians Only* was the first significant history of the Restoration Movement written from the "Independent" perspective. Yet Murch suffered from a massive ego, and he was always eager to relate how significant he was in Brotherhood affairs. As a result, his writings about himself cannot be trusted to be objective, fair, or even truthful. His autobiography, *Adventuring for Christ in Changing Times: An Autobiography of James DeForest Murch* (Louisville: Restoration Press, 1973), is a classic case in point. The reader of this book is led to wonder how the Restoration Movement, indeed even the entire evangelical persuasion, could ever have gotten along without him.

[31]Garrett, p. 637.

[32]Garrett, p. 639.

[33]Arant, p. 89.

[34]Garrett, p. 640, quoting from *Christian Standard*, 1940, p. 735. Welshimer was president of the NACC three times (1927, 1929, and 1940), the only person so honored.

[35]Garrett, p. 640, quoting Raphael Miller in *Christian-Evangelist*, 1940, p. 492.

down the wall of division that separated the two fellowships. One of the men present suggested to Murch that he contact Claude F. Witty, a Noninstrumental minister in Detroit who had similar hopes.[36]

A year of correspondence between Murch and Witty resulted in a meeting held in Cincinnati on February 23, 1937, with an equal number of Instrumental and Noninstrumental leaders present. In the next few years, at least half a dozen meetings were held. In 1939 bolder plans were laid with a "national" meeting planned for Detroit in May, which drew over a thousand persons. Again, several similar meetings were held in succeeding years.

Murch and Witty co-edited the *Christian Unity Quarterly* to provide a forum to encourage discussion on the relevant topics. Hundreds of thousands of copies of a tract, *Christian Unity: Churches of Christ and Christian Churches*, were distributed. Several periodicals encouraged the work, speaking from all sides of the Brotherhood, even the *Christian-Evangelist*. After a few years, however, Witty and other Noninstrumentalists took offense when the address of one of the Noninstrumentalists, an address that was considered damaging to the traditional acappella position, was clandestinely reproduced and circulated.[37] After this loss of confidence, the meetings withered away.

It is difficult to gauge the success of the whole endeavor. On the grassroots level, numerous individuals who participated in the meetings came to appreciate their brethren from the other side of the issue. Some attitudes were being changed, and some openness cultivated. However, after the blowup, the situation reverted to the status quo. There were no visible institutional results of the series of meetings.

It was also during this same period, the decades of the '30s and '40s, that the division between the independent Christians and the organized Disciples filtered down to another level. Up to this time, most of the polarization had occurred relative to national agencies—such as the UCMS and the International Convention. But in the decade of the '30s the strife reached down to the level of the state organizations. These state societies had been in existence since 1839. For decades they had been agencies of encouragement for new church planting, Sunday School development, and camaraderie of the churches within particular states. But when individuals sympathetic to liberalism began to take

---

[36]Murch talks about the discussions with Witty most fully in his *Adventuring for Christ*, pp. 126-133; somewhat more condensed in *Christians Only*, pp. 274-276; Garrett also discusses the event, pp. 664-666.

[37]Murch, *Adventuring for Christ*, p. 132.

over the high offices, conservatives in these states began to distrust the state societies. Sometimes the state secretary (usually the principal executive officer carried this title) used his position to support open membership, to try to silence conservatives in the annual meetings, or even to ostracize conservative leaders. The national division of 1926-1927 was being duplicated on the state level in the 1940s.

Even more tragic was when such disputes got down to the congregational level itself. By the 1940s and 1950s, numerous local churches began to polarize over the issues of liberalism that had been festering within the Brotherhood over the past half century. Sometimes this focused on the disposition of missionary money (to the UCMS or elsewhere), sometimes with the selection or retention of a preacher, sometimes with the practice of open membership itself. Whatever the specific issue, the result was the cleavage of a particular local congregation.

The hottest dispute then came when both factions claimed to be the legitimate owner of the church building and sued the other side for exclusive possession. There were a couple of dozen such court cases where one portion of the church sued the other portion for ownership of the building. Each side called in "expert" witnesses to give testimony— missionary society officials on one side, ministers, evangelists, or professors of independent Bible colleges on the other.

Institutionally, one of the major arguments made by the "Co-operatives" was that the building was built with money loaned through the Board of Church Extension, which was now one of the agencies incorporated in the organized Disciples work. This was a strong argument, but it was often ably refuted by the conservative claim that at the time the building was built, the people that supported the Board of Church Extension believed what the independent Christians still believed, while the Disciples of Christ organization had changed their belief structure. Most courts decided in favor of the continuity of belief rather than the continuity of institutions.[38] Thus, most of the court cases resulted in the buildings being given to the Independent Christian factions (eight of fourteen). In six cases, however, the court decided the other way. On several occasions (four out of the six), the Independents who lost their case on the first hearing appealed the decision. In every such situation, the appellate court reversed the lower court decision. Whenever the organized Disciples appealed a case they lost in the first

---

[38]Dr. Lewis A. Foster, professor at CBS since 1950, testified as a witness in several of these cases. He later compiled a chart (see p. 336) covering fourteen of these cases illustrating the basic pattern of the judges' decisions.

COURT TRIALS

Date	For "Disciples"	Against "Disciples"
1922		Redlands, California
Jun 1948		Harrisonburg, Virginia
May 1949	Pontiac, Illinois (not appealed)	
Nov 1950		Smithers, West Virginia
Aug 1951	Eldora, Iowa	
Dec 1951		Smithers, West Virginia—affirmed by Supreme Court of appeals of West Virginia
Mar 1952		Lair vs. Elmore, U.S. District Court at Des Moines, Iowa
Aug 1952	Oxford, Indiana (not appealed)	
Nov 1952	Brookville, Indiana	
Nov 1952		Eldora, Iowa, lower court decision reversed by Iowa Supreme Court
Feb 1953		Salem, Illinois
Oct 1953		Decision in Lair-Elmore case affirmed by U.S. Circuit Court of Appeals at St. Louis, Missouri
Nov 1953	Chaplin, Kentucky	
Feb 1955		Chaplin decision unanimously reversed by Kentucky Court of Appeals
Feb 1955		Salem, Illinois; affirmed by Illinois Court of Appeals
1957		Olney, Illinois
1958		Brookville, Indiana; lower court decision unanimously reversed by Supreme Court of Indiana
Aug 1960		Wayne, Nebraska
Dec 1964	Level Green Christian Church, New Castle, Virginia	
Apr 1966		Clarksdale, Mississippi
Jan 1967		New Castle, Virginia; lower court decision unanimously reversed by Supreme Court of Virginia

(This chart was prepared by Dr. Lewis Foster, Distinguished Professor of New Testament at The Cincinnati Bible Seminary.)

round (three times), they lost the second round as well. The result was that most of these court cases were decided in favor of the Independents (twelve out of fourteen) including all cases (seven) that went to the appellate level.

Regardless of the disposition of the court cases, however, the Brotherhood as a whole lost through this development. Irrespective of who wound up owning the property, a local church that had gone through a public court battle found it hard to present a congenial picture of Christianity at work. After all the church's dirty linen had been aired in public, it was difficult for the church members to conduct evangelism in their communities. This whole process further accelerated the separation between the Independents and the Disciples as numerous conservative Christian Churches became fearful for their property if they remained identified with the Disciples.

An additional step toward separation came unintentionally through an effort to bring more efficiency and order to the fund-raising engaged in by many of the national agencies of the organized work. There were literally dozens of these agencies all competing for the same missionary dollars from the same churches. This made things awkward for the churches to decide in a given month whether to subsidize a new church building in Africa, buy shoes for orphans, provide Bibles for a destitute inner city mission, help a Christian hospital purchase needed equipment, help a college build a necessary dormitory, or even help plant a new church in a nearby community. Most churches found it difficult to respond to these emergency appeals every month. In addition, all these agencies were spending a vast amount of money in postage and printing in sending out such appeals.

One answer was Unified Promotion, adopted by the International Convention in 1935.[39] Under this plan, those agencies approved by the organized work all consolidated their appeals through one agency. All the money raised through Unified Promotion was then divided among the various agencies according to an agreed formula. Thus the agencies were no longer fighting each other for the same financial support, and the mailing of appeals was coordinated through a single office, not duplicated by dozens of offices.

On the one hand, this was a reasonable approach to organizing financial appeals for the Brotherhood. On the other hand, it had sinister overtones. Agencies that were not "approved" did not share in the distribution formula. Originally Unified Promotion claimed that any

---

[39]Garrison and DeGroot, pp. 507-509; McAllister and Tucker, pp. 398-399.

agency that was willing to open its books for financial inspection could share in the unified program. Later, however, "approval" became "endorsement," which could be withheld from certain agencies. By that time, Unified Promotion became a matter of "recognizing" what were the "legitimate" agencies of the organized Disciples.[40] The conservatives saw this as one more step in hierarchical control and ecclesiasticism. Thus, what started out as an effort to streamline fund-raising became a litmus test of loyalty and fellowship.

Another tenuous bridge between the various branches of the Restoration Movement has been the World Convention of Churches of Christ. This was formally organized and held in conjunction with the International Convention in Washington on Pentecost of 1930. Eight thousand delegates attended, and similar conventions have been held at roughly five-year intervals. They have been held in the United States, Canada, Australia, New Zealand, Mexico, Puerto Rico, and Scotland. The Noninstrumentalists have had only token involvement in these meetings; although the Independent Christian Churches have participated in many of the most recent conventions, the bulk of the planning, involvement, and attendance has come from the Disciples. The purpose of the convention is for fellowship, inspiration, and mutual helpfulness. The conventions do not seek to control the theology or policies of the churches that participate.[41] Nevertheless, the members of the two more conservative branches of the Stone-Campbell Movement do not look to the Disciples for inspiration or help; and because of the theological tensions, they feel awkward at the fellowship, which seems artificial in light of the deep theological differences.

Another common thread in the Restoration Movement today is the Disciples of Christ Historical Society. Historian Errett Gates proposed a historical society as early as 1901,[42] but it was not until 1939 that the International Convention appointed a committee to investigate the possibility. The society was formally organized in 1941, with headquarters temporarily located at Culver-Stockton College in Canton, Missouri. In 1952 the Society moved to new facilities in Nashville and in 1958 dedicated the Thomas W. Phillips Memorial Building near Vanderbilt University.[43] The Society represents the most significant collection of documents of the history of the Movement, and it is available to all

---

[40]Murch, *Christians Only*, p. 290; McAllister and Tucker, pp. 398-399.
[41]Garrison and DeGroot, p. 531; McAllister and Tucker, pp. 391-392.
[42]See the references in McAllister and Tucker, p. 399.
[43]*Ibid.*, p. 400.

branches of the Movement. Membership on its board of trustees is shared among the three camps, although the Disciples provide the majority of financial support.

The year 1959 saw the birth of another attempt to reconcile and resolve the problems of division within the movement. At a Consultation on Ecumenical Christian Unity held at Phillips University in Enid, Oklahoma, James B. Carr, Professor of Missions at Manhattan Bible College, insisted that principles used as a basis for urging ecumenical unity ought also to be applied within the Restoration Movement. This initiated a discussion that led to a call for a Consultation on Internal Unity held that same year in Wichita. About two hundred individuals from Oklahoma and Kansas attended, with approximately equal representation from the Disciples and Christian Churches.[44]

Two years later a second consultation was held, but it was marked by the insistence of A. Dale Fiers, then president of the United Christian Missionary Society, that a unified Brotherhood demanded "a common structure for the administration of inter-congregational responsibility."[45] Fiers' emphasis on organizational cohesion reminded too many of the [Independent] Christian Church folk of the heavy-handed policies four decades earlier, and they were unwilling to follow Fiers' lead. Additional consultations were held every year until 1966, but they accomplished nothing further. Also, by that time the Disciples leaders were well into their plans for Restructure, and further discussions with the Independents seemed pointless.

Restructure

Restructure was the key buzzword for the Disciples in the 1960s. As early as 1948, a number of Disciples leaders recommended a commission to review organizational structure and program. A "Conference on Unification" was held in Indianapolis in 1958, attended by 250 national and area leaders; they put a priority on the unification of state and area boards. That same year, a Council of Agencies meeting focused on complete restructure of Disciples organization and program. A Study Committee on Brotherhood Structure began meeting in 1959 under the chairmanship of W. M. Wickizer, and it reported its findings to the International Convention in 1960. Initial plans were for the leadership

---

[44]Webb, pp. 362-363.

[45]Webb, p. 363, quoting Charles Gresham (ed.), *The Second Consultation on Internal Unity* (Oklahoma City: n.p., n.d.), p. 145.

to be vested in the convention itself and for all agencies to be ready for changes.[46]

In the process of this, the UCMS and the Board of Higher Education sponsored the appointment of the Panel of Scholars in 1957 "to restudy the doctrines of Disciples of Christ."[47] The panel met semiannually over the next several years, critiquing papers and harmonizing a perspective. The result was finally a three-volume publication, *The Renewal of Church: The Panel of Scholars Reports*, edited by W. B. Blakemore, Dean of the Disciples Divinity House of the University of Chicago. The papers in these volumes fairly consistently reflected a liberal perspective. More than just the musing of scholars, these papers became the accepted theological foundation upon which restructure was built. As the official history of the Disciples states, "There can be little doubt that the work of the Panel of Scholars greatly influenced the discussions and decisions on structure and organization which came later."[48]

The 1960 International Convention enlarged the Committee on Brotherhood Restructure to 120 persons, attempting to make it as representative as possible of all the churches. A rationale for restructure was provided in Resolution 30 adopted that same year. After acknowledging that traditionally the Disciples distrusted organizations and feared ecclesiasticism, it continued:

> Much of the problem that the Disciples of Christ have had with organization stems from the fact that as a religious body we have had almost no theology of *Church* beyond the local congregation. The Church was only the sum

---

[46]Restructure developments are discussed in Webb, pp. 365-373 and McAllister and Tucker, pp. 419-423, 443-451. Wickizer as chairman of the first Committee is mentioned by McAllister and Tucker on p. 367.

[47]This is the phrase used by W. M. Wickizer, Executive Secretary of the Division of Home Ministries with the UCMS (the rough equivalent of the old ACMS), in his prefatory statement in *The Renewal of Church: The Panel of Scholars Reports*, 3 Vols., edited by W. B. Blakemore (St. Louis: The Bethany Press, 1963), vol. 1, p. 8. Wickizer was the one who addressed the issue of reorganization at the 1958 meeting of the Council of Agencies (McAllister and Tucker, p. 421), and Webb calls him "The Father of Restructure" (Webb, p. 366). It may be significant, as Webb points out, that the Panel of Scholars "was not appointed by the International Convention and thus did not represent the 'Brotherhood,' but only two of its agencies" (Webb, p. 366).

[48]McAllister and Tucker, p. 434, adding a reference to Loren E. Lair, *The Christian Church (Disciples of Christ) and its Future* (St. Louis: The Bethany Press, 1971), pp. 32 ff. Lair's book contains a detailed history of the Commission on Restructure and the development of the Provisional Design (McAllister and Tucker, p. 436).

total of autonomous congregations and it was thought congregational autonomy should be protected . . . at all costs. . . .

Furthermore the conviction has come to us that the *Church* is something more than the sum total of local congregations, that it has a very real and vital total entity that should be reflected in its corporate structure.[49]

This portion of the resolution virtually endorsed denominational reorganization of the local congregations and the various agencies into one structure. Although many Disciples were willing to reorganize the agencies into a more efficient model, they were concerned that Resolution 30 would transform "the inherited congregational polity into a well-defined supra-congregational structure."[50] As it turned out, such concerns were justified.

The term *church* was no longer to be confined to a local body of believers. It was claimed that such a restriction obscured the wholeness of the Brotherhood. Furthermore, the term *agency* failed to convey the concept that the service being performed was really the work of the church. A proper understanding of *church*, it was argued, must embrace the work of the church at all levels and in its broadest dimension. Thus the gathering of Christians at a state convention is not properly understood as a "convention" but rather as "the church" functioning at the state level. Similarly, the International Convention of Disciples of Christ is improperly conceived as a mass meeting of disciples and a reporting body for the separate agencies. It is more properly a manifestation of the "church" functioning at the national or international level. This being the case, it was only appropriate that these bodies be designated as "church" (assemblies) and that the former "state secretary" of a society become the "minister" to the church at this level. The General Secretary of the International Convention would be designated as the General Minister of the Christian Church (Disciples of Christ).[51]

By 1963 the Commission on Restructure had decided that the three manifestations of the church were to be: the congregation, the region (state, province, or area), and the general. By 1964 the Commission had agreed upon some basic guidelines, two of which were:

1. The structure will be designed so that the Christian Church (Disciples of Christ) in all its manifestations at all levels reflects its oneness and the unity of the church.

---

[49]*1960 Year Book (July 1, 1959 - June 30, 1960) of Christian Churches (Disciples of Christ)*, (Indianapolis: International Convention of Christian Churches [Disciples of Christ]), 1960), p. 27.

[50]Webb, p. 367.

[51]Webb, p. 368.

2. The Christian Church will follow the principles of representative government through the structuring of delegate bodies.[52]

These two guidelines in particular pave the way for a denominational structure. It is ironic that Resolution 30 of 1960 acknowledged that the Disciples traditionally feared denominational structure and ecclesiasticism, and three years later the Commission adopted guidelines that would institute these very things. It is further noteworthy that the official Disciples history, written by McAllister and Tucker, then state, "These guidelines were consistent with the traditions and historic practice of the Disciples."[53] The irony is that when the Bible colleges established statements of faith for their faculty, McAllister and Tucker claimed that "the dissidents distorted the Disciples tradition when it served their purpose to do so."[54] Claiming that the guidelines adopted in 1963 were "consistent with the traditions and historic practice of the Disciples" is a flagrant distortion of Disciples tradition and practice, but it served McAllister and Tucker's purpose to do so.

When the International Convention met in Detroit in 1964, they were faced with an amendment to the bylaws that would convert it into a delegate assembly. Since the Disciples had a long tradition—going all the way back to the Synod of Kentucky and the Redstone Baptist Association—of resistance to authoritative assemblies, there was great opposition to this, but it was adopted nonetheless. One purpose for this action was the acknowledgment that numerous Independent Christian Churches were still officially listed as Disciples churches but had not participated in Disciples meetings. (The Independent churches were afraid that involvement would jeopardize their independent standing and ownership of their church buildings or even put them under legal obligation to accept decisions of future assemblies.) Transforming the International Convention into a delegate convention would eliminate the possibility that these churches might show up at the last minute and vote against the Restructure package. Not only did the bylaws eliminate these potentially troublesome votes, but they also provided significant voting representation to the agency officials; the combination virtually guaranteed a favorable response to Restructure.[55]

It may be significant that at the same convention in Detroit in 1964, the respected Disciples historian, W. E. Garrison—himself a liberal, but

---

[52]McAllister and Tucker, p. 439, quoting Lair, p. 70.
[53]McAllister and Tucker, p. 439.
[54]*Ibid.*, p. 384.
[55]Webb, pp. 368-369.

one attuned to the Disciples tradition—spoke at a ministerial breakfast. Entitling his address "A Fork in the Road," he indicated his belief that the Disciples were facing a decision between two directions, and he voiced his concern that they would choose the wrong fork. He later indicated that in fact he did believe they had chosen the wrong one.[56]

Opposition to Restructure took form beyond the pleading of a senior statesman. An anonymous Committee for the Preservation of the Brotherhood appeared and distributed two anonymous pamphlets entitled "Freedom or Restructure?" and "The Truth About Restructure." Four copies of each of these were mailed to every congregation listed in the Disciples *Year Book*. The committee had actually been organized at First Christian Church of Canton, Ohio, under the encouragement of James DeForest Murch, who also wrote both documents. The expense of printing and distribution was underwritten by B. D. Phillips of Butler, Pennsylvania. In addition, Phillips commissioned Murch to write a "scholarly and definitive" treatise on *The Free Church*, which he did. When the book was published in 1965, Phillips sent out one thousand free copies to key churches. Most of the concern of this committee had to do with perceived threats to the freedom of local congregations and their property rights in their church buildings.[57]

Much of the leadership of the Committee for the Preservation of the Brotherhood came from "Independents." But there also arose another committee completely from the ranks of those who had been longtime loyal supporters of the International Convention. Robert W. Burns, longtime preacher at the Peachtree Christian Church in Atlanta and a respected Disciple leader throughout the South, and others formed the Atlanta Declaration Committee in 1967. Burns had written *The Atlanta Declaration*, and his concern was again focused on congregational autonomy and local church property rights.[58] Neither of these efforts, however, had any effect in changing the outcome of Restructure.

Instead, Restructure continued to move right along. In 1966, the International Convention adopted the Commission's suggestion that the convention be transformed into a delegate convention for 1967 to pave the way for the adoption of the Provisional Design for the Christian Church (Disciples of Christ)—otherwise known as Restructure. The 1967

---

[56]McAllister and Tucker, p. 445. See Garrett, p. 709 for the story of how McAllister and Tucker initially whitewashed Garrison's judgment, then corrected it after being chided by A. T. DeGroot.

[57]McAllister and Tucker, p. 444; Webb, pp. 370-371; Murch, *Adventuring for Christ*, pp. 287-291.

[58]McAllister and Tucker, pp. 445-446; Webb, pp. 371-372; Murch, *Adventuring for Christ*, pp. 291-293.

International Convention met in St. Louis as a delegate assembly. It made some revision to the Provisional Design but basically adopted the package. The package was then submitted to the states, areas, and agencies, needing an approval from two-thirds of them. By the time of the 1968 meeting in Kansas City, the necessary votes were in, and the delegates at Kansas City almost unanimously approved the transformations that Restructure represented. When the votes were final, the assembled delegates spontaneously broke out into the Doxology.[59]

There were a number of things accomplished by the adoption of Restructure. One of the most significant was the departure of numerous "Independent" congregations that were still listed in the Disciples *Year Book*. Earlier in the century, the Disciples *Year Book* had listed all churches that were identified with the Stone-Campbell movement with the exception of those Noninstrumental congregations that had already withdrawn. When the divisions of 1926-1927 and beyond occurred, most congregations were still listed in the *Year Book*. The listing was a convenience, after all, and for clergy there was some advantage in being included—qualifying for railroad passes, for instance. Some of the Independent congregations took no initiative in getting out of the *Year Book* because there seemed no need to do so. The list was harmless, and most congregations did not bother about trying to clarify the distinctions. But once Restructure was adopted, the question of property rights came to the fore. Once a delegate convention was set up and all congregations listed in the *Year Book* were officially represented in the General Assembly, then the decisions of that Assembly would become legally binding on all congregations thus represented. The legal implication was that congregations listed in the *Year Book* were under the decisions of the Assembly, even if those particular congregations did not have representatives at the meeting. To be listed in the *Year Book* was to be included with the Disciples churches. If the Assembly decided upon a certain course of action and the local congregation dissented, could it lose its church building? This was a live possibility, though no one knew the exact answer to it. But the chances were potentially scary enough that Independent congregations did not want to take the chance. Similarly, there was also talk about the General Assembly beginning to move toward merger with other denominations. If the Assembly voted in favor of a merger, could this vote force a local congregation into such a merger against its will? Again, nobody knew for sure, but the Independents were unwilling to risk their property and their local existence.

---

[59]McAllister and Tucker, pp. 441-443; Webb, pp. 368-372.

That is why, shortly after Restructure was voted in at Kansas City, thousands of congregations officially requested that their name be removed from the *Year Book*.[60] Thus one immediate result of Restructure was a paring down of denominational statistics. The resulting numbers were smaller, but certainly more accurate.

Other results were to implement what Restructure was all about. A new denominational headquarters was established, with A. Dale Fiers becoming the first general minister and president of the restructured church. A new name was put into place. Previously the official name had been "Christian Churches (Disciples of Christ)." Now it became "Christian Church (Disciples of Christ)." The difference was small—the plural ending "es" was removed from "Christian Churches." Symbolically, this indicated that whereas previously the Disciples were made up of a series of local churches, now they were simply one body, *the church*. From being a series of associated congregations, they had now become a denominational entity. The annual International Convention was replaced by a biennial General Assembly.

Seven divisions, four councils, and several auxiliary units now replaced all the bureaucracy of previous Disciples agencies. The United Christian Missionary Society was now divided into a Division of Homeland Ministries and a Division of Overseas Ministries. The UCMS became only a holding company, distributing its money to the two divisions.[61]

Change also occurred on the publishing level. *The Christian* was the

---

[60]The exact number is somewhat uncertain. McAllister and Tucker state that 3,000 congregations with an estimated membership exceeding 750,000 took legal action to withdraw from the fellowship (p. 386). In another context, they state that 2,300 requested removal by 1970, that is, within two years, and "many more congregations" did so in the next three years (p. 446). An initial 2,300 plus "many more" could total 3,000. This departure left the Disciples with 4,046 congregations in 1970. In effect, they had lost about one-third of their strength. But actually the losses were less meaningful than that. Most of these congregations were deadwood as far as the Disciples program was concerned: they sent no money to Unified Promotion and did not participate in any way in the Disciples activities. The 1967 *Year Book* (p. S343) lists 4,794 participating congregations and 3,253 nonparticipating for a total of 8,047. The 1968 *Year Book* (p. S314) lists, respectively, 4,225 and 1,715, for a total of 5,940. The 1970 *Year Book* (p. 213) lists 4,046, and 1,112, for a total of 5,158. The totals of 1967 and 1970 thus show a drop of 2,889. Having these congregations withdraw from the *Year Book*, then, only served to clean up the paperwork left over from the 1926-1927 polarization. The Disciples organization was glad to see these churches depart, for most such churches were nonproductive with regard to the Disciples program. McAllister and Tucker estimate that these departures cost the denominational budget less than $100,000 per year (p. 446).

[61]McAllister and Tucker, p. 449.

continuing magazine that was once the *Christian-Evangelist*, edited by J. H. Garrison. *World Call* was the organ of the UCMS, which in turn had replaced individual papers that the CWBM, the ACMS, and the FCMS had each published. But in 1974, *World Call* and *The Christian* were merged to form *The Disciple*, the official publication of the restructured denomination. Initially a biweekly, this was slightly modified in 1975 to be semimonthly,[62] and it is now published monthly.

There was also no doubt that the new organization reflected a good deal of liberal theology. The leadership of the Disciples was overwhelmingly liberal. The professors at Disciples seminaries and the leadership of the denominational agencies were all committed to liberalism. Perhaps as many as half of all Disciples churches were practicing open membership. Most professors in Disciples seminaries often rejected the physical resurrection, the inspiration of Scripture, supernatural miracles as recorded in Scripture, and even the deity of Christ. Express social concerns, certainly satisfactory in themselves, replaced any allegiance to traditional Scripture teaching; the liberals regarded the traditional doctrines of Christianity as based on ignorance, shallowness, and unacceptable exclusivism. This was another reason why the Independents, certainly much more conservative in theology, desired to remove themselves from the Disciples organization and its theological liberalism.

Later Developments

Yet it is important to note that although the leadership of the Disciples was now liberal, there were still numerous ministers and churches that were not. These churches soon formed a bulwark against continuing denominational drift toward liberalism. The Disciples upper-level leadership has continued in liberal directions, but there are numerous Disciples ministers and churches that are not pleased with these tendencies.

One effort at trying to prompt meaningful unity and fellowship between the three branches of the Restoration Movement was vested in the magazine *Fellowship*, which began publication in 1974. The three editors of the magazine represented the three branches, and its editorial board was composed of leading thinkers and writers from all camps. It lasted only three years, but it served as a platform for serious appeals to unity. The fact that it accomplished so little suggests that there was little chance of real *rapprochement* over the issues at the time.[63]

---

[62]*Ibid.*, p. 451.
[63]Garrett, pp. 661-662.

As we have mentioned repeatedly in this book, the Restoration Movement began with a twofold commitment to Christian unity and biblical authority. The Noninstrumental Churches of Christ have continued to hold that commitment to biblical authority, often at the expense of any meaningful concern for Christian unity. The Disciples of Christ, on the other hand, have usually felt a strong commitment to Christian unity, even though their liberalism has cut them off from any real commitment to the authority of Scripture.

In the twentieth century, the Disciples have continued to demonstrate their interest in Christian unity. They have been participants in the Federal Council of Churches since virtually its very beginning. When the Federal Council changed into the National Council of Churches in 1950, they continued their involvement in these ecumenical concerns. The Disciples were also represented at the Edinburgh Missionary Conference in 1910, which is considered the beginning of the modern ecumenical movement. In 1948 when the Missionary Conference became the World Council of Churches, the Disciples were involved, and continue to be. In fact when Ruth Rouse and Stephen Neill wrote their two-volume history of the Ecumenical Movement, they dedicated it to the Disciples for their long-standing tradition of commitment to ecumenical unity.[64]

In 1960 Eugene Carson Blake of the United Presbyterian Church delivered an address in which he invited major American denominations to participate in a plan of union to establish a church "catholic and reformed." By 1962 the Consultation on Church Union (COCU) was established, with participation from the Presbyterians, Episcopalians, Methodists, United Church of Christ, Disciples of Christ, Evangelical United Brethren (EUB), and three black Methodist denominations. One result of COCU was that the EUB and the Methodists merged in 1969 to form the United Methodists.

In addition, the United Church of Christ and the Disciples of Christ set up preliminary discussions that have continued to look toward possible merger. The UCC and the Disciples are both liberal in theology, and the accepted practice of open membership in Disciples Churches does not see the infant baptism of the UCC as a problem. Discussions between the UCC and the Disciples continue. Although no firm calendar of merger has been established, it is likely that these two groups will ultimately

---

[64]"To the Disciples of Christ Whose untiring ecumenical spirit has once again been manifest in the generous provision of the funds which have made possible the writing and Publication of this History of the Ecumenical Movement." Rouse and Neill, p. v.

merge into a single ecclesiastical body. It is ironic that Alexander
Campbell and the leaders of the Smith-Jones Movement once resented
each other so bitterly, but their spiritual descendants now are courting
denominational merger.

It is obvious that the modern Disciples are continuing to move in liberal and ecumenical directions, but there are significant exceptions within the organized body of the Christian Church (Disciples of Christ). As
mentioned previously, there have been numerous ministers and churches
within the Disciples who have adhered to a conservative theology and
practice. Having become increasingly dissatisfied with the official leadership of the Disciples, some of them formed, about 1985, a group called
Disciple Renewal. These people want to continue a steadfast biblical witness among the Disciples and try to swing the majority of the denomination away from liberalism and back to an acceptance of biblical teaching.
They publish a magazine called *Disciple Renewal*, edited by Kevin Ray
and Richard Bowman, both of central Illinois.

The Disciple Renewal people do not want to leave the Disciples organization. They are not interested in another split; they want to remain as
agents of biblical Christianity within the denomination and strive for
reform from within. In 1987, at the General Assembly in Louisville, they
submitted two proposals that reached the floor of the assembly. One resolution was a condemnation of homosexuality. This was rejected by
majority vote of the Assembly. A second resolution stated that there was
salvation in no other name but the name of Jesus. This resolution was
tabled for further discussion and was assigned to a Commission on
Theology.[65] Two years later the Commission brought their report in a
thirteen-page statement that avoided the real issue.[66] In the floor discussions on the issue, the members of the panel that had prepared the
report affirmed that God does not desire any one to perish;[67] since God
is sovereign, we can expect that all people will be saved, through names
other than that of Jesus.[68]

The leaders of Disciple Renewal were responsible for both of the
disturbing resolutions in 1987, and they have continued to question
the liberal directions of headquarters in Indianapolis. When Michael

---

[65]One feels certain that the apostle Peter, who first made the statement in Acts
4:12, would not think that the statement needed further discussion.

[66]*Report of the Commission on Theology: "Salvation in Jesus Christ"* (Indianapolis:
Council on Christian Unity, Christian Church [Disciples of Christ, 1989]).

[67]The reference is to 2 Peter 3:9.

[68]The floor discussions were taped, and the audio cassettes from this session
bear out this information.

Kinnamon was nominated for the position of general minister and president, to be elected at the 1991 General Assembly, the Renewal people were very disturbed because of Kinnamon's acceptance of homosexuality and his favorable attitude toward the prospect of ordaining homosexual ministers. He needed a two-thirds vote of all delegates, but the conservatives cut him short. Out of 5,623 votes, 3,679 voted for his election, 1,944 against, and 28 abstained. Kinnamon missed election by about 65 votes.[69] Disciple Renewal did not account for all of the 1,944 negative votes, but they were a major voice in his defeat.

Disciple Renewal continues to work for a steadfast witness from within the Disciples organization. Yet many of the Disciple congregations that support Disciple Renewal are also open membership. The Disciple Renewal group of people are an interesting combination of the two key original commitments that began the Restoration Movement. Some of their personnel have spoken at the North American Christian Convention, as the NACC has tried to encourage the biblical orientation of the Renewal folk.

Another significant development that has occurred in the last decade has been the continued meetings of the Restoration Forum. About 1983 Don DeWelt of the Instrumental Christian Churches, and Reuel Lemmon, Noninstrumentalist and editor of *Firm Foundation,* began talking about the possibility of holding some discussions between the two groups. This led in 1984 to a forum held at Ozark Christian College with an invited attendance of about fifty individuals on each side. This initial meeting was billed as a "Unity Forum," which was unfortunate. The label led some people, particularly Noninstrumentalists, to believe the Noninstrumentalists who attended were going to abandon their position and merge with the Instrumentalists. Later meetings have been called the "Restoration Forum," a label that both sides can be comfortable with.

In the first several of these meetings attendance was by invitation only, since many of the Noninstrumentalists did not want some of their more belligerent brothers coming and disrupting the delicate beginnings of harmony and fellowship. Even some of those who attended were there at risk, not wanting the other people back home to know of their involvement. Some who attended were "written up" in brotherhood journals and attacked as apostates, or at least as weak and no longer trustworthy.

---

[69]See the article by C. J. Dull, "Showdown in Tulsa," *Christian Standard*, March 15, 1992, pp. 6-8. See also articles in *Disciple Renewal* on the topic.

There have been eleven such Restoration Forums so far, the latest held in Joplin, Missouri in November, 1993.[70] Normally at each such meeting, an individual from each side speaks on an assigned topic or issue. This stimulates thinking, sharing, and an exchange of views. Both sides have come to learn that they have often misunderstood the position of the other. Yet no one has abdicated his position. Often the topics assigned cut right to the heart of the issues—the use of musical instruments in worship, discussions of the nature of worship, discussion of the principles of biblical hermeneutics. Yet through such discussions, many have come to realize they are brethren in Christ, and this overrides any differences. Friendships have developed, an acceptance of brotherhood and fellowship. There has also come the realization that terminology and custom often are the backbone of the differences, rather than substantial disagreement on principles.

There has also come a growing perception that many of the Noninstrumentalists no longer hold the issue as a test of fellowship. They certainly prefer to worship without the instrument, but many no longer consider its use a sin, particularly among the younger generation of preachers. There is no indication that numerous noninstrumental churches will now move instruments in, but at least there is more of an open attitude of fellowship with other members of the Restoration Movement. Such openness is a healthy forecast for the future.

Another interesting series of developments also began in 1983. A number of individuals in the conservative Christian Churches/Instrumental Churches of Christ thought that the group had stagnated in recent years. They proposed getting a number of representative leaders and thinkers together to suggest ways in which the Restoration Movement could move again. What could be done to stimulate some real life, energy, and vision into the Christian Churches? They planned a meeting in St. Louis in 1984 called "The Open Forum on the Mission of the Church." This has led to a series of annual meetings in the spring to investigate topics of Brotherhood concern. The first meeting was by invitation only, and this aroused the suspicion of numerous others who feared a select group of wheeler-dealers was trying to "take over the brotherhood." Thus the next several meetings featured an open microphone in the center of the floor. This was to be an "open" forum with no hidden agenda and no restrictions on freedom of speech.

---

[70]Many of the addresses given at these Forums have been printed in book form, through College Press in Joplin. This applies specifically to Forums Five through Nine.

The Open Forum in Indianapolis in 1988 focused on controversial topics of Brotherhood disturbance: women's role in the church, biblical inerrancy, and concern for Christian unity. Ironically it was Michael Kinnamon, then at Christian Theological Seminary in Indianapolis, who was invited to speak on ecumenical concerns. Reflecting his ecumenical involvement through the Disciples, he chided the conservative Christians for their ideal of unity about which they had done absolutely nothing. Feeling the justified sting of his remarks, members of the Convening Committee of the Open Forum talked about exploring some attempt at Christian unity. The suggestion arose of talking to the Church of God, Anderson, because their doctrine and practices were so close to those in the mainstream of the Restoration Movement.

Thus the Open Forum in 1989 met in Indianapolis and hosted speakers from the Church of God, Anderson.[71] The Church of God, Anderson, allows full use of women as elders and preachers. They practice the ordinance of footwashing. They observe the Lord's Supper occasionally, although it is not a weekly practice for them. They baptize by immersion, although they do not connect it to the remission of sins. In 1990, the Church of God hosted the Open Forum in Anderson, Indiana, and in 1991, both groups met in Lexington, Kentucky, to continue their discussions and exchanges. In 1993, they met at St. Joseph, Michigan. Both groups have discovered they share an interest in Christian unity, a return to the primitive church, a commitment to biblical authority, local congregational autonomy, and worldwide missions outreach. With all this in common, they continue to explore their differences in the context of Christian fellowship, acceptance, and a growing sense of brotherliness. No one is talking merger or consolidation. Both sides continue to be excited as they explore the future of an expanding sense of Christian unity, whatever form it may take.

In 1992, the Open Forum met again as a limited number of leaders to brainstorm on the future of the Brotherhood. Discussions at this time

---

[71]Because there are about two hundred different groups in the United States that claim identity under the label "Church of God," it is necessary to designate exactly in this regard. The Church of God (Cleveland, Tennessee) is pentecostal; in fact, there are fourteen different pentecostal groups called the Church of God, and five of them have national headquarters in Cleveland, Tennessee. They are splinters off one another. But the Church of God (Anderson, Indiana) is not pentecostal but Wesleyan in background. Daniel S. Warner experienced entire sanctification in 1877, but he was not allowed to develop this preaching in the General Eldership of the Church of God in North America (Winebrennerians). By 1881 he had brought together the beginnings of a movement that became the Church of God (Anderson).

focused on continuing to prepare leaders for global missions outreach, including preparing a curriculum for the colleges to adapt to prepare workers for specific fields. Double Vision (doubling the number of congregations in the movement by the year 2000) was one of the initial outgrowths of the Open Forum back in 1984, and it continues to draw attention to the need for church planting. The 1992 meeting included a discussion of Double Vision plans to provide a resource center for networking funds, personnel, and methodology for church planting and church growth. Discussions continue with the Open Forum Convening Committee as to how they can encourage the Disciple Renewal people without compromising them. A continuing concern for Christian unity stimulated suggestions to continue the discussions with the Church of God, Anderson, as well as branch out and discover other groups to talk with that may provide similar fruit.

Thus, as the Restoration Movement approaches the end of the twentieth century, the original ideals of Christian unity and biblical authority continue to operate as magnets of interest. It is tragic that the Movement itself has splintered into three portions; but within all three portions there are numerous individuals and leaders who desire to fulfill the original dream of Thomas Campbell and B. W. Stone to unite the church on the basis of biblical teaching. Progress is being made, both within the Movement and as it strikes up contact with parallel evangelical groups. The future of the Restoration Movement may still be very exciting.

Chapter 13

A Current Challenge

The thesis of this book is that the Restoration Movement centers on two major concepts—the concern for the unity of all believers, and the concern for the authority of Scripture alone as the basis of Christian teaching and identity. Throughout this work we have followed these two emphases. In the early years, the two usually worked conjointly; unfortunately, in later years, the tendency has normally been for the two to work in isolation, and often in opposition. It has been very easy in the history of the Restoration Movement for a person to take one of the two concerns and work on it to the exclusion of all else. Usually this has created difficulties; often it has resulted in division in the Movement.

Understanding the Issues

We have seen what happens when people consistently place all their emphasis on biblical authority to the exclusion of any concern for unity. The tendency is to create an isolated group that becomes sectarian in its outlook and activity. Much of the Noninstrumentalist movement has fallen into this trap. We have also seen what happens when people consistently place all emphasis on unity, without any concern for biblical standards. The result is the acceptance of denominational structure and ecumenicity. Unity may result, but it is no longer a Christianity that is modeled on New Testament teaching. The Christian Church (Disciples of Christ) fully represents this tendency. Both of these extremes are perversions of the Restoration Movement.

It is easy for the Christian Churches and Churches of Christ to stand in the middle of this polarization and point out the foibles of both

extremes. We can see the narrow-mindedness of the Noninstrumentalists
on our right, and the liberalism of the Disciples on our left. How good it
is to stand in the middle of the road! Unfortunately, however, this viewpoint is too simplistic. The tension between union and biblical authority
is an ongoing dynamic. To understand the tension between the two concerns through history is both illuminating and interesting. But if this is
all we see, then it remains little more than an interesting intellectual clas-
sification. But it is more. The dynamics between unity and biblical
authority are not just useful handles to understand our past; they are
important devices to continue to have a handle on the present.

Currently the Restoration Movement is at a crossroads. Numerous
individuals are viewing the Movement and wondering if it has the ability
to survive the pressures and issues that modern Christianity is facing in
late twentieth century America. Many are abandoning the Movement for
other identities. The tragedy is that many people from within the
Movement are leaving it at the very time when many outside the
Movement are looking for the very ideals that the Movement represents.
The modern failure of the Restoration Movement has been twofold: (1)
we have failed to properly educate our own constituency, and (2) we have
failed to make our plea known to the searching world. In the first
instance, all disclaimers aside, we have often viewed the Movement as a
denomination all to itself. We have expected our people to be loyal to
our identity, rather than loyal to the ideals of the Movement and the
pristine Christianity that it desires. It is no wonder if numerous of our
young people, and many of our dynamic younger preachers, are weary;
they see the Restoration Movement as little more than a complacent
middle class aggregation of fossilized Campbellites. In the second
instance of failure, we have lacked both the knowledge of what our
Movement really stands for as well as the confidence that its ideals are
still applicable and practice-able. As a result, we have dropped the enthusiasm that animated the early pioneers of the movement, an enthusiasm
that led them into confident dialogue with other members of the evangelical community of the nineteenth century. Out of that dialogue came
converts—not converts to Campbellism per se, but converts to a
Movement that envisioned the unity of all Christians upon the simple
basics of New Testament Christianity. Because we have lost that enthusiasm, we have allowed the Restoration Movement to solidify into a philosophy of maintaining the status quo rather than carrying on the ideals of
the Movement itself.

We need to recapture the vision of what the Movement really represents, and this means a new awareness of the twin goals of unity and

biblical authority. If we forget our twin roots, then we have little to say to the modern world. But if we recall what we are, we have a magnificent ministry to the Christian world. Beyond that, we still have the primary ministry of evangelizing the lost. We must never forget that evangelism is the basic need of our generation. But evangelism is always restricted when the Christian message is clothed in division, sectarian bitterness, or suspicion. To facilitate evangelism, we need a church that is restored in its unity and in its commitment to biblical authority.

Thus we need to keep in mind the twin roots of the Movement to prevent the continuing polarization and resplintering the Movement has already experienced in tragic proportions. There are numerous issues that continue to bedevil the peace of our churches. Normally our churches tend to react in one of two ways—ways that have become deeply grooved in our automatic responses to the last century.

On the one hand, when a controversial issue comes up, one group insists that the issue violates a principle of Scripture. To tolerate the aberration means to abandon our commitment to biblical authority. Therefore, they say, we must fight the innovation and maintain biblical purity. All those who practice, accept, or tolerate the innovation must be marked as those unworthy of our fellowship. This response is not new, as previous chapters have indicated.

On the other hand, many of the same issues are greeted by people who feel there is no sacrifice of biblical principle involved. The issue is a matter of opinion or perspective. Therefore, to make the issue a test of fellowship is not only foolish, but also contrary to the principles of the Movement. Instead, we must maintain our Movement's commitment to Christian unity and embrace people on both sides of the issue as Christian brothers and sisters. We must not, they say, sacrifice our unity on the altar of sectarian divisiveness. This response is not new either, as previous chapters have indicated.

Where, then, does this place the Restoration Movement? At a crossroads. How we face these modern issues will determine our future. We can face these issues with a narrow, defensive attitude of maintaining our status quo, or we can face the issues with a nonchalant attitude of inclusiveness. Both responses are dangerous and counterproductive. What we need is that proper balance of unity and biblical authority that has marked the Movement in its best light since its beginnings. Properly applied, these principles will save the current Movement from disaster as well as open a new scope of ministry to the evangelical community that is searching for a biblical faith without sectarianism.

All this is easily said, but often difficult to implement. It is easy for us to stand from the modern perspective and gauge what should have been done on former issues—issues that are useful to us now only as historical reference points. But the issues we face are much more alive, and therefore the proper response is much more elusive. Where exactly *is* that proper balance between unity and biblical authority? We do not want to go too far one way or the other, but finding that difficult middle ground is often no easy matter. Still, we must make up our mind that we will avoid both the Scylla of sectarianism as well as the Charybdis of ecumenical compromise. What are the issues we face? I suggest a few.

Role of Women in the Church

One issue that has rocked the church for the past few decades, and one that will undoubtedly continue to challenge the church for some decades into the future, is the role of women in the church. On the one hand are the traditionalists who contend that women are to be silent and subservient to men; that God has placed church leadership and authority exclusively in the hands of men. On the other hand are the women's liberationists who believe that such views are not only old-fashioned, but virtually un-Christian; they contend that women are equal to men and ought to have equal access and appointment to all church positions and offices.

How is the Christian Church to respond to this difficulty? At the core of the dispute is the tension between unity and biblical authority. The traditionalists argue that the liberationists are undermining the teaching of Scripture; they are false teachers, and unless they repent, they should be cut off from the circle of true Christians. Some liberationists are willing to break fellowship with the traditionalists because of the latter's narrow-mindedness against the *true* import of biblical Christianity. In contrast to these extremes, but more normative to most liberationists, are those who urge the cause of unity. The New Testament, they say, reflects some of the male chauvinism of the first century and therefore must be adjusted to reinforce the more mature modern ideals of sexual egalitarianism. Thus we have some people pushing biblical authority at the expense of unity, while others push unity at the expense of biblical authority.

Both sides must look at the real issue very closely and objectively. If in fact the liberationists are willing to sacrifice the integrity of biblical teaching, they must be marked as apostate and rejected. But the issue is probably not that simple—just as it is not that simple for the traditionalist. True, the traditionalist can quote Scripture for his position: 1 Timothy 2:12 ("I do not permit a woman to teach or to have authority over a man;

she must be silent"); Ephesians 5:24 ("As the church submits to Christ, so also wives should submit to their husbands in everything"); and 1 Corinthians 14:34 ("Women should remain silent in the churches. They are not allowed to speak, but must be in submission"). Yet people on the other side of the issue also quote Scripture, namely Galatians 3:28 ("There is neither Jew nor Greek, slave nor free, male nor female, for you are all one in Christ Jesus").

When both sides quote Scripture, it is not a matter of biblical authority versus unity. More properly it is a question of the *interpretation* of that biblical authority. Often two different passages of Scripture can be made to appear contradictory. But if we accept the inspiration of Scripture, it is axiomatic then that God does not lie and his Word is not self-contradictory. If two Scriptural passages seem to contradict, it may be necessary to make one of the passages the primary principle and understand the other as an exception because of certain circumstances. The problem then is to determine which passage is the primary principle, and which reflects the nuances of unusual circumstances.

For instance, Acts 2:38 states that we are to repent, be baptized, and then receive the gift of the Holy Spirit. Then in Acts 8 we are told the Samaritans had been baptized but had not received the Holy Spirit. Rather than see the two passages as contradictory, it is helpful to understand that different gifts of the Holy Spirit are referred to here. A resolution of the problem is to see the Acts 2 passage as referring to the Spirit's indwelling presence and the Acts 8 passage as referring to miracle-working ability.

The issue of properly understanding biblical teaching is further complicated by the necessity of trying to sift the eternal teachings of Scripture out of the temporary cultural forms of first-century Christianity. A parallel situation can be seen in the use of the holy kiss and foot washing in the first century. In five different passages of Scripture the apostles Paul and Peter command Christians to greet one another with a holy kiss (Romans 16:16, 1 Corinthians 16:20, 2 Corinthians 13:12, 1 Thessalonians 5:26, and 1 Peter 5:14). Yet modern Christians are quite willing to dismiss this as a first-century custom not binding on twentieth-century culture. J. B. Phillips even translates the phrase, "a hearty handshake." To accuse modern Christians of not believing in the authority of Scripture because they do not practice the holy kiss is to beg the question. Furthermore, most modern Christians do not practice foot washing, in spite of the explicit command of Christ (John 13:14). Most Christians today acknowledge these two references as dealing with first-century culture.

What then are we to make of the Scriptural passages quoted by the traditionalists? There is no doubt what these passages mean. But the question is one of interpretation. Given the male-dominated society of the first century, are these Scriptural references given simply to accommodate Christians to a lifestyle that will not offend the first century? Or did Paul and Peter (and thus God, using the Holy Spirit to speak through these two men) intend that these commands be literally implemented by all cultures and societies?

It will not do to glibly say, "The Bible says it, I believe it." We obviously do not apply that same glib reasoning to the holy kiss and foot washing. Thus, the issue calls for serious Bible study. To what extent are the Scriptural words influenced by human culture and therefore of temporary import only? Yet serious Bible study will also point out that in the very context where Paul discusses women's role, he also discusses creation and the Fall. In 1 Corinthians 11:8-9 Paul concludes that man was not created for woman, but woman was created for man. In 1 Timothy 2:13-14 he states that Adam was formed first, not Eve, but it was Eve who was deceived in the temptation. Thus the issue becomes more complex. In light of the possible influences of first-century society, as well as the apparent connection between women's role and Creation/Fall, what *is* the proper biblical teaching on the role of women in the church, the home, and the society?

Problems in Application

Further to the point, how does this issue affect the application of the twin principles of the Restoration Movement? Does this issue represent a sufficiently important point of biblical teaching that those who do not accept it are to be cut off as apostate, ejected from the fellowship of true Christians? Or can the issue be treated as a matter of opinion, with Christian unity tolerating both positions, without compromising our commitment to biblical authority? This is the key point. Only serious Bible study and a careful application of the total biblical teaching can point to a resolution. Simplistic, glib answers will not suffice, on either side.

Charismatics

Another issue that represents a continuing difficulty for modern Christians is the question of those who advocate modern charismatic gifts, or, more properly, speaking in tongues. At the core of the issue is the same concern about the tension between unity and biblical authority.

Some charismatics believe their position is Scriptural, and any who resist that position are fighting against the teaching of Scripture. Yet many noncharismatics believe the charismatic position is wrong, that those who advocate it are supporting false teaching, and that the position itself represents an undermining of biblical authority. Both groups have virtually no fellowship with each other. There are also the unionists, either charismatic or noncharismatic, who believe that the continuance of Christian unity is more important than uniformity in the practice. Again, what is the church to do in this situation? Can the church tolerate differences over this issue, or must disfellowshipping occur?

Some noncharismatics are strong in insisting that the charismatic gifts ceased in the first century, that modern tongues speaking cannot be a valid spiritual experience (some even suggest it is satanic in origin), and that therefore the charismatics cannot be tolerated. First Corinthians 13:8-10 is often used to conclude that the compilation of the New Testament (the "perfect") precludes the possibility of valid speaking in tongues (the "imperfect"). The charismatics who see their experience as normative insist that one must be able to speak in tongues in order to be a mature Christian. One must search for the gift, seek out the gift, and pray for the gift of tongues. Again, serious Bible study is necessary on this issue.

The deductive argument that tongues have ceased because the apostles are dead is not a convincing argument. However, there is no doubt that most charismatics do not abide by the guidelines that Paul laid down in 1 Corinthians 14—that no tongues speaking should occur without proper interpretation, that all should be done to the edification of the body, and that tongues and prophesying are conducted in the presence of an unbeliever only for the purpose of bringing him to a saving knowledge of Christ, not for sensationalism or overawing him. Otherwise, Paul states, the unbeliever will simply dismiss the Christians by saying, "You are out of your mind" (1 Corinthians 14:23).

Obviously, the proper use of tongues was an occasion of controversy and disturbance within the Corinthian church. But it was not a cause of division. Paul's whole point in 1 Corinthians 12 was to emphasize the unity of the body, despite the variety of gifts. Today some doubt whether these gifts are even available, but there is still no reason to sunder the fellowship of the church on the topic. Regardless of one's presuppositions about tongues, careful Bible study will show no division in the New Testament churches over this issue. As long as there is no undermining of biblical teaching, unity over the question of charismatic tongues can prevail.

Inerrancy

The current dispute over inerrancy may be the most significant controversy with respect to the future of the Restoration Movement. Again, the dispute represents at its core the key concerns of the Movement in terms of biblical authority and Christian unity.

Many in the Movement today are advocating a position of biblical inerrancy. They insist that anything less than this is an undermining of biblical authority. If we admit that the Bible has errors, they contend, then the entire structure of biblical teaching is undermined, leaving open the opportunity to deny or dismiss any biblical instruction whatsoever. Those on the other side, sometimes called "limited inerrancy," deny this. They point out that the Bible does not include the word "inerrant." They argue that to make a term of human origin a symbol of faithfulness to Scripture is to erect a creed in much the same way as the Westminster and Philadelphia Confessions of Faith were unacceptable in the days of Campbell and Stone. They refuse to allow such a human term to become a test of fellowship.

Further than this, many who deny the "inerrancy" of Scripture are in favor of referring to the Bible as "infallible." The distinction, they maintain, is that "inerrancy" means the Bible is without any mistake in chronology, historical reference, geography, or any other area. This, they say, is going too far based on the evidence currently available. Instead, the Bible is infallible, that is, its teaching in the area of morals and salvation is sufficient for us to know God's will and find salvation in Christ. The Bible thus performs God's intended purpose in informing us of the way to salvation; but it was never God's purpose to write a treatise on scientific or historical accuracy.

It is important to note that neither group wants to disparage biblical authority. Both defend it, but they define it in different ways. The "anti-inerrant" group has a smaller corpus of Bible to defend than the "inerrant" people. One side contends that mistakes in arithmetic and history do not compromise the value of the Bible as God's Word to us; the other side says they do. The inerrantists argue that if the Bible is in error in some references, how can we know that it faithfully speaks God's Word to us in the areas of religious and ethical instruction? The "anti-inerrantists" claim that the inerrantists are dividing the body of Christ over a human opinion. The other side contends that it is not human opinion that is the issue, but the integrity of the Bible itself. They claim it is the "anti-inerrantists" who are erecting a human opinion and making it divisive.

Thus both groups contend for their position, each convinced that its position is closer to the ideal of the Restoration Movement than the other. This whole dispute has a remarkably familiar cast to it, for it is similar in many ways to the dispute over liberalism that wracked the Movement early in the century. The liberals contended they still adhered to the Bible, although there is no doubt that the Bible meant something different to them than it did to the conservatives, and certainly something different from what it meant to the nineteenth-century leaders of the Movement. The conservatives saw liberalism as a body of teaching that basically undermined biblical teaching; they were adamant in resisting it. The liberals argued that the conservatives (whom they liked to identify as "fundamentalists") were erecting an unbiblical hermeneutic into a test of fellowship and thus making it a barrier to unity. Yet the conservatives countered that it was the liberals who were erecting their opinions into issues that would break the unity of the Movement because it meant a sacrificing of biblical authority. The same arguments are currently being made over the inerrancy dispute.

The question then is, can inerrancy be considered a matter of opinion in order to keep the unity of the faith, or does inerrancy stand so close to the commitment to biblical authority that it must be maintained, even at the cost of unity, if necessary? It is interesting to observe, however, that the inerrantists have never stated that inerrancy is to become a test of fellowship or a test of church membership. They only wonder if inerrancy ought to be a factor in considering leadership and financial support within the Movement. The inerrantists argue that "limited inerrancy" is an undermining of biblical authority; therefore they who advocate it are really taking a stand against the authority of the Bible. Should such people be respected as brotherhood leaders? Should schools that include such persons on their teaching faculty be supported by churches of the Movement that are still committed to biblical authority? Is the denial of inerrancy the beginning of a whole new wave of liberalism painfully similar to the one experienced early in this century? Can biblical inerrancy be waived in the name of Christian unity, or is this issue so important that no compromise can be tolerated? The issue represents a significant test of the validity of the Restoration Movement with its twin goals, so apparently irreconcilable here. How one sees the issue determines his response.

Baptism

To anyone familiar with the history of the Christian Churches/Churches of Christ, it may seem incongruous that baptism would be a source of controversy in the Movement. Yet it certainly is. Earlier in this century, the Movement experienced the severe contest epitomized in the phrase "open membership." The liberals were willing to waive baptism by immersion for those who were transferring from churches (denominations) that did not have the practice. The conservatives saw this as a lapse in respect to biblical authority, and the battle was fiercely fought for a half century. For the independent Christian Churches that rejected open membership, baptism was a *sine qua non.*

But baptism as an issue has come up again. Now it is not so much the practice of immersion as the theology of baptism and its place in the process of salvation. The Restoration tradition has always seen baptism as being "for the purpose of remission of sins." This emerged in Campbell's debates with Presbyterians, and it was also one of the points of friction between himself and the Baptists. The textual evidence for this position is weighty: Acts 2:38, Acts 22:16, 1 Peter 3:21, and others. This position has long been one of the cherished marks of identity of the Movement.

This position was held so adamantly that Campbell was even charged with being a water regenerationist—it was the water that saved. As we mentioned earlier in our discussion of the Lunenburg Letter, there were certainly people within the Movement at the time who placed so much emphasis on immersion as to make it appear to be the be-all and end-all of Christianity. In calm moments, of course, virtually no one asserts that a ritualistic dunking in water grants salvation. But discussions on baptism rarely remain calm for very long. As a result, baptism has become a symbol: for intelligent reading of the Scriptures, for loyalty to the traditions of the early pioneers, for faithfulness to the authority of Scripture and the teaching of Christ himself. In this charged atmosphere, people often make vehement statements that have unfortunate nuances. Many people even within the Movement have recognized that baptism has sometimes been turned into a magical sacrament apart from faith, trust, and general obedience.

In addition, there is conflict with the rest of the evangelical Christian community. More and more groups are accepting the practice of baptism by immersion. These same people, however, believe that Christians are saved by faith, not by their works. When they hear the traditional presentation on baptism by Christian Churches, it sounds legalistic and mechanical. They take it as a denial of the necessity of a person having faith in Christ in order to be saved. Unfortunately, this is not an either/or situation, though it is often perceived in that way.

People outside the movement see us as having this wooden, legalistic view on baptism, and many people even within the Movement have been persuaded of the same. As a result, many ministers within the Movement seem to be abandoning the traditional understanding of baptism as an element in the process of salvation. They are more comfortable with baptism as a matter of obedience and a testimony of one's faith, but not "for remission of sins." Since this is so similar to the traditional Baptist position, we have an abundance of snide comments about "Baptist preachers in Christian church pulpits."

Ministers of this persuasion see themselves as being more faithful to the spirit of the gospel of Christ than their more traditional Christian Church brethren who emphasize the *purpose* of baptism. Again, it is not a matter of denying biblical authority, but of understanding biblical teaching in its entire context. So again we have conflict over defining the limits of biblical authority and unity. Many of the more traditional brethren see the others as "soft" on baptism and therefore undermining the authority of the Bible because they do not teach or apply the actual New Testament teaching on the purpose of baptism. They conclude that such people ought to be rejected from the brotherhood, not allowed to speak at the North American Christian Convention or at major conferences, nor lauded from pulpit, press, or classroom.

The other side, of course, sees the traditionalists as being narrow-minded legalists who have a mechanical view of salvation that focuses on the *process* rather than on the *result*. Some of them welcome rejection as an indication that the mainline of the Restoration Movement has in fact become sectarian and ought to be abandoned. Others resist the rejection and contend they are faithful both to the Restoration Movement and to the authority of the Scripture and the Christ who provided it. So the issue comes down to a dispute between unity and biblical authority. Can those who de-emphasize the purpose of baptism be included in the fellowship? Does the adjustment in this new practice represent such an undercutting of biblical authority that separation is the better course? This is the issue—and it will be a long time in finding resolution.

Participation in Evangelical Activities

The other issues discussed up to this point may or may not be live issues for numerous ministers and churches. Because of geography, culture, or strong personalities, questions on these issues may never come to the surface. But every minister, every church faces the question of how it will interact with other evangelical congregations in its area. These questions may focus on token issues of insignificant import, or they may focus on larger questions of policy and community perception.

Should a church of the Restoration Movement participate with other churches (Methodist, Nazarene, Presbyterian, Baptist, Church of God, Roman Catholic, etc.) in such activities as community Good Friday services? What about community VBS programs? How about participation in Billy Graham crusades? Should a church allow a minister from an evangelical Protestant church to assist in a wedding ceremony? What about a Catholic priest assisting in a wedding in a Christian Church? Should ministers be involved in interdenominational ministerial associations?

These are not always simple questions. Again, at the core of the problem is the struggle to find the comfortable median point within the tension produced by the polarizing inclinations toward Christian unity and adherence to biblical authority. Granted that various evangelical churches are "wrong" on a number of points of doctrine and practice. Some of them are silent where the Bible speaks; others speak authoritatively where the Bible is silent. What should be the response of Christian Church ministers to such people?

One is to affirm that such groups have failed to follow the teachings of Scripture, or at least they have added other teaching to the Bible and therefore have compromised the integrity of biblical teaching. As a result, such people ought not to be identified as Christians, and we can have no fellowship with them in things religious. We may live in the same town as they do as American citizens, but we can do nothing in common with them in the name of worship or specifically religious activity. They are outside the bounds of the Bible, and therefore outside the bounds of Christian unity. To be faithful to the ideals of the Restoration Movement, we must stand apart as Christians only.

Yet there are impressive arguments on the other side as well. The more unity-minded brethren point out that the Restoration Movement has always claimed, "We are not the only Christians, but we are Christians only." Therefore, since other people are Christians, we need to cooperate with them in the name of Christian unity. In addition, they claim, if we isolate ourselves from all suspected religious practitioners, we will have no opportunity to influence them with the principles of the Movement and can never bring such people to a fuller knowledge of biblical teaching and the inclusiveness of Christian fellowship.

The major need, of course, is to find the area where we can draw the lines. How much participation can we engage in without compromising our stand on the Bible as sole authority? If we participate with other local churches in such community activities, isn't that saying that we don't care what they believe, because we are all Christians anyway? How can we sponsor Billy Graham's preaching when he so patently leaves out a major part of the gospel plan of salvation, namely baptism by immersion for remission of sins? If we participate openly with other churches, will our members get the impression that it doesn't matter what they believe; all churches are essentially alike and the differences are insignificant? How far can we go in the name of Christian unity without sacrificing our ideal of being Bible people?

Yet this also raises the basic question of what we mean when we talk about Christian unity. Unity with whom? on what basis? in what sense? Of course, we are not talking about corporate mergers with denominational bodies. Nor are we talking about joining a Christian Church to a denominational congregation. But what *do* we mean when we talk about Christian unity? Initially Thomas Campbell saw denominational divisions as a horrid evil; if we cooperate with denominational divisions in community joint services, isn't that accepting and indeed "blessing" those same denominational divisions? At stake is the very crucial question of how one blends these twin concerns without seeming to lean too far one way or the other.

This question is very much to the fore in the dialogue continuing with the Church of God, Anderson. Some members of Christian Churches have criticized the discussions because the Church of God uses women ministers, does not baptize for remission of sins, and does not observe the Lord's Supper weekly. Therefore, they conclude, these people are not following New Testament teaching, and if we meet with them as equals, then we are obviously soft on biblical teaching and are compromising the integrity of Scripture. Even to use the label "Christian unity" in our dialogue with the Church of God unacceptably suggests we are going to merge with them and thus "sell out" traditional Restoration Movement positions. The same questions—or perhaps even worse ones—will apply if dialogue begins with such other groups as the Nazarenes, Free Will Baptists, or some others. The crucial question here is whether we can dialogue with other evangelical groups without compromising our adherence to Scripture. Many think we can; others think we cannot.

A further consideration down the same road is the fine line between supporting community charities and denominational initiative. Assume the local Presbyterian church is sponsoring a Boy Scout troop, and the scouts are raising funds through a paper drive. They knock on your door and ask for your old papers. If you give, what are the implications of your material support to what is manifestly an arm of the Presbyterian church? Have you compromised your biblical loyalty? Or have you expressed a spirit of Christian charity that rises above sectarian distinctions? Assume that the time is early December and when you exit from the grocery store, there is the Salvation Army collecting Christmas donations. If you contribute, are you endorsing their faith-only soteriology? Or is your gift a matter of aiding those who are less fortunate during the Christmas season? Again, where do you draw the line? Is the issue of biblical teaching sufficient to justify refusing support in such cases? Or is the charitable support sufficiently important for Christian witness that the secondary aspect of theological error can be dismissed? Answers to these kind of questions are rarely black-and-white in their determination.

Project for the Future

The concern for Christian unity has been one of the driving forces behind and within the Restoration Movement ever since its founding. In realistic terms, how is that to be applied to the Movement in the present and the future? The entire history of the Movement has wrestled with the matter of implementation and priorities. Some groups within the movement have insisted that until the denominations are willing to accept the pattern of New Testament order, there can be no outreach to them in the name of Christian unity. As we have seen, the tendency of this is sectarianism. Yet to adopt full Christian unity without any commitment to biblical authority is self-defeating and leads only to ecumenical compromise. Therefore, it is not a matter of which principle to implement first. It is a matter of implementing a joint project. If we try to implement one ideal first before making any progress on the other, the Restoration Movement will never restore anything.

But working on the two ideals jointly has led to the problems and questions of the previous pages. How can we do both without jeopardizing or abandoning one or the other? The question is a matter of degree rather than exclusion. We must avoid being too narrow in the area of biblical authority while at the same time we avoid being too open in the area of Christian unity. Perhaps we can say that the more a group reflects proper biblical teaching, the more we can be united with them in Christian activity. This sliding scale thus avoids the problem of clear-cut yes-and-no answers. If people adamantly reject all that the Bible teaches, then obviously there is no area of Christian activity in which we can share. That is why we have no desire to initiate dialogue on Christian unity with denominations of liberal persuasion. If they do not accept the inspiration of Scripture (and virtually by simple definition the liberals do not), then obviously we do not have enough in common with them to engage in serious dialogue. But throughout this context, we are not talking about dialogue with liberals—we are talking about discussions with groups that accept the inspiration and authority of Scripture. The closer people stand to Bible teaching, the more we have in common with them.

One of the problems many of our churches and ministers face is that they don't even know how much we have in common with so many groups in the evangelical community. What separates our churches from the Nazarenes, the Open Bible churches, the Churches of God, and various other independent congregations? Can we honestly plead that we are interested in Christian union if we have made no overtures to conservative churches in our own community to find out how much we have in common? It may be that for many such groups, our only difference is the name over the church door and a few optional practices. Is this sufficient to stand in the way of mutual Christian fellowshipping, perhaps even sharing worship services, as on a Sunday evening?

What is the attitude the communities in general have toward our churches? Do other churches know of our commitment to Christian unity? Or do they simply believe that the Christian Churches are a bunch of self-righteous people who believe they are the only ones going to heaven? Do they see us as a closed, sectarian group? If so, why? Have we earned such a reputation in that community? If not, what can we do to show that this is not a true picture of our congregations and our fellowship as a whole? The other churches in the community undoubtedly know we practice baptism by immersion, but why do they know this and not other things? Have we preached Christian unity as much as we have preached baptism? Could we present the basic position of our churches in such a way that would elicit interest and acceptance by other churches? Perhaps our efforts toward Christian union have been so minimal because we have been "hearers" of this part of the plea, but not "doers." What would it take in your community for the Christian Church/Church of Christ to become known as a congregation that is interested in Christian unity on the basis of the Bible? Is your church's reputation such in the community that people would not believe you are interested in union on the Bible? What would it take to change your church's reputation? Are you willing to do that? Would you be willing to sacrifice your congregation's identity, perhaps even your building, for the cause of Christian unity in your community? Would people think you sincere if you approached them in the name of Christian union? Or would they only think this was some sort of a gimmick to "con" people into "joining" our churches? These are not easy questions; the answers aren't easy either. But it may represent the kind of thinking and planning we will have to do to implement the concern of the Restoration Movement for Christian union.

In the name of the Restoration Movement, how sacred is the identity of a separate fellowship known as the Christian Churches/Churches of Christ? Would we be willing to have our fellowship go out of existence if it could advance the cause of Christ? The Stone Movement began the *Last Will and Testament of the Springfield Presbytery* with the statement, "We will that this body die, be dissolved, and sink into union with the body of Christ at large." If our identity as "Campbellites," or even as "Christian Churches," has become a barrier to the unity we seek, are we willing that the Restoration Movement die, be dissolved, and sink into union with the body of Christ at large? Or is our love for the Movement and its visible institutional embodiment greater than our love for the unity of Christ's church, His body?

What will it take to bring about a greater measure of unity among Bible-believing people without sacrificing our obedience to Scripture? No one wants to abandon Bible teaching or compromise biblical authority. But have we been so adamant on one part of the Restoration Plea that we have forfeited the other part? Again, where can we draw the line in the tension between the polar attraction of Christian union against biblical authority?

I would suggest that there are two keys to be kept constantly in mind as we analyze our attitudes and responses to the conservative evangelical Christian world. We have a basis for Christian union with all people who will accept (1) the authority of Scripture, and (2) the lordship of Christ. The more they accept these, the more we have in common with them and are already in Christian unity in mind and heart, and perhaps also in action. If people do not accept the authority of Christ and His Word, then it will be difficult if not impossible to have much to do with them in the name of Christian activity. Again, that is why involvement with theological liberals is not even considered here. The Lordship of Christ and the authority of His Word is foundational. If we and other groups have this in common, we have a basis to build upon. Now it may be that other people say they accept the authority of Scripture, but then add that they don't see it as teaching baptism by immersion for the remission of sins, or weekly communion, or the organization of the church under elders and deacons, or any of a number of things. But if they accept the authority of Scripture, at least we have a common base of authority and from there it is only a matter of patient and loving teaching. It may take a great deal of teaching and a long time. But unity on the authority can bring about unity in faith and practice. This is what our forefathers believed many generations ago.

So then, the Restoration Movement stands at a crossroads. How do we understand our basic position? Are we interested in biblical authority? Are we interested in Christian union? Do we see the two as antithetical, or can the two be held in harmonious tension? What are we willing to do to see the Restoration Movement accomplish its long-term goals—not the erection of an identifiable fellowship, but the unity of the world according to the prayer of Jesus as recorded in John 17: that we may be one that the world may be won. This is our project for the future.

Bibliography

Ahlstrom, Sydney E. *A Religious History of the American People.* New Haven: Yale University Press, 1972.

Ames, Van Meter (ed.). *Beyond Theology: The Autobiography of Edward Scribner Ames.* Chicago: The University of Chicago Press, 1959.

_____, (ed.). *Prayers and Meditations of Edward Scribner Ames.* Chicago: Disciples Divinity House of the University of Chicago, 1970.

Andrews, Edward Deming. *The People Called Shakers.* New York: Dover Publications, Inc., 1963.

Averill, Lloyd J. *American Theology in the Liberal Tradition.* Philadelphia: The Westminster Press, 1967.

Bailey, Kenneth K. *Southern White Protestantism in the Twentieth Century.* New York: Harper & Row, Publishers, 1964.

Baxter, William. *Life of Elder Walter Scott.* Nashville: Gospel Advocate Company, n.d.

_____. *Pea Ridge and Prairie Grove: or, Scenes and Incidents of the War in Arkansas.* Cincinnati: Poe and Hitchcock, 1866.

Beazley, George G., Jr. (ed.). *The Christian Church (Disciples of Christ): An Interpretative Examination in the Cultural Context.* n.p.: The Bethany Press, 1973.

Blakemore, Wm. Barnett. *Quest for Intelligence in Ministry: The Story of the First Seventy Years of Disciples Divinity House of the University of Chicago.* Chicago: The Disciples Divinity House of the University of Chicago, 1970.

_____, (ed.) *The Renewal of Church: The Panel of Scholars Reports.* 3 vols. St. Louis: The Bethany Press, 1963.

Bower, William Clayton. *Through the Years: Personal Memoirs.* Lexington, Kentucky: Transylvania College Press, 1957.

_____ and Roy G. Ross (eds.). *The Disciples and Religious Education*. St. Louis: Christian Board of Publication, 1936.

Brodie, Fawn. *No Man Knows My History: The Life of Joseph Smith the Mormon Prophet*. New York: Alfred P. Knopf, 1945.

Buckley, James M. *A History of Methodism in the United States*. New York: Harper & Brothers, Publishers, 1898.

Cairns, Earle E. *Christianity Through the Centuries: A History of the Christian Church*. Revised and Enlarged Edition. Grand Rapids: Zondervan Publishing House, 1981.

Campbell, Alexander. *Memoirs of Thomas Campbell*. Cincinnati: H. S. Bosworth, 1861.

_____. *Debate on Christian Baptism Between Mr. John A. Walker, A Minister of the Secession, and Alexander Campbell*. Second Edition Enlarged. Pittsburgh: Eichbaum and Johnston, 1822.

_____. *A Public Debate on Christian Baptism, Between the Rev. W. L. Maccalla, a Presbyterian Teacher, and Alexander Campbell*. London: Simpkin and Marshall, 1842.

_____. *A Debate Between Rev. A. Campbell and Rev. N. L. Rice, on the Action, Subject, Design and Administrator of Christian Baptism*. Lexington, Kentucky: A. T. Skillman and Son, 1844.

Campbell, Selina Huntington. *Home Life and Reminiscences of Alexander Campbell*. St. Louis: John Burns, Publishers, 1882.

Campbell, Thomas. *Declaration and Address*. Lincoln, Illinois: College & Seminary Press, n.d.

Cartwright, Peter. *Autobiography of Peter Cartwright*. New York: Abingdon Press, 1956.

Cauthen, Kenneth. *The Impact of American Religious Liberalism*. New York: Harper & Row, Publishers, 1962.

Centennial Convention Report: One Hundredth Anniversary of the Disciples of Christ, Pittsburgh, October 11-19, 1909. Cincinnati: The Standard Publishing Company, 1909.

Cochran, Louis. *The Fool of God: A Novel Based Upon the Life of Alexander Campbell*. New York: Duell, Sloan and Pearce, 1958.

Conkin, Paul. *Cane Ridge: America's Pentecost*. Madison: The University of Wisconsin Press, 1990.

Davidson, Robert. *History of the Presbyterian Church in the State of Kentucky*. New York: Robert Carter, 1847.

Davis, M. M. *How the Disciples Began and Grew: A Short History of the Christian Church*. Cincinnati: The Standard Publishing Company, 1915.

_____. *The Restoration Movement of the Nineteenth Century*. Cincinnati: The Standard Publishing Company, 1913.

DeGroot, A. T. *Church of Christ Number Two*. Birmingham, England: Published by the Author, 1956.

_____. *New Possibilities for Disciples and Independents*. St. Louis: The Bethany Press, 1963.

Donan, P. *Memoir of Jacob Creath, Jr*. Indianapolis: Religious Book Service, n.d.

Dowling, Enos E. *An Analysis and Index of the Christian Magazine, 1848-1853*. Lincoln, Illinois: Lincoln Bible Institute Press, 1958.

_____. *The Restoration Movement*. Cincinnati: The Standard Publishing Company, 1964.

Dunnavant, Anthony L. (ed.) *Cane Ridge in Context: Perspectives on Barton W. Stone and the Revival*. Nashville: Disciples of Christ Historical Society, 1992.

Filbeck, David. *The First Fifty Years: A Brief History of the Direct-Support Missionary Movement*. Joplin, Missouri: College Press Publishing Company, 1980.

Fitch, Alger Morton, Jr. *Alexander Campbell: Preacher of Reform and Reformer of Preaching*. Joplin, Missouri: College Press Publishing Company, 1988.

Fletcher, David W. (ed.). *Baptism and the Remission of Sins: An Historical Perspective*. Joplin, Missouri: College Press Publishing Company, 1990.

Fortune, Alonzo Willard. *Adventuring with Disciple Pioneers*. St. Louis: The Bethany Press, 1942.

_____. *The Disciples in Kentucky*. n.p.: The Christian Churches in Kentucky, 1932.

Franklin, Joseph and J. A. Headington. *The Life and Times of Benjamin Franklin*. St. Louis: John Burns, Publishers, 1879.

Garrett, Leroy. *The Stone-Campbell Movement: An Anecdotal History of Three Churches*. Joplin, Missouri: College Press Publishing Company, 1981.

Garrison, James Harvey. *Memories and Experiences: A Brief Story of a Long Life*. St. Louis: Christian Board of Publication, 1926.

_____, (ed.). *The Old Faith Restated: Being a Restatement, by Representative Men, of the Fundamental Truths and Essential Doctrines of Christianity as Held and Advocated by the Disciples of Christ in the Light of Experience and of Biblical Research*. St. Louis: Christian Publishing Company, 1891.

_____, (ed.). *The Reformation of the Nineteenth Century*. St. Louis: Christian Publishing Company, 1901.

_____. *The Story of a Century.* St. Louis: Christian Publishing Company, 1909.

Garrison, Winfred Ernest. *An American Religious Movement: A Brief History of the Disciples of Christ.* St. Louis: Christian Board of Publication, 1945.

_____. *Religion Follows the Frontier: A History of the Disciples of Christ.* (New York: Harper & Row, Publishers, 1931.

_____. *Variations on a Theme: "God Saw That It Was Good."* St. Louis: The Bethany Press, 1964.

_____, (ed.). *Faith of the Free.* Chicago: Willett, Clark & Company, 1940.

Garrison, W. E. and Alfred T. DeGroot. *The Disciples of Christ: A History.* Revised Edition. St. Louis: The Bethany Press, 1958.

Gates, Errett. *The Disciples of Christ.* New York: The Baker & Taylor Co., 1905.

_____. *The Early History of Relation and Separation of Baptists and Disciples.* Chicago: The Christian Century Company, 1904.

Gerrard, William A., III. *A Biographical Study of Walter Scott: American Frotier Evangelist.* Joplin, Missouri: College Press Publishing Company, 1992.

Goodspeed, Thomas Wakefield. *William Rainey Harper: First President of the University of Chicago.* Chicago: The University of Chicago Press, 1928.

Gresham, Charles (ed.). *The Second Consultation on Internal Unity.* Oklahoma City: n.p., n.d.

Grob, Gerald N. and Robert N. Beck (eds.). *American Ideas: Source Readings in the Intellectual History of the United States.* 2 vols. New York: The Free Press, 1963.

Hailey, Homer. *Attitudes and Consequences in the Restoration Movement.* Second Edition. Rosemead, California: The Old Paths Book Club, 1952.

Haley, J. J. *Debates That Made History: The Story of Alexander Campbell's Debates with Rev. John Walker, Rev. W. L. McCalla, Mr. Robert Owens, Bishop Purcell, and Rev. Nathan L. Rice.* n.p., n.p., 1920.

_____. *Makers and Molders of the Restoration Movement: A Study of Leading Men Among the Disciples of Christ.* St. Louis: Christian Board of Publication, 1914.

Hall, Colby D. *Rice Haggard: The American Evangelist Who Revived the Name Christian.* Fort Worth: University Christian Church, 1957.

Hanna, William Herbert. *Thomas Campbell: Seceder and Christian Union Advocate.* Cincinnati: The Standard Publishing Company, 1935.

Harrell, David Edwin, Jr. *A Social History of the Disciples of Christ, vol. 1, Quest for a Christian America: The Disciples of Christ and American Society to 1866.* Nashville: The Disciples of Christ Historical Society, 1966.

Harrison, Ida Withers. *Forty Years of Service: A History of the Christian Woman's Board of Missions, 1874-1914.* n.p., n.p., n.d.

Hayden, A. S. *Early History of the Disciples in the Western Reserve.* n.p., n.p., [1875].

Hooper, Robert E. *Crying in the Wilderness: A Biography of David Lipscomb.* Nashville: David Lipscomb College, 1979.

Hudson, Winthrop S. and John Corrigan. *Religion in America: An Historical Account of the Development of American Religious Life.* Fifth Edition. New York: Macmillan Publishing Company, 1992.

Humble, Bill J. *Campbell and Controversy: The Story of Alexander Campbell's Great Debates with Skepticism, Catholicism, and Presbyterianism.* n.p.: Old Paths Book Club, 1952.

Jennings, Walter Wilson. *The Origin and Early History of the Disciples of Christ.* Cincinnati: The Standard Publishing Company, 1919.

Jones, Abner. *Memoirs of the Life and Experiences, Travels and Preaching of Abner Jones.* Exeter, New Hampshire: Norris & Sawyer, 1807.

Keith, Noel L. *The Story of D. S. Burnet: Undeserved Obscurity.* St. Louis: The Bethany Press, 1954.

Kershner, Frederick D. *The Restoration Handbook: Studies in the History and Principles of the Movement to Restore New Testament Christianity.* Cincinnati: The Standard Publishing Company, 1920.

Kilgore, Charles Franklin. *The James O'Kelly Schism, in the Methodist Episcopal Church.* Mexico City: Casa Unida De Publications, 1963.

Lair, Loren E. *The Christian Church (Disciples of Christ) and Its Future.* St. Louis: The Bethany Press, 1971.

Lamar, James Sanford. *Memoirs of Isaac Errett.* 2 vols. Cincinnati: The Standard Publishing Company, 1893.

Last Will and Testament of the Springfield Presbytery. Lincoln, Illinois: College & Seminary Press, n.d.

Locke, John. *A Letter Concerning Toleration.* Introduction by Patrick Romanell. Indianapolis: The Bobbs-Merrill Company, Inc., 1955.

Loetscher, Lefferts A. *A Brief History of the Presbyterians.* Fourth Edition. Philadelphia: The Westminster Press, 1978.

Lunger, Harold L. *The Political Ethics of Alexander Campbell.* St. Louis: The Bethany Press, 1954.

Marshall, Robert and John Thompson. *A Brief Historical Account of Sundry Things in the Doctrines and State of the Christian, or as it is Commonly Called, the Newlight Church.* Cincinnati: J. Carpenter and Company, 1811.

Mathes, James M (ed.). *Works of Elder B. W. Stone, to which is added a few Discourses and Sermons (original and Selected).* Second Edition. Cincinnati: Moore, Wilstach, Keys & Co., 1859.

McAllister, Lester G. *Thomas Campbell: Man of the Book.* St. Louis: The Bethany Press, 1954.

_____. *Alexander Campell at Glasgow University, 1808-1809.* Nashville: Disciples of Christ Historical Society, 1971.

McAllister, Lester G. and William E. Tucker. *Journey in Faith: A History of the Christian Church (Disciples of Christ).* St. Louis: The Bethany Press, 1975.

McBeth, H. Leon. *The Baptist Heritage.* Nashville: The Broadman Press, 1987.

McNemar, Richard. *The Kentucky Revival.* Cincinnati: John W. Browne, 1807.

MacClenny, W. E. *The Life of Rev. James O'Kelly and the Early History of the Christian Church in the South.* Indianapolis: Religious Book Service, 1950.

McLean, Archibald. *The History of the Foreign Christian Missionary Society.* New York: Fleming H. Revell Company, 1919.

Mead, Frank S. *Handbook of Denominations in the United States.* New York: Abingdon-Cokesbury Press, 1951.

Mills, Dean. *Union on the King's Highway: The Campbell-Stone Heritage of Unity.* Joplin, Missouri: College Press Publishing Company, 1987.

The Missouri Christian Lectures, Delivered at Independence, Mo., July, 1883. St. Louis: John Burns, Publishers, 1883.

Moore, William Thomas. *A Comprehensive History of the Disciples of Christ.* New York: Fleming H. Revell Company, 1909.

Morro, W. C. *"Brother McGarvey": The Life of President J. W. McGarvey of The College of the Bible, Lexington, Kentucky.* St. Louis: The Bethany Press, 1940.

Murch, James DeForest. *Adventuring for Christ in Changing Times: An Autobiography of James DeForest Murch.* Louisville: Restoration Press, 1973.

_____. *Christians Only.* Cincinnati: The Standard Publishing Company, 1962.

Nichols, James Hastings. *History of Christianity, 1650-1950: Secularization of the West.* New York: The Ronald Press Company, 1956.

Olmstead, Clifton E. *History of Religion in the United States.* Englewood Cliffs, New Jersey: Prentice-Hall, Inc., 1960.

Power, Frederick D. *Sketches of Our Pioneers.* Chicago: Fleming H. Revell Company, 1898.

Purviance, Levi (ed.) *The Biography of Elder David Purviance.* Dayton, Ohio: B. F. and G. W. Ells, 1848.

Report of the Commission on Theology: "Salvation in Jesus Christ." Indianapolis: Council on Christian Unity, Christian Church (Disciples of Christ), 1989.

Richardson, Robert. *Memoirs of Alexander Campbell,* 2 vols., Cincinnati: The Standard Publishing Company, 1913.

Rogers, John (ed.). *The Biography of Eld. Barton Warren Stone, Written by Himself: With Additions and Reflections.* Cincinnati: J. A. & U. P. James, 1847. Reprinted in Hoke S. Dickinson, *The Cane Ridge Reader,* n.p., n.p., 1972.

_____, (ed.). *The Biography of Elder J. T. Johnson.* Cincinnati: Published for the Author, 1861.

Rogers, John I. (ed.). *Autobiography of Elder Samuel Rogers.* Fourth Edition. Cincinnati: The Standard Publishing Company, 1909.

Rouse, Ruth and Stephen Charles Neill (eds.). *A History of the Ecumenical Movement, 1517-1948.* Philadelphia: The Westminster Press, 1954.

Rudolph, L. C. *Francis Asbury.* Nashville: Abingdon Press, 1966.

Shaw, Henry K. *Buckeye Disciples: A History of the Disciples of Christ in Ohio.* St. Louis: Christian Board of Publication, 1952.

_____. *Hoosier Disciples: A Comprehensive History of the Christian Churches (Disciples of Christ) in Indiana.* n.p., The Bethany Press, 1966.

Shackleford, John, Jr. *Life, Letters, and Addresses of Dr. L. L. Pinkerton.* Cincinnati: Chase & Hall, Publishers, 1876.

Shelley, Bruce L. *A History of Conservative Baptists.* Wheaton, Illinois: Conservative Baptist Press, 1971.

Shriver, George H. (ed.). *American Religious Heretics: Formal and Informal Trials.* Nashville: Abingdon Press, 1966.

Smith, Elias. *The Life, Conversion, Preaching, Travels, and Suffering of Elias Smith.* Portsmouth, New Hampshire: Beck & Foster, 1816.

Smith, H. Shelton, Robert T. Handy, and Lefferts A. Loetscher (eds.). *American Christianity: An Historical Interpretation with Representative Documents, Vol. I.* New York: Charles Scribner's Sons, 1960.

Stevenson, Dwight E. *Walter Scott, Voice of the Golden Oracle: A Biography.* Joplin, Missouri: College Press, n.d.

_____. *Lexington Theological Seminary, 1865-1965: The College of the Bible Century.* St. Louis: The Bethany Press, 1964.

_____. "The Bacon College Story: 1836-1865," *The College of the Bible Quarterly*, vol. 29, no. 4 (October, 1962).

Stewart, David. *The Seceders in Ireland, With Annals of Their Congregations.* Belfast: Presbyterian Historical Society, 1950.

Survey of Service: Organizations Represented in International Convention of Disciples of Christ. St. Louis: Christian Board of Publication, 1928.

Sweet, William Warren. *Religion in Colonial America.* New York: Cooper Square Publishers, Inc., 1965.

_____, (ed.). *Religion on the American Frontier, 1783-1840: A Collection of Source Materials. Vol. II, The Presbyterians.* New York: Cooper Square Publishers, Inc., 1964. Originally published by Harper & Brothers, Publishers, 1936.

Tucker, William E. *J. H. Garrison and Disciples of Christ.* St. Louis: The Bethany Press, 1964.

Tulga, Chester E. *The Foreign Missions Controversy in the Northern Baptist Convention.* Chicago: Conservative Baptist Fellowship, 1950.

Tyler, Benjamin B. *A History of the Disciples of Christ.* American Church History Series. New York: The Christian Literature Co., 1894.

Wade, John W. (ed.). *Pioneers of the Restoration Movement.* Cincinnati: The Standard Publishing Company, 1966.

Walker, Hugh. "The Apostasy of Craighead." In *The Tennessean.* Nashville, February 27, 1977.

Ware, Charles C. *Barton Warren Stone, Pathfinder of Christian Union: A Story of His Life and Times.* St. Louis: The Bethany Press, 1932.

Webb, Henry E. *In Search of Christian Unity: A History of the Restoration Movement.* The Cincinnati: Standard Publishing Company, 1990.

Welshimer, P. H. *Concerning the Disciples: A Brief Resume of the Movement to Restore the New Testament Church.* Cincinnati: The Standard Publishing Company, 1935.

West, Earl Irvin. *Life and Times of David Lipscomb.* Henderson, Tennessee: Religious Book Service, 1954.

_____. *The Search for the Ancient Order: A History of the Restoration Movement.* 4 vols. Nashville: Gospel Advocate Company, 1974-1987.

West, William Garrett. *Barton Warren Stone: Early American Advocate of Christian Unity.* Nashville: The Disciples of Christ Historical Society, 1954.

Whitly, Oliver Read. *Trumpet Call of Reformation.* St. Louis: The Bethany Press, 1959.

Wilburn, James R. *The Hazard of the Die: Tolbert Fanning and the Restoration Movement.* Austin, Texas: Sweet Publishing Co., 1969.

Willett, Herbert Lockwood. *Our Plea for Union and the Present Crisis.* Chicago: The Christian Century Company, 1901.

Willett, Herbert Lockwood, Orvis F. Jordan, and Charles M. Sharpe (eds.). *Progress: Anniversary Volume of the Campbell Institute on the Completion of Twenty Years of History.* Chicago: The Christian Century Press, 1917.

Willett, Herbert Lockwood and Lillian Reynolds Philputt (eds.). *"That They May All Be One": Autobiography and Memorial of James M. Philputt, Apostle of Christian Unity.* St. Louis: Christian Board of Publication, 1933.

Williams, D. Newell (ed.) *A Case Study of Mainstream Protestantism: The Disciples' Relation to American Culture, 1880-1989.* Grand Rapids: William B. Eerdmans Publishing Company, 1991.

Williams, John Augustus. *Life of Elder John Smith.* Cincinnati: R. W. Carroll, 1870.

Winebrenner, John (ed.). *History of All the Religious Denominations in the United States.* Harrisburg, Pennsylvania: n.p., 1849.

Wright, John D., Jr. *Transylvania: Tutor to the West.* Lexington: The University Press of Kentucky, 1980.

Yearbook of Christian Churches (Disciples of Christ).

Young, Charles A. (ed.). *Historical Documents Advocating Christian Union.* Chicago: The Christian Century Company, 1904.

Articles

Duncan, Pope A. "Crawford Howell Toy: Heresy at Louisville." In George H. Shriver (ed.), *American Religious Heretics: Formal and Informal Trials.* Nashville: Abingdon Press, 1966.

Mathisen, R. R. "Evangelical Alliance." In *Dictionary of Christianity in America,* edited by Daniel G. Reid. Downers Grove, Illinois: InterVarsity Press, 1990.

Rogers, John. *"The Life and Times of John Rogers, 1800-1867, of Carlisle Kentucky."* Transcribed by Virginia M. Bell and Abridged by Roscoe M. Pierson and Richard L. Harrison Jr. Lexington: Lexington Theological Seminary, 1984. [Volume XIX, Nos. 1 and 2 of Lexington Theological Quarterly, January-April, 1984.]

Rogers, Max Gray. "Charles Augustus Briggs: Heresy at Union." In George H. Shriver (ed.), *American Religious Heretics: Formal and Informal Trials.* Nashville: Abingdon Press, 1966.

Sarvis, Guy. "A Perspective of Missions." In Winfred Ernest Garrison (ed.), *Faith of the Free.* Chicago: Willett, Clark & Company, 1940.

Wasson, Woodrow W. "Approaches to the Understanding and Use of the Bible Among the Disciples of Christ." *Scroll,* vol. 57, no. 2 (1965).

Periodicals

American Christian Review.
Campbell Institute Bulletin.
Christian Baptist.
Christian Century.
Christian-Evangelist.
Christian Herald.
Christian Messenger.
Christian Oracle.
Christian Palladium.
Christian Standard.
Disciple Renewal.
Evangelist.
Gospel Advocate.
Gospel Luminary.
Herald of Gospel Liberty.
Lard's Quarterly.
Millennial Harbinger.
Morning Star and City Watchman.
New Christian Quarterly.
Scroll.

Manuscripts

Ames, Edward Scribner. "Christian Union and the Disciples, A Sermon for the Hyde Park Church of the Disciples, Chicago, January 11, 1903." N.p., n.d.

Annual Proceedings of the American Christian Bible Society.

Annual Register of the University of Chicago.

Bushnell, George W. "The Development of the College of the Bible Through Controversy." Unpublished B.D. Thesis at the College of the Bible, Lexington, Kentucky. 1934.

"Campbell Institute Record, 1896-1921." A bound volume of minutes and reports in the library of the Disciples Divinity House of the University of Chicago.

"Chicago Christian Missionary Society Minutes." In the Library of the Disciples Divinity House of the University of Chicago.

DeGroot, Alfred Thomas. "The Practice of Open Membership Among the Disciples of Christ."Unpublished B.D. Thesis at the College of Religion, Butler University, Indianapolis, Indiana. 1929.

Freeman, Samuel P. "Trends of Disciple Preaching on Christian Unity." Unpublished M. A. Thesis, University of Chicago Divinity School, Chicago, Illinois, 1936.

Minutes of the Redstone Baptist Association.

Rice, Perry J. "The Disciples of Christ in Chicago and North-Eastern Illinois, 1839-1939." Bound, typed manuscript in the library of the Disciples Divinity House of the University of Chicago.

Willett, Herbert Lockwood. "The Corridor of Years: An Autobiographical Record." Introduction and edited by Herbert Lockwood Willett III. Typed, photocopied, and bound, 1967. On file at the library of the Disciples Divinity House of the University of Chicago.

Index